EQUAL EMPLOYMENT OPPORTUNITY

SOCIOLOGY AND ECONOMICS
Controversy and Integration

An Aldine de Gruyter Series of Texts and Monographs

SERIES EDITORS

Paula S. England, *University of Arizona, Tucson*
George Farkas, *University of Texas, Dallas*
Kevin Lang, *Boston University*

Values in the Marketplace
James Burk

Equal Employment Opportunity:
Labor Market Discrimination and Public Policy
Paul Burstein (ed.)

Industries, Firms, and Jobs
Sociological and Economic Approaches
[Expanded Edition]
George Farkas and Paula England (eds.)

Beyond the Marketplace:
Rethinking Economy and Society
Roger Friedland and A. F. Robertson (eds.)

Social Institutions:
Their Emergence, Maintenance and Effects
Michael Hechter, Karl-Dieter Opp and Reinhard Wippler (eds.)

The Origin of Values
Michael Hechter, Lynn Nadel and Richard E. Michod (eds.)

Parents' Jobs and Children's Lives
Toby L. Parcel and Elizabeth G. Menaghan

Power, Norms, and Inflation: A Skeptical Treatment
Michael R. Smith

EQUAL EMPLOYMENT OPPORTUNITY
Labor Market Discrimination and Public Policy

PAUL BURSTEIN
Editor

ALDINE DE GRUYTER
New York

About the Editor

Paul Burstein is Professor of Sociology and Adjunct Professor of Political Science at the University of Washington, Seattle. His 15 years of research on equal employment opportunity and civil rights have been supported by the National Science Foundation and other organizations. He is the author of *Discrimination, Jobs, and Politics* (University of Chicago Press), and his articles have appeared in numerous journals.

Copyright © 1994 Walter de Gruyter, Inc., New York

ALDINE DE GRUYTER
A division of Walter de Gruyter, Inc.
200 Saw Mill River Road
Hawthorne, New York 10532

This publication is printed on acid-free paper ⊗

Library of Congress Cataloging-in-Publication Data

Equal employment opportunity : labor market discrimination and public
  policy / Paul Burstein, editor.
        p.   cm. — (Sociology and economics)
    Includes bibliographical references (p.   ) and index.
    ISBN 0-202-30475-2. — ISBN 0-202-30476-0 (pbk.)
    1. Discrimination in employment—United States.   2. Discrimination
  in employment—Law and legislation—United States.
  3. Discrimination in employment—Great Britain.   4. Discrimination
  in employment—Japan.   I. Burstein, Paul.   II. Series.
  HD4903.5.U58E793   1994
  331.13′3—dc20   94-10601
                                                                       CIP

Manufactured in the United States of America

10 9 8 7 6 5 4 3 2 1

Contents

III. LEGAL DEFINITIONS OF "DISCRIMINATION": CONTROVERSY AND CONFLICT

IV. ECONOMIC AND ORGANIZATIONAL CONSEQUENCES OF EQUAL EMPLOYMENT OPPORTUNITY LAWS

Theoretical Issues

Consequences for Workers

Introduction

The struggle against employment discrimination has been one of the defining features of American life for decades. It was at the heart of the civil rights movement. At the 1949 hearings on equal employment opportunity (EEO) in the U.S. House of Representatives, both Clarence Mitchell, testifying on behalf of the National Association for the Advancement of Colored People (NAACP), and Representative Adam Clayton Powell, one of the chief congressional proponents of civil rights legislation, emphasized that passage of an EEO bill had first priority in their legislative program, taking precedence over bills dealing with voting, lynching, and segregation in public accommodations.

EEO is at the heart of the contemporary women's movement as well. The National Organization for Women (NOW) was founded in 1966 partly out of anger at the federal government's refusal to take seriously the prohibition of sex discrimination included in Title VII of the Civil Rights Act of 1964. NOW's first demonstration—perhaps the first feminist demonstration in five decades—was a protest against the U.S. Equal Employment Opportunity Commission's (EEOC) failure to enforce the law (Harrison 1988). For Jews, Mexican-Americans, and other groups as well, the fight against employment discrimination was central to their struggle to become full participants in American society (Burstein 1985).

This should be no surprise. As Herbert Hill, former national labor director of the NAACP has written (1977 [excerpted here]), work is "one of the most creative of human tasks, . . . the most significant source of identity for western men and women." Without access to work for which one is qualified, the social theorist T. H. Marshall has said (1964), one cannot be fully a member of a modern community. Deprive someone of the opportunity to work, Hill concludes (1977, p. 34), and the result is profound alienation and despair.

Since the movement for federal EEO legislation begin in the early 1940s, much has changed. Most notably, the movement succeeded, though only after a long fight. Title VII of the Civil Rights Act of 1964 prohibits employment discrimination on the basis of race, religion, national origin, and sex. Discrimination is prohibited by a number of executive orders, other laws, and major judicial decisions as well. (This includes discrimination against white men; legally, all races and both sexes are protected equally.) Growing experience in enforcing the

EEO laws has led many people to change their ideas about discrimination and about how to eliminate it; this in turn has led to amendments to Title VII, most recently in the Civil Rights Act of 1991. Economic and sociological theories about discrimination have changed and so, as a result, have ideas about what to do about it. The struggle against discrimination has broadened to incorporate other groups (in the United States, there are now prohibitions against discrimination on the basis of age and disability, for example) and to include many other countries around the world. The debate about discrimination has become much more complex, as some of those involved demand ever-stronger measures on behalf of minorities and women, while others argue that the main problem the United States now faces is reverse discrimination victimizing white men (Lynch 1989; Epstein 1992). EEO is a constant concern in the workplace, the courts, the media, and the halls of Congress.

Important as the issue of EEO is, it is difficult to learn about it in a systematic way. Scholarly work on EEO is found in journals in law, economics, sociology, political science, and other fields, as well as books, pamphlets, popular magazines, and the reports of research institutes. It would take a great deal of work for anyone to acquire a reasonably comprehensive overview of what we know and think about EEO and its consequences. Books are not really a substitute for the work to be found in journals because, although many books on EEO have been published, most are either quite specialized or highly polemical. Thus the need for this book. In *Equal Employment Opportunity: Labor Market Discrimination and Public Policy,* I have tried to bring together an important but widely scattered body of work on EEO. Those in particular fields—law, economics, or sociology, for example—will find here some pieces they are already familiar with, plus many others they would not come across in the course of their ordinary reading or research. Those interested in a broad introduction to EEO will find classic pieces from a variety of fields and perspectives, and thus will have the opportunity to learn about crucial issues and controversies from a single book. The introductions to each section place the issues in context, explain important points where necessary, and often suggest additional readings for those who want to pursue the issues further. Many sections describe particularly significant controversies pertaining to EEO—controversies about what discrimination is, the economic consequences of EEO laws, and affirmative action, for example—and include works presenting the major competing views. It is seldom possible to convince those involved in an intense controversy that their point of view has been presented as fully as they would like, but readers should get a good sense from this book of what some the most intense controversies are and what arguments and evidence have been used by those involved.

The book should be useful for several groups of readers. Social scientists and lawyers interested in EEO will find here a range of materials that they would probably not see otherwise. Students in graduate and undergraduate courses on discrimination, critical issues in American politics, labor markets, and business will find much that is informative and useful here. Many managers and professionals—including human resources managers, attorneys, and journalists—concerned about EEO, affirmative action, workplace diversity, and related issues will find an introduction to the best recent work on issues of continuing importance for American business, politics, and social change. And educated readers simply interested in EEO will find the book interesting— provided they are willing to make their way through some legal and social-scientific terminology and statistical data.

The book is organized as follows. Section I briefly portrays the history of labor market discrimination against minorities and women in the United States, and describes the development of federal EEO policies.

The next section presents theories of labor market discrimination and its consequences, and considers how different theories lead to different suggestions for policies intended to end discrimination.

The articles in Section III ask, What is "labor market discrimination"? Much of the political and legal debate over EEO and affirmative action stems from fundamental disagreements about what discrimination is. It is impossible to understand current controversies about EEO without an awareness of what the disagreements are and how they developed.

What are the economic and organizational consequences of EEO laws and policies? Many economists would predict that EEO laws cannot help minorities and women, and that enforcing such laws will undermine the efficiency of American business. Other scholars argue that the laws do help their intended beneficiaries, at little or no cost to business; indeed, EEO laws might even make business more efficient. These controversies are addressed in Section IV.

The next section considers issues raised by ethnic diversity and gender difference in the workplace. As the American labor force becomes more heterogeneous, and as demands increase for employers to adapt to the needs of working mothers (and fathers), attempts to enforce the EEO laws continually raise questions about whether EEO implies no more than treating everyone alike, or whether, alternatively, it can lead to the productive accommodation of diversity.

The United States is hardly the only nation dealing with labor market discrimination against minorities and women. Many other countries have adopted EEO laws, some willingly and some seemingly to accommodate pressures from international organizations and public opinion. Some of the laws draw, at least in part, on the American experience with EEO, while others have quite an independent history. Section VI describes labor market discrimination in Great Britain and Japan and considers those nations' attempts to deal with it.

Some of the most intense conflicts about EEO concern affirmative action. Many Americans believe that women and minorities are the beneficiaries of reverse discrimination, and resist enforcement of the EEO laws ostensibly for that reason. Others think that affirmative action is a way of achieving EEO that is both reasonable and necessary. Some of the key political, legal, and philosophical issues raised by the fight over affirmative action are addressed in the articles in Section VII.

Some things to note: This book deals with discrimination on the basis of race, religion, national origin, and sex—the subjects of Title VII of the Civil Rights Act of 1964, the nation's most important civil rights law. Although discrimination on the basis of age, disability, and veteran status are also prohibited by federal law (and other kinds of discrimination are prohibited in some states by state law), this book does not deal with them, nor does it deal with proposals to extend prohibitions to discrimination on other bases, such as sexual orientation. This does not suggest that other types of discrimination are unimportant, only that the focus here is on the types of discrimination that were so central to the nation's politics from the 1940s on (or from the 1960s, in the case of sex discrimination).

A word on terminology is in order. Economists use the term *labor market discrimination,* where lawyers use *employment discrimination.* I will use the terms interchangeably, and there should be no confusion in the context in which they occur. The law refers to *sex* discrimination where the term preferred by many social scientists and legal scholars today is *gender.* I will often use the term *sex* in the legal context, particularly when referring to laws that use that term, and *gender* elsewhere.

The works presented here have all been edited for length so that a wide range of subjects and views could be included in a book of reasonable size. Major deletions of text are identified by ellipses (. . .). Where tables, figures, and footnotes have been deleted, those remaining have been renumbered. In addition to the end-of-chapter references there is a selected bibliography at the end of the book, where additional references from the law review chapters are cited as well as references relevant to the subject. The writers' arguments have been presented as completely as possible; nothing is "taken out of context." Obviously, if readers want to get all the nuances in an argument or to see all the supporting data, they need to refer to the original sources.

Finally, I would like to thank the authors of the chapters in this book. I am grateful for their willingness not only to let their works be reprinted here, but for their willingness to let me edit them as well. Without their support for the scholarly norm of making intellectual work widely available, it would not have been possible to include so wide a range of excellent material in a single book.

I

Discrimination Against Minorities and Women: Some Historical Background

Most Americans think that the labor market generally operates fairly, that people get ahead through hard work and that they can normally expect to be rewarded for what they do. Many have a vague sense that some groups have been discriminated against, particularly blacks and women, but know little about it and tend to think of it as having occurred long ago. Even members of groups that have suffered greatly from employment discrimination have only general ideas about how it has affected them and how it has changed over time.

Thus, it is important to begin with a brief history of labor market discrimination. The first point to convey is how pervasive labor market discrimination has been and how great are its consequences. Virtually all groups except white Protestant men of northwest European ancestry have suffered from intense discrimination at one time or another. Irish Catholics were its victims from the time they started arriving in the United States in large numbers in the 1840s and 1850s; Italians, Poles, and other European groups were seen as distinct and inferior "races," and kept out of many jobs; Jews suffered from widespread anti-Semitism well on into the 1950s; and of course blacks, Asians (Japanese, Chinese, Filipinos, and others), Hispanics, and American Indians have been the victims of discrimination as well (see, e.g., Lieberson 1980; Takaki 1989). Women of all groups were denied access to many jobs, and were denied pay equal to men's in the jobs they won.

Much of the discrimination was blatant in ways that people would find astonishing today. It was not a matter of "glass ceilings" preventing employees' rise to the highest levels of the corporate hierarchy, subtly biased employment tests, or verbal harassment on the job. Instead, discrimination often meant total (or virtually total) exclusion—from jobs, from firms, even from entire occupations and industries. In the nineteenth century, employers routinely posted No Irish Need Apply signs on their businesses, and in the twentieth, job ads sent to employment agencies and newspapers often made it very clear that no blacks, Jews, or Catholics would be considered for many jobs. Sex discrimination was so common, and so much taken for granted, that there was no need to mention it in specific ads;

1

the very structure of the classified advertisements in newspapers, with one section for Help Wanted—Male and another for Help Wanted—Female showed that women would not even be permitted to apply for men's jobs (or men for women's—but women's jobs were fewer and paid much less). Many labor unions restricted membership to white men, and many employers—major national corporations as well as small local businesses—would not hire minorities for any but the most menial jobs.

Most people have little sense of the importance of labor market discrimination in American history, in large measure, because there is so much less discrimination now than there used to be. Particularly with regard to white ethnic and religious minorities, including Irish Catholics, Jews, and groups from Southern and Eastern Europe, discrimination has declined so much that most people are unaware of the little that remains, and members of such groups (particularly the men) are more likely to be seen as perpetrators of discrimination than as its victims. Many groups that once suffered greatly from discrimination have even raised their earnings above the national average (see Neidert and Farley 1985 [excerpted here]; Farley 1990; Takaki 1989; Lieberson 1980).

This decline in discrimination against some groups has been interpreted in three major ways. The first (and most common) interpretation is that the experience of Irish Catholics, Jews, and other groups will be shared by all other groups, because so many fundamental aspects of American society work against discrimination that it will inevitably disappear. In the not too distant future, according to this view, the United States will be a society in which everyone's labor market outcomes depend on skill and effort, not on skin color, religion, ethnic background, or sex. This view is consistent with the general American belief in progress; with Gunnar Myrdal's suggestion that Americans' belief in fairness and equality should undermine their practice of discrimination (1962); and with economists' theories predicting that discrimination will disappear in modern market economies because it is economically inefficient (see Becker 1957, and discussions of the relevant theories in Donohue 1986 and Goldin 1991 [excerpted here]; England in this volume, and Lieberson 1980).

The second interpretation is that continuing discrimination against some groups does not mean that the United States is simply somewhat slow in bringing discrimination against them to its inevitable end. Instead, it may show that American society may be willing to make room for new groups and eventually treat them fairly only so long as they are white and male; nonwhite minorities and women are too "different," too threatening, too often seen as inferior for them to have any hope of winning true equality. Among minorities, blacks in particular have always been treated worse than others (except perhaps American Indians), and—some would argue—there is no reason to expect their victimization to be brought to an end by Americans' vague commitment to fairness and equality or by economic advance (see the arguments reviewed in Lieberson 1980).

The third interpretation is more complex than the first two and, possibly for that reason, is the one least often expressed. Discrimination against minorities is common in virtually all multiethnic and multiracial societies, and discrimination against women is common everywhere. Some of this is easy to understand—some workers may gain economically by reducing competition through discrimination—and some of the reasons for it remain mysterious, but the pervasiveness of discrimination is obvious; it is hardly a characteristic only of American society. What is less obvious is that discrimination is a dynamic and contingent phenomenon. Discrimination against particular groups can rise and fall, and its intensity varies from country to country and over time. Discrimination may be affected by general attitudes (those favoring equality, for example) and by the market, but it is influenced by specific organizational, cultural, and political forces as well.

From this point of view, there is nothing inevitable about discrimination except, probably, the likelihood that in every society some people will feel the temptation to exclude others from jobs on the basis of ascribed characteristics. Discrimination may decline, but it may also increase; it may be directed consistently at particular groups, or its focus may change. And both discrimination and the reduction of discrimination are likely to require considerable effort.

This is essentially the message of Herbert Hill, Claudia Goldin, and many others (e.g., Lieberson 1980; Takaki 1989; Milkman 1987; Bielby and Baron 1986; Jaynes and Williams 1989). Hill shows how well blacks could have done economically after the American Civil War. Many blacks had been highly trained before the war, so that they would be more valuable to the slave owners; at the end of the war, a high proportion of skilled workers in the South were black, and many whites as well as blacks saw black workers as at least as capable as whites. And blacks' desire to make use of their skills and to acquire more education was intense (see also Lieberson 1980). Their desires were thwarted, however, because whites succeeded in restricting their access to jobs, education, and political power. Whether this was inevitable is difficult to say. But it could not have seemed inevitable to whites at the time, because those who wanted to institutionalize the oppression of blacks felt they had to devote tremendous effort to doing so. It took decades of effort, legal and illegal, to institute the Jim Crow system of racial oppression (which some whites as well as blacks opposed), and continuing effort to prevent challenges to it from whites as well as blacks. Nor, as Hill and many others in this volume argue, was the dismantling of the system of racial oppression the inevitable result of progress or good intentions. It too required tremendous struggle, which continues today (see also Burstein 1985; Lawson 1976; Garrow 1978).

Goldin tells a story about women similar in important ways to Hill's about blacks. She shows that employment discrimination against women has neither declined steadily (as the first interpretation would suggest) nor been unchanging (as the second interpretation might lead one to expect). Indeed, wage discrimination against women seems to have increased between 1900 and 1940, partly because large corporations in the most advanced and rapidly growing sectors of the economy adopted discriminatory personnel policies. Women's labor market outcomes have improved in recent years, Goldin argues, not only because of broad patterns of economic and demographic change, but also because of the rise of feminist ideology and the growth of women's political power.

Political power has, indeed, been central to the fate of many groups in American society, white ethnic groups as well as blacks, Hispanics, other nonwhite minorities, and women. Many scholars believe that the economic advance of white ethnic groups was made possible in part by their ability to influence the political process, and that other groups have done less well economically because they were denied the right to vote and other modes of access to power (Lieberson 1980; cf. Jaynes and Williams 1989). It is power that gives group access to education, government jobs and contracts, and other advantages. Even scholars opposed to EEO laws argue that political power has affected groups' economic success, contending, for example, that the racist policies of white-run state governments seriously impeded blacks' economic advance before the civil rights laws were adopted in the 1960s (Epstein 1992).

Blacks, Jews, and other groups began to push for a federal EEO law in the 1940s. It was a long struggle (see Burstein 1985). The first such law was not adopted until 1964, as Title VII of the Civil Rights Act, and it was only with adoption of the Equal Employment Opportunity Act of 1972 that the executive branch was given significant power to enforce the law. Passage of EEO laws was an important step in the fight against employment discrimination, but only a step. As David Rose shows in his article, "Twenty-Five Years Later," passage of the laws was followed by continuing and intense struggles over how they were to be interpreted and implemented. Rose's message is consistent with those of Hill and Goldin: The struggle for economic advance and against discrimination is in important ways a political struggle, one that continues for a long time, in a variety of arenas, with the outcome not guaranteed.

1

Black Labor and the American Legal System: Race, Work, and the Law

Herbert Hill

HISTORICAL SOURCES OF RESISTANCE TO CHANGE

A great irony lies at the heart of slavery in the United States. Although slaves were not legally recognized as persons, central to the institution of slavery was the requirement that these less-than-human chattels, or "articles of commerce" (by legal definition), perform one of the most creative of human tasks: work. It was largely in the condition of involuntary servitude that black people in America acquired a great variety of skills by which they labored for their masters and were instrumental in creating their masters' wealth.

In 1965, a hundred years after the end of the Civil War and the abolition of slavery, federal legislation went into effect to eliminate the continuing barriers that deny black citizens equal opportunity to work and to share in the rewards of work. By then, many forces had combined to push the descendants of black men and women, both slave and free, into a subordinate position in the American labor force. A dual racial labor system had been established. Whites derived substantial economic and social gains from the subordination of blacks, and both employers and organized white workers repeatedly resisted compliance with new civil right statutes. . . .

Title VII, with its 1972 amendments, has led to a new stage in the struggle against job discrimination. Prior to the emergence of this law federal executive orders requiring nondiscrimination in employment by government contractors were honored more in the breach than in the observance, and although many states had fair employment laws, they were seldom enforced. . . .

Employer resistance to the requirements of Title VII of the Civil Rights Act

Excerpts reprinted with permission from *Black Labor and the American Legal System: Race, Work and the Law.* Originally published 1977 by the Bureau of National Affairs, Inc. Reissued in 1985 by the University of Wisconsin Press. Copyright © 1977 by Herbert Hill.

often came from a desire to maintain labor tranquility by not disturbing established systems of hiring, promotion, and job assignment. Stiff resistance also resulted from attempts to perpetuate the racial exclusiveness of certain all-white occupations, especially among professional, technical, and supervisory personnel. National corporations—in heavy industry, public utilities, banking and insurance, retailing, consumer goods manufacturing, transportation, and elsewhere—not only failed to use their power and influence to obtain compliance with the new law but instead persisted in retaining and defending illegal discriminatory employment practices. This resistance was intensified by assumptions of the inferiority of nonwhite workers and in some instances by management's commitment to racial segregation. . . .

[T]he response of unions as defendants in Title VII cases repeatedly revealed that labor organizations have become the institutional defenders of white male workers' job expectations, expectations which have become the norm and are based in large part upon the systematic deprivation of black workers; any alteration of this norm is considered to be "reverse discrimination." An account of organized labor's resistance to Title VII must take into consideration the advantages that discriminatory employment patterns give to white male workers in training, promotion, higher job status, and better wages. In fact, organized labor's efforts to evade the new legal requirements are incomprehensible without an understanding of its history in both generating and codifying the job expectations of white workers at the expense of blacks.

White workers' claims to more desirable job classifications and to "inherent" white employment privileges—which had a long history in the contentions for access to work between whites and blacks—were reinforced by labor unions in a variety of crafts and industries. In most craft occupations, if blacks were excluded from union membership they were thereby almost entirely excluded from the craft labor force; and when they were included in industrial unions on a segregated or inferior basis, they did not share equally in the benefits of unionization. Through the collective bargaining process, organized labor has played a crucial role in institutionalizing a variety of discriminatory practices in diverse sectors of the economy. . . .

When Title VII became effective—on July 2, 1965—two centuries of American history had created formidable obstacles to its acceptance. Not only were many powerful institutions involved in perpetuating the racial status quo in employment, but popular belief had come to question the capacity of blacks to do acceptable work. Consistent with the self-fulfilling prophecy, the high rates of black unemployment and the concentration of black workers in low-wage occupations were considered proof of their inherent limitations. The condition of black workers was increasingly held to be a deserved consequence of the overall inadequacy of the black population.

To appreciate fully the influences that fostered the notion that low job status is a result of black cultural attitudes toward work, and to trace to some degree the history of black labor, it is necessary to go back to the period of slavery. It was the "peculiar institution," slavery itself, that created not only the familiar images of field hands and domestic servants but, far less widely depicted in popularizations of the American past, the skilled workers and artisans of the southern labor force. The more skilled the slave, the more profit for the master.

Although there is tangible evidence of the presence of skilled slave craftsmen in the American colonies during the seventeenth century, Negro mechanics and craftsmen did not become important factors in the colonial economy before the eighteenth century. In the earliest period slaveowners feared, as historian Leonard Stavisky argues, that educating slaves and giving them access to tools might provide them with weapons to be used against their masters. The hostility of white artisans and general assumptions about the Negro's inferior capacity contributed to the reluctance to employ slaves in any pursuit other than heavy agricultural labor. Declining tobacco prices and a concurrent shortage of skilled labor during the early eighteenth century, however, forced reconsideration of the issue, and plantation owners in Virginia and elsewhere began to train their slaves in the home manufacture of shoes and cloth goods, as well as building construction. . . .

Stavisky also reminds us that a minimum of specialization existed in the eighteenth century crafts, so that every trade embraced a wide variety of operations. A Negro blacksmith, for example, could work in iron and fashion his own tools. A carpenter would also be a wood turner, pattern maker, and so on.

The use of slaves in the wide range of skilled work required on the colonial plantation is illustrated by advertisements for the sale of slaves. An advertisement in the *South Carolina Gazette* in 1751 offered "About Fifty Valuable Slaves, among which are sundry tradesmen, such as Bricklayers, Carpenters, Coopers, Sawyers, Shoemakers, Tanners, Curriers, and Boatmen." . . . Slaves also worked at manufacturing trades in the colonial towns. . . .

A significant characteristic of the southern economy in the eighteenth and early nineteenth centuries was that large plantations functioned virtually as self-contained economic units. . . . By 1850 more than 20 percent of the 3.2 million slaves in the South were engaged in activities other than large-scale agriculture. It has been estimated that 400,000 of these were urban slaves and the balance were in rural areas. Altogether, blacks performed a large share of the nonagricultural labor tasks in the antebellum South. Domestic and personal service accounted for the largest number of nonagricultural jobs for Negroes, but slaves, both rural and urban, as well as free blacks in the towns, also engaged in a variety of other occupations too. Slaves built the plantations and at a later period kept the large ones supplied through small-scale local manufacturing. Slave artisans were worth considerably more money than ordinary field hands; well-trained mechanics sometimes sold for as much as $2,000, compared to a price of $800 to $1,000 for a strong plantation hand. . . .

Whether owned directly by their employers or hired out, urban blacks followed a wide variety of occupations. . . . There was a heavy concentration of blacks in the building trades, including the most highly skilled classifications. The Charleston, South Carolina, municipal census for 1848, for example, showed that black workers outnumbered whites as bricklayers, house and ship carpenters, plasterers, wharf builders, and coopers, and that as many blacks as whites were painters and millwrights. The same general pattern was true for Savannah, New Orleans, and other urban communities. Quite frequently private companies bought black workers to build canals, and most of the railroads in South Carolina were to a large extent constructed with slave labor. In many instances cities, towns, and villages purchased slaves for the purpose of building municipal projects. . . .

Though historians have held conflicting views regarding the degree and the significance of southern industrialization in the antebellum period, a growing body of evidence establishes that, to the extent that southern industry existed, slaves constituted the basic work force at virtually all levels. The employment of slaves in industry was not merely an extension of the "southern way of life" and less costly than the use of wage workers. It was, from the viewpoint of the slaveowners, an essential instrument for maintaining their hegemony over the flow of capital in the South and securing their class position against the emergence of independent entrepreneurial groups. . . .

The widespread domination by slaves of the skilled trades in the South impeded the growth of a free white working class, so that by the beginning of Reconstruction the great majority of skilled workers in the South were black. A federal census of occupations taken in 1865 revealed 100,000 blacks among the 120,000 artisans in the South. It is as though history were making sport of present-day shibboleths when we read the accounts and warnings in antebellum records of the undesirability of employing white immigrants—among them the Dutch and the Irish—as industrial workers and craftsmen in the South because of their drunkenness, shiftlessness, instability, and lack of commitment to what now would be described as the "work ethic," along with the fear that free whites would demand "rights" as workers, including the right to organize, strike, and command higher wages. White immigrants with skills were in the minority. The few who were master craftsmen were valued for training other workers, but proper training was long and costly. The belief in the unreliability of white workers (a consequence of slavery was that it demeaned work and workers), the higher wage base required, and white workers' insistence on better living conditions than slaves combined to discourage the training and hiring of whites for skilled employment.

In the North, where free persons of color were denied equal citizenship rights and where free blacks were not the essential human tool in industrialization, black workers were concentrated in a variety of service and unskilled jobs but were also part of the skilled labor force, especially in the early part of the nineteenth century. In Philadelphia, which had the largest free black population of any northern city, the Society of Friends compiled in 1838 a hierarchy of black occupations that included such skilled jobs as cabinetmaker, plumber, printer, sailmaker, ship's carpenter, and stone cutter, among other crafts.

At the same time, especially in the South, there was a growing movement toward displacing the black worker and restricting permissible occupations. . . . A major example of how considerations of race subsumed conflicts of class occurred in South Carolina in the early 1850s, when widespread action was taken to eliminate black workers from the textile industry. The decision of employers to manufacture textiles with white workers exclusively was based upon the warnings of James H. Hammond and other political leaders, who perceived a potential danger to the stability of the social order if poor whites continued to be excluded from the textile industry. Thus was begun the practice of black exclusion from the major manufacturing industry of South Carolina, a practice which was to be adopted later in other southern states, and which would accelerate in the post-Reconstruction era. . . .

The Thirteenth Amendment legally ended the institution of slavery, but left unresolved the fundamental issues of land reform and the protection of black labor. The former slaveowners made a successful and determined effort to salvage what they could of their "security as a class" by forcing inferior caste status on the newly emancipated slaves and thwarting the legal rights guaranteed by the Thirteenth, Fourteenth, and Fifteenth Amendments.

The failure to "reconstruct" the South left the black freedman without an independent economic or political base. Once the emancipated black was defined as inferior in a series of court decisions and by social practice, and the Federal Government did little or nothing to insure equal treatment, his economic position continued to deteriorate, thus reinforcing the notion of racial inferiority. In the North (as southern leaders never tired of repeating as evidence of Republican Party hypocrisy) the rights of blacks had seldom been protected—either before Emancipation or after Reconstruction.

After 1877 the willingness of national Republican administrations to make local and state governments responsible for law enforcement on racial matters contributed to the steady and disastrous degeneration of the freedman's political and economic condition; one of the results was the extension of segregated racial employment patterns in the North and South alike. In the latter, it was further institutionalized by law; in the former, it was served by custom. In both, it was enforced by violence. In the post-Reconstruction era, national economic and social forces, together with the proliferation of the infamous Black Codes and Jim Crow laws, conspired to deliver newly freed blacks to the statutory status of nonslaves but not to the equal rights of American citizenship; they were still the bondsmen of subjugation and exploitation.

By the 1880s, with the failed effort of Reconstruction ended and with urbanization and industrialization well under way, black wage earners, in the face of overwhelming difficulties, struggled to participate in the industrial transformation of the nation.

At the beginning of the twentieth century . . . [t]he status of black workers was becoming increasingly tenuous, however, as the process of racial occupational eviction was accelerated. After Reconstruction, as industrialization increased in the South, new jobs were created that required new skills. White artisans learned their trades under the apprenticeship system of the advancing craft unions, which usually excluded blacks. . . .

During this period of industrial expansion, white labor unions organized strikes and took other action to force the displacement of black workers from jobs they had long held. In 1890 the Brotherhood of Locomotive Trainmen petitioned the Houston and Texas Central Railroad demanding that all black workers be replaced by whites, and in 1909 white workers struck against the Georgia Railroad to protest the company's practice of hiring black firemen.

Violence frequently accompanied organized labor's efforts to replace black men with white union members, as in a strike called in 1911 to protest the employment of blacks by the Cincinnati, New Orleans and Texas Pacific Railroad, which resulted in the killing of ten black firemen. Similar events were to occur in the railroad industry over a period of many years.

By the turn of the century the process of racial job displacement that had begun in the South was also well under way in the North. Here too economic expansion and the quickened pace of industrialization gave rise to new and more attractive jobs, to which blacks were denied entry. As Gunnar Myrdal wrote in *An American Dilemma,* "[p]rogress itself seems to work against the Negro" (Myrdal 1962 [1944] p. 206). At the same time, the emergence of labor unions that excluded blacks on the basis of race also hastened the occupational eviction of northern blacks from skilled jobs. . . .

The emergence of the organized labor movement in the post-Reconstruction period was an important factor in the process of racial occupational eviction. A few unions succeeded in organizing both black and white workers and for a relatively brief period tried to build labor organizations based upon interracial working class unity. Among these were the Knights of Labor, the Brotherhood of Timber Workers, the Industrial Workers of the World, and in its early years the United Mine Workers of America, founded in 1890. But the dominant labor influence at the beginning of the twentieth century, the American Federation of Labor, was to have an adverse effect on the status of black workers, both in the North and South.

In the 1880s and 1890s the success of the American Federation of Labor as a national organization also led to its power and to its ability to determine the policies and practices around which labor unions were to coalesce. With the rise of the AFL, organized labor could have chosen to include black workers in a single, racially unified labor movement. Instead, most unions chose to drive black workers out of competition with white organized workers. This end was achieved with the assent and cooperation of employers, who saw benefits to themselves in policies that guaranteed a supply of cheap black labor, unorganized and unprotected.

The unions affiliated with the AFL and the independent railroad brotherhoods attained their restrictive goals by a variety of methods. These included exclusion of blacks from membership through racial provisions in union constitutions or in the ritual bylaws of local unions; exclusion by tacit agreement in the absence of written provisions; racially segregated units; separate racial lines of seniority and job assignment in union contracts; union control of licensing boards; refusal to admit nonwhites into union-controlled apprenticeship training programs; negotiating discriminatory labor agreements that directly affected black workers while excluding them from union membership and preventing their participation in collective bargaining; and denial of access to hiring halls and other union-controlled job referral systems.

Early in its history, the American Federation of Labor affirmed the principle that "working people must unite and organize, irrespective of creed, color, sex, nationality or politics."[1] The 1890 AFL convention passed a resolution declaring that the federation "looks with disfavor upon trade unions having provisions which exclude from membership persons on account of race or color."[2] At the same convention the AFL refused to admit the National Association of Machinists (later the International Association of Machinists) because the national constitution of the Machinists union limited membership to white persons exclusively. During the 1890s some unions affiliated with the AFL helped black workers in their struggle for labor organization and union recognition. Most important was the historic New Orleans General Strike of 1892, in which thousands of black and white workers joined together in an expression of interracial unionism. But for the most part these were brief and episodic events that soon gave way to the conservative and racially exclusive craft union policies of the AFL. . . .

Early in the twentieth century the configuration of the racial employment pattern was fixed. The changes in the economic, political, and social order begun after Reconstruction had become clearly defined. Immigrant workers satisfied the increased demand for labor and further served to displace black workers. Despite early hostility toward the impoverished new arrivals who were willing to work for a pittance, the trade union movement was ultimately willing to absorb them while still denying membership, and thus access to skilled craft jobs and labor union protection, to blacks. Farm labor, domestic service, and menial jobs in industry were all that remained open to the black wage earner. . . .

Almost as quickly as blacks were displaced from skilled jobs, the myth that they were incapable of doing skilled work was born and took root in the American consciousness, among whites and even among some blacks. During the early 1900s, as blacks were being more and more restricted to menial and unskilled jobs at the lowest pay and losing the share of skilled jobs they had once possessed even as slaves, Booker T. Washington was calling upon blacks to demonstrate their virtues by discipline and hard work in occupations that would keep them out of competition for jobs with whites. According to his precepts, the black who was willing to work diligently within limited job contexts—performing either humble jobs or work that serviced only the black community—was precisely the black who did not threaten the white worker and who could elicit benevolent tolerance from the white establishment.

The great majority of blacks still lived in the South, where they worked mainly in agriculture or domestic service. But throughout the country they were without the protection of organized labor and were prevented from holding any but the meanest jobs. They were compelled to accept whatever wages they were offered or not work at all. When blacks were able to enter new industries, they were limited almost exclusively to inferior positions with little chance of advancement. At the same time, displacement from their traditional work in the railroad industry, in the longshore industry, in skilled construction work, and in the higher status service occupations continued—reaching its peak in the 1930s. . . .

Under the Wagner-Connery Act of 1935, which became the National Labor Relations Act, the right of workers to organize into unions of their own choosing was given legal sanction and the employer's obligation to engage in "good faith" collective bargaining was established within a comprehensive legal structure. As a result of the failure of Congress to address issues of racial discrimination in the Act—despite pressure from civil rights organizations that it do so—the power of labor unions to engage in a variety of discriminatory racial practices was reinforced by law.

This was also the period when the industrial unions, with a different approach from that of the AFL craft unions, made their great drives to organize industrial workers. Arriving late on the labor scene, the Congress of Industrial Organizations[3] had fresh possibilities of pursuing nondiscriminatory policies. When the industrial union movement arose the CIO adopted a formal policy of racial equality. Although unevenly implemented and often ignored by its affiliates, the CIO's egalitarian program was an important break with the AFL tradition. The protectionist, guildlike spirit of the AFL craft unions was contrary to the aims and growth potential of industrial unionism, which required the inclusion of all employees in large collective bargaining units as a source of plantwide unity (and then industrywide unity) to exert pressure on employers. Within the industrial unions, organized on vertical lines rather than in the horizontal craft structure of the AFL unions, the forms of racial discrimination changed. Informal discriminatory job practices often became more rigid when separate seniority and promotional lines based on race were structured through provisions in collective bargaining agreements of many CIO industrial unions.

Despite some skepticism based upon their earlier experiences with labor unions, thousands of black workers soon came to accept the CIO. But within a few years they found that they had again become the victims of a different kind of discriminatory pattern. For example, in the southern steel industry, where racial job assignment had been somewhat casual, more classifications had been available to black workers before unionization. In many industries collective bargaining agreements systematized seniority practices in which job assignment, promotion, furlough, and dismissal were based on race. Furthermore, such discriminatory systems were routinely enforceable through union contracts. In the South this was done explicitly by designating racial lines of job progression; in the North, through a variety of euphemisms and through the operation of departmental seniority.

Protests by black industrial workers against such discriminatory practices in the North as well as in the South began in the 1940s. The *First Report* of the Fair Employment Practice Committee, established by a federal executive order in 1941, provides the details of a work stoppage by black steelworkers that began on February 25, 1944, at the coke plant of the Carnegie-Illinois Steel Corporation in Clairton, Pennsylvania:

> The stoppage in the coke plant which occurred at midnight, February 25, 1944, was the result of a long series of incidents dating back as far as 1933. Prior to 1933 the entire coke works was manned by Negroes, but thereafter management began to introduce white workers who were taught the various processes in the plant by Negroes. As soon as the white workers became proficient in the operations of the various machines, the Negro workers were transferred to other departments and jobs of a lower classification. Various incidents of this type continued to occur up to December 1943.
>
> The Negro workmen, realizing that they were being steadily barred from all the higher jobs formerly held by them, decided that the only way to regain what they had lost was to tie up the plant by striking. . . . Negro workmen on the midnight shift at the byproducts plant refused to work, claiming that they were denied promotions and were actually being passed over by white men with far less seniority.[4]

Typical of action by black steelworkers during the 1950s and early 1960s was the petition to the national offices of the Steelworkers union dated February 5, 1958, from black members of Local 2401 of the United Steelworkers of America, which stated in part that "all the undersigned are employed at the Atlantic Steel Company plant in Atlanta, Georgia, and are members of the Steelworkers Union. For many years we have been denied the right to be upgraded and promoted . . . all the colored workers are kept in laborer jobs while the whites with less seniority are promoted over us."[5] Interestingly enough, many of the aggrieved black workers had played a decisive role in organizing the union at this plant. When the international union failed to respond, the black workers filed complaints with the President's Committee on Government Contracts and the National Labor Relations Board against both the company and the union. But despite the protests of black workers against the discriminatory pattern, local and national union leaders in Atlanta and elsewhere continued to trade off the rights of black workers to obtain greater benefits for whites. . . .

A consequence of federal labor laws that gave unions legal privileges and immunities was that the government itself became a party to the discriminatory practices of organized labor. . . . Compliance with the requirements of the law as it developed in Title VII litigation has been resisted by the two organized groups that have repeatedly been ordered to initiate changes by the courts: employers and labor unions. There are, however, certain notable differences in the forms and the degree to which each has resisted compliance. . . .

[E]mployer resistance to change is in large part based on the desire to keep an enterprise operating with a minimum of disruption to established methods. The legally required elimination of discriminatory practices may involve extensive financial costs and the dismantling of long-established employment procedures. In these terms, employer resistance to change is not only a mirror of the racial prejudice of the society at large, it is also rooted in traditional management objections to government interference, although corporate enterprise is the direct beneficiary of many forms of vital government assistance.

The resistance of organized labor is far more complex. For example, because of his race the white worker historically has enjoyed certain specific benefits in employment which, in turn, have created a highly exploited class of black labor that is rigidly blocked from advancing into the all-white occupations. The white plumber, printer, or electrician, by virtue of the exclusion of blacks from the trade, does not have to compete with an entire subclass within the working population. Similarly, in desirable classifications in industrial plants white workers are also exempted from competition with blacks; they are assigned job classifications with a high wage base and have access to better paying, more skilled jobs. Thus white workers have expectations of both the opportunity for employment and the opportunity for earnings and promotion which are based in varying degrees (depending on the industry) on the denial of equal opportunity to blacks. The elimination of racial disadvantages in employment necessarily affects the expectations of white workers, since it compels competition with black workers and other minority group members where none previously existed. White workers, therefore, feel directly "victimized" by legislation, administrative action, and court orders that provide not only for equal job opportunity but for measures that attempt to compensate for the present effects of past discrimination. What the white male worker believes to be at stake is his likelihood of getting a job, his status in the job, his promotion, seniority, and susceptibility to layoff—the entire constellation of expectations which he tacitly assumes are his rights. . . .

The enactment of civil rights laws, especially those prohibiting racial discrimination in employment, in conjunction with a variety of social programs begun during the past two decades, promised a new and better future for black Americans. Because the hope is so great, the promise becomes all the more vivid. But as the promise and the hope fail to materialize, the despair and alienation become more profound. This alienation is rooted in the most significant source of identity for western men and women—work.

NOTES

1.   Federation of Organized Trades and Labor Unions, Fourteenth Annual Convention, *Proceedings,* 1894, p. 55.

2.   American Federation of Labor, Tenth Annual Convention, *Proceedings,* 1890, p. 31.

3.   Formed in 1935, as the Committee for Industrial Organization, the CIO was expelled from the AFL and reorganized in November 1938 as the Congress of Industrial Organizations. In 1955 it merged with the AFL to form the AFL-CIO.

4.   *First Report,* July 1943-December 1944 (Washington, D.C.: Fair Employment Practice Committee, 1945), pp. 81–82.

5.   Petition of Negro steelworkers employed at the Atlantic Steel Company, Atlanta, Georgia, to Boyd Wilson, international representative, United Steelworkers of America, CIO, February 5, 1958. (Copy in NAACP files.)

REFERENCES

Myrdal, Gynnar. 1962. *An American Dilemma.* New York: Harper and Row. Originally published 1944.

2

Understanding the Gender Gap: An Economic History of American Women

Claudia Goldin

Recent research on gender differences in earnings and occupations has produced a discouraging set of findings. The ratio of female to male earnings among full-time workers was roughly constant from the 1950's to the early 1980's, and the segregation of occupations by sex is substantial and has declined only slightly across the last century. Only since the early 1980's has the ratio of female to male earnings begun to rise. One might have hoped and expected economic progress to have narrowed differences in earnings and occupations between men and women. Gender differences in earnings and occupations appear impervious to the broad social and economic changes that have operated in other spheres, such as labor force participation and the political arena.

[I] hope to clarify the long-term aspects of the stability and persistence of gender differences and point to changes in some indicators that have been hidden from view. At other points, I discuss features of the historical record that appear discouraging and even paradoxical, such as the apparent lack of a relationship between the ratio of female to male earnings and female labor force participation. Some of these features are, in reality, easily explained. . . .

The examination of the historical record, presented in this chapter, reveals that the ratio of female to male full-time earnings was not as constant before 1950 as it has been since. Rather, it rose from the early nineteenth century to the 1930's. The reliance on the last three decades of earnings data owes not to their greater relevance, but to their greater availability. . . . But there is little solace to be gained from the narrowing in the gender gap in earnings from 1815 to 1930, or from the possible decline in occupational segregation by sex. "Wage discrimination"—and by that I mean a statistical concept developed to measure the degree to which earnings differences between men and women are not accounted for by differences in their productive attributes—increased over time.

17

"Wage discrimination" emerged sometime between 1890 and 1940 and has remained at roughly the same level since. . . .

Economic progress over the long run ought to reduce differences between the earnings of men and women. By economic progress, I mean the use of machinery, the reliance on mental as opposed to physical power, the increase in schooling for all, the general expansion of the market for goods and services, and the breakdown of norms and ideologies that have constrained both women and men. The labor market's rewards to strength, which made up a large fraction of earnings in the nineteenth century, ought to be minimized by the adoption of machinery, and its rewards to brainpower ought to be increased. Formal education, supplied by the employee, should replace on-the-job training possibly denied individuals who, as a group, have brief life-cycle employment. As more women enter and remain in the labor market, their experience in jobs and with firms should approach that of the male labor force. With the broadening of markets in goods and services, there is less gain to specialization by men and women in the home and to household production. Economic progress, it seems, should narrow and eventually eliminate differences in the earnings of females and males.

The Ratio of Female to Male Full-time Earnings

Recent trends in the gender gap appear to contradict the hypothesis that economic progress brings with it a narrowing in the differences between the sexes. . . . Even among full-time, year-round workers the ratio of female to male earnings has been far below 1 for all of American history and was about .60 until the early 1980's. In the 1970's, the 59 cents on the dollar figure became synonymous with inequality between men and women in the labor market. It symbolized the failure of the marketplace to ensure equal treatment and became a banner for the women's movement.

. . . .

"Wage discrimination" means that one group, here females, is paid less than another group, here males, even when the characteristics of each are identical. It measures the degree to which equal characteristics are given a different value by the market. The interpretation of "wage discrimination" and its empirical counterpart, however, are considerably more complicated than the definition.

The concept could measure the extent to which prejudices against women in the labor market lower their earnings compared with those of men. But prejudice could be more extensive than indicated by "wage discrimination" if women are denied job training and education, or if jobs are segregated by sex. It could, alternatively, overestimate the extent of discrimination if the earnings function omits relevant variables such as strength, intensity of work, hours, and responsibility. . . . "[W]age discrimination" emerged sometime between 1890 and 1940 in the white-collar sector of the economy. Even though manufacturing employment was highly segregated by sex, . . . wages between men and women were more equal, given the characteristics of the two groups, than they have been since. As women began to extend their time in the labor force and compete directly with men for jobs in the white-collar sector, substantial amounts of "wage discrimination" started to appear. Accounting for unexplained differences in earnings between men and women cannot be precise, but several prime suspects are revealed in the historical evidence.

One is a form of "statistical discrimination." Because most women would leave the labor force at the time of marriage, employers denied them access to various job ladders, and women were tracked into various dead-end positions or ones involving very limited mobility (see also Thurow, 1975). Historical surveys concerning the jobs offered males and females in office employment reveal policies designed to segregate workers in this fashion.

A related reason is that male workers and employers had a distaste for working with or under the direction of women. There was, in other words, simple discrimination against women workers with a multitude of possible origins. Male workers may have feared the introduction of females would lower their earnings and dilute the skills required through the division of labor and increased capital intensity. In the nineteenth and early twentieth centuries, male manufacturing workers knew the impact that mechanization and the division of labor had in the tobacco and canning industries. The molders' union, for example, instituted fines for teaching a woman the trade of core making and did not allow women into the union during World War I (U.S. Department of Labor, 1920; also Greenwald, 1980). Another possibility is that male workers believed the introduction of females would lower the prestige or status attached to their occupation (Goldin, 1988).

The search for a monocausal explanation for differences between the earnings and occupations of men and women can only produce frustration. Current distinctions in the labor market affect future distinctions through conceptions of appropriate behavior, through the prejudices of workers, customers, and employers, and through individual expectations. A highly segregated workplace, where pay for women's work is less than that for men's work, will lead men to increase their prejudices against having women work in their occupation; increased prejudice, in turn, reinforces the status quo. A highly segregated work force will render the woman who seeks employment in a man's occupation a deviant, and the stigma could have an impact on other spheres of social interaction, such as marriage.

The determinants of earnings for both men and women are many. The more schooled, trained, and experienced tend today to be better paid than the usual lot, as do those who are just smarter and more able. But schooling and training amount to little in an economy with low demand for such skills. Education has not always commanded the substantial premium it does today. In the manufacturing sector of the late nineteenth century, strength and stamina were more highly valued traits than the formal skills acquired at school. But in the emerging white-collar sector of the early twentieth century, education became highly rewarded for both men and women. . . .

Several large-scale surveys of female manufacturing and sales workers were undertaken at the federal and state levels from 1884, the date of the Massachusetts report *Working Girls of Boston* (1889), to 1907, that of the U.S. Senate, *Report on Condition of Woman and Child Wage-Earners* (1910–1911). . . . These various surveys are used here to explore the determinants of earnings among working women in the period 1888 to 1907. . . . The difference in average (full-time) annual earnings between male and female factory operatives was substantial. Female operatives working full-time across the United States earned 54% of the average male operative in 1890, 55% in 1900, and 56% in 1905. . . .

Part of the difference between the earnings of males and females can be attributed to the considerably longer work and occupational experience of the male labor force. Males, on average, had three times the total work experience of females, almost three times the duration in current occupation, and one and one-half times the years with current employer. Much of the difference between the earnings of female and male workers might then be due to the considerably longer lifetime of work for men than women in the late nineteenth century, less so their greater attachment to particular firms. The longer duration on the job and at an occupation may, in turn, have been due to the greater ability of young men to obtain apprenticeships, either formal or informal.

The remaining portion of the difference in earnings would then result from how males and females were paid given their attributes. As is apparent from the discussion of female occupations in manufacturing, their job ladders were relatively short, and even though their wages rose rather steeply at first their earnings reached a plateau early. Males, however, had longer job ladders and garnered skills valued across firms and occupations. . . .

The measure of "wage discrimination" can be easily applied to the data on male and female earnings in manufacturing for the late nineteenth and early twentieth centuries. In the California sample, for which both female and male earnings are given, mean earnings of a female operative are $6.70 per week and those of a male are $14.69, yielding a ratio of 0.456. Had the average female worker been rewarded for her characteristics as if she were a male, her earnings would have been $8.81. The difference between the earnings of the male, $14.69, and those of the conjectural female, $8.81, is a consequence of his greater job, occupation, and firm experience. The difference between the earnings of a female worker, $6.70, and those of the conjectural female, divided by the difference in the earnings of male and female workers, is a measure of "wage discrimination," and is 35% in this case (using the log values). "Wage discrimination" results from the differential evaluation of equivalent characteristics in the marketplace and from differences in the constant terms, here the earnings of a worker with no job experience. . . .

[S]ome of the difference between male and female earnings may be due to occupational barriers, the results of which can be seen in the extraordinary degree of sex segregation of industries and occupations around 1890. But another part of the difference may be due to disparities in average strength and intensity of work. . . .

Given the virtual absence of women in male-intensive industries and the very few occupations in which there were both males and females, it is difficult to judge the returns to strength and work intensity. There is, however, a small group of occupations that paid by the piece and had large groups of male and female workers within the same firm. In a sample of piece-rate occupations, males earned 25% more than females, even when the work was identical, the piece rate was the same, and both worked for the same firm. . . . It is conceivable that male workers were better trained and that part of the 25% difference is due to differences in experience and training that should already be accounted for in the "wage discrimination" partition. But even in unskilled, menial work, for which women of greater strength must have been selected and for which training was unnecessary, men earned about 15% more on average than women. . . .

The 15% figure can be taken as a lower bound for initial differences in productivity in manufacturing. Initial differences are built into the earnings of workers with no work experience, but ought not be blamed on "wage discrimination." Adjusting the constant term for females by 15% raises average earnings in the example above to $7.78 (from $6.70) and narrows the unexplained portion to slightly more than $1.00, or 19.5% of the difference in the logs of male and female earnings.

Even at its initial, unadjusted level of 35%, "wage discrimination" in manufacturing around 1900 was slight in comparison with that found in more recent studies. At its adjusted level of 19.5%, "wage discrimination" in the manufacturing sector was extremely low.[1] Modern, empirical discrimination studies, summarized above, generally find that "wage discrimination" accounts for at least 55% of the difference in the logs of male and female earnings. An unexplained difference of 55% is hard to rationalize by the absence of various factors that are difficult to measure or are unobserved. One of 19.5% seems far easier to explain by such omission, particularly since it is for a sector in which strength demands, intensity of work, and the work environment may have favored male over female workers.

The low ratio of earnings of females to males in late-nineteenth-century manufacturing jobs was due largely to differences in attributes, primarily job experience, despite the extraordinary segregation of industries and occupations between the sexes. But attribute differences may, in turn, be due to discriminatory factors. It has already been noted that young women had few incentives to work hard. They kept very little of their own earnings, they stood almost no chance of being promoted, and their work taught them little of use outside their particular factory. Not surprisingly, they looked to marriage and a home of their own as an escape. Occupational and industrial sex segregation may have had little net effect on the ratio of female to male earnings, but sex segregation may not be as benign as the data on "wage discrimination" imply. . . .

CLERICAL WORK AND CLERICAL WORKERS

The share of all female workers in the clerical sector expanded from just 4% to 21% over the period 1890 to 1930. The clerical sector had been 15% female in 1890 but was more than 50% by 1930, and while male employment in the sector rose as well, the proportion of all employed men in the sector increased trivially, from 3% to 6%. The clerical sector grew primarily by hiring female workers. . . .

Male and female clerical workers began their work careers with apparently similar skills, but males were placed on a different track. The resulting occupational distribution was highly segregated at the upper end, while beginning positions were often integrated. Advancement to secretary for most women clerical workers was the highest achievable rank, and although secretaries earned 40% more than typists, they were paid considerably less than comparably experienced men. . . . There is ample proof that women were excluded by firm policy from virtually all office jobs involving substantial advancement within the firm. . . . Women could not have achieved the male earnings function because they were barred from most jobs with promotional possibilities. The evidence regarding firm-level policies is probably unique to the period examined when discrimination on the basis of sex and marital status was not illegal and when it was often considered public-spirited because of the Depression. It is likely that firms had similar policies before and after the Depression.

Women were prohibited from entering various clerical positions through the personnel policies of most firms, and . . . married women were barred from many of the largest and highest paying firms. The firm-level records of the Women's Bureau study, just used to measure "wage discrimination," termed here the 1940 Office Firm Survey, contain answers to two questions concerning occupations reserved for men and for women by firm policy. The precise questions were "Which [office] jobs are open to men only?" and "Which [office] jobs are open to women only?"

Across the three large cities in the sample, 74% of all firms had formal policies restricting occupations to "women only," and these restrictions affected 79% of the female employees in the sample. . . . Firms barred women from occupations of authority (executive, department head), and from those for which high skill was required (engineer, draftsman). They often prohibited women from entering the accounting division (accountant, teller, collector, cost controller, paymaster), to which men were often advanced when they demonstrated initiative and drive in the unskilled jobs. But firms also barred women from the unskilled entry-level positions of mail boy, errand boy, and messenger. New York Life Insurance Company considered male office boys a "source of future staff," and Philadelphia Transportation Company likewise hired male messengers "because they are source of raw material" (1940 Office Firm Survey). . . .

"Wage discrimination" rose from at most 20% of the difference in male and female earnings around 1900 in manufacturing to 55% in office work in 1940. The origins of "wage discrimination" are thus to be found in various policies that transformed labor from the spot market of the manufacturing sector to the wage-setting arena of modern firms, in which earnings do not contemporaneously equal a worker's value to the firm. These conscious policies were designed to elicit appropriate effort, to screen for suitable employees, and to bind employees to the firm, among other reasons. Promotion from within, adopted by most large firms in the Women's Bureau 1940 sample, enabled managers to alter worker effort and select for the most able among large groups of workers. There was, as well, real training both on and off the job.

In this newly established labor arena, female white-collar workers were treated differently from men for several reasons. Firms in office work and in manufacturing found it profitable to treat women not as individuals, but as a group. As a group, they were less likely to aspire to positions of responsibility; as a group, they were less likely to remain in the labor force. But because women could conceivably enter the male occupational track in office work—they did, after all, commence work with identical earnings—they would have to be barred from certain occupations if firms (or their employees) did not want them to enter. The situation differed from the manufacturing sector. Formal barriers were infrequently encountered there. Instead, actual requirements, say, strength and various normative influences that defined certain industries as male only, deterred women from requesting entry. The fact that so many entire industries had no female operatives suggests the force of societal norms in the manufacturing sector. In office work, however, such appeal could not be made, and both men and women were instead barred by firm policy from certain occupations.

The overall impact of the new labor policies was to have consciously sex-segregated occupations. Differences in expected tenure on the job may have been responsible for some distinctions in the job ladders offered men and women. But these differences were reinforced by a long history of occupational segregation and by a society that had formed a consensus around the virtue of sex segregation and the appropriateness of differentiating on the basis of sex. They were also enabled by the absence of an opposing ideology that would eventually lead women as individuals to become discontent with their treatment as a group.

. . . .

Discrimination against women is manifested in a variety of ways. In its most typical form, no prescribed barriers exist. Rather, employers, employees, and customers can express their prejudices against women workers by preferring not to associate with them. This form of discrimination is often inferred from its effects on earnings and occupations. In other instances, custom and tradition are dominant, and individuals are penalized for deviating. Prescribed barriers against the training and employment of women are perhaps the most easily observed forms of discrimination. Rules have existed barring the education and training of women, as in the professions of law and medicine and among certain medieval guilds and more modern unions (see Morello, 1986, on law; Harris, 1978, on the professions in general). In other circumstances, rules restricted the employment of women, as in the armed forces, post office, local fire departments, and legal profession. The distinction between the two types of discrimination—the more or less subtle revealing of preferences and the rather obvious prohibitions—is often blurred when written rules do not exist but custom dictates the result.

Bars concerning the hiring and firing of married women, termed "marriage bars," arose in teaching and clerical work from the late 1800's to the early 1900's and provide the most numerically important form of all prohibitions in their impact on the employment of married women. In 1920 just 11% of all married women in the labor force were teachers and clerical workers, yet by 1970 the percentage nearly quadrupled, to 41%. The prohibitions covered what were to become the most frequent occupations for married women in the post-1950 era. In contrast, prohibitions against the training and employment of women as doctors and lawyers, probably the best known of all bans, affected a trivial percentage of women. . . .

Marriage bars were instituted in public-school teaching sometime in the late 1800's and were expanded in the early 1900's. Extensive surveys of local school districts beginning with 1928 indicate that 61% of all school systems would not hire a married woman teacher and 52% would not retain any who married while on contract. . . . Both types of bars increased during the Depression, and on the eve of American entry into World War II, fully 87% of all school districts would not hire a married women and 70% would not retain a single woman who married. But sometime during World War II, both bars disappeared. By 1951 only 18% of the school systems had the hire bar and 10% the retain bar.

The extent of the marriage bar in office work can be inferred from information in two comprehensive surveys conducted by the Women's Bureau (U.S. Department of Labor, 1934b, 1942), called here the 1931 Office Firm Survey and the 1940 Office Firm Survey.

In 1931, 12% of all firms in the sample had a formal policy of not retaining single women when they married, but 25% of all female employees were in firms having such a policy. The policy, therefore, increased with firm size. Some firms did not have a strict marriage bar policy but had discretionary rules allowing them to retain able workers, to hire married women when single were unavailable, or to leave the policy up to department heads. About 35% of all female employees were working in firms that would not retain them if they married as a condition of both policy and discretion. Considerably more firms had policies against hiring married women than against the retention of single women who married. About 29% of all firms had such policies in the 1931 survey, and the policies affected 36% of all female employees across these firms. More than 50% of all firms in the sample would not hire married women as a condition of policy and discretion, and more than 50% of all female employees in the sample were employed by those firms.

. . . .

ORIGINS OF DISCONTENT

Few American women before the 1960's would admit that discrimination on the basis of sex affected their earnings and employment. I do not mean that women had not felt discontent with their treatment in the labor market before the 1960's. Educated women, in particular, had often expressed indignity with prohibitions against their employment, particularly in the professions; mass dismissals of women in both post–world war periods were met with outrage; and the marriage bars of the 1930's, certainly the firing of married women by the federal government, led many women to speak publicly about their treatment. Yet most women were silent about their exclusion from promotion and training and about the resulting earnings differences given equal experience and education. Their silence, moreover, was a product of custom and prejudice, just as the silence of black Americans was. Women required a perception of injustice and an ideology to awaken and unify them. Discontent was finally articulated in the 1960's by large numbers of college-educated, middle-class women, and they ultimately produced the feminist revival of the 1960's and 1970's (Freeman, 1975). Although the discontent described by Betty Friedan in her 1963 book was apparent as early as the 1920's (Cowan, 1983a), college-educated women whose expectations greatly exceeded their realizations incited a mass movement.

Perceptions of Discrimination

The use of the word "discrimination" to describe unequal outcomes in earnings and occupations by sex, given identical inputs, is rather recent. In the nineteenth and early twentieth centuries, when most paid labor was in manufacturing and agriculture, inequality of earnings was most commonly viewed as arising from inherent differences between men and women in strength, endurance, drive, and ambition. . . . Some differences were admitted to have been socially determined; for example, apprenticeships were denied female workers not only because they were not expected to remain with the trade, but also because it was considered socially improper to give or receive training. . . .

"[W]age discrimination" increased considerably with the growth of occupations in the clerical, sales, and professional sectors that substituted brain power for strength and formal education for on-the-job training. . . . At issue here is why women rarely commented on what appears now to be obvious and substantial inequities that widened over time.

Part of the reason concerns norms that define appropriate behavior and that somehow punish deviance. Occupations assume an "aura of gender," informing individuals which should be pursued by each sex. . . . Consequently, there may be circularity in the contentment of female workers. Sex-segregated occupations quickly become associated with gender distinctions that are not necessarily part of the original rationale for segregation. For a woman to express dissatisfaction would be to reject one set of traits and embrace another.

. . . .

NOTES

1.   Various biases concerning the self-selection of workers may afflict the earnings data for women. Although these cannot be assessed using current data, they do not seem important. The problem, in general, is that individuals who remain on the job for long periods may differ from those who leave early. To the extent that those who leave early are the most productive and able, for which there is no reliable indicator, the earnings function will be biased in favor of discrimination. One possibility is that women who are most able in the labor market are also most productive in the household and, because of this, marry earlier. It seems more likely that young women who were highly productive in the labor market married later, not earlier. Thus the possible biases from self-selection do not appear, in this case at least, to have been important. Further, the range of possible occupations for females in manufacturing around the turn of the century was sufficiently limited that biases of this nature could not greatly alter the results presented above.

REFERENCES

Cowan, Ruth Schwartz. 1983. "Two Washes in the Morning and a Bridge Party at Night: The American Housewife between the Two Wars." In Lois Scharf and Joan M. Jensen, editors, *Decades of Discontent: The Women's Movement, 1920–1940*. Westport, CT: Greenwood Press.

Freeman, Jo. 1975. *The Politics of Women's Liberation*. New York: Longman.

Goldin, Claudia. 1988. "A Pollution Theory of Discrimination: Male and Female Differences in Earnings and Occupation." Manuscript, University of Pennsylvania.

Greenwald, Maurine Weiner. 1980. *Women, War, and Work: The Impact of World War I on Women Workers in the United States*. Westport, CT: Greenwood Press.

Harris, Barbara J. 1978. *Beyond Her Sphere: Women and the Professions in American History*. Westport, CT: Greenwood Press.

Morello, Karen Berger. 1986. *The Invisible Bar: The Woman Lawyer in America, 1638 to the Present*. New York: Random House.

U.S. Department of Labor, Women's Bureau. 1920. *The New Position of Women in American Industry*. Bulletin of the Women's Bureau, No. 12. Washington, DC: U.S. Government Printing office.

United States Department of Labor, Women's Bureau. 1934. *The Employment of Women in Offices*, by Ethel Erickson. Bulletin of the Women's Bureau, No. 120. Washington, DC: U.S. Government Printing Office.

United States Department of Labor, Women's Bureau. 1942. *Office Work in [Houston, Los Angeles, Kansas City, Richmond, and Philadelphia]*. Bulletin of the Women's Bureau. Nos. 188–1, 2, 3, 4, 5. Washington, DC: U.S. Government Printing Office.

3

Assimilation in the United States: An Analysis of Ethnic and Generation Differences in Status and Achievement

Lisa J. Neidert and Reynolds Farley

A fundamental question for both social science and political policy throughout this century is how this nation incorporates immigrants who come from differing countries and cultural backgrounds. Do we have a melting pot in which immigrants not only contribute to the nation's culture, but are rapidly assimilated so that their occupational achievements are not very different from those of the native-born population? Or is our society thoroughly divided by race and ethnicity such that the Anglo-Saxons who founded the country are much more successful than others, perhaps because of discrimination and exploitation? . . . Fortunately, there is a new body of data which allows us to resolve questions about the assimilation process. . . .

In preparation for the decennial enumeration, the Bureau of Census, in November, 1979, asked a national sample the birthplace, ancestry and language questions which appeared on the Census of either 1970 or 1980. This is an important new data source for three reasons. First, for the first time, we can investigate the achievements of ancestry groups classified by their generations in the United States. For example, the educational attainment and occupational prestige of people born in Mexico may be compared to that of U.S.-born people who also claim Mexican ancestry. Second, the sample size, approximately 170,000, is sufficiently large to both classify ethnic groups by generation and to identify the characteristics of newly-arriving groups. In this paper, we use the terms ethnicity and ancestry interchangeably. Third, information about ancestry or ethnicity is available by generation for the entire population. . . .

The nature of these data is illustrated in Figure 1 which shows the ancestry composition of the population in 1979. Data are presented for all groups reported by one million or more.

Excerpts reprinted with permission from the *American Sociological Review* 1985, vol. 50: 840–850. Copyright © 1985 by the American Sociological Association.

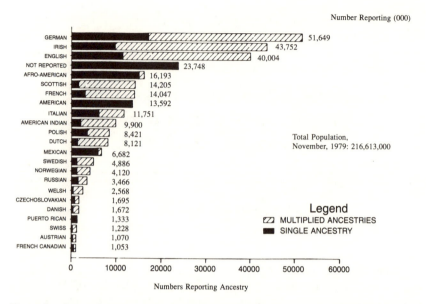

Figure 1. Ancestries reported by one million or more persons, November, 1979. *Source:* U.S. Bureau of the Census, Current Population Reports, Series P-23, No. 116.

Figure 1 reports that just under one-quarter of the population claimed German ancestry while about one-fifth reported Irish or English. The next largest ancestry groups—Afro-American, Scottish and French—were much smaller, about one-third the size of the largest ancestries. Italian was the only other origin claimed by more than ten million. Only four other groups—American Indians, Polish, Dutch and Mexican—were reported by more than five million.

For each ancestry, we indicate what proportion of responses were given singly and the proportion given in combination with other ancestries. Overall, about six out of ten who answered this question gave only one response while the rest gave multiple ancestries. Among white groups, the proportion with multiple reports is roughly proportional to their duration of residence in this country, undoubtedly a consequence of ethnic intermarriage. Only 22 percent of those asserting Irish ancestry gave a single response, while 88 percent of the Mexican origin population reported only one ancestry.

ETHNIC DIFFERENCES AMONG FIRST-GENERATION IMMIGRANTS

To study assimilation, we looked at the characteristics of men age 20 to 64 in 1979.[1] We wished to know whether those in the core cultural group—men of

English ancestry—enjoyed an advantage in socioeconomic status. We analyzed data for three generations: those who were born abroad (first-generation immigrants), those who were born in the United States but had one or both parents born abroad (second generation) and those born in the United States of U.S.-born parents (third and higher generations).

Within every generation, men from each ancestry group are compared to men of the core culture group—that is, men of English origin—on four measures of status. Two pertain to education: average school years completed, and the proportion who finished at least one year of college.

We wished to analyze ethnic differences in earnings; however, the data were not available since the November Current Population Survey did not ask about earnings. It included only one income question and that involved the total income of the entire household. To describe economic differences among these groups, we determined per capita household income.[2] These amounts reveal large differences in the prosperity of the groups but they are influenced by ethnic differences in earnings, family size and receipt of transfer payments.

A fourth measure of achievement is the average socioeconomic occupational score for a group. The Census Bureau's survey reported the detailed occupation of every employed man and the usual job for those who were out of work. A score was assigned using the scale developed by Duncan (1961; Blau and Duncan, 1967:118–120; Featherman and Hauser, 1978). These range from a high of 96 assigned to dentists to a low of 3 for mine-equipment operatives. . . .

One component of this investigation determines whether the educational attainment, occupational achievements and per capita income of various ancestries equal those of the core group—the English. However, we wished to go beyond that comparison. Do men of English origin have an advantage in the competition to get prestigious jobs or do all groups have similar rates of occupational achievement? If there is discrimination in the labor market such that Anglo-Saxons are favored, or if some groups have cultural values which enhance their achievement, we should find significant ethnic differences in the rate at which ancestries convert educational attainment into occupational status.

To test this, the socioeconomic occupational index was regressed upon years of education and a series of control variables that influence achievement. These were the man's age, his marital status: a dichotomous variable which distinguished married-spouse-present men from others, region of residence: South or non-South, and language. For the first generation, this is a dichotomous variable indicating whether or not the man reported he spoke English well, while for the second and third generations, language is measured by a variable which distinguished men with a non-English mother tongue from those whose mother tongue was English.

The Bureau of the Census coded approximately 400 ancestries. To facilitate the analysis, we grouped some of these. Our aim was to create groups which were homogeneous with regard to cultural and geographic origin and included a total sample size (uninflated) of 50 or more men age 20 to 64. There was no problem in dealing with such ethnicities as Italians and Germans, but other ethnicities such as Jamaicans, Haitians and other Caribbeans were all too small to consider on their own. One alternative was to exclude these ethnicities; the other was to form groups such as "other southern Europeans" and "Caribbeans". Some ancestries appear in one generation but not in others. Filipinos, for example, are sufficiently numerous to be included in the first generation but not the third, while older immigrant groups such as Afro-Americans appear chiefly in the third generation. For the majority of respondents, there was no problem in assigning ancestry since they reported only once. However, 38 percent gave two or more ancestries (U.S. Bureau of the Census, 1982: Table A). People who listed multiple ancestries were classified by their first report. A man who listed French-Norwegian, for example, was treated as French.

Table 1 provides information about that 5 percent of the population that was foreign-born. Data are shown for the English ancestry group and for the thirteen other ancestries that were sufficiently large. English men completed an average of 13.2 years of schooling and 43 percent finished one or more years of college. Their educational attainment exceeded that of most other groups. Asians, Filipinos and men from northwest Europe had greater attainments but the only significant difference involved the extensive college education of two groups: Asians and Filipinos. At the other end, several foreign-born groups reported significantly less attainment than the English; among these groups were Italians, other southern Europeans, Caribbeans and the Hispanic groups. These educational differences in the first generation are, in part, the outcome of migration selectivity. Two of the easiest ways to migrate legally to the United States are to have relatives here or to have a skill—often a profession—which is in short supply. . . .

Turning to occupational status, we find that the status of no group exceeds that of the English. Men from several ancestries including Italians, Caribbeans and the Hispanic groups worked at significantly less prestigious jobs. The per capita income data show that first-generation English have a favorable economic status. No foreign-born group has an income exceeding that of the English, and many are significantly poorer. Mexicans reported exceptionally low incomes: less than 30 percent that of the English.

We next considered the rate at which ancestry groups convert their educations into occupational achievement. For the first generation group, it would have been desirable to distinguish education received in the United States from that obtained elsewhere. Unfortunately, this topic was not investigated in the November 1979 CPS. . . .

For English men, each additional year of schooling netted a man 4.5 socioeconomic index points. Stated differently, remaining in school three additional years leads to an increment of 14 points for an English migrant or creates the difference between an auto mechanic and a bookkeeper. No ancestry had a

Table 1. Foreign-Born Men 20 to 64 Classified by Ancestry, Characteristics of Groups and Occupational Returns for Educational Attainments

| | | Characteristics of Groups | | | | Regression Analysis | | |
| | | | | | | Returns for Education[a] | | |
Ancestries	Population (000)	Median Years of School	Percent with Some College	Mean Occupational Score	Per Capita Income (000)	R^2	b	Standard Error of b
English	123	13.2	43%	50	$9,400	39%	4.5	0.8
British Isles, Not England	123	13.6	52	47	10,500	39	4.9	0.7
German	167	13.2	48	42	9,900	29	4.3	0.8
Other N.W. Europe	148	13.4	52	44	9,600	49	5.3	0.6
Italian	184	10.0*	15*	32*	6,000*	30	2.7	0.5
Other South Europe	127	10.2*	17*	28*	5,000*	29	1.6*	0.5
Russian/East Europe	271	13.1	47	44	8,800	49	4.5	0.4
Asian	202	14.2*	64**	44	5,200*	46	5.4	0.5
Other Spanish	281	11.1*	28*	31*	4,800*	38	3.5	0.4
Mexican	587	6.9*	9*	18*	2,700*	16	0.9*	0.2
Puerto Rican	123	8.7*	5*	27*	3,300*	20	2.2	0.8
Cuban	131	12.0*	41	37*	5,800*	30	3.3	0.8
Filipino	88	13.9	76**	38*	5,300*	36	3.8	0.8
Caribbean	147	9.9*	25*	27*	4,900*	55	4.7	0.6

[a]The value of b indicates the change in occupational status associated with a one-year change in educational attainment. The model regresses the occupational socioeconomic score upon years of schooling completed, age, marital status (a dichotomy distinguishing married-spouse-present men from all others), region (a dichotomy distinguishing those in the South) and ability to speak English (a dichotomy distinguishing those who speak English well from those who speak it not well or not at all).

* Mean, proportion or coefficient is *significantly smaller* than comparable parameter for the English ancestry group (.05 level).

** Mean, proportion or coefficient is *significantly larger* than comparable parameter for the English ancestry group (.05 level).

Source: U.S. Bureau of the Census, Current Population Survey: (November, 1979) Public Use Tape File.

significantly greater rate of return for its educational attainment in the first generation than the English and only two groups—other southern Europeans and Mexicans—did significantly less well. . . .

ETHNIC DIFFERENCES AMONG SECOND-GENERATION MEN

Data for American-born sons of foreign or mixed parentage are shown in Table 2. Because the second generation is larger than the first—11 percent of the population had a foreign-born parent in 1979—more ancestries are represented, including Scandinavians, Poles and French. . . .

There were differences in educational attainment among the second generation: the English were extensively educated compared to others. Only Russians exceed them in attainment but the difference is not significant. Many ethnicities—including old stock groups—report significantly lower attainments than the English. Second-generation Mexicans were distinctive because of their exceptionally limited attainment; they averaged almost four fewer years of schooling than the English.

With regard to occupational status, men of English origin are also in a favorable position since no other group had a significantly greater achievement. Several second-generation ancestries were significantly lower in occupational status. They represent a variety of different origins: Germans and the Irish from northern Europe, Italians from the South, Poles from eastern Europe, Asians and the two Hispanic groups. . . .

Economic differences—as assessed by per capita income—among the second generation were smaller than among the first. The English were prosperous, but Russians and the other western European group—a group composed primarily of Dutch and Belgians—had even higher incomes. Three second-generation ancestries were significantly poorer than the English. Mexicans remained at the bottom of this financial ranking.

Although second-generation men of English ethnicity have an occupational advantage over other ancestries, there is little evidence that they are more effective in converting their educational attainment into occupational status. Table 2 shows the occupational returns for investments in education using a model similar to that described for the first generation. An additional year of education added 5.5 points to the occupational score of English men. No group had a significantly greater rate of return. Indeed, the coefficients for almost all ancestries were lower than that for the English but only two groups—Mexicans and the Lithuanian/Latvian/Ukranian combination—had significantly lower rates of return. This once again provides support for the assimilation view since most second-generation ancestries were not at a disadvantage vis a vis the English in converting their investments in education into occupational status.

Table 2. Native-Born Sons Age 20 to 64 of Foreign or Mixed Parentage, Characteristics of Groups and Occupational Returns for Educational Attainment

Ancestries	Population (000)	Characteristics of Groups				Regression Analysis Returns for Education[a]		
		Median Years of School	Percent with Some College	Mean Occupational Score	Per Capita Income (000)	R^2	b	Standard Error of b
English	318	13.8	56	50	$9,000	41	5.5	0.5
Scottish/Welsh	162	13.4	52	47	8,700	35	5.3	0.8
German	624	12.6*	37*	41*	8,400	32	4.6	0.3
French	205	11.9*	27*	37*	7,000*	24	4.1	0.6
Irish	324	12.6*	40*	40*	8,400	33	4.6	0.4
Scandinavian	355	13.7	55	48	8,700	32	4.9	0.5
Other West Europe	218	12.8*	39*	44*	10,100	36	5.3	0.6
Italian	907	12.1*	30*	43*	7,900	34	4.9	0.3
Other South Europe	153	12.5*	38*	39*	8,400	38	5.1	0.7
Polish	470	12.1*	30*	39*	8,000	45	5.0	0.4
Other East Europe	317	12.4*	32*	42*	8,600	32	4.8	0.6
Russian	259	14.4	64	55	10,900	30	4.5	0.6
Lithuanian, Latvian and Ukranian	87	12.8*	43	42*	7,700	31	4.1*	0.1
Asian	108	13.6	56	44*	8,400	42	7.2	0.9
Other Spanish	160	12.0*	41*	37*	6,400*	39	4.0	0.5
Mexican	371	10.1*	21*	30*	5,000*	21	2.6*	0.3
Canadian	120	12.6*	38*	43*	7,000	35	6.3	0.8

[a] The value of b indicates the change in occupational status associated with a one-year change in educational attainment. The model regresses the occupational socioeconomic score upon years of schooling completed, age, marital status (a dichotomy distinguishing married-spouse-present men from all others), region (a dichotomy distinguishing those in the South) and ability to speak English (a dichotomy distinguishing those who speak English well from those who speak it not well or not at all).

* Mean, proportion or coefficient is *significantly smaller* than comparable parameter for the English ancestry group (.05 level).
Source: See Table 1.

ETHNIC DIFFERENCES AMONG THIRD-GENERATION MEN

The term third generation describes American-born sons of parents who were both born in the United States. This includes many higher generations since the forebears of some of these men arrived in the colonies in the 1600s. . . .

Several ancestries reported greater educational attainment than the English: Scottish/Welsh, Russians, and Asians. An array of third-generation ancestries completed fewer years of schooling than the English, including several old stock groups, the Hispanic ancestries and two which are racial minorities: American Indians and Afro-Americans. Looking at occupational rankings, we find three groups—the Scottish/Welsh, Russians and the east Europeans—worked at significantly higher-status jobs than the English while many groups had average socioeconomic indexes lower than those of English ancestry men.

Per capita income in third-generation households varied widely. Russians and Asians had significantly larger incomes than the English. Indeed, the richest group—the Asians—had per capita incomes about 40 percent in excess of those of the English. On the other hand, many ancestries were significantly poorer than the English, including the French, Germans and Irish. Ancestries with the lowest per capita incomes, however, were Americans, Indians, Afro-Americans and, at the very bottom, Mexicans, who had incomes only 60 percent of those of the English.

To determine whether membership in a particular ancestry was an advantage or a liability for occupational achievement, we once again looked at the returns for investments in education. Presumably, if employers prefer members of one ancestry or if some groups have cultural values which give them an edge, we find differences in the rate at which education is converted into occupational status.

[A]n additional four years of schooling netted a third-generation Englishman 21 occupational points. Several ancestries had greater returns for their investments in education: an identical amount of schooling netted an Asian 30 points; a Russian, 28 points; and other east Europeans, 26 points. The ancestries at a disadvantage in the occupational achievement process were American Indians and Mexicans who derived only 14 occupational points from four additional years of schooling. Those who claimed Afro-American or American as their ethnic origin were also significantly behind the English.

The hypothesis that ancestry has no significant effect on occupational attainment in the third generation should be rejected. However, most of the European-origin groups achieve at about the same rate as the English. There is no evidence that Poles, the Irish, Italians or Scandinavians are at a disadvantage in the competition for good jobs. Consistent with previous studies, we find that Russians are unusually successful. . . . There is consensus that this group is largely Jewish. . . . Third-generation Asians, however, were even more successful than Russians in converting their educations into prestigious jobs. The groups at a disadvantage were the descendents of three groups who have traditionally experienced hostile treatment: Mexicans, Indians and blacks.

Those who claim American ancestry were distinctively low in educational attainment and occupational status, and their returns for investment in schooling were significantly smaller than those of the English. These people differ from others in that they had to persist in saying "American" after having been prodded for some other response. Relative to the other ancestries, they are highly concentrated in the South, have limited educations, and about one-quarter of them are black. . . .

The assimilation model contends that immigrants become similar to the core cultural group the longer they remain in the United States. Presumably, a first-generation migrant is at a disadvantage because he lacks information about the labor market, because he cannot speak English well or because of discrimination. If assimilation occurs, we expect ancestries to become more similar to the English as the number of generations in this country increases.

Ideally, this hypothesis should be tested with longitudinal data covering several generations and many decades. Such data are not available, but with this unique data set we can see if ethnic differences in occupational achievement disappear by the third generation, controlling for differences in age, region, marital status, English language ability and education. . . .

We lack the longitudinal data needed to investigate whether ancestries differ in the way they transmit their advantages or liabilities from one generation to the next. However, findings from these cross-sectional data provide strong support for the assimilation model for European groups. . . . On the basis of these data, we drew five conclusions about migrants, ethnicity and the assimilation process in the United States.

First, immigrants and their children in 1979 were not at a great disadvantage in social or economic status. The selectivity of immigration helps to account for the high status of first-generation migrants but second-generation migrants differ only a little from third and higher generations in educational attainment, occupational status or per capita household income.

Second, there are significant ethnic differences in education, occupational rankings and per capita income in all generations. Even among those stock groups who have been in the United States since the nineteenth century, we find that some are higher in status than others. In most comparisons, the educational attainment, occupational standing and economic status of the core cultural group—the English—exceeds that of other ethnicities. The ancestries also differ among themselves. For example, third- and higher-generation Afro-American men complete three and one-half fewer years of schooling than Russians, and per capita income in third-generation Mexican households is less than half that in Asian households.

Third, in the process of occupational achievement, European-origin groups are not at a disadvantage compared to those of English ancestry. Many ancestries spend fewer years in school than the English, but in the competition for prestigious jobs, these groups are not significantly disadvantaged.

Fourth, several groups stand out for their low levels of achievement in the third generation: Mexicans, Afro-Americans and American Indians. Third-generation Mexicans were the least effective of any group—even less effective than Afro-Americans—in translating their educational attainment into occupational prestige (Chiswick, 1978:921; Duncan and Duncan, 1968:364; Poston et al., 1976; Poston and Alvirez, 1973; Featherman and Hauser, 1978: Table 8.16). Numerous investigations of racial differences report that blacks are not very successful in converting their education into occupational prestige and this undoubtedly explains the low returns shown for Afro-Americans (Seigel, 1965; Duncan, 1968; Hauser and Featherman, 1977:133–36). Even though we are describing an unusual group of American Indians, since most of them claim this as their ancestry but not their race, we find that they were also at a significant disadvantage in the attainment process since their rates of return for education were close to those of Mexicans and Afro-Americans, not to those of European-origin ancestries.

Fifth, at least in the third generation, Russians and east Europeans are significantly more successful than the English in using their educational credentials to obtain prestigious jobs. Asians were also very successful in all generations. There is now a popular image of Asians in the United States as highly educated and financially secure but this is strongly influenced by the selectivity of current migration. When we turn to those Asians whose forebears arrived in the United States before World War I, we find that they are even more successful in the occupational achievement process than the descendents of Russians who arrived at the same time.

Has assimilation occurred in the United States in the manner described by Park? Obviously, one cross-sectional survey cannot provide a definite answer but it tells us about contemporary ethnic differences. If assimilation means that third-generation ethnic groups will be indistinguishable from the core English group with regard to education, occupation or per capita income, the answer is definitely not. Even when the analysis is restricted to European-origin groups, we find significant differences on these indicators of status. On the other hand, if assimilation means that ethnic groups are neither favored nor at a disadvantage in the process of occupational achievement, then there is strong evidence to support the theory. Among European-origin ancestries, only Russians and east Europeans are significantly different from the English and they are more successful.

NOTES

1.   An effort was made to study the occupational achievements of women classified by ethnicity and generation. However, the small number of employed women limited this analysis.

2. The ethnicity of a household was determined on the basis of the ancestry reported by the head or co-head of the household.

REFERENCES

Blau, Peter M. and Otis Dudley Duncan. 1967. *The American Occupational Structure.* New York: Wiley.

Chiswick, Barry R. 1978. "The effect of Americanization on the earnings of foreign-born men." *Journal of Population Economy* 86:891–921.

Duncan, Beverly and Otis Dudley Duncan. 1968. "Minorities and the process of stratification." *American Sociological Review* 33:356–64.

Duncan, Otis Dudley. 1961. "A socioeconomic index for all occupations." Pp. 109–38 in Albert J. Reiss, Jr., *Occupations and Social Status.* New York: Free Press.

———. 1968. "Inheritance of poverty or inheritance of race?" Pp. 85–110 in Daniel P. Moynihan (ed.), *On Understanding Poverty.* New York: Basic Books.

Featherman, David L. and Robert M. Hauser. 1978. *Opportunity and Change.* New York: Academic.

Park, Robert E. and Ernest W. Burgess. 1921. *Introduction to the Science of Sociology.* Chicago: University of Chicago Press.

Poston, Dudley L., Jr., David Alvirez, and Marta Tienda. 1976. "Earnings differences between Anglo and Mexican American male workers in 1960 and 1970: changes in the 'cost' of being Mexican American." *Social Science Quarterly* 57:618–31.

Siegel, Paul M. 1965 "On the cost of being a Negro." *Sociological Inquiry* 35:41–57.

U.S. Bureau of the Census. 1982. *Current Population Reports*, Series P-23, No. 116.

4

Twenty-Five Years Later: Where Do We Stand on Equal Employment Opportunity Law Enforcement?

David L. Rose

I. INTRODUCTION

[T]he Civil Rights Act of 1964, which was the first comprehensive legislation to address the problems of discrimination in American society, became the cornerstone of modern civil rights law, including equal employment opportunity law.

The leaders in the struggle to adopt the Civil Rights Act have largely passed from the public scene, and a new generation has reached adulthood with little knowledge of the conditions that called for its adoption. The time is ripe for review.

The ability of this country to integrate the diverse ethnic elements of its inhabitants stands in stark contrast to the experience of much of the rest of the world. While bitter rivalries over the years have separated French and German, Polish and Hungarian, and Catholic and Protestant Irish, their descendants have lived together in this country in relative harmony and have worked together to create an economy and a democracy which is the envy of much of the world.

The countries that have not been able to resolve equitably the differences between the different ethnic groups who live within their borders are numerous. Cyprus, Ethiopia, India, (Northern) Ireland, Israel, Lebanon, Sri Lanka, Somalia, South Africa, and the Sudan are but a few. The tensions and bitterness exemplified in those countries not only deprive the subordinate ethnic group of political freedom and economic opportunity, but they also threaten the fabric of society and the safety and well being of the entire populations.

In this country, political freedom and economic opportunity have been avail-

Excerpts reprinted with permission from the *Vanderbilt Law Review* 1989, vol. 42:1121–1181. Copyright © 1989.

able for the great bulk of the population—if not to many of the immigrants themselves, at least to their children and grandchildren. Yet, the color line for many years prevented political and economic integration. Indeed, racial integration was contrary to the views of the great majority of the population at least until the recent past. Political and economic integration of the minority racial communities into the mainstream of American society was not possible until the country came to grips with the concept of equality of opportunity inherent in the Declaration of Independence and the fourteenth amendment, and adopted the Civil Rights Act of 1964.

The question of whether the political, economic, and social system in this country can incorporate persons of different color with the same success that it has with persons of different national origin remains unanswered, and the issue of whether this or any other country can fully utilize the capabilities of its women remains to be seen. Thus, the question of whether equality of opportunity can be translated from an ideal into more nearly a reality is for the future.

In my view, effective enforcement of the equal employment opportunity law in the next decade is a necessary, if not sufficient, predicate for the social and economic well being of the Nation. This Article reviews the accomplishments and shortcomings of federal equal employment opportunity law[1] over the last twenty-five years in the hope that the questions set forth above can be answered in the affirmative.

II.   HOPES AND ASPIRATIONS: THE HISTORICAL CONTEXT, LEGISLATIVE HISTORY, AND CONVENTIONAL WISDOM

A.   The Situation in 1964

Although the Civil War had been fought over the issue of slavery, and corrective legislation was enacted during Reconstruction, patterns of segregation and discrimination in employment quickly were formed and maintained in the post-Reconstruction era and remained virtually unaltered until the early 1960s.

The executive and judicial branches had been in the forefront of the civil rights battles in the 1940s and 1950s. Every president from Franklin Roosevelt to Lyndon Johnson had adopted executive orders on equal employment opportunity. . . .

Despite the expressed policies of the executive branch since President Truman's Executive Order 9980 in 1948, employment in the federal government remained largely segregated in the 1950s and the early 1960s, with sharply defined jobs for whites and blacks. Segregation and discrimination also continued with little change in the private sector and in most state and local governments, despite executive orders on equal employment opportunity and the adoption of fair employment laws by twenty-five states in the postwar period (mostly the larger industrial states outside of the South).

Blacks were excluded from traditionally "white" jobs and were limited to lower paying, less desirable jobs throughout the South. While the discriminatory practices of employers and unions in other regions were frequently less explicit and less rigid, custom, inertia, seniority and referral systems, union pressure, and informal practices accomplished much the same result throughout the rest of the country. For example, in the trucking industry only whites were allowed to drive trucks in the higher paying "long haul" or "over the road" jobs, while blacks were relegated to "city" driving in some locations and were excluded from all positions except janitor or janitor and dockworker in others. In the paper industry, blacks worked in the woodyard while whites operated the equipment inside. In the steel industry, blacks held the physically strenuous, hot and dirty jobs, while the better paying supervisory positions were reserved for whites.

Although discrimination by unions had been declared unlawful as early as 1944, many unions retained their "white only" clauses, while others deleted the clauses but not the practices underlying them. Segregated unions continued to exist.[2] While the industrial unions such as the United Automobile Workers and the Steel Workers tended to admit blacks as well as whites, they did little to break down the established job hierarchies.

While tradition and the nature of the work played an important role in the racial identification of jobs, in my view the principal determinant was the rate of pay. For example, when the Teamsters organized the trucking industry in the South in the 1950s, the rate of pay doubled for the dockworkers in Memphis, where dockworkers traditionally had been black. The employer immediately changed the job from an all-black gang with a black "caller" (who would call out the destination) and a white "reader" (who would read the bill of lading) to a "one man gang" in which each worker was in theory supposed to read the bill of lading and determine where the cargo was to go. Literacy tests were given and a number of the black dockworkers were fired. The seniority roster showed that every person hired as a dockworker in Memphis after 1957 until the effective date of Title VII was white. Other minorities had made some progress during and after World War II, but pay rates showed that they too continued to be subject to overt discrimination in many parts of the country. In 1962, nonwhite males earned only 59.9 percent the income of white males, and nonwhite females earned only 50.3 percent the income of white females.

The role of women in employment also was severely circumscribed by custom, social pressure, and practice. During World War II, women worked throughout industry, and successfully performed many jobs previously restricted to men. After the war, the prevailing view that these jobs should be reserved for men to support their wives and children was used to oust the women from these jobs. When the "boys" came home from the war, the "girls" went home to become mothers and housekeepers, or were relegated to traditionally female jobs. While some professional schools opened their doors to women in the postwar era, the number of women entering professions other than teaching and nursing was small, and their employment opportunities were severely limited. . . .

The Civil Rights Act of 1964, a comprehensive piece of legislation with eleven titles, included provisions mandating nondiscrimination in public accommodations, public facilities, public education, and federally assisted programs, as well as in employment. . . . The legislative history is particularly difficult to decipher because so many different issues were being considered, because the bill was sent directly to the floor of the Senate, and because Title VII was amended on the floor of the Senate during the filibuster. . . .

Apparently for tactical reasons, the House Judiciary Committee Report on the full bill was uninstructive on the purposes and scope of Title VII. . . . The portion of the Judiciary Committee Report dealing with Title VII simply paraphrased Title VII's provisions with no elaboration or explanation. . . .

The views of the Republican members of the Judiciary Committee, like the Report of the House Committee on Education and Labor, shed more light on the objectives of the bill. In order to support their opinion that the evidence of widespread employment discrimination was "overwhelming," the Republicans relied upon reports from the Department of Labor showing that nonwhite unemployment was 11.4 percent, as compared to 4.9 percent for whites, that the jobs for employed nonwhites were concentrated in the semiskilled and nonskilled positions, that the median annual wages and salary incomes of employed nonwhite males were only 59.9 percent of those of white males, and that the median income for nonwhite women was only 50.3 percent of the median income for white females. Republican Congressman William M. McCulloch and his colleagues noted that the "severe inequality" in employment in the United States created a "condition of marginal existence" for the average black. The Republicans also pointed out the economic inefficiency caused by restricting the employment opportunities of blacks. In particular, the Republicans argued that these discriminatory practices limited purchasing power and acted as a brake upon potential increases in the gross national product. The Republicans concluded:

> Aside from the political and economic considerations, however, we believe in the creation of job equality because it is the right thing to do. We believe in the inherent dignity of man. He is born with certain inalienable rights. His uniqueness is such that we refuse to treat him as if his rights and well-being are bargainable. All vestiges of inequality based solely on race must be removed in order to preserve our democratic society, to maintain our country's leadership, and to enhance mankind.

The Senate Committee on Labor and Public Welfare held hearings on an equal employment opportunity bill, including the bill proposed by Senator Hubert Humphrey, in the summer of 1963. That Committee issued its report on February

4, 1964, while the omnibus civil rights bill was on the floor of the House. . . . [T]he Senate Labor Committee relied upon the same kinds of statistics from the Department of Labor that were relied upon by the House Committee on Education and Labor and the Republican members of the Judiciary Committee in drafting their reported views on the proposed legislation. The Senate Committee found that "overt or covert selective devices, intentional or unintentional, generally prevail throughout the major part of the white economy" and recommended the Humphrey bill, which contained procedures different from Title VII but substantive provisions that directly paralleled those of Title VII. That bill was designed specifically to prohibit all "institutionalized . . . discrimination," particularly that discrimination "preserved through form, habit or inertia." The Committee noted that if the black labor force, at its then present educational level, had been fairly and fully utilized, the gain to the national economy would have been thirteen billion dollars. . . .

Congress adopted the Equal Employment Opportunity Act of 1972 to amend Title VII of the Civil Rights Act of 1964. The legislative history of this Act shows that it was designed primarily to improve the administration and effectiveness of Title VII. . . . An additional objective of the Act was to broaden the coverage of Title VII to include employees of state and local governments and the federal government. . . .

Although the congressional adoption of the Civil Rights Act of 1964 was viewed with enthusiasm in the areas of public accommodations, public facilities, and education, the leadership of the civil rights community was disappointed with Title VII and felt that it was largely unenforceable. The EEOC had been modeled on the National Labor Relations Board. Clarence Mitchell, the Director of the Washington Bureau of the NAACP, had participated in enforcing President Roosevelt's Executive Order as a member of the Fair Employment Practices Commission during World War II. He and other leaders of the civil rights groups decided that effective enforcement of any equal employment opportunity legislation could be accomplished only through administrative cease and desist authority of the kind held by the NLRB. Yet the EEOC had been stripped of cease and desist authority in the House bill in order to attract sufficient Republican support.

The commentators viewed Title VII with skepticism for several reasons. The fair employment practice laws adopted by twenty-five states, including most of the larger states, had little effect (Hill 1964). Title VII contained elements of various state laws that already had proven to be unsuccessful, including the establishment of a commission with authority to conciliate, but no power to compel action. Enforcement was limited to suits by private persons or the Attorney General. The commentators saw the success of the measure as dependent primarily upon the willingness and ability of the Attorney General to bring suits, and the interpretation of the law by the courts.[3]

III. ENFORCEMENT OF FEDERAL EQUAL EMPLOYMENT OPPORTUNITY LAW

A. The Early Years (1965–1969)

From July 2, 1965, when Title VII went into effect, at least through 1967, little progress was made in the desegregation of jobs or job opportunities under either Title VII or the executive orders intended to prevent discrimination in employment.

Because the EEOC had no enforcement authority, but only the authority to investigate and to attempt conciliation, it was unable to enforce the Civil Rights Act by itself. Moreover, Congress also had deprived the EEOC of the authority to adopt substantive interpretive regulations. Thus, the Commission was limited to promulgating record-keeping and reporting regulations, and to formulating interpretive "guidelines," which if followed would exempt an employer from liability[4]. . . .

The EEOC adopted in 1966 the first "Guidelines on Employment Testing Procedures," which interpreted the term "professionally developed ability test" in the Act to mean "a test which fairly measures the knowledge or skills required by the particular job or jobs which the applicant seeks, or which fairly affords the employer a chance to measure the applicant's ability to perform a job or class of jobs." In its regulations and guidelines the EEOC usually took an expansive view of the meaning and coverage of Title VII, except in matters of sex discrimination[5]. . . .

Although the Commission had anticipated receiving only 2000 charges of discrimination in its first year, it received 8856. The number of charges rose to 12,148 in 1969, and to 71,023 in 1975. Thus, almost from the beginning, the Commission was swamped by charges, and it began to fall further and further behind in its response to the charges. With the vast number of charges filed, the uncertainty of what the law required, the lack of expertise among most of the personnel, and the lack of an internal check on what kinds of evidence were necessary and appropriate, the investigations usually were not marked by care or thoroughness.

While numerous private suits were filed during the early years of Title VII, few of those suits reached trial because of the many procedural issues that were presented. . . . While the initial procedural rulings favored a broad interpretation of the rights of minorities, private litigation provided little guidance to employers, labor organizations, or to the government enforcement agencies on the substantive obligations under the law.

The Labor Department's Office of Federal Contract Compliance took an aggressive posture in the mid-1960s in enforcing the executive orders regulating federal contractors. Lack of clarity in the law on testing and seniority, however, and lack of direct control over building trades unions—with whom the federal government had no direct contractual relationship—slowed the program and tended to result in requests for assistance from the Justice Department, rather than administrative proceedings to bar the awarding of contracts.

The Civil Rights Division of the Justice Department decided after passage of the Civil Rights Act to give priority first to public accommodations, then to voting, and then to school desegregation. As a result, only two employment law suits were brought in 1965 and 1966 by the Division. . . .

By the summer of 1967 there still were no substantive appellate decisions and only two significant district court decisions interpreting Title VII. At that time, however, the Attorney General, probably in response to the Leadership Conference on Civil Rights and at least in part because little progress had been made elsewhere, decided to give priority to employment litigation.

The Justice Department's objective for the next two years was to obtain substantive determinations from the courts so that employers and unions would know their obligations, blacks and other employees and applicants would know their rights, and the enforcement agencies (principally the EEOC and the Labor Department) would know how to process charges of discrimination. . . .

From the earliest cases the chief issue in employment discrimination law was whether Title VII and Executive Order 11,246 prohibited only purposeful discrimination, or whether they also prohibited unnecessary practices that were neutral on their face but had a discriminatory impact. The Department of Justice sought to clarify this issue by raising in its first three suits the question of whether nepotism and other neutral practices violated Title VII. The first of these suits involved the Asbestos Workers Local 53, a union consisting only of white journeymen, and their practice of restricting membership to the sons (or nephews raised as sons) of union members. The District Court not only found that this practice was unlawful, but also ruled unlawful the practices of relying upon recommendations of present members and of requiring a majority vote for admission to membership.

B. Years of Growth and Development (1969–1975)

The first four substantive appellate decisions on the merits of claims brought under Title VII's equal employment opportunity provisions were rendered in 1969. The Department of Justice was a plaintiff in each of these four suits. . . . In each of the first three cases, the courts of appeals ruled that Title VII not only prohibited purposeful discrimination, but also that it prohibited unnecessary practices that were discriminatory in effect[6]. . . .

The broad interpretation of Title VII previously adopted by the federal appellate courts was threatened when a divided Fourth Circuit ruled in *Griggs v. Duke Power Co.*[7] that an employer could lawfully require employees to be high school graduates and to pass written "ability" tests before being transferred or hired into previously all-white jobs. Even though these requirements had not been used in the past and thus were not necessary, the court upheld the testing and educational requirements as long as they were applied fairly and their adoption had not been motivated by a racial or other invidious purpose. . . . In a unanimous opinion issued on March 8, 1971, the Supreme Court reversed the Fourth Circuit and held that facially neutral "practices, procedures, or tests" that are discriminatory in effect cannot be used to preserve the "status quo" of employment discrimination. . . .

When Richard Nixon assumed the Presidency in 1969, his record of supporting a positive policy designed to achieve nondiscrimination by government contractors and subcontractors was well established. In June 1969, Nixon's Assistant Secretary of Labor Arthur Fletcher soon promulgated the Philadelphia Plan, which required bidders on federally assisted construction contracts in the five county Philadelphia area to set numerical goals for using blacks and other minorities in six building trades. Minorities traditionally had been excluded from the unions and from participation in the trades. . . .

The adoption of the Philadelphia Plan by the Department of Labor and support for the Plan from the Attorney General, the President, and the courts had far reaching results. Regional plans like the Philadelphia Plan were adopted by the Department of Labor for building trades in most large metropolitan areas. More significantly, numerical goals and timetables were incorporated into the obligations of industrial and other federal procurement contractors and subcontractors in 1970 by "Order No. 4," which later became a regulation issued by the Secretary of Labor (41 C.F.R. pt. 60-2, 1988). . . .

The government sought back pay in employment discrimination suits for the first time in the fall of 1969 in order to provide employers with an incentive to come promptly into compliance with the law. Having approved the imposition of goals and timetables in the Philadelphia Plan even absent a judicial finding of discrimination, the Justice Department began in the fall of 1969 to seek relief in the form of goals and timetables on a regular basis as a part of judicial decrees entered by consent or after litigation.[8]

With the unanimous decision of the Supreme Court in *Griggs v. Duke Power Co.*, the initial work of securing interpretation of the substantive provisions of Title VII was complete. The Justice Department's equal employment opportunity litigation program next sought to secure precedents for effective remedies and broad impact. . . .

Perhaps the greatest accomplishments by the government in the field of equal employment opportunity occurred during the years 1972 through 1975. For example, the EEOC's efforts to bring the Bell System's employment practices before the Federal Communications Commission in 1973 led to a consent decree with American Telephone & Telegraph (AT&T) under which over thirty-one million dollars in back pay was awarded to employees.[9] While this award was modest in the amount paid per person, the size of the suit, covering over 500,000 employees, and the size of the award captured the attention of businessmen across the country. Successful suits by the Department of Justice against Bethlehem Steel and United States Steel were followed by a nationwide suit in 1974 against the entire basic steel industry, which covered more than 700,000 employees.[10] Similarly, successful suits by the Department against a number of trucking companies led to a nationwide suit against a defendant class of over 250 trucking companies in that same year and a consent decree against the employers.[11] These three suits combined brought over two million employees under the coverage of consent decrees with goals, timetables, and back pay. The suits in the steel and trucking industries, following on the heels of the *A.T.& T.* case, led to fear in the business community that, unless the equal employment opportunity problems received prompt attention and were remedied, major litigation with a high risk of bad publicity and large back pay awards would follow.

During this period substantial movement and enforcement occurred in the contract compliance program. After the Philadelphia Plan was sustained in the Congress and in the courts, the federal government incorporated goals and timetables formally into the obligations of employers who had federal contracts or subcontracts. These employers included most large corporations and many smaller ones. . . .

The first ten years of Title VII were capped by the decision of the Supreme Court in *Albemarle Paper Co. v. Moody* in June 1975. . . . The Court affirmed the two major holdings of the Fourth Circuit and confirmed the obligations of district courts: To grant back pay when there have been violations of the Act without racial or other invidious purposes; and to hold tests that have a discriminatory impact unlawful absent proof from the employer that the tests meet professionally acceptable standards.

C.   The Middle Years (1975–1982)

In the years after the *Albemarle* decision there occurred consolidation, continued enforcement, and relatively little change in the structure of employment discrimination law. . . . During the mid-1970s, the federal government coordinated its efforts to ensure nondiscrimination in employment. In 1978, the five federal agencies with enforcement responsibilities under federal equal employment opportunity law adopted the Uniform Guidelines on Employee Selection Procedures, which were applicable to the United States as an employer as well as to private, and state and local government employers.[12] These Guidelines provided employers, the psychological profession, and the courts with uniform federal guidance on the kind of evidence necessary to validate a test or other selection procedure.

Under President Carter's Reorganization Plan Number 1 of 1978, the EEOC gained "lead agency" status in efforts to combat discrimination in employment.

The EEOC was given the responsibility to coordinate all equal employment opportunity matters, as well as responsibility for enforcement of the Age Discrimination in Employment Act and the Equal Pay Act. . . .

The Equal Employment Opportunity Act of 1972 amended Title VII by extending its coverage to state and local governments and to the federal government itself, and by granting the EEOC the authority to bring its own suits. . . . Along with its enhanced responsibilities, the EEOC continued to receive many more charges than it was able to handle, so that by 1979 its backlog of unprocessed charges had risen to 70,000. . . .

Under the leadership of Eleanor Holmes Norton in the late 1970s, the Commission adopted a number of procedural reforms to expedite the processing of charges, including the "rapid charge process" and the placement of lawyers from the Office of General Counsel in district offices to work with equal employment opportunity specialists under the supervision of district directors. She also directed the creation of systemic discrimination units within each district office and an early litigation identification program. These reforms sharply reduced the backlog.[13]

As a result of these reforms, however, most charges of discrimination were investigated only to ascertain the rights of the individual concerned, and the EEOC adopted a directive precluding its investigators from examining the broader or classwide implications of a charge, except for those charges designated for either systemic investigation or the early litigation program. By 1981, with the systemic discrimination program barely off the ground, the EEOC issued its first seven systemic discrimination charge "reasonable cause" decisions. Thus, in nine years after it had received litigation authority and seven years after that authority had become exclusive, the EEOC had filed only one systemic suit under Title VII. . . .

From 1975 through 1982, the Department of Justice brought numerous suits, particularly pattern or practice suits, against state and local governments. . . . The testimony of Assistant Attorney General William Bradford Reynolds before the Subcommittee on Employment Opportunities of the House Education and Labor Committee foreshadowed the Reagan Administration's commitment to equal employment opportunity. Reynolds announced that the Department of Justice would no longer insist upon or support hiring or promotion goals. Reynolds, however, pledged a vigorous program to enforce the federal equal employment opportunity law as it had been interpreted to date, including the adverse impact ruling in *Griggs*. . . .

In apparent contrast to Reynolds's testimony, J. Clay Smith, Jr., Acting Chairperson of the EEOC, testified before the same Subcommittee and made clear the EEOC's adherence to the concept of affirmative action, including hiring and promotion goals, as interpreted by nine of the courts of appeals. He also supported and explained the affirmative action guidelines previously adopted by the EEOC. Similarly, the Director of the Office of Contract Compliance explained to the Subcommittee modified approaches to enforcement of Executive Order 11,246, but advocated further adherence to the overall scheme of self-imposed goals and timetables to correct for underutilization.

Thus, while the nature of decrees sought and obtained by the Justice Department changed during the first years of the Reagan Administration, enforcement of the law as it had been interpreted previously continued and there was little or no change in the stated policy or direction at the EEOC or the Department of Labor.

D. The Later Years (1983–1988)

In January 1983, the Civil Rights Division of the Justice Department filed an amicus brief in *Williams v. City of New Orleans* (792 F.2d 1554, 1984) a private suit against the New Orleans police department, and argued that racial goals or quotas are unlawful under Title VII. . . .

The brief in *Williams* established the de facto administrative primacy of the Justice Department in employment discrimination matters. The EEOC had not been consulted about the brief. . . . The Justice Department followed its brief in *Williams* with a brief in *Firefighters Local Union No. 1784 v. Stotts.*[14] A court order had required the City of Memphis to lay off more senior whites and retain more junior blacks. The government's brief on appeal to the Supreme Court urged the Court to overrule a court-ordered racial override of the last-in-first-out seniority provisions of a collective bargaining agreement. . . .

After the Supreme Court struck down the court order in *Stotts,* Justice Department officials announced that the decision had sounded the death knell for race-conscious affirmative action and began a systematic effort to revise consent decrees with approximately fifty-one public employers in order to eliminate their numerical goals. Thereafter, in numerous speeches and briefs, the Justice Department officials argued strenuously on both constitutional and statutory grounds against race-conscious relief in Title VII cases, race- or sex-conscious voluntary affirmative action plans, and race- or sex-conscious goals or set-asides in government contracting. Moreover, the Department filed a number of other briefs siding with employers on questions such as: Whether Title VII preempted provisions of a state law that offered greater protections to pregnant workers than Title VII; and whether the discriminatory impact principles from *Griggs* applied to subjective employment practices.

The Justice Department briefs in these cases made no reference to nor did they rely upon the applicable regulations or guidelines of the agencies charged with administering federal equal employment opportunity law. . . . Thus, the Justice Department during these years approached equal employment opportunity issues in court as if the regulations and guidelines adopted by the agencies charged with administering equal employment opportunity law did not exist, or at least were not binding upon the government. That approach reflected an apparently conscious decision by the Reagan Administration to seek change in civil rights law through the courts, rather than through acts of Congress or changes in agency regulations and guidelines.

While the Supreme Court did not make the sweeping changes urged by Justice Department, the cumulative effect of the Justice Department's positions was that the lawyers for the executive branch, who had been in the forefront of advocating the civil rights of blacks, other minorities, and women since the days of President Truman, became the advocates for a restrictive interpretation of the civil rights laws. The roles of the EEOC and the Department of Labor were diminished during this period. . . .

Clarence Thomas became Chairperson of the EEOC in May 1982. . . . When he testified at his confirmation hearing in 1982, he stated that goals and timetables are necessary to monitor progress, and he initially resisted the efforts of the Justice Department to file a brief challenging the lawfulness of goals and timetables under Title VII in *Williams*. By 1984, apparently after the *Williams* brief and the Supreme Court's *Stotts* decision, Chairperson Thomas eschewed support for these decisions and by 1985 described the use of "hiring and promotion quotas, so-called goals and timetables" as "fundamentally flawed."

Chairperson Thomas also expressed opposition both to the adverse impact interpretation of Title VII and to the use of statistics to prove purposeful discrimination. Despite Thomas's opposition, the EEOC did not change either its Uniform Guidelines on Employee Selection Procedures, which embodied and attempted to implement the adverse impact branch of Title VII, or its affirmative action guidelines, which encouraged employers to adopt and follow affirmative action plans with goals and timetables. . . .

Chairperson Thomas's hostile views toward the adverse impact branch of Title VII became known throughout the EEOC, and according to Congressman Augustus Hawkins, were determinative in the Commissioners' decisions on whether to bring class action suits. Chairperson Thomas, however, denied in his 1986 confirmation hearings that there was any policy against bringing suits to enforce the adverse impact branch of Title VII.

The Commission brought no testing or other adverse impact suits from 1983 to January 1989, and only one such proposed suit has been approved by the Commission; that approval came in the summer of 1988. Thomas's views, therefore, were sufficient to discourage law suits either to enforce the adverse impact branch of Title VII or to prove purposeful discrimination through the use of statistics. Without making any changes in the EEOC regulations or guidelines, or even in written statements of policy, therefore, the Commission in effect decided not to enforce one of the most important aspects of Title VII and declined to bring new suits using methods of proof that had been approved repeatedly by the Supreme Court. . . .

Approximately five years ago, two leading practitioners noted the increased difficulties facing lawyers in bringing and maintaining class actions on behalf of plaintiffs in equal employment opportunity cases. The trend continued, and appears to have accelerated in the last five years. The number of class action, job discrimination lawsuits filed each year fell steadily from 1174 in 1976, to 326 in 1980, 156 in 1983, and only 48 in 1987. While the decision of the Supreme Court in *General Telephone Co. v. Falcon*[15] in 1982 may have played some role, the sharp decline preceded that decision by several years. Of course no one can know what number of equal employment opportunity suits should be filed in order to enforce the law effectively. The sharp decline in the filing of class action suits, however, suggests strongly that it has become increasingly difficult for those harmed by discriminatory employment practices to find counsel who can and will represent their interests effectively. . . .

The enforcement role of the Office of Federal Contract Compliance Programs of the Department of Labor (OFCCP) since 1983 is more difficult to document. Media accounts have suggested that the Department of Justice attempted to have President Reagan evoke Executive Order 11,246 or amend it to remove the affirmative action provisions. No such changes have been made in the Order itself or in the affirmative action regulations, and no other regulatory initiatives have been taken. . . . Nevertheless, there appears to have been no major administrative litigation undertaken during the Reagan Administration, and the accomplishments of the OFCCP in the last few years are not apparent to the public. . . .

NOTES

1. While the Article is written in commemoration of the twenty-fifth anniversary of the Civil Rights Act, I use the term federal equal employment opportunity law to include not only Title VII of the Act, but also Executive Order 11,246 and its predecessors, and other provisions of federal law prohibiting discrimination in federal and federally assisted programs and activities.

2. *See Local 189, United Papermakers,* 416 F.2d at 980; in *Local 189, United Papermakers,* the suit was brought against Local 189, the white local, whose threat to strike against a new seniority system demanded by the Department of Labor precipitated the suit. Local 189A, the black ("colored") local, included all the black employees and supported the government's suit.

3. *See,* e.g., Rachlin 1966; Schmidt 1966.

4. On September 24, 1965, President Johnson issued Executive Order 11,246, which transferred enforcement responsibility for federal contractors and subcontractors from the President's Committee to the Secretary of Labor, but left the substantive and enforcement procedures otherwise unchanged. Exec. Order No. 11,246, 30 Fed. Reg. 12,319 (1965). He amended that Order in 1967 to insert the word "sex," where race, color, and national origin appeared, so as to provide for equal employment opportunity and affirmative action for women. Exec. Order No. 11,375, 32 Fed. Reg. 14,303 (1967).

5. The original EEOC guideline on sex as a bona fide occupational qualification was not favorable to the equal employment opportunity rights of women. That guideline, for example, recognized that most states had enacted laws which were intended to protect women in employment. The Commission set forth its belief that Congress did not intend to disturb such laws which were intended to and had the effect of protecting women against

exploitation and hazard, so that compliance with a state law which prohibited women from being employed in jobs which required them to lift more than a specified number of pounds would not be considered a violation of Title VII. That guideline is quoted and discussed in Bowe v. Colgate-Palmolive Co., 416 F.2d 711 (7th Cir. 1969). The courts of course held that the ability to lift specified amounts without danger should be determined on an individual basis. The Commission adopted a much more liberal set of Guidelines on Discrimination Because of Sex in 1972. 37 Fed. Reg. 6836 (1972) (codified at 29 C.F.R. pt. 1604 (1988)).

6.   Local 53, Int'l Ass'n Heat & Frost Insulators v. Vogler, 407 F.2d 1047 (5th Cir. 1969); Local 189 United Papermakers v. United States, 416 F.2d 980 (5th Cir. 1969), *cert. denied,* 397 U.S. 919 (1970); *St. Louis Arch* case, 416 F.2d at 123.

7.   420 F.2d 1225 (4th Cir. 1970).

8.   Numerical relief in the form of referrals had been sought and obtained in Local 53, International Association Heat & Frost Insulators v. Vogler, 407 F.2d 1047 (5th Cir. 1969), but that case was viewed within the Division as an exception warranted by the particularly harsh discrimination shown by the record. The first fruit of the new policy seeking more impact and clearer relief was in the Seattle building trades suit against five unions in the Seattle area, which was brought in the fall of 1969, and in which relief was obtained in June 1970 against all five of the unions and their apprenticeship programs. United States v. Ironworkers Local 86, 443 F.2d 544 (9th Cir. 1971), *aff'g* 315 F. Supp. 1202 (W.D. Wash. 1970), *cert. denied,* 404 U.S. 984 (1971).

9.   *See* EEOC v. American Tel. & Tel. Co., 556 F.2d 167 (3d Cir. 1977), *cert. denied sub nom.* Communications Workers of Am. v. EEOC, 438 U.S. 915 (1978).

10.   United States v. Allegheny-Ludlum Indus., 517 F.2d 826 (5th Cir. 1975), *cert. denied sub nom.* NOW v. United States, 425 U.S. 944 (1976). Predecessor suits were United States v. Bethlehem Steel Corp., 446 F.2d 652 (2d Cir. 1971), and United States v. United States Steel Corp., 5 Empl. Prac. Dec. (CCH) ¶ 8619, at 7814 (N.D. Ala. 1973).

11.   *See In re* Trucking Indus. Employment Practices Litig., 384 F. Supp. 614 (J.P.M.L. 1974).

12.   *See* 29 C.F.R. pt. 1607 (1988); *see also* 5 C.F.R. § 300.103(c) (1988) (regulations of Office of Personnel Management); 28 C.F.R. § 50.14 (1988) (regulations of Justice Department); 29 C.F.R. pt. 1607 (1988) (EEOC Guidelines); 31 C.F.R. § 51.53 (1988) (regulations of Treasury Department); 41 C.F.R. pt. 60-3 (1988) (regulations of Labor Department). The regulations of the Treasury Department were issued under the Revenue Sharing Act.

13.   By the fall of 1981, the backlog had been reduced from almost 70,000 charges to less than 24,000.

14.   (467 U.S. 561, 1984).

15.   457 U.S. 147 (1982).

REFERENCES

Hill, Herbert. 1964. "Twenty Years of State Fair Employment Practices Commissions." *Buffalo Law Review* 14:22–69.

Rachlin, Carl. 1966. "Title VII: Limitations and Qualifications." *Boston College Industrial and Commercial Law Review* 7:473–94.

Schmidt, Charles T., Jr. 1966. "Title VII: Coverage and Comments." *Boston College Industrial and Commercial Law Review* 7:459–72.

II

Theories About Discrimination and What to Do About It

The traditional view of labor market discrimination is that it "consists of acts causing economic harm to an individual that are motivated by personal antipathy to the group of which that individual is a member" (Blumrosen 1972 [excerpted in this volume]). From this point of view, it is obvious what should be done to end labor market discrimination: Prohibit individuals from acting on the basis of their prejudices, and punish them if they do. Labor market discrimination will disappear when employers become ashamed of their prejudices and abandon them, and those who remain prejudiced stop discriminating because they fear legal action.

This is not the view of social scientists who analyze labor market discrimination. Of course they are aware that minorities and women are harmed by prejudiced employers, but their ideas about labor market discrimination differ from the traditional view in important ways, and so do the policy proposals that stem from their understanding of how labor markets work.

Modern theorizing about labor market discrimination began with Gary Becker's book, *The Economics of Discrimination,* first published in 1957. Like those holding the traditional view of discrimination, Becker assumed that some employers had an antipathy toward members of particular groups—he called this, using economists' language, a "taste for discrimination"—which led them to refuse to pay members of such groups as much as they deserved on the basis of productivity. In fact, employers' taste for discrimination is measured in terms of how much less they pay members of the groups they dislike than they pay others; an employer with a strong taste for discrimination might be willing to pay a black worker only 50 percent as much as an equally productive white, for example, while an employer with a weak taste for discrimination would be willing to pay 90 percent as much.

Why employers had a taste for discrimination was not Becker's concern. Instead, he was more interested in its consequences. One of his most important conclusions (described in more detail in Paula England's article) was that in a competitive labor market, discrimination by employers should eventually disappear, because it is economically inefficient: Employers who do not pay workers what they are worth (because of their taste for discrimination), in terms of productivity, will eventually be driven out of business by employers who do. (Becker also considers the implications of employees and customers having a taste for discrimination; see Becker 1971, 1957; Ehrenberg and Smith 1991:ch. 14.)

Becker's model remains the starting point for most serious discussions of labor market discrimination, but it has also been criticized, most obviously because his prediction that discrimination would disappear has not, in the eyes of most analysts, been borne out. As England and Baron write in their chapters, three alternative approaches have been developed, one accepting many of Becker's assumptions about markets but reaching different conclusions about the future of discrimination, and two rejecting some of Becker's key assumptions.

The first alternative is the concept of "statistical discrimination." To a substantial extent, this concept was developed in response to the quandary presented by Becker's work: If employers are rational and markets competitive, why doesn't employment discrimination disappear? For economists, the best way to confront this question would be to show that rationality and efficiency can lead to the continuation of discrimination rather than its demise. Their basic approach (elaborated on in a number of ways since the initial formulation in the early 1970s) was to add what they saw as an important factor to Becker's model of labor markets: the cost of information about worker productivity. It can be costly for employers to learn about the likely productivity of job applicants. They want to keep this cost (like other costs) as low as possible, of course, and one way to do so is to rely on generalizations—or stereotypes—about the productivity of members of different groups. It may be expensive to gauge the productivity of individuals, but it is easy to ascertain their race or gender. If employers believe that whites are more productive than blacks or men more productive than women, on the average, it may be economically rational for them to use race or gender as a screening device, hiring members of the group they see as more productive for the better jobs. The more productive members of the groups less favored by employers will be paid less than they are worth (because they are being evaluated as group members and not as individuals) and under some circumstances labor market outcomes for the group as a whole will suffer. Because such statistical discrimination is economically rational, it can continue for a long time. In addition, as Lundberg points out (1989 [excerpted here]), statistical discrimination can lead to a self-fulfilling prophecy. If blacks or women see that employers fail to reward them on the basis of productivity, they may conclude that it is not worthwhile devoting time or money to improving their skills (since they wouldn't be rewarded for doing so anyway); but their failure to do so will buttress employers' conclusions about group differences in productivity, and thereby contribute to the continuation of the statistical discrimination.

The statistical discrimination model accepts Becker's assumptions about rationality and efficiency in labor markets, but reaches some different conclusions. The other two approaches to discrimination reject at least some of his assumptions.

In the "monopsony" model described by England (also see Ehrenberg and Smith 1991:ch. 14), the labor market is not competitive in the sense posited by Becker and most other economists. Women are kept out of good jobs by collusion among men, as employers, workers, legislators, and husbands; a similar argument would apply to whites discriminating against blacks and to other forms of discrimination.

The organizational approach of Baron and others (cf. Cohn 1985; Milkman 1987; also see Goldin 1991 [excerpted here]) challenges Becker and most other economists in another way. Its proponents argue that employers are not "rational" in the sense economists typically assume them to be. Rather than making employment decisions on strictly economic grounds, employers are influenced by cultural and normative factors both when making decisions about individual workers and, crucially, when establishing the personnel procedures that govern how workers are hired, promoted, and paid in large organizations. For example, some jobs may be done mostly by women at some firms because they were seen as "women's work" when the firm was founded and the assignment of women to the jobs became part of the firm's standard personnel procedures. In addition, because the jobs were seen as women's work, they may have been assigned low rates of pay because women were seen by male employers as needing or deserving less money than men. Once established, such procedures and pay scales may affect women and minorities for generations, even after the reasons for creating them have been forgotten and the norms that justified them have changed (also see Eichner 1988 [excerpted here]). In addition, and most importantly, employers adopting particular practices for cultural and normative reasons will *not* necessarily be driven out of business by employers less influenced by them.

These four approaches to discrimination are not necessarily contradictory; each may hold true to some extent in parts of the labor market. But their implications for policy differ in some significant ways. Because Becker's model suggests that discrimination by employers will disappear in competitive markets, its adherents often argue that the law should do no more than see to it that labor markets are competitive, for example by prohibiting employers or unions from colluding to preserve jobs for favored groups. Indeed, some prominent scholars (e.g., Epstein 1992) believe that labor market discrimination would disappear most rapidly if all EEO laws were repealed; many more doubt that laws regulating employers—as EEO laws do—can do more good than harm (see the debate between Donohue and Posner [excerpted here]). Adherents of the monopsony approach might feel the same way, but wish to prevent collusion outside the labor market as well (with regard to access to education, for example).

Those who see discrimination either as potentially efficient under some circumstances (in statistical discrimination) or as built into personnel procedures take another view. For many of them, EEO laws are needed to end discrimination because employers have to be compelled to rethink their procedures; employers also need incentives to develop better ways to evaluate workers. EEO laws directed at individuals motivated by a taste for discrimination are likely to be less effective than laws based on an understanding of how discrimination is institutionalized in ways leading even unprejudiced employers to harm minorities or women.

Lundberg (1989 [excerpted here]) focuses on what policies are likely to be effective against statistical discrimination. She argues that it is important to distinguish between what she calls an "equal opportunity" approach to ending discrimination, which focuses on regulating employers' procedures, and an "affirmative action" approach, focusing on outcomes. Because it is difficult to monitor employers' procedures effectively, EEO enforcement efforts might focus on whether employment outcomes for women and minorities are in accord with some basic notions of equal opportunity, leaving employers considerable discretion as to how to achieve the goal of EEO.

Sociologists who emphasize the normative, cultural, and organizational bases of discrimination devote less attention than economists do to analyzing the likely effectiveness of different types of EEO policies. They do argue, however, that effective EEO policies require building concerns about EEO into the basic rules and policies that govern organizational activities, particularly personnel procedures (Baron, and Edelman 1992 [excerpted here]). And firms must be monitored to see that the rules they adopt are more than symbolic gestures having little impact on employment outcomes.

The first modern EEO bills were written in the 1940s, well before Becker's work (Burstein 1985), and reflect the traditional view that the way to end discrimination is to seek out and punish individuals who put their prejudices into practice. As originally adopted, Title VII manifested this 1940s' approach, for the most part, making it possible for legal scholars and the Department of Justice to argue in later years that only actions that intentionally harm identifiable individuals on the basis of race or other ascribed characteristics can be considered discriminatory (Gold 1985; Department of Justice 1987 [excerpted here]).

Yet Title VII was also ambiguous in crucial ways, particularly with regard to defining discrimination and spelling out what employers and unions could be required to do to end it (see Blumrosen 1972 [excerpted here]; Burstein 1990). The ambiguity has permitted those involved in EEO enforcement to develop a variety of new approaches to employment discrimination since the 1960s. The "adverse impact" approach accepted by the U.S. Supreme Court in *Griggs v. Duke Power Co.* (401 U.S. 424, 1971; see Blumrosen 1972 [excerpted here]) prohibits the use of convenient but relatively inaccurate employment criteria, and has been described as potentially suitable for attacking statistical discrimination (Burstein 1990; cf. Lundberg 1989 [excerpted here]). Both the adverse impact approach and affirmative action programs focusing on labor market outcomes (rather than personnel procedures) may be seen as attempts to end discrimination brought about by information costs and organizational routines. It is not at all clear that EEO enforcement has been directly influenced by developments in theories about discrimination—the history of that relationship has yet to be written—but there can be little doubt that both theories and enforcement have been affected by the experiences of those trying to end discrimination and the difficulties they have confronted in attempting to do so.

5

Neoclassical Economists' Theories of Discrimination

Paula England

There is a paradox in the literature by economists on discrimination. Although economists have developed a number of models of discrimination, orthodox neoclassical economists believe that the long-term persistence of most types of discrimination by employers is unlikely if labor markets are competitive. This paper reviews neoclassical models of discrimination, and explains why most neoclassical theorists believe that many forms of discrimination will gradually disappear because of competition in markets. Here I provide neither a critique of the theoretical positions nor an assessment of how well empirical evidence supports their contentions. Rather, the goal here is to explain the distinctive deductive logic of neoclassical economic reasoning about discrimination. Most of the models discussed below were originally developed as scholars thought about racial discrimination. However, their logic generally can be applied to discrimination based upon sex, ethnicity, or age as well.

TASTE DISCRIMINATION

Becker's (1957) taste model posits that employers, workers, or customers may have a taste for discrimination. Such a "taste" refers to a preference in favor of or against hiring, working with, or buying from a group such as women or minorities. To economists, whether one is willing to pay an extra amount of money for something is indicative of whether one has a taste for it. Thus, a taste for discrimination implies that discriminators are willing to pay extra to hire the group that is preferred. Becker saw tastes for discrimination as explained by premarket factors.

An employer with a taste for discrimination against women is unwilling to hire women *unless* they offer themselves at a wage enough below the wage paid to men that it completely offsets the distaste they experience by employing women. How low this wage must be will depend upon the extent of the employer's taste for discrimination. Thus, Becker, like most economists, saw an inextricable link between discrimination in wages and hiring; they are not seen as distinct types of discrimination.

Some employers discriminate, not because of their own tastes, but as a response to their customers' tastes. Yet, we would not expect customer discrimination to be widespread, but rather to occur only in service firms (e.g., stores) where employees meet customers. In manufacturing and extractive firms, and even in many service firms, customers do not know the race or sex of workers, so customer-induced taste discrimination should not be pervasive.

Employers may also discriminate in response to their workers' tastes. For example, male workers may object to working with women (Bergmann and Darity 1981), requiring a higher wage to do so.

STATISTICAL DISCRIMINATION

Models of statistical discrimination are a part of the "new information economics," the key insight of which is that it is costly to gather information relevant to decisions. These models focus on the fact that employers make decisions about hiring in the absence of full information about each applicant's productivity. The idea is that it is virtually always too expensive and perhaps impossible to get full information on each individual applicant for a job. Thus, employers often use statistical generalization about the race or sex group to which an individual belongs to make hiring decisions.

However, Thurow (1975:172) confuses the issue when he says that statistical discrimination "occurs whenever an individual is judged on the basis of the average characteristics of the group or groups to which he or she belongs rather than upon his or her own characteristics." Thurow is correct that the use of group averages is one of the defining characteristics of this model of statistical discrimination. However, his implication that nondiscriminators use "individual characteristics" rather than "group averages" makes no sense unless we are to consider virtually all hiring decisions discriminatory. All individual characteristics (e.g., test scores, education) define groups (e.g., the group with SAT scores over 1,100, the group of college graduates). Thus, there is no operational difference between basing decisions on individual characteristics or on group means. Productivity is always estimated from individual characteristics of applicants that define groups, whether these groups are defined by achieved characteristics, such as education, or characteristics ascribed at birth, such as sex or race. The only exception to this is the case where the relevant individual characteristic *is* a direct measure of productivity on the job. But on-the-job productivity is virtually never measured before hire.

Thus, it is the fact that *group* statistics (averages, variances, or reliabilities) are used that makes us call a screening process *statistical* (whether an ascribed criterion such as sex or an achieved criterion such as education defines the group). It is the fact that *ascribed* criteria such as sex or race define the groups for which averages are compared that makes us label the process *discrimination.* Thus statistical discrimination occurs when differences between groups that are defined by ascribed criteria such as race or sex are used to make employment decisions.

There are several models of statistical discrimination. I will discuss models based on average differences in productivity between groups (e.g., women and men, or blacks and whites), those based on differences in the variances of groups' productivity, and those based on group differences in how reliably or accurately screening instruments (such as tests) predict their productivity.

Let us consider the model of statistical discrimination in which hiring decisions are made on the basis of race or sex group *averages* on ability to be productive in the job (Arrow 1972:96–97; Phelps 1972:660; Lloyd and Niemi 1979:11). These models assume that it is too expensive for the employer to measure each individual's ability, but that group differences in *average* productivity are correctly known. Thus, members of the group with a higher average productivity are preferred.

Since race or sex groups have overlapping distributions on virtually all characteristics, using one group's average to estimate individual characteristics results in mistaken predictions about individuals who are qualified in a way unusual for their race or sex. But, since sex and race can generally be observed almost costlessly, in the absence of other cheap screening criteria, it may improve the average productivity of an employer's work force to choose all workers from the group with the higher average. This model does not imply that group differences are innate; it simply implies that they were not created by the employer who is engaging in the statistical discrimination. The differences may have been created by patterns of discrimination in the family or in schools or by other broad social forces.

Could a model of statistical discrimination based on average difference in productivity-related characteristics explain discriminatory wage differentials disadvantaging women or blacks as a group? Aigner and Cain (1977) argue that, even if groups differ in potential productivity, the model cannot explain discriminatory wage differentials between groups. They claim that statistical discrimination based on averages does *not* reduce the *average* earnings of the race or sex group with the lower average productivity. If we assume that group means on productivity are the basis of hiring and pay decisions, they argue that groups will receive an average level of pay commensurate with their average productivity. For example, if women are 10 percent less productive at some jobs, employers will be unwilling to hire any women in such jobs unless they will work for 10 percent less than is paid to men. The "error" involved in statistical discrimination is that individuals who are atypical for their group will be paid more or less than their individual productivity, although, under the assumptions of the model, on average the group will be paid commensurate with its productivity. For example, the woman who, compared to the average woman, knows an unusually large amount of auto mechanics will not find a job as a mechanic or she will have to settle for a lower wage than she would in the absence of statistical discrimination. This is because all women will be treated like the average woman, and all men will be treated like the average man (holding constant observed indicators of productivity such as schooling). In sum, they argue that statistical discrimination based on group averages should not lead to group differences in *average* earnings in excess of *average* productivity differences between groups (Aigner and Cain 1977).[1]

A second type of statistical discrimination hinges on race or sex group differences in *variances* rather than averages (Phelps 1972; Aigner and Cain 1977). Suppose that women have the same average as men on a productivity-relevant characteristic, but the women's distribution has a larger variance, indicating more women than men at both extremely high and extremely low scores. If the cost of finding a better indicator of productivity and using it to screen each individual applicant is prohibitively high, will it pay employers to prefer the group with the smaller variance? The answer to this question depends upon whether employers are risk-averse (Aigner and Cain 1977). If they are not risk-averse, the expected value of productivity for women and men will be determined by the respective means of the two groups, and if these means are the same, it is not rational to engage in statistical discrimination. However, if the employer is risk-averse, the group with the smaller variance will be preferred even when group means are equal.

The relevance of risk-aversion to preferring a group with a smaller variance can be seen by making an analogy to how people decide what stock investment to make. Suppose you have two investment possibilities, and each has an expected payoff of 9 percent in the next year. Your generally accurate broker tells you that investment A has an expected return of 9 percent, and the return is unlikely to fall outside the range of 8–10 percent. She estimates that investment B also has an expected return of 9 percent, but sees a reasonable chance of either losing all your money or making a 200 percent return on B. If you are at all risk-averse, you will pick investment A over B, although they have the same "average" (i.e., expected) return. Likewise, in hiring, the risk-averse employer will engage in discrimination against a more internally variable group because there is more risk of hiring an especially bad worker from this group. If employers are risk-averse, statistical discrimination based on variances *can* produce sex or race differences in average earnings that are in excess of sex differences in average productivity.

A third model of statistical discrimination posits race or sex differences in the degree of accuracy with which ability is measured by tests or other selection devices (Phelps 1972; Aigner and Cain 1977; Borjas and Goldberg 1978; Lang 1988; Lundberg and Startz 1983). For one group, the "error term" in a regression predicting productivity from the selection device is larger, and the R^2 is smaller. Thus the selection device has lower reliability for the group with the larger error term. This does *not* mean that productivity is consistently underestimated for the group for whom the screening devices are less reliable. Most models assume that men and women (or whites and minorities) with any given score on the selection device have the same average productivity, but that there is more variability or dispersion around the regression line for women or minorities. And there is no assumption of *any* difference in the groups' distributions on productivity; both means and variances may be equal. If the cost of finding and using a more reliable indicator of productivity is prohibitively high, will it pay employers to prefer the group for whom the available indicator has greater predictive power? As with models of statistical discrimination based on differences in variances in productivity, risk-averse employers will discriminate. Even in the absence of risk-aversion among employers, it is possible for this sort of discrimination to create discriminatory wage differences through creating incentives for groups for whom selection devices are worse predictors to invest less in unobservable forms or more in observable forms of human capital or other "signals" of productivity (Lundberg and Startz 1983; Lang 1988).

MONOPSONY MODELS OF DISCRIMINATION

Economists define monopsony as the situation in which there is only one buyer, so the market lacks competition.[2] Madden's (1973) monopsony model of sex discrimination posits that women are kept out of good jobs by collusion among men, as husbands, employers, legislators, and workers. The model starts from the observation that men have substantial power over women's decisions to accept jobs. For example, women's options were limited in the past by laws barring them from some jobs. Even today they are limited by patriarchal customs in which husbands have the right to dictate in which city a couple will live in. This creates monopsony-like power for employers who hire women. The real situation is not so extreme that all women face a single employer so there is no competition for their labor. But the model's insight is to work out the implications of a situation where, because of various forms of male power, women are closer to being in a situation of having only one potential employer than are men. Monopsonistic employers can pay lower wages to women than they would be able to if they were in competition for female labor. The classic example of monopsony power is the labor market for nurses, particularly in small towns that only have one hospital. Such a situation benefits men *as a group* at the expense of women as a group. Indeed, members of any group will make relative gains if they can exclude nonmembers from opportunities. Thus, analogous models could be devised to discuss racial discrimination.

THE EROSION OF DISCRIMINATION IN COMPETITIVE MARKETS

Most neoclassical economists believe that discrimination sows the seeds of its own destruction because its practice costs money. Becker (1957) realized that this was a tension in his discrimination theory (Arrow 1972). The erosion of many types of discrimination should happen as long as labor markets are "competitive," by which economists mean that there are a number of possible buyers of labor for each seller of a particular type of labor and vice versa. Let us examine the process by which economists believe discrimination should eventually disappear. I will use sex rather than race in the illustrative examples below, but the reader should bear in mind that the same logic applies for race discrimination.

Suppose that the discrimination is based on employers' tastes, but employers differ in the strength of their discriminatory tastes. Some employers' tastes not to hire women will be so strong that they will hire no women, regardless of how cheaply women offer to work. At the other extreme are employers we will call "nondiscriminators"; they are indifferent between men and women, so they are open to hiring either or both men and women, and paying them equal wages. Employers with an intermediate level of discriminatory tastes are willing to hire some women, but only if the women will work for a lower wage than they are willing to pay men. How much lower the wage would have to be to make them indifferent between men and women is a measure of the severity of their discriminatory taste.

In such a setting, what will the nondiscriminators, those who are indifferent between men and women, do? Since women are available at a lower wage than men despite equivalent productivity, they will choose to hire the cheaper women. Employers whose tastes for discrimination are so extreme that they are unwilling to hire women no matter how low the price will hire all men. Employers whose tastes for discrimination are intermediate will hire women if the difference between the female and male market wage is great enough to offset their distaste, but will hire men if it is not. Employers whose taste (by coincidence) requires exactly the same wage differential to make them indifferent between men and women as the difference between the female and male market wage may hire some of each sex. These employers will pay men the male market wage and women the female market wage.

In this scenario, "nondiscriminators" are taking advantage of the exploited status of women, paying them a lower wage than men are making at other firms. Thus, in one sense, we might not want to call them nondiscriminators. Economists, however, label them nondiscriminators because, if other employers' discriminatory tastes had not provided them with cheapened labor, they would have been willing to pay men and women the same wage. Further, these "nondiscriminators" who hire women cheaply are not the source of women's discriminatory low wage; indeed, they are part of the mechanism of the erosion of discrimination. Such employers are like arbitrageurs in stock markets who buy up stocks that others are undervaluing.

Such "nondiscriminators" contribute to the demise of discrimination because their relatively low labor costs give them an advantage in competitive product and capital markets. Because they can sell their products for a lower price and/or offer higher returns on investments in the firm, such firms should come to sell an increasing share of the product market and hire an increasing share of the labor market in their industry. Because of their higher labor costs, employers with more taste for discrimination may go bankrupt. Alternatively they will be bought out by employers with less or no taste for discrimination. Eventually, the theory predicts that expansion of employment in the least discriminating firms will bid up the job opportunities and wages of women, leading women's wages and job distributions to converge toward men's. At this point, the wage at which women must offer to work to get hired is only as low as consistent with the tastes of the least discriminatory employer. Through this process, competition is said to bring about the demise of taste discrimination in the long run. Of course, the length of the "long run" is an empirical question that theory cannot specify.

This economic reasoning implies that the *eventual average* amount of discrimination in the economy depends, not on the *average initial* level of discriminatory tastes, but upon the amount of discriminatory taste held by the *least* discriminatory employers. This latter amount will be the *eventual average* level of discrimination after the "arbitrage" has occurred.

The description above of the demise of discrimination applies generally if the discriminatory tastes belong to employers. It will not occur in the case of customer tastes causing discrimination since customers do not "go out of business" for paying to indulge their tastes. However, the sex or race of those who work in a job is generally not visible to customers. Thus, neoclassical theory would predict that taste discrimination based on customers' tastes will fail to erode only in service jobs where customers interact with workers. In the case of discrimination based on workers' tastes, the erosion process should lead to enduring sex segregation by firm. However, this segregation by firm should not generate wage differences between men and women.

Goldberg (1982) has pointed out an exception to the notion that taste discrimination will necessarily erode in competitive labor markets. (His discussion refers to race discrimination; I have adapted it here to sex discrimination.) The argument hinges on the distinction between two types of taste discrimination: antifemale discrimination, in which women are paid less than the contribution of the marginal worker to revenue (hereafter called marginal product) while men are paid marginal product, and promale discrimination, in which men are paid more than marginal product while women are paid marginal product. The latter involves selective altruism toward men because the employer finds employing them rewarding in a nonpecuniary sense. Goldberg (1982) shows that antifemale discrimination will eventually erode in competitive markets (to the level of the least discriminatory employer) by the process described above. However, his point is to show that the discrimination I have called altruistic promale discrimination need not erode in competitive markets. The essence of the argument is that employers engaging in altruistic promale discrimination can survive in the long run if the nonpecuniary utility they get from what they pay men makes them willing to take a lower-than-market profit rate, and leads them to reject buyout bids from owners who are less (or non-) discriminatory, and thus could run the business more profitably. In contrast, if one is engaging in antifemale discrimination, the same buyout offer from a less (or non) discriminatory employer will be compelling. The two models of taste discrimination, altruistic promale discrimination and antifemale discrimination, are different in their ability to survive in competitive markets, despite having several things in common. Both types of discriminators are willing to take less profit than the maximum possible in order to indulge their taste for discrimination, so neither model assumes that employers are profit-maximizers as economists typically assume. The critical difference between the two models is that in the altruistic promale model, the value of the firm is greater to one with more rather than less (or non-) discriminatory tastes, so nondiscriminators can't buy out discriminators. In the antifemale model, the pecuniary gain that a nondiscriminator can make (at least temporarily) from hiring women at their cheapened wage makes it possible that the firm is more valuable to the nondiscriminator than the discriminator. This is because, if women are hired at their market price, the two employers have the same profit level but the discriminatory suffers the disutility due to the antifemale taste that the nondiscriminatory doesn't suffer. Goldberg (1982) points out that Becker (1957) incorrectly assumed that the two types of taste discrimination are identical with respect to their tendency to erode in competitive markets.

The concept of statistical discrimination has had great appeal to economists because it seems more capable than other models of discrimination of explaining the anomaly of the persistence of discrimination in competitive markets. Unlike taste or error discrimination, it is profit-maximizing for employers to engage in statistical discrimination if the costs of the error it creates in predicting individuals' productivity are less than the expense of developing and administering screening instruments with greater predictive power. The latter costs exist because of limitations in the "technology" of personnel administration. They are examples of what economists call "information" or "search" costs. Because of these costs, and to the extent that there is no fear of the costs of a lawsuit,[3] there is no pecuniary advantage to ceasing statistical discrimination, as there is for taste or error discrimination. Why would an employer want to abandon a cheap method of estimating productivities when it is expensive to develop screening devices that allow one to find those individuals whose productivities are above the average of their sex? If employers are already using the most effective screening technology that is cost-effective, statistical discrimination will be able to endure in competitive markets precisely because it does not cost money.

Statistical discrimination is distinct from the other types of discrimination in that it cannot erode entirely through the pure market forces of "arbitrage" as the others can. However, it is important to recall that only those models of statistical discrimination involving variances or the reliability of screening instruments can produce group wage differentials in excess of productivity differentials. Models of statistical discrimination based on different group means will not produce such differentials.

What of the monopsony models of discrimination? How do economists think that discrimination involving this noncompetitive feature can disappear, since the very competition through which market forces work is not present to the usual degree? As long as the situation of monopsony persists, economists concede that the discrimination will persist. But many economists would question whether it is not a gross exaggeration to say that women face monopsonistic employers. Even if women are geographically constrained, most occupations have numerous employers competing in each local labor market.

CONCLUSION

To summarize, most forms of discrimination tend to self-destruct in competitive labor markets in the long run, according to orthodox neoclassical reasoning. Taste discrimination should erode from arbitragelike market forces alone unless it is altruistic discrimination that entails paying the privileged group more than marginal revenue product. Discrimination based on monopsony is seen as an unusual situation. Statistical discrimination based on group differences in means should not produce group differences in earnings. However, statistical discrimination based on variances or differential reliability of screening devices may persist; it will not erode through arbitragelike market forces alone.

These theoretical deductions affect how neoclassical economists respond to evidence of persistent job and wage differentials by race and sex that cannot be explained by available measures of human capital or compensating differentials. Some deny that any significant amount of market discrimination still exists. When challenged to square this conclusion with the many studies showing that women and minorities earn less than white men after adjustments for education, test scores, experience, and seniority, such theorists point to the possibility of supply-side explanations that hinge upon group differences in preferences or human capital that have gone unmeasured in past research. Some of those who deny the existence of market discrimination will concede that premarket (i.e., familial or societal) discrimination or past market discrimination may explain these supply-side differentials, at least in part. Others concede only statistical discrimination, the type of discrimination that economists view as most likely to persist (e.g., Fuchs 1988). Discrimination arising because of an altruistic tendency by employers to pay an advantaged group more than the contribution of the marginal worker to revenue (as in Goldberg's 1982 model) is as likely to persist as statistical discrimination, but is nonetheless unpopular among economists because they generally assume selfishness rather than altruism in market relations (England 1993). Still others believe that discrimination of various types does seem to be able to persist even in the face of market competition, and view this as an unsolved theoretical anomaly for economic theories (Arrow 1972).

NOTES

1.   This conclusion may not follow in the presence of heterogeneous jobs when this is combined with one group being easier to match with jobs than the other. To see this, consider an example with equal number of men and women and two jobs, each employing half the workers. Assume also that individual productivity is unobserved, but sex-specific mean productivities are observed in each job, and that men produce 12 in job A but 8 in job B whereas women produce 10 in every job. In equilibrium, neoclassical theory would predict that all men will be employed in job A and earn 12, whereas all women will be employed in job B and earn 10. In this case, unequal wages can result from statistical discrimination, even though men and women's mean productivity is equal.

2.   Monopoly is defined as the situation in which there is only one seller. However, sometimes the term *monopoly* is used more broadly to cover both monopoly and monopsony, or more generally, a situation in which actors are engaged in collective collusion rather than competing with each other. Thus, sometimes this will be called a monopoly model.

3.   This is an important proviso since statistical discrimination has generally been found by the courts to be illegal. An employer cannot lawfully adopt a policy of not hiring any blacks because of knowledge that, at any given level of education, blacks have lower test scores. However, employers may lawfully use test scores as screening criteria unless they are not job relevant.

REFERENCES

Aigner, D. J. and G. G. Cain. 1977. "Statistical Theories of Discrimination in Labor Markets." *Industrial and Labor Relations Review* 30:1975–87.

Arrow, Kenneth. 1972. "Models of Job Discrimination" Pp. 83–102 in *Racial Discrimination in Economic Life,* edited by A. Pascal. Lexington, MA: Lexington, Heath.

Becker, Gary. 1957. *The Economics of Discrimination,* 1st ed. (2nd ed., 1971). Chicago: University of Chicago Press.

Bergmann, Barbara and William Darity. 1981. "Social Relations in the Workplace and Employee Discrimination." Pp. 155–62 in *Proceedings of the Industrial Relations Association.*

Borjas, George J. and Matthes S. Goldberg. 1978. "Biased Screening and Discrimination in the Labor Market." *American Economic Review* 68(5):918–22.

England, Paula. 1993. "The Separative Self: Androcentric Bias in Neoclassical Assumptions." Pp. 37–53 in Marianne A. Ferber and Julie A. Nelson, eds., *Beyond Economic Man: Feminist Theory and Economics*. Chicago: University of Chicago Press.

Fuchs, Victor R. 1988. *Women's Quest for Economic Equality*. Cambridge, MA: Harvard University Press.

Goldberg, Matthew S. 1982. "Discrimination, Nepotism, and Long-Run Wage Differentials." *Quarterly Journal of Economics* 97:308–19.

Lang, Kevin. 1988. "A Sorting Model of Statistical Discrimination." Unpublished manuscript. Department of Economics, Boston University.

Lloyd, Cynthia and Beth Niemi. 1979. *The Economics of Sex Differentials*. New York: Columbia University Press.

Lundberg, Shelly J. and Richard Startz. 1983. "Private Discrimination and Social Intervention in Competitive Labor Markets." *American Economic Review* 73:340–47.

Madden, Janice F. 1973. *The Economics of Sex Discrimination*. Lexington, MA: Lexington.

Phelps, Edmund. 1972. "The Statistical Theory of Racism and Sexism." *American Economic Review* 64:659–61.

Thurow, Lester. 1975. *Generating Inequality*. New York: Basic Books.

6

Organizational Evidence of Ascription in Labor Markets

James N. Baron

Theories of discrimination and labor markets have, at least until recently, treated organizations or firms for the most part as black boxes.[1] Organizations are assumed to structure work, design rewards, and allocate personnel so as to satisfy some broad technical or societal imperative, which is taken as exogenous and determinative. Organizations are simply the arenas in which these larger imperatives are played out. This black box treatment of organizations has been as conspicuous in sociologists' functional theory of stratification (Davis and Moore [1945]; Lenski [1966]; Treiman [1977]) as in economists' human-capital models of labor-market attainment. The former theory argues that firms must pay an occupation what it is worth, where worth is determined by societal importance; according to the latter (human-capital) theory, firms must pay workers what they are worth, where worth is determined by the value of the skills and training needed in a given line of work and the relative supply and demand of individuals available to perform that work. Both theories thus implicitly assume that organizations design wage rates so as to allocate and motivate labor efficiently. Enterprises allocate individuals to their highest and best use because if they did not do so, some other organization would bid away the individual's services by offering a higher wage, which could be paid because the individual would be more productively employed. Returns to individual ability and experience are similarly rationalized in these accounts. . . .

This inattention to organizational arrangements is equally puzzling when one considers public policy concerns. For example, debates about the likelihood of reducing long-standing inequalities by increasing educational attainment among women and nonwhites hinge on assumptions about when, how, and why firms use educational criteria in staffing decisions. Yet few studies of inequality have

Excerpts reprinted with permission from Richard Cornwall and P. V. Wunnava, eds., *New Approaches to Economic and Social Analyses of Discrimination,* pp. 113–143, published by Praeger Publishers, an imprint of the Greenwood Publishing Group, Inc., Westport, Conn. Copyright © 1992.

examined that topic directly (e.g., Collins [1975]; Cohen and Pfeffer [1986]). Moreover, most social policies aimed at changing the distribution of labor-market opportunities and outcomes are targeted toward organizations, rather than individuals, if only because it is much more difficult administratively and politically to design, implement, enforce, and evaluate policy interventions aimed at individuals or households than at workplaces. Given that fact, inattention to organizational arrangements and policies shaping the distribution of rewards is all the more unfortunate.

To be sure, recent economic models concerning transaction costs, firm-specific human-capital investment, efficiency wages, gift exchange, implicit contracts, and the like have provided much greater richness to economists' investigations of organizations and labor markets. However, as Granovetter ([1985], [1988]) has observed, when economists tackle issues of internal organization, they typically propose formal models that represent institutions, contracts, and governance arrangements as optimal solutions to ubiquitous problems of moral hazard, adverse selection, and aversion toward effort and risk. Granovetter noted some of the conceptual and empirical shortcomings of such adaptive stories. Because work organizations are arenas of ongoing social and political interaction, and not simply combinations of factor inputs and atomized individuals, organizational arrangements are influenced by cultural, political, and social psychological forces, and not simply by technical considerations and the logic of "principal-agent" relationships.

Understanding something about the sociology and social psychology of work organizations is therefore likely to inform our understanding of employment outcomes, including the extent of ascription in labor markets. Organizations influence the observed distribution of career outcomes in at least three key ways: by deciding what a given job entails (and drawing boundaries among jobs); by determining what a given job is worth; and by matching specific types of workers to particular positions.

Accordingly, I begin by surveying some results from recent research on these three issues, which illustrate how models of efficient labor markets and rational employers seem to miss some important empirical facts. The evidence suggests that social forces and discriminatory cultural beliefs prevalent when a job or organization is founded condition the way that positions are defined, priced, and staffed, becoming institutionalized within the formal structure and informal traditions of the enterprise. After surveying various strands of this evidence, I try to weave them together. . . .

I. WHAT IS A JOB? ORGANIZATIONAL ARRANGEMENTS AS SOCIALLY ENDOGENOUS

Economists tend to view organizational arrangements, such as the specification of duties and the structure of reporting relationships, as deriving from a technologically mandated production function. Organizations structure activities in order to maximize productive efficiency and then staff positions accordingly. However, there is substantial evidence to suggest that the way in which roles and organizations are structured and evaluated is not independent of who is performing a specific activity. In other words, one organizational basis of ascription glossed over in economic accounts is the tendency for positions occupied by women and minorities to be structured and evaluated differently.

For instance, members of high-status social groups (e.g., males, especially whites) are substantially more likely to be allocated to unique job titles in organizations. . . . In 415 organizations that we studied, there were 2,699 one-person jobs. Men occupied 91.9 percent of these jobs, while they represented 79.9 percent of the 206,335 employees in the sample. . . . [S]everal types of evidence support the interpretation that ascriptive characteristics play a causal role. First, a wealth of recent theory and research addresses cognitive and social psychological biases governing social categorization (Brewer and Kramer [1985]). That work indicates an "in-group" bias in social categorization whereby more elaborate and differentiated schemas are adopted to describe in-group members and their activities. . . .

An important corollary result from the social psychological literature is that the process of categorization is self-perpetuating. A set of categories, once in place, reinforces perceptions of distinctiveness across those categories, even if the categorization is entirely capricious. Numerous controlled experiments show that arbitrary categorizations of subjects into groups that are presumed to have different abilities or qualities can induce the distinctions in attitudes and behaviors that were expected and that were ostensibly the justification for the categorization. . . . Social psychological studies also highlight how categorization and differentiation can be used strategically by high-status individuals or groups to segregate themselves from those of lower status, preserving their advantaged position and distinctive status within the larger society. . . .

The tendency documented above for men and whites to monopolize one-person organizational job titles illustrates these processes. White men typically have preeminent influence in most organizations, and they enjoy a privileged position within the larger social order. Accordingly, it seems plausible that white men have a more elaborate and differentiated schema of the work that they do than they do of "women's work" and "minority work," which has become institutionalized within the formal structure of organizations. . . .

Another form of evidence that ascriptive characteristics help mold how jobs are defined is archival. "Smoking guns" are rare in contemporary efforts to unearth discrimination, but there were fewer taboos about such things in previous decades. Accordingly, in many of the data sets I have studied, one finds explicit statements by those charged with designing employment systems averring that race and sex were taken into account in designing jobs and pay systems. For instance, in a recent class-action sex-discrimination lawsuit against the state of California, the judge was particularly struck by an internal memorandum drafted in 1934 by a state government official explaining job-classification procedures. The document stated that in establishing the initial salary schedules for civil-service jobs, in addition to market and skill factors, "certain supplemental factors were also taken into consideration, namely, the . . . age, sex, and standard of living of the employees normally recruited for a given [job]" (Becker [1934:62]). Presumably the specifications of jobs and divisions among them were equally influenced by ascriptive stereotypes. . . .

In short, there are powerful cultural and psychological forces shaping the design of organizational arrangements that are often given short shrift in efficiency-oriented models of labor markets and firms. While unequal labor-market outcomes are obviously due in part to differences in the kinds of positions occupied by members of different social groups, presumed differences among social groups are also an important *cause* of distinctions among work roles within an organizational division of labor. The historian Margo Conk [1978] has noted how, for instance, the U.S. Census Bureau imposed distinctions among detailed occupations based on perceived sociocultural distinctions (e.g., of sex and race) among the kinds of people who typically did different kinds of jobs. Ironically, variations in occupational distributions have subsequently been invoked to "explain" differences in socioeconomic standing by sex and race, when these differences helped to define the occupational classification in the first place!

Why does the social basis of organizational and occupational categorization matter? One reason it matters is that various studies, which I review below, show that jobs done by in-group and high-status members are also likely to be judged as worth more than other jobs. This in-group bias favoring job categorization is therefore quite significant for pay discrimination. . . . In short, conceptualizing and operationalizing discrimination solely in terms of unequal returns to individual human-capital or occupational characteristics ignores the subtle (yet powerful) ways that ascriptive distinctions are incorporated into organizational structures governing jobs, pay, and promotions.

II.   WHAT IS A JOB WORTH? THE ORGANIZATIONAL CONTEXT OF BIAS

Evidence from diverse sources suggests that positions dominated by women and nonwhites are evaluated as worth less than positions that are otherwise comparable (in terms of skills and requirements) but dominated by men and whites. . . . Some of my recent work has examined how organizational arrangements, the prevalence of various interest groups, and characteristics of jobs affect the tendency toward biased judgments of job worth (Baron and Newman [1989], [1990]). We analyzed how the prescribed pay rates attached to jobs in the California civil service vary (net of job requirements) with the demographic composition of incumbents. We focused on the officially prescribed entry pay rates attached to jobs within the civil-service salary system, rather than analyzing the average wages received by job incumbents. This dependent variable obviously ignores variations in the actual pay received by incumbents in a given job. However, it has the virtue of being unaffected by sex or race differences in human capital, productivity, and the like among workers in a job. In other words, ours is a measure of prescribed or normative wages. If one observes, for instance, that female-dominated jobs are ranked lower in the normative wage hierarchy than otherwise comparable male-dominated jobs, this cannot be attributed to unmeasured human-capital or productivity differences among incumbents. To assess the net effects of sex and race composition on the perceived worth of jobs, we controlled for job content by using various detailed occupational distinctions (used by the state itself to represent differences in job requirements and responsibilities), as well as estimates of educational and experience requirements listed in civil-service job descriptions (see Baron and Newman [1989]).

Like other researchers, we found substantial net penalties associated with the presence of women and nonwhites in jobs, both cross-sectionally and in longitudinal analyses examining how changes in demographic composition between 1979 and 1985 affected a job's standing within the pay hierarchy of California state government. However, the magnitude of these penalties depended on various contextual factors. Among jobs dominated by women or nonwhites, the devaluation of pay was substantially greater when there were fewer objective criteria for gauging performance. This result is consistent with social psychological work documenting that decision makers rely on social criteria of proof more in settings lacking objective evaluative standards (Cialdini [1988]). . . .

Our analyses uncovered certain organizational conditions that mitigate biased evaluations of job worth. Strong collective bargaining units committed to pay equity by sex, for instance, have lessened the devaluation of "women's work" within the California civil service (Baron and Newman [1990]). So, apparently, has employment growth. Theories of occupational crowding imply that the entry of women (or nonwhites) into a line of work depresses the wage rate by creating excess supply. If a work role becomes typed as worth less when women enter it, one might expect that women's entry would be less conspicuous and threatening to male occupants under conditions of growing demand for the job or occupation than under circumstances of decline. We found this to be the case in longitudinal analyses of prescribed pay rates of jobs between 1979 and 1985 within the California civil service (Baron and Newman [1989]).

In sum, the organizational and occupational context and the presence of various interest groups influences the extent of ascription in gauging what positions are worth. We have found the same to be true in studying the extent of gender-based job assignment (or sex segregation) within organizations. I turn next to that research.

III. WHO GETS WHAT JOB? ORGANIZATIONAL AND ENVIRONMENTAL FACTORS AFFECTING THE SUCCESS OF JOB INTEGRATION EFFORTS

A.   Historical Founding Conditions and Structural Inertia

Organizational theorists have argued that environmental conditions present at the time an enterprise is founded tend to be indelibly imprinted on its structure (Stinchcombe [1965]). Organizations adopt structures and procedures that are not only appropriate economically at the time of founding, but that also correspond to broader social understandings about how a specific type of enterprise ought to look and ought to be run. Once rationalized systems of personnel administration became accepted as an essential component of modern bureaucratic enterprise, for instance, they spread quickly to new firms and industries lacking many of the characteristics (such as high turnover, large size, and a unionized work force with firm-specific skills) that had supposedly necessitated such innovations in the first place (Meyer and Rowan [1977]; Tolbert and Zucker [1983]; Baron, Dobbin, and Jennings [1986]).

Once in place, organizational structures and procedures demonstrate considerable inertia. . . . The influence of historical founding conditions and inertial pressures on labor-market outcomes has been documented in several empirical studies my colleagues and I have conducted. For instance, we recently studied patterns of job integration by sex in California state agencies between 1979 and 1985 (Baron, Mittman, and Newman [1991]). . . . Consistent with theories of organizational inertia, our longitudinal analyses revealed that younger state agencies, established during an era of intense concern with workplace equity, exhibited somewhat faster progress toward gender integration than older organizations did. Similar evidence of the effects of founding conditions existed at the job level; there was less devaluation by race and sex among civil-service jobs founded after the late 1970s, when the state government began paying closer attention to comparable worth, than among otherwise comparable jobs founded previously (Baron and Newman [1989], [1990]; also see Kim [1989]). These results call into question an assumption underlying many economic models of organizations and labor markets, namely, that the structure of jobs and organizations observed reflects the exigencies of productive efficiency. Rather, the organizational literature underscores the inertia associated with structures and procedures. Jobs and organizations are designed in ways that conform to economic pressures and sociocultural understandings present at the time of founding, which are likely to persist unless subject to intense pressures for change.

Organizational theorists have claimed that structural inertia is greater not only in old organizations, but also in large organizations compared to small ones. Large organizations invariably must decentralize their activities, and the delegation of authority and power usually impedes coordinated, centralized efforts by organizations to adapt to environmental pressures and changes. Consistent with that prediction, our analyses of state agencies and other studies in diverse samples of establishments document that larger organizations are more segregated and are slower to integrate over time (see Bielby and Baron [1984]; Lyson [1985]). . . .

B.   Interests

Various groups within organizations are likely to perceive an interest in either sustaining or undoing ascriptive job assignments and reward allocations. Because discriminatory organizational arrangements are often inert and may provide substantial economic and social benefits to the majority, the rate at which they abate in a given organizational setting is likely to depend on the constellation of interests favoring or opposing equal treatment.

Obviously, the aggrieved minorities themselves represent potentially important interest groups opposing such practices. Sociologists have argued that minority groups are more powerful and prone to collective action when their relative numbers increase in an organizational setting (Kanter [1977]). In a sample of predominantly small organizations in California's private sector, which had been studied by the U.S. Employment Service between 1959 and 1979, job segregation varied inversely with the percentage of female employees in an establishment, even after controlling for occupational composition and other organizational characteristics likely to affect segregation levels (Bielby and Baron [1984]). Similarly, in longitudinal analyses of California state government agencies between 1979 and 1985, organizations employing a sizable (and increasing) proportion of women displayed faster gender integration than otherwise comparable agencies, again even controlling for relevant organizational and occupational constraints (Baron, Mittman, and Newman [1991]).

Of course, these effects might have nothing to do with the political actions of the minority groups involved, but rather simply reflect labor-supply constraints. For instance, agencies having a large (or increasing) percentage of women may integrate faster because they are less constrained by sex-specific labor supply than other organizations. However, while labor supply obviously shapes gender-based job allocations within organizations, it is far from the entire story. I base this inference on four facts. First, we have found persistent segregation across jobs and organizations even in settings where gender-based differences in labor supply seem minimal, such as detailed occupations that employ both men and women (Bielby and Baron [1986]). In occupations involving a mixture of traditionally "male" and "female" characteristics (e.g., physical lifting and repetitive dexterous work, respectively), both women and men were employed, but hardly ever in the same job classes or organizational settings. In other words, both sexes were available for this kind of work, but their assignment to specific work settings appeared to depend principally on whether a specific employer typed the role as more "appropriate" for men or women. This brings me to the second piece of evidence undercutting labor-supply explanations: Employment Service analysts explicitly recorded employers' ascriptive stereotypes with amazing frequency; a number of illustrations are cited in Bielby and Baron [1986].

Third, in analyzing segregation trends in the California civil service, labor-supply constraints affecting an agency's capacity to integrate were proxied in several ways. For instance, we allowed the agency target to depend on the overall percentage of women in the organization, and our specification of the speed of adjustment controlled for the occupational composition of each agency. Fourth, we conducted numerous supplementary analyses to examine whether the effect of having a large contingent of women on rates of gender desegregation merely reflected labor-supply differences across organizations. For instance, we examined alternative measures of job segregation for each agency that standardized for the degree of segregation within the civil service as a whole, examining only how segregated each agency is in its jobs relative to the degree of segregation in the statewide occupational labor markets from which it draws. In these supplementary analyses, the effects pertaining to the percent female in each agency were weakened, but not eliminated. The evidence, then, suggests that the relative size of disadvantaged constituencies in an organization has a direct net effect on the speed with which discriminatory job assignments abate, which is not due solely to labor-supply considerations. . . .

C.   Organizational Leadership

Some perspectives on organizational evolution emphasize the role that leaders play in adapting organizations to the environment. In economic models, two rational employers facing the same production function are typically presumed to organize in roughly the same way and pursue similar objectives. In contrast, the organizational literature has suggested and documented that leaders can matter in shaping organizational evolution.

Our analyses of state government agencies revealed that organizations headed by female leaders were slightly faster to integrate by sex than otherwise comparable agencies run by men. We also found a positive effect of turnover among agency leaders on speed of job integration by sex. In the public sector, however, executive succession is closely linked with changes in political administration. Indeed, the effects of the gender and turnover of leaders on agencies' adjustment toward their integration targets appear to be due principally to the change of political administration that occurred in 1982–83, when the Republican George Deukmejian replaced the liberal Democrat Jerry Brown. Integration was occurring fairly consistently at the time most Brown appointees were replaced (1983 to early 1984) and then declined precipitously during the first year (1984–85) that Deukmejian's appointees (disproportionately men) had complete control over budgets and hiring. This was also the period of lowest executive succession, following the spate of postelection political appointments (see Baron, Mittman, and Newman [1991]). Thus the widespread turnover of leaders that occurred after the 1982 election definitely wrought change in agency practice, consistent with other organizational research showing that leadership succession is a key way in which bureaucracies overcome inertia and realign themselves with a changing environment. . . . However, given the lag between the Deukmejian appointments and agency responses, it appears that executive succession associated with the Republican gubernatorial victory in 1982–83 actually *depressed* progress toward gender-integration targets. In other words, changes at the top did indeed facilitate organizational change in this case, but not in the direction of reducing ascription.

It might be argued that we found effects of leader characteristics and turnover on segregation patterns only because we were looking at a sample of public-sector organizations. Economists have frequently observed that state governments operate in a protected environment, sheltered from competitive pressures that might reduce or eliminate the latitude for leaders to shape organizational practice in their own vision. This may be true. However, there appears to be considerable anecdotal evidence that top-level organizational commitment has also influenced antidiscrimination efforts in the private sector (e.g., Shaeffer and Lynton [1979]; O'Farrell and Harlan [1984]; Bielby and Baron [1984]). . . .

D. Environmental Pressures and Constituents

Finally, organizational theory and research also provide some clues about how an organization's success at reducing ascriptive job assignments might be affected by its environment. Although organizations are subject to inertia, they are not immune to external pressure. Like other researchers (e.g., Salancik [1979]; Freeman [1981]; Beller [1984]; Leonard [1984]), we found that state agencies subject to the strongest external pressures for reform exhibited faster integration. For instance, agencies that had been targeted and sanctioned by the state government's own watchdog organization, the State Personnel Board, integrated more rapidly (Baron, Mittman, and Newman [1991]). Similarly, agencies whose mandate makes them most subject to oversight by the state legislature integrated faster than agencies having more autonomy. . . .

IV. LOOSE COUPLING AND ORGANIZATIONAL RESPONSES TO ANTIDISCRIMINATORY PRESSURES

Organizational scholarship also reminds us of the distinction between formal organizational structures and policies on the one hand and actual practices on the

other. The less than perfect correlation between the two is probably not acciden-
tal, but rather an important way that organizations retain the flexibility necessary
to adapt to uncertain and rapidly changing environments (Weick [1976]). Just as
organizations are not realistically portrayed by the production functions of economic theory, neither are they meaningfully represented by the organization
charts and policy manuals of administrative science.

This point is important because it helps explain, I believe, why we often find
more evidence of egalitarian *reforms* by organizations than we do of egalitarian
outcomes. For example, examining field notes prepared by U.S. Employment
Service analysts, Bielby and I found fewer employers explicitly mention-
ing policies restricting women's employment based on physical demands of
work after 1971—when the California Supreme Court declared such policies
unconstitutional—than beforehand. However, we found that women were actually somewhat more likely to be excluded from jobs involving heavy lifting after
1971 than they had been previously (Bielby and Baron [1986:784–785]).

Our analyses of California government agencies uncovered similar evidence of
the limits of antidiscriminatory reforms. I noted above that gender integration
was faster in state agencies cited for past discrimination by the State Personnel
Board. The board identified certain targeted job classifications in which specific
employment objectives were to be reached, but their sanctions were also intended
to reduce segregation throughout the entire job structures of the agencies involved. Yet segregation declines in the cited agencies were entirely attributable to
integration in the targeted job classes; in fact, in two of the three organizations
involved, the remaining job classifications actually became slightly more segregated over the period studied (Baron, Mittman, and Newman [1991]).

This result brings to mind Smith and Welch's (1984) findings: comparing
occupational distributions obtained from employers (via the Equal Employment
Opportunity Commission [EEOC]) and from employees (via the Census Bureau),
they concluded that much of the apparent "job integration" in response to the
targeting of industries by the EEOC and Office of Federal Contract Compliance
Programs (OFCCP) simply reflected cosmetic reclassifications of disadvantaged
workers into "managerial" and related categories. These findings suggest the
ability of organizations to segregate their desegregation efforts, as it were, com-
partmentalizing their activities to respond to specific internal constituencies and
external pressures without undertaking wholesale reforms (also see Leonard
[1989]). While this might reflect a conscious effort to subvert the intended aims
of targeting, an intriguing alternative is that it simply illustrates the tendency for
social systems to respond to pressures for costly or disruptive changes in a
selective and limited way. That tendency, of course, generally has tremendous
adaptive value, as ecologists have demonstrated, since overresponsiveness to
environmental forces could quickly cripple any complex system. This is not
to endorse the outcome in this case, but only to offer a possible explanation
for it. . . .

In sum, attention to what goes on inside organizations underscores the difference between organizational "accounts" and actual practices and suggests when antidiscriminatory policies and reforms may mask the perpetuation of ascriptive outcomes. There is a methodological implication here as well. Social scientists and policymakers often assess labor-market trends (including discrimination) based on official statistics reported by organizations to government agencies, statistics that represent a particular kind of organizational account or social construction. The organizational context of labor-market outcomes is thus critical not only because they can manipulate the very statistics and perceptions that frame public policies and discussions concerning discrimination. The examples described above should serve to illustrate how the social scientist's datum or trend is often the manager's strategically created fiction. . . .

VI. SUMMARY AND IMPLICATIONS FOR FUTURE RESEARCH

In the organizational world I have described, the extent of ascription is affected not simply by employer tastes, labor supply, the legal environment, and economic transaction costs, but also by psychological, political, and normative factors shaping organizational change and sustaining the status quo in a given setting. Drawing on my own research, I have described how some of these factors affect three facets of discrimination: how ascriptive characteristics figure in the way jobs are defined, evaluated, and staffed in organizations. . . .

Economists of various stripes have begun paying greater attention to the role of organizational arrangements in shaping employment relations and labor-market outcomes. By encouraging their efforts, perhaps this chapter abets the raiding of sociologists' turf by the economists (who would no doubt call this intellectual rent seeking). However, integrating economic and sociological insights into organizations is likely to improve our understanding of discrimination, our policies to eliminate it, and the quality of scholarship in both disciplines.

ACKNOWLEDGMENT

This chapter was partially completed while the author was a fellow at the Center for Advanced Study in the Behavioral Sciences; support from the Alfred P. Sloan Foundation and from the center staff is gratefully acknowledged. The National Research Council's Panel on Pay Equity Research, the Stanford Graduate School of Business, and faculty fellowships from tthe Business School Trust and from Robert M. and Anne T. Bass helped support the research described in this chapter, for which the author is appreciative. I thnak Pamela Pommerenke for research assistance and thank David Baron, William Bielby, James Heckman, Rod Kramer, Ed Lazear, Jeffrey Pfeffer, John Roberts, and the Middlebury Conference participants for very helpful comments on the ideas in this chapter.

NOTES

1. I use the terms *discrimination* and *ascription* in this chapter to refer to job assignments or reward allocations influenced directly (intentionally or not) by employees' ascriptive characteristics—in other words, where group membership has an effect on opportunities and outcomes that is not simply due to straightforward differences in human capital and labor supply across social groups.

REFERENCES

Baron, James N. and William T. Bielby. 1984. "The Organization of Work in a Segmented Economy." *American Sociological Review* 49, 4 (August):454–473.

Baron, James N., Frank Dobbin, and P. Devereaux Jennings. 1986. "War and Peace: the Evolution of Modern Personnel Administration in U.S. Industry." *American Journal of Sociology* 92, 2 (September):350–383.

Baron, James N., Brian S. Mittman, and Andrew E. Newman. 1991. "Targets of Opportunity: Organizational and Environmental Determinants of Gender Integration within the California Civil Service, 1979–1985." *American Journal of Sociology* 96, 3 (May):1362–1401.

Baron, James N. and Andrew E. Newman. 1989. "Pay the Man: Effects of Demographic Composition on Prescribed Wage Rates in the California Civil Service." pp. 107–130 in Michael, Hartmann, and O'Farrell [1989].

————. 1990. "For What It's Worth: Differences Across Organizations, Occupations, and the Value of Work Done by Women and Nonwhites." *American Sociological Review* 55, 2 (April):155–175.

Beller, Andrea H. 1984. "Trends in Occupational Segregation by Sex and Race, 1960–1981." pp. 11–26 in Reskin [1984].

Bielby, William T. and James N. Baron. 1984. "A Woman's Place Is with Other Women: Sex Segregation within Organizations." pp. 27–55 in Reskin [1984].

————. 1986. "Men and Women at Work: Sex Segregation and Statistical Discrimination." *American Journal of Sociology* 91, 4 (January):759–799.

Brewer, Marilynn B. and Roderick M. Kramer. 1985. "The Psychology of Intergroup Attitudes and Behavior." *Annual Review of Psychology* 36:219–243.

Cialdini, Robert B. 1988. *Influence.* 2d ed. Glenview, Ill: Scott, Foresman.

Collins, Randall. 1975. *The Credential Society.* New York: Academic Press.

Conk, Margo A. 1978. "Occupational Classification in the United States Census, 1870–1940." *Journal of Interdisciplinary History* 9, 1 (Summer):111–130.

Davis, Kingsley and Wilbert E. Moore. 1945. "Some Principles of Stratification." *American Sociological Review* 10, 2 (April):242–249.

Freeman, Richard B. 1981. "Black Economic Progress After 1964: Who Has Gained and Why?" pp. 247–294 in Sherwin Rosen (ed.) *Studies in Labor Markets.* Chicago: University of Chicago Press for the National Bureau of Economic Research.

Granovetter, Mark. 1985. "Economic Action and Social Structure: The Problem of Embeddedness." *American Journal of Sociology* 91, 3 (November):481–510.

————. 1988. "The Sociological and Economic Approaches to Labor Market Analysis: A Social Structural View." pp. 187–216 in George Farkas and Paula England (eds.) *Industries, Firms, and Jobs: Sociological and Economic Approaches*. New York: Plenum Press.

Kim, Marlene. 1989. "Gender Bias in Compensation Structure: A Case Study of Its Historical Basis and Persistence." *Journal of Social Issues* 45, 4 (Winter):39–50.

Lenski, Gerhard. 1966. *Power and Privilege: A Theory of Social Stratification*. New York: McGraw-Hill.

Leonard, Jonathan S. 1984. "The Impact of Affirmative Action on Employment." *Journal of Labor Economics* 2 (October):439–463.

————. 1989. "Women and Affirmative Action." *Journal of Economic Perspectives* 3, 1 (Winter):61–75.

Lyson, Thomas A. 1985. "Race and Sex Segregation in Occupational Structures of Southern Employers." *Social Science Quarterly* 66:281–295.

Meyer, John W. and Brian Rowan. 1977. "Institutionalized Organizations: Formal Structure as Myth and Ceremony." *American Journal of Sociology* 83, 2 (September):340–363.

Michael, Robert T., Heidi I. Hartmann, and Brigid O'Farrell (eds.) 1989. *Pay Equity: Empirical Inquiries*. Washington, D.C.: National Academy Press.

O'Farrell, Brigid and Susan Harlan. 1984. "Job Integration Strategies: Today's Programs and Tomorrow's Needs." pp. 267–291 in Reskin [1984].

Reskin, Barbara F. (ed.) 1984. *Sex Segregation in the Workplace: Trends, Explanations, Remedies*. Washington, D.C.: National Academy Press.

Salancik, Gerald R. 1979. "Interorganizational Dependence and Responsiveness to Affirmative Action: The Case of Women and Defense Contractors." *Academy of Management Journal* 22, 2:375–394.

Shaeffer, Ruth G. and Edith F. Lynton. 1979. *Corporate Experiences in Improving Women's Job Opportunities*. Conference Board Report no. 755. New York: Conference Board.

Stinchcombe, Arthur L. 1965. "Social Structure and Organizations." pp. 142–193 in J. G. March (ed.) *Handbook of Organizations*. Chicago: Rand McNally.

————. 1979. "Social Mobility in Industrial Labor Markets." *Acta Sociologica* 22, 3:217–245.

Treiman, Donald J. 1977. *Occupational Prestige in Comparative Perspective*. New York: Academic Press.

Weick, Karl E. 1976. "Educational Organizations as Loosely Coupled Systems." *Administrative Science Quarterly* 21, 1 (March):1–49.

7

Equality and Efficiency: Antidiscrimination Policies in the Labor Market

Shelly J. Lundberg

I. INTRODUCTION

During recent years, a move away from government regulation of, and intervention in, the U.S. economy has occurred. This trend has been broad based. It has affected policies as diverse as welfare and antitrust and has inevitably extended to enforcement of antidiscrimination legislation. A sharp decrease in federal activities in this area has occurred, as have reduced budgets, confusion, and inactivity in the principal enforcement agencies. The ever-controversial set of policies known as affirmative action has come under particular criticism, though recent Supreme Court decisions have upheld the essentials of affirmative action. The decline of antidiscrimination activism, together with increased scrutiny of both the purpose and the methods of existing enforcement activities, will likely continue in the near future.

One important criticism of antidiscrimination programs is that they are inefficient and costly. Because the economy has been relatively stagnant for many years, government actions reducing the economy's productivity are increasingly difficult to justify to the public. Of course, administrative costs are part of any regulatory effort, but most concern over antidiscrimination efforts centers on the additional costs resulting from distorted private hiring and promotion decisions. Government pressure to employ and promote women and minorities may force firms to misallocate labor and thus suffer production losses. Proponents usually cite the offsetting benefit of progress toward a social goal of greater equality. As the driving force behind initial measures such as the Civil Rights Act, this factor deserves much weight. However, one can make another case for antidiscrimination efforts more in keeping with the current concern over productive efficiency.

If two equally productive groups of workers are treated differently by employ-

Excerpts reprinted with permission from *Contemporary Policy Issues* 1989, vol. 7:75–94. Copyright © 1989 by Western Economic Association Int'l.

ers in hiring and compensation, then discrimination exists in the labor market. Given this definition, one may reasonably regard discrimination as a market failure, that is, a departure from economists' paradigm of a perfect market. In a perfectly functioning market, workers of equal ability are compensated equally.

If discrimination is due to market failure, then one can justify government intervention so as to correct the problem on efficiency grounds. Most discussion on discrimination as a constitutional issue has contrasted two sets of individual rights: (i) employers' right to unhindered operation of their private business and (ii) employees' right to equal treatment. Introducing an efficiency criterion changes the focus to a trade-off between the employers' individual interests and the public's interest in an efficient allocation of society's resources. . . .

The following sections survey briefly the federal government's antidiscrimination efforts and the economic theories of discrimination. I then outline a simple theory of discrimination based on imperfect information. Competitive firms pay wages equaling each worker's expected contribution to output. Due to imperfect information about individual abilities and productivity, these wages will not lead to the most efficient allocation of resources. In particular, workers will face inadequate incentives to invest in training. One may show that if employers possess better information about employees of a particular sex or race, then those employees eventually will be better paid than others even though the two groups are initially equally productive.

There is a potential for the government to improve this situation, and this paper considers several possible remedies. The first is an equal opportunity rule that an omniscient government enforces. The paper considers both the possibility of firms' evading this rule and the problems involved in monitoring and enforcing compliance. The second policy considered is analogous to "disparate impact" judgments in which the type of information that employers can use in personnel decisions is regulated. Finally, the paper considers an affirmative action-type policy monitoring the outcomes, rather than the process, of hiring and compensation decisions. Each policy is examined in terms of both its efficacy in remedying the distorted training incentives that discrimination causes and its costs to private firms through misallocation of labor.

II.   FEDERAL ANTIDISCRIMINATION PROGRAMS

Beginning during the 1960s, the federal government constructed an administrative and legal apparatus designed to combat discrimination in employment. This process began when the Equal Pay Act was passed in 1963. The two most important components, however, have been Title VII of the Civil Rights Act

(1964) and Executive Order No. 11246 (1965), which prohibited discrimination by federal contractors. . . .

Title VII prohibits discrimination in employment and compensation. The Equal Employment Opportunity Commission (EEOC) is charged with investigating and mediating complaints under the Civil Rights Act (the Act) and since 1972 has been empowered to bring suit against employers. The courts have developed standards as to which employer practices constitute discrimination. The Office of Federal Contract Compliance Programs (OFCCP) was established to monitor the employment practices of federal contractors. Firms with federal contracts above a certain size must submit reports analyzing their employment of women and minorities relative to those groups' availability in the qualified labor force. If these reports reflect that such protected groups are "underutilized," then the employer must prepare an affirmative action plan—including goals and timetables—for remedying such underutilization. Ineligibility for federal contracts is the ultimate, if seldom invoked, penalty for failing to make good-faith efforts to implement an acceptable plan. . . .

Two standard objections to such programs exist. The first charges that activities of both the EEOC and the OFCCP are likely to reduce the total productivity of the economy. The charge that government regulation is inefficient is widespread and is by no means limited to antidiscrimination measures. More specifically, costs are associated with any regulatory effort. These include administrative costs involved in monitoring compliance, litigation costs, and costs involved in distortions of private firms' personnel decisions. Government pressure to increase the hiring and promoting of female and minority workers may lead firms to misallocate labor and thus cause production losses.

A second criticism is that affirmative action pressures firms into engaging in "reverse discrimination," or preferential treatment of women and minorities. One may regard this as a direct violation of equal opportunity laws and so may render affirmative action objectionable on *a priori* grounds.

The standard counterargument to both charges involves asserting a state purpose—achieving economic progress for disadvantaged groups of workers whose members have suffered from labor market discrimination. Many economists have concluded that equal pay or equal opportunity hiring constraints placed on firms involve an equity–efficiency trade-off. That is, while such constraints transfer resources so that income is divided more equally among groups, they also cause efficiency losses. Justifying such policies on the basis of equity considerations requires making a social judgment as to the value of redistributing society's resources, and then setting this value beside the more easily measured efficiency cost. Society inevitably must make such judgments in many circumstances. I admit to their validity but would argue that justifying equal opportunity enforcement activities, including affirmative action, need not rest solely on equity grounds.

III.   ECONOMISTS AND DISCRIMINATION

Economists tend to exhibit a strong bias toward *laissez faire* operation of the economy, and for good reason. Perfectly competitive markets, under certain well-defined conditions, have been shown to function in an optimal manner. That is, desired goods and services are produced efficiently in response to the signals of prices, so that no individual can be made better off without someone else's being made worse off. If the distribution of resources resulting from the free play of markets is considered socially undesirable, then resources are best redistributed through lump-sum taxes and transfer payments rather than through direct interference in production. Government interventions in this ideal economy— e.g., minimum wages, safety regulations, proportional income taxes—generally will be inefficient in that they distort incentives and reduce the quantity of goods and services available in the economy.

The common notion that antidiscrimination efforts involve an efficiency cost seemingly derives from this set of optimality theorems and the belief that the U.S. economy closely approximates the ideal economy that such theorems require. If this is so, then labor market discrimination could not arise in the first place, since paying equally productive individuals different wages is incompatible with profit maximization in perfect markets. In fact, economists have had some difficulty in constructing theories of discrimination in which wage differentials will persist in a reasonably well-functioning labor market. One quite intuitively appealing model, in which discrimination is based on employers' personal prejudice, produces wage differentials that persist only if all employers in the market are equally prejudiced. An unprejudiced employer will earn higher profits by hiring relatively underpaid women and minorities, and eventually will drive all other firms out of business. Discriminators will be penalized by the marketplace, and wage differentials will disappear (Becker, 1957; Arrow, 1973).

An alternative model attributes discrimination to employers' lack of information about individual workers' productivity. Wage differences may be caused by differential information about two groups of workers. This is usually called "statistical discrimination" (Phelps, 1972, pp. 659–661; Aigner and Cain, 1977, pp. 175–187). Employers cannot measure the exact productivity of job applicants and thus must use whatever information is available to estimate that productivity. Besides using obvious indicators such as education, previous experience, references, and test results, employers will use worker characteristics such as race or sex if they believe such characteristics to be informative. This will result in stereotyping: Individuals will be assigned, to some extent, the qualities of the group to which they belong. This may seem unfair but is to some extent inevitable in a world of imperfect information. For example, college graduates generally will be assumed to be more productive than high school graduates, though in many individual cases this will not be true.

If all employers are equally ill informed, then this type of discrimination is consistent with profit maximization and thus with long-run persistence of discrimination. In the statistical discrimination model of Aigner and Cain (1977), no differences exist in average compensation for groups that on average are equally productive. An extension allowing for feedback from employers' incentives to workers' decisions to invest in their own skills and training, however, leads to an evidently discriminatory outcome.

IV.   AN IMPERFECT INFORMATION MODEL OF DISCRIMINATION

If one recognizes that individual decisions regarding education and training are affected by anticipated labor market rewards, then one can construct a model in which imperfect information does lead to labor market discrimination (Lundberg and Startz, 1983, pp. 340–347). In this economy, competitive non-prejudiced employers find it optimal to offer different wage schedules to two groups of workers who have, on average, equal abilities. These different wage schedules affect future workers' incentives to invest in training and so lead to differences in both average productivities and average wages. Government intervention in the form of equal opportunity rules may be efficient.

A.   Employers Cannot Measure the Productivity
of Individual Workers Exactly

Personnel decisions are made in an atmosphere of uncertainty. Potential workers vary in their skills and abilities, and these will affect their productivity with the firm. One could reasonably suppose that employers know how productive an "average" worker is and have some notion as to how ability is distributed over the labor force, but must consider that employers cannot observe the productivity of a particular worker directly. Instead, they can acquire for each individual a "test score" predicting productivity with some error, in the same way that a typing test predicts actual on-the-job typing proficiency or a SAT score predicts college performance. This test score need not result from a single test since it represents the employer's best guess as to an applicant's future effectiveness as a worker. In particular, such a test may include the subjective evaluation of a well-intentioned but not omniscient personnel officer.

B.   Employers Have "Better" Information About Some Workers
Than About Others

Each applicant belongs to one of two easily observable groups. These groups may be defined by sex, race, ethnic group, or any other characteristic not directly related to productive abilities. I will call these group 1 and group 2 so as to avoid limiting the discussion to one type of discrimination. The essential ingredient of a statistical theory of discrimination is that the test score predicts productivity more accurately for type 1 workers than it does for type 2 workers. . . .

This type of differential reliability could arise if all personnel managers are members of group 1 and are more effective at assessing workers who are members of their own group. Personnel professionals are skilled at reading the signals of character and ability that candidates produce during interviews. However, if applicants from a different group produce those signals, then cultural differences may obscure such signals and lead to a less reliable composite test score. One would expect this uncertainty to erode over time. But if type 2 workers are relatively recent arrivals in a particular industry or profession, then a long track record relating observable qualities to eventual performance may not have been built up.

For example, suppose that a firm wishes to avoid workers likely to quit during the early years of employment and that individuals vary in their propensity to quit. The personnel director may be very effective at detecting signs of employment instability in male candidates. . . . The same manger, however, may be unable to predict the propensity to quit of female candidates. . . . Note that this approach does not require any difference in the average quit rates of male and female workers. It merely implies that one can predict individual quit behavior more accurately for one group than the other.

C. Competitive Wages Will Be Based on Both Group Average and Individual Characteristics

Because the firms in this labor market are competitive, they will pay each individual a wage equal to his or her expected contribution to total product. This expectation is based on two pieces of information: (i) the individual's test score and (ii) the average productivity of the group to which he or she belongs. The wage paid will be a weighted average of these two measures. Wages will be calculated differently for group 1 than for group 2. Because the test score measures productivity more accurately for type 1 workers, the test score will receive greater weight—relative to group average productivity—in calculating wages for these workers. Wages for type 2 workers will place less weight on the individual test score since it is less reliable, and will place more weight on the group average.

Consider an individual applicant with a higher-than-average test score. The employer will discount part of this high score as resulting from random testing error—e.g., good luck, an "on" day, less-than-frank references—so that wages will not rise proportionately with test scores. However, the employer will place relatively more weight on this high score as indicating high productivity if the applicant belongs to group 1. Therefore, we observe two wage schedules: Group 1 workers' wages will rise more rapidly with test scores than will group 2 workers' wages, and the reward for improving one's test score is smaller for type 2 workers.

D. Workers' Incentives to Improve Their Skills Will Be Inhibited by the Offered Wage Schedules

Productivity will likely depend not only on innate abilities but also on skills and knowledge that workers have acquired during school or previous work experience. This distinction is important since individuals cannot choose their level of innate ability but may choose whether to invest in training. In making such a decision, workers will weight the costs of training against the anticipated reward of higher wages in the labor market.

Acquired skills increase productivity, yet employers cannot observe such skills except through their effect on the test score. That is, it is not years of schooling *per se* but the amount actually learned in school that increases productivity, where this is to some extent under individual control. Kenneth Arrow (1973, p. 27) describes these human capital investments in the more general sense: "Hence, the investments are not the usual types of education or experience, which are observable, but more subtle types of personal deprivation and deferment of gratification which lead to the habits of action and thought that favor good performance in skilled jobs". . . .

Differences in these acquired abilities likely constitute much of the difference between a good worker and a bad worker. For example, two teenagers' resumes may list similar after-school jobs in fast-food restaurants. One teenager may have developed good work habits and acquired some knowledge of how to deal with the public, while the other teenager may not have developed such habits or acquired such knowledge. Such learning would have been costly in terms of greater attention and effort expended and less time fraternizing with other employees, but the difference in acquired skills may show up imperfectly in a subsequent job interview or in a reference from a supervisor. . . .

E. Workers of the "Better Known" Type Will Invest More and Be Better Paid

For type 1 and type 2 workers, the cost of increasing one's expected test score through such activities is the same but the benefits are not the same. If the employer knows that testing errors are greater for group 2, then the employer will discount a high test score to a greater extent and will offer a smaller wage increase for type 2 than for type 1 workers. Thus, the incentive is weaker for type 2 workers to distinguish themselves through productive investment, and so they rationally will invest less in imperfectly observable skills.

Plotting wages against test scores for the members of each group will reveal that group 2 workers receive lower average wages than do group 1 workers, corresponding to the former's lower average productivity. . . .

F.   Is This Discrimination?

Certainly, employers treat members of the two groups differently, but the difference in average wages corresponds exactly to the difference in productivity due to less acquired skills among type 2 workers. Because of competition in the labor market, each worker is paid a wage equaling his or her expected marginal product. In deciding what wage to pay, employers efficiently use all available information—including group membership—so as to predict productivity. Thus, this different treatment is due not to prejudice or aversion to type 2 workers but to employers' inability to distinguish between more- or less-skilled workers of group 2.

On the other hand, the observed difference in average productivity between the two groups is due entirely to the incentives that firms offer. The two groups began with equal average abilities but rationally chose different investment strategies due to the different rewards inherent in the two wage schedules. One may argue that inherently equal workers in the labor market are treated such that their economic rewards are very different. This is labor market discrimination, though it involves no invidious prejudice on the part of employers.

Little question exists as to the legal status of the wage schedules paid by profit-maximizing employers in this model. The essence of statistical discrimination is that individuals are judged partly on the basis of employers' perceptions of group averages or "stereotypes." The courts have established that this tendency to attribute the characteristics of particular groups to an individual employee is discriminatory.

V.   EFFICIENT GOVERNMENT INTERVENTION: EQUAL OPPORTUNITY LAWS

Imperfect information in this labor market constitutes a market failure in that total welfare is lower than it would be in a world of perfect information. Employers' inability to assess the productivity of job applicants is a fundamental and realistic source of market failure. Because employers use information about group average productivity to estimate an individual's worth, no person in the group receives full credit for self-improvement efforts. If the test score predicted productivity perfectly, then each additional point on the test would yield an equivalent increase in wages: No discounting for testing error would occur. Because the reward for investing in skills would be higher, both groups would undertake more of such investment and total labor productivity would increase. . . .

An antidiscrimination policy can improve the efficiency of this economy. Suppose that employers can be prevented from offering wage schedules varying by group membership. Henceforth, a type 1 worker and a type 2 worker with the same test score must be offered the same wage. . . .

If this policy restricts the actions of competitive employers, then how can it improve the efficiency of the economy? By equalizing the quantity of skills that the two groups of workers acquire, the policy ensures that workers use educational resources more effectively. I have assumed that a unit of training increases the productivity of type 1 workers by the same amount as it does that of type 2 workers. However, in the discriminatory equilibrium, group 2 workers receive less training than do group 1 workers. The social cost of education in this economy can be reduced without impairing total labor productivity by allocating training more evenly among individuals. (If one employs the standard assumption that the costs of training increase with the amount of training received, then the last unit of training that type 1 workers purchase is more expensive than the last unit that type 2 workers purchase in the discriminatory equilibrium.) Because the initial discrepancy in training was not due to any real differences in the productivity of training across groups, eliminating this discrepancy enhances efficiency. The antidiscrimination policy accomplishes this. In this case, no equity–efficiency trade-off occurs. Equality and efficiency go hand in hand.

This model is a simple and stylized representation of the labor market. Is it a special case generating atypical results? I think not. This example illustrates that if discrimination results from imperfect markets—and discrimination, properly defined, could hardly arise in a perfect labor market—then government intervention may be efficient. This holds even when employers are competitive and are not prejudiced in the sense of having an aversion to one group of workers.

This does not mean that an actual government policy along the lines of that suggested above will in fact achieve this increase in efficiency. An antidiscrimination policy involves costs that must be weighed against the reduced training costs. First, production losses are likely to occur due to greater mismatches between workers and jobs when employers are forbidden to use information that they had previously found useful. Employers will minimize such losses by using all available information, including group membership, when allocating workers. In addition, enforcement costs will arise, as they do in maintaining any sort of social policy inconsistent with the private incentive structure. Type 2 workers with high test scores—and type 1 workers with low test scores—will, under the antidiscrimination rules, be paid a wage higher than their expected marginal product, so that firms will have an incentive to avoid hiring such workers. . . . The problem of monitoring compliance with such a program is more difficult. What does it mean to offer wage schedules not dependent on group membership, and how can the government tell when a firm is doing so?

VI.   PROBLEMS WITH ENFORCING EQUAL OPPORTUNITY LAWS

The actual process by which hiring, promotion, and compensation decisions are made is inherently unobservable to a government agency charged with enforcing equal opportunity laws, nor is it observable to the courts. Subjective evaluations may play as large a role as do easily measured qualifications in personnel decisions, but the former are difficult for the firm to justify and for the government to proscribe. In this section, I discuss a simple case where firms easily evade the equal opportunity rule and where government's efforts to enforce compliance lead to a familiar quandary.

A.   Evasion

In the previous section, we considered an antidiscrimination policy in which the government forbids using group membership to determine wages. Because group membership provides information about how to interpret the observed test score, employers have an incentive to evade this regulation. Suppose that employers are aware of some other type of information, such as height. Let height bear no relationship to workers' productive abilities but be correlated with group membership. That is, type 1 workers are more likely to be tall than are type 2 workers.

Before antidiscrimination regulations are enforced, employers do not use height to determine hiring or wages since height provides no useful information. Once employers are prohibited from considering group membership, however, height becomes a useful index. . . . To be optimal, employers will use height as a type of imperfect proxy for the proscribed index, group membership, and so will evade the equal opportunity laws.

In the new equilibrium, short workers will have less incentive to invest in training than will tall workers. In the long run, short workers will have lower average productivity. These disadvantaged workers will be from both groups but predominantly from group 2, so that wage differentials between the two groups will still exist. . . .

B.   Disparate Impact Rules

Employers' use of height as a proxy for group membership is reminiscent of cases to which courts have applied the disparate impact standard. In *Griggs v.*

Duke Power Co., a unanimous Supreme Court held that intent to discriminate is not necessary for a firm to violate Title VII. The employer's written examinations and educational requirements acted as a bar on the promotion of black workers: These facially neutral criteria had a disparate impact on black workers in the same way that height has a disparate impact on group 2. Employers may use such tests only if they show that the tests are related to job performance. As the Supreme Court declared, "Tests must measure the person for the job; not the person in the abstract". . . .

A principal difficulty in applying the disparate impact standard has been in ascertaining when personnel policies are in fact measuring the person for the job. Generally, a narrow view has been taken: Criteria demonstrably correlated with job performance but not shown to have a direct link with required skills have been disallowed. Educational achievement in many blue-collar jobs is a good example. Word-of-mouth recruiting, a time-honored method of acquiring good applicants while minimizing screening costs, tends to perpetuate past discrimination and in many circumstances is prohibited. Generally, apparently neutral policies that help perpetuate the effects of past discrimination on the workforce composition have been suspect.

Should the use of height be prohibited in hiring and promotion decisions by our hypothetical employer? In the case where height itself is not related to an individual's ability but is used as a proxy for group, the use of height as such clearly should be prohibited, if possible. In a more realistic case, height itself may be informative about productivity and be correlated with group membership. . . .

It seems clear that enforcing equal opportunity legislation by such means is a difficult business. Employers have a strong incentive to look for apparently neutral characteristics correlated with race or sex and to introduce such characteristics into personnel decisions. Usually, this simply will involve changing the weights assigned to legitimate indicators already used. No malice need characterize this procedure: A computer programmed to minimize deviations between marginal product and wages paid to each worker would use all available information in this way.

If the government's arsenal of enforcement techniques is limited to regulating the process by which wages are set, as is characteristic of actions under Title VII, then the government is unlikely to do more than either allow or disallow the use of specific worker qualifications. For example, the EEOC and the courts could not possibly rule on the exact way in which an individual firm should use education in setting wages, though this might be the optimal policy. Each indicator must either be used as the employer sees fit or not be used at all. Disallowing useful indices imposes costs on firms, while permitting the use of such indices countenances a *de facto* evasion of equal opportunity laws. Even more serious is the shortcoming that the government may be unable to observe all factors that firms use: The government cannot prevent employers from using subjective impressions from interviews with applicants, and such assessments may be among the most damaging for minority and female workers.

Generally, regulating personnel policies directly to enforce equal opportunity is an intrusive and costly way to combat statistical discrimination. . . .

VII.   AFFIRMATIVE ACTION

I now turn to affirmative action-type policies. I use this term to denote measures that attempt to enforce equal opportunity by monitoring the outcomes of the firm's hiring and promotion decisions rather than monitoring the process itself. The ideal antidiscrimination policy would forbid using group membership to determine wages, but this is ineffective if the firm can use substitute indicators such as the test scores that Duke Power used. The government cannot feasibly prohibit the use of all such substitutes: They will be different for each firm, and some substitutes may also be legitimate qualifications that have assumed a dual purpose. One may regard an affirmative action policy as a practical response to a situation in which the government has insufficient information about individual firms' personnel policies to effectively monitor and enforce non-discrimination.

A.   Distinguishing Features

In its narrowest sense, affirmative action is the activity required of federal contractors so as to demonstrate that they are in compliance with equal opportunity laws. Contractors must analyze the extent of their underutilization of women and minorities and then submit a plan to remedy any such underutilization. These plans generally include numerical goals and schedules, and the contractor must make "good faith" efforts to implement the plan. Underutilization exists when a job category contains fewer women or minorities than might be expected based on their presence in the pool of qualified available labor. . . .

The rationale of such a policy is that if the firm is not discriminating, then one might expect the number of minority employees in each job category to be roughly proportional to their representation among "qualified" prospective employees. If they are underrepresented, then their underutilization is *prima facie* evidence of discrimination. The catch, obviously, is that making the term "qualified" operational is difficult.

Two important characteristics differentiate affirmative action from other antidiscrimination measures. One is that affirmative action concentrates not on the procedures that firms follow but on the outcomes of firms' decisions in terms of employment patterns. The second is that affirmative action requires firms to eliminate the effects of past discrimination from their labor forces. . . .

B. A Stylized Example of an Affirmative Action Policy: Observed Wage Schedules Must Be Equal for Type 1 and Type 2 Workers

In our simple model, suppose that the government elects not to regulate the indices that firms may use in setting wages and instead requires that wage schedules be identical for each group, conditional on some set of easily observable indicators of productivity. Admitting regression analyses of earnings as evidence in many court cases is consistent with this approach, as are the utilization studies that affirmative action requires. If the government can observe the test score and regards the score as a reasonable indicator of a worker's qualifications, then the rule might be that a regression of wages on the test score should be the same for both groups. Therefore, firms may use any information they like in setting wages so long as average outcomes satisfy the affirmative action restriction.

Consider the previous case where height is informative to employers only insofar as it acts as a proxy for group membership. If the government cannot prohibit the use of height—either because it cannot establish that height is unrelated to ability or because it cannot reliably observe the use of height—then the government may impose such a policy restricting wage outcomes. Under these circumstances, this requirement will have the same effect as will a disparate impact judgment forbidding the use of height. Given the restriction that apparent wage schedules conditional on the test score must be identical, firms will have no incentive to use height in their true underlying wage schedules. If firms cannot use height to differentiate between the two groups, then height will not be used at all and an equal opportunity outcome will result.

By contrast, if height is informative about productivity, then firms will continue to base wages on height as well as the test score—in a restricted way, however, so as to conform to the affirmative action constraint. In general, firms optimally will offer tall workers a more steeply sloped wage schedule than they will offer short workers if the former's test scores are more reliable indicators of productivity. However, because type 1 workers are more likely to be tall and because wages must average out at each test score, firms will offer tall type 2 workers a steeper schedule than they will offer tall type 1 workers. To meet the affirmative action restriction, firms will offer type 2 workers of each height a higher return on base qualifications relative to the workers' type 1 equivalents. Employers will feel that this requires them to provide "preferential treatment" to type 2 workers.

What effect will such an affirmative action policy have on efficiency? The private cost to employers of misallocating labor will be higher than it is under *laissez faire*, in which employers can use all available information freely. On the other hand, the incentives of type 1 and type 2 workers will be brought closer together than they are under *laissez faire*, and this will reduce the total cost of training in this economy. The relative magnitude of these costs and benefits is theoretically indeterminate, and a policy decision must also consider the contribution of greater income equality to social goals.

If height itself is informative about productivity, then firms should prefer an affirmative action-type policy, which regulates the wage outcomes, over a disparate impact-type policy, which forbids the use of height. One can easily show that firms' allocation losses will be higher under the disparate impact ruling than they would be under the affirmative action policy, which would permit use of the height index in a restricted way. If a policy allows the use of particular indices but requires that evidence of their use is not observable in firms' employment and compensation patterns, then firms retain more freedom of action than they would if their personnel policies were regulated directly.

C. Preferential Treatment

The affirmative action policy described above does not overtly require that employers provide preferential treatment for group 2 workers. From the firms' viewpoint, however, such preferential treatment is inevitable if they are to continue complying with the regulation. . . . The parallel with actual affirmative action policies, which monitor the relationship between a firm's labor force and some loosely defined pool of available labor, is fairly obvious.

Suppose that a firm is required, under its affirmative action plan, to ensure that the proportion of black managers is consistent with the proportion of college-educated black workers in its labor pool. The firm wishes to take into account indicators other than years of education—such as an aptitude test score, which the firm believes signals higher productivity but which also is strongly correlated with race. As a result, high scores on the aptitude test will increase the likelihood of both black workers' and white workers' being promoted, but black workers will not need as high a score to be promoted as will white workers. The firm must engage in such preferential treatment if it wishes to employ the test score in its internal decision process but still ensure that the proportions of black and white managers are consistent with the representation of college graduates in the labor force.

Compare this solution to the case of a disparate impact judgment, in which the firm is explicitly forbidden from using the aptitude test score as a qualification for promoting a worker to management. The firm feels that workers who score high on the test will be discriminated against in this equilibrium relative to other college graduates. That is, the firm will be prohibited from rewarding such high scorers' expected higher productivity by taking the test score into account in promotion decisions. (Also, the firm will not be allowed to use the test score as a proxy for race.) Because these high scorers will be predominantly white, the firm feels that black college graduates will, on average, be overpromoted. Forbidding the use of any type of information that the firm finds useful will be viewed as requiring preferential treatment. We are less likely to call this reverse discrimination than we are in the affirmative action case, though the outcome is quite similar: Black and white workers are apparently treated in the same manner, conditional on the information that the firm is permitted to use. In both cases, training efficiency will be increased by providing black and white workers with more equal incentives than under *laissez faire*.

Much of the current debate over the merits of affirmative action concerns the use of temporary preferential treatment to achieve true equal opportunity in the labor market. This dispute, most abstractly, involves weighing the value of fairness in procedures against that of fairness in outcomes. That is, should the government be enforcing equal treatment of individuals in the labor market or equal treatment of well-defined groups of workers? If discrimination is due to imperfect information about the productivity of individuals, then I am not sure that this philosophical argument—important as it may be—is particularly relevant to policy decisions. One consequence of this deficiency in the labor market is that firms necessarily treat workers as members of identifiable groups with known characteristics. This need not involve any invidious prejudice: Profit-maximizing entities are merely attempting to use all available information in allocating labor. No one can be treated entirely as an individual if his or her abilities cannot be known with certainty. If equal opportunity legislation prevents personnel departments from overtly using race or sex, then they will alter their use of other types of information correlated with race or sex—such as height or aptitude test scores—for the same purpose. Attempting to enforce truly race- or sex-blind hiring and compensation in this market is hopeless.

Affirmative action policies may be realistic responses to imperfect information in two ways: They accept that it is infeasible to enforce laws demanding that each individual be judged on his or her merits alone, and they accept that the government can regulate only behavior that it can observe. The second principle leads to regulating economic outcomes rather than decision processes within firms, and the first principle implies that the regulations themselves reintroduce the practice of explicitly considering group membership in employment. Herein lies the aspect of affirmative action to which many object: Because these policies recognize that rational employers will use race or sex implicitly if they do not do so explicitly, such policies attempt to eliminate discrimination by leaning against firms' tendency to underemploy or undercompensate certain groups.

VIII.   CONCLUSION

In economics, labor market discrimination is objectionable not only on moral grounds but also because the unequal treatment of equally productive workers is inefficient. Discrimination, properly measured, results from a market failure, and one may consider a role for government in alleviating the consequences of this failure. Government intervention to combat discrimination is necessarily costly in terms of both the public resources devoted to monitoring and enforcing and the private costs involved in distorted personnel decisions. An effective and well-directed antidiscrimination policy will minimize such costs, but lack of information about each firm's actual personnel policies prevents discrimination from being prohibited outright. The incentives to evade equal opportunity rules are likely great, and achieving an optimal outcome by directly regulating each firm's hiring and promoting process is infeasible.

One may consider affirmative action-type policies as second-best responses to these enforcement problems. It is easier to regulate directly things one can observe (such as the outcome of employment and compensation decisions) rather than things one cannot observe (such as the role of sex or race in such decisions). The effect of such regulation on efficiency is uncertain: A more efficient allocation of training and other investment in human capital, plus the social benefits of greater equality, must be set against the private costs of misallocating workers among jobs and the public costs of enforcing a policy that runs counter to private incentives. It should be possible, however, to design effective affirmative action plans that may leave firms better off than do disparate impact standards, which control the information that a firm may use in personnel decisions. Whether actual affirmative action plans achieve this second-best optimum is an open question.

REFERENCES

Aigner, D. J., and G. G. Cain, "Statistical Theories of Discrimination in Labor Markets," *Industrial and Labor Relations Review, January* 1977, 175–187.

Arrow, K. J., "The Theory of Discrimination," in O. Ashenfelter and A. Rees, eds., *Discrimination in Labor Markets,* Princeton University Press, Princeton, N.J., 1973.

Becker, G. S., *The Economics of Discrimination,* University of Chicago Press, Chicago, 1957.

Lundberg, S. J., "The Enforcement of Equal Opportunity Laws Under Imperfect Information: Affirmative Action and Alternatives," working paper, University of Washington, Seattle, 1987.

Lundberg, S. J., and R. Startz, "Private Discrimination and Social Intervention in Competitive Labor Markets," *American Economic Review,* June 1983, 340–347.

Phelps, E. S., "The Statistical Theory of Racism and Sexism," *American Economic Review,* September 1972, 659–661.

III

Legal Definitions of Discrimination: Controversy and Conflict

If there is one thing that should be clear by now in discussions of EEO, that would be what discrimination is. Nevertheless, thirty years after employment discrimination was prohibited by Title VII, one of the most bitter controversies about efforts to end discrimination concerns exactly that issue.

Title VII itself is rather vague. It prohibits some specific practices—for example, "to fail . . . to hire . . . because of . . . race, color, religion, sex, or national origin" (42 U.S.C. 2000e, sec. 702(a))—but then adds that it shall be an "unlawful employment practice . . . otherwise to discriminate" without saying what that means.

For many, Congress had no need to say more because the definition is so obvious. To discriminate, Belz writes (1991:9, 15–16), is intentionally to use race or another ascribed characteristic as a basis for employment decisions. It means being "color-conscious" rather than "color-blind" (Glazer in Nieli 1991:5). "The discrimination Congress meant to outlaw," Gold has written (1985:492), "was purposeful, intentional and motivated by racial animus or stereotyped thinking." It means that "motivated by a worker's race [or color, religion, sex, or national origin], an employer treats the worker less favorably than a worker of another race would have been treated" (Gold 1985:431).

But not everyone agrees that the definition is so obvious. Edelman (1992: [excerpted here]) writes that the definition is "ambiguous" and notes that although Title VII defines eleven terms in great detail—including *employer* and *person,* the definitions of which might also seem obvious—it does not so define *discrimination.*

There have been many disagreements since Title VII was adopted over whether specific practices constitute discrimination. Is it discrimination on the basis of sex to treat pregnant women less favorably than other workers? The Supreme Court said in 1976 that it was not, stating that the employer was not distinguishing between men and women, but rather between "pregnant women and nonpregnant persons" (*General Electric Co. v. Gilbert,* 429 U.S. 125 at 138). Congress overruled the Court, however, by adopting the Pregnancy Discrimination Act of

1978 and defined differential treatment based on pregnancy to be sex discrimination (Schlei and Grossman 1983:12). Is it discrimination on the basis of religion
to treat members of one religion less favorably than others because they refuse to
work on their sabbath? Again, there has been disagreement, with the EEOC
arguing that this constituted discrimination, the courts disagreeing, Congress
amending the law, and the courts limiting the scope of the congressional amendment (Beckley and Burstein 1991 [excerpted here]; Schlei and Grossman
1983:7). There have been many such disputes, suggesting that the definition of
discrimination may not be obvious to everyone.

By far the most serious disagreement about what constitutes discrimination
concerns what has come to be known as "adverse impact." Beginning in the
1960s, some lawyers and civil rights activists began to contest the widely held
view (see the quotation from Gold above) that only deliberate consideration of
race (or other ascribed characteristics) constitutes discrimination. They argued
that many seemingly fair employment practices, such as requiring all applicants
for particular jobs to have certain educational credentials or test scores, had been
adopted to reduce minorities' or women's chances for advancement. Going further, some argued that practices that adversely affect minorities or women should
be considered discriminatory, even if those adopting them had not intended to
harm minorities or women, unless the employer could demonstrate that they
really helped distinguish good employees from poor ones.

In 1971, the Supreme Court adopted this view in *Griggs v. Duke Power Co.*
(401 U.S. 424), expanding the definition of discrimination to encompass not only
intentional disparate treatment, but many practices having a disparate (or adverse) impact on minorities or women (unless justified by "business necessity")
as well (Schlei and Grossman 1983:ch. 1). As a result of this and other Supreme
Court decisions, guidelines issued by the EEOC, executive orders, and congressional action, the *legal* definition of discrimination has changed dramatically
since Title VII was adopted.

For some, this change has absurd and disastrous consequences. Those favoring
the traditional definition of discrimination object to the *Griggs* decision because,
they argue, its definition of discrimination distorts an important concept in order
to win preferential treatment for minorities and women. Under a "disparate
impact" standard, they claim, any negative labor market outcome can, with
sufficient imagination, be interpreted as the result of "discrimination." Depar-
tures from the discriminatory intent definition lead to quotas, a concern with
group representation in the workplace rather than justice for individuals, and a
new (reverse) racism (see, e.g., Glazer 1991; Abram 1986 [excerpted here];
Scalia 1991; Gold 1985).

Those supporting the changed—and still changing—definition, in contrast,
assert that relying on the traditional definition would make it impossible to end
many employment practices that perpetuate the subjugation of blacks and other
groups. The economists Ashelfelter and Oaxaca argue (1987:322), for example,

that "It is not hard to see that the appearance of disparate treatment [that is, intentionally differential treatment—the "traditional" definition of discrimination] is easy for an employer to eliminate without making any change in behavior at all. . . . To most economists the insistence on finding 'smoking gun' evidence of discriminatory actions, intent, or motivation seems quite irrelevant to determining whether labor market discrimination exists" (cf. Posner 1987:517–18 [excerpted here]). The history and complexity of modern employment practices are such that practices harming particular groups can be institutionalized without there being any way to attribute discriminatory intent to anyone (as the Supreme Court concluded had happened at Duke Power; see, e.g., Blumrosen 1972 [excerpted here]; Bielby and Baron 1986; Eichner 1988 [excerpted here]).

Similar controversies exist over the definition of affirmative action (Burstein 1992). These disputes over definitions are important because their outcomes have potentially important consequences. Both those who favor the "obvious" definition, emphasizing intention, and those who favor a flexible definition including impact, seem to agree that legal adoption of the obvious definition of discrimination would slow the advance—deserved or undeserved—of minorities and women, while adopting the newer definition would hasten it. How discrimination is defined, and whether the definition is more or less "fixed" or subject to change by Congress and the courts, is likely to affect employer behavior and labor market outcomes for minorities and women.

The two works excerpted here exemplify the competing positions in the controversy over how discrimination should be defined. Blumrosen's "Strangers in Paradise: *Griggs v. Duke Power Co.* and the Concept of Employment Discrimination" (1972) represents the view that a broad and flexible definition of discrimination, incorporating concern with the impact of employment practices as well as their intent, is crucial if minorities and women are to have truly equal opportunities in the labor market. "Redefining Discrimination: 'Disparate Impact' and the Institutionalization of Affirmative Action," published in 1987 by the Office of Legal Policy of the U.S. Department of Justice, constitutes a vigorous response to both the revised view of discrimination and Blumrosen personally. The competing points of view are strongly held and have very different implications for the struggle over equal opportunity; because each has been adopted by important political groups as well as by scholars, the controversy over how discrimination should be defined will play a role in legislative and legal disputes over EEO for years to come (Burstein 1990).

8

Strangers in Paradise: Griggs v. Duke Power Co. *and the Concept of Employment Discrimination*

Alfred W. Blumrosen

I. PROLOGUE: THE OCCASION FOR A DECISION

In March 1966, the Equal Employment Opportunity Commission (EEOC) negotiated an extensive agreement with the Newport News Shipyard to eliminate employment discrimination. The outcome of these negotiations—which were conducted by the Office of Conciliations which I then headed—was the first major achievement for the EEOC under title VII of the Civil Rights Act of 1964. Following that episode, Ken Holbert, Deputy Chief of Conciliations, and I decided to try to negotiate a model conciliation agreement on the subject of discriminatory employment testing. We knew that many companies had introduced tests in the 1950's and early 1960's when they could no longer legally restrict opportunities of blacks and other minority workers and that the tests had proved to be major barriers to minority advancement. We therefore sought to negotiate a solution that would induce industry either to stop using these tests, or, at the least, to modify their use so that they did not have a discriminatory effect.

Our attempt failed completely. We chose as the springboard for obtaining the model settlement a finding of the Commission that there was reasonable cause to believe a paper company in Louisiana had violated title VII, because the finding had mentioned the use of tests. However, when we attempted to negotiate on the testing issue, company officials pointed out that the reasonable-cause finding had merely alluded to the issue of employment tests. They maintained that their tests for general ability were important in enabling them to secure generally competent workers and that by using these tests, the company had developed a capable work force. They would not give up the tests unless compelled to do so. And we could not persuade the officials that title VII required the abandonment of these devices.

Excerpts reprinted with permission from the *Michigan Law Review* 1972, vol. 71:59–110. Copyright © 1972.

As we flew back to Washington, we reflected on the setback we had just received. We concluded that further conciliation efforts concerning testing would be useless unless the Commission published a clear official statement delineating what the law required. . . . As a result, the Commission issued its guidelines on employment testing on August 24, 1966.

The guidelines represented the EEOC's interpretation of section 703(h) of title VII, which permits the use of a "professionally developed" ability test so long as that test is not "designed, intended or used" to discriminate. They rejected the position that the use of *any* test developed by a professional in the field of institutional or industrial testing was protected under title VII and thus laid to rest one of the arguments presented by employers in conciliation conferences. The guidelines also interpreted the phrase "professionally developed" to refer to tests measuring an employee's ability to perform the specific job or class of jobs for which he has applied, and thereby rejected the argument that an employer could test for "general ability or promotability." The remainder of the guidelines constituted a Commission endorsement of contemporary psychological testing standards developed by professional associations.

For those of us involved in title VII's administration, the guidelines provided the basis for a determination that certain testing practices were illegal. On this authority, our Office resumed efforts at conciliation. . . . When negotiations failed or were not undertaken because of the huge backlog of work at the Commission, suits were frequently brought in federal court under title VII, often with the litigation conducted by attorneys of the NAACP or the Legal Defense and Education Fund, Inc.

One such case was *Griggs v. Duke Power Co.* (401 U.S. 424, 1971). It reached the Supreme Court and provided the first occasion for the high court to determine the nature and scope of the prohibition on racial discrimination in employment under the Civil Rights Act of 1964. Although issued without fanfare, *Griggs* is in the tradition of the great cases of constitutional and tort law which announce and apply fundamental legal principles to the resolution of basic and difficult problems of human relationships. The decision has poured decisive content into a previously vacuous conception of human rights. It shapes the statutory concept of "discrimination" in light of the social and economic facts of our society. The decision restricts employers from translating the social and economic subjugation of minorities into a denial of employment opportunity. . . .

The assumption underlying *Griggs* is that the Civil Rights Act of 1964 protects the interests of minority groups and their members in securing and improving employment opportunities. *Griggs* views discrimination not only as an isolated act by an aberrant individual wrongdoer that affects only an individual complainant, but also as the operation of industrial-relations systems that adversely affect minority group members. Title VII law thus focuses on the harm to both the group and the individual.

Griggs redefines discrimination in terms of consequence rather than motive, effect rather than purpose. This definition is new to the field of employment discrimination, in which a subjective test had previously been used. The Court applied this new definition to invalidate hiring standards based upon education and testing, and in the process gave strong legal sanction to the EEOC's statutory interpretations.

Significantly, the *Griggs* opinion was written by Chief Justice Burger, and concurred in by seven of his brethren (Justice Brennan absented himself from the case). The case was decided during a time in which the Supreme Court appeared to be shifting toward a cautious approach to constitutional issues. Yet, it is a sensitive, liberal interpretation of title VII. It has the imprimatur of permanence and may become a symbol of the Burger Court's concern for equal opportunity. Although the Court may take a more cautious approach to constitutional rights of minorities, *Griggs* makes clear that sympathetic interpretation of *statutory* rights is the order of the day. . . .

II. EQUAL-OPPORTUNITY DAY FOR BLACK WORKERS IN THE SOUTH

In *Griggs,* the Supreme Court dealt with an archetype of the subordination of black workers in the South. This pattern . . . involved a broad range of industrial-relations devices and understandings that defined the "place" of black workers.

In enacting the 1964 Civil Rights Act, Congress provided a one-year delay in the effective date to give labor and management an opportunity to comply voluntarily with the Act's provisions, and to allow the EEOC and the Department of Justice to "tool up" for the enforcement of the Act. Neither of these events occurred. During this one-year moratorium, southern industry engaged in a flurry of activity that sometimes involved genuine changes in industrial-relations systems, but more often produced only a "cosmetic change"; many employers adopted seemingly neutral personnel policies, which, in fact, perpetuated the subordinate position of black workers. Tests and educational requirements were adopted extensively in the early 1960's to achieve this result. The tests could be justified as "sound" personnel practices and would also permit an employer to continue the subordination of minorities.

Before 1965 at the Duke Power Company, blacks were assigned only to the labor department to perform janitorial and low-level maintenance work throughout the Dan River Steam Station. All jobs in other departments were reserved for whites. The economic bite of the discrimination was clear. The top rate of pay in the "black" department was $1.55 per hour, which was fourteen cents below the bottom rate in the white departments and nowhere near the white departments' top rates, which ranged from $3.18 to $3.65 per hour. The company did not have formal criteria for employment when this system of segregation was first implemented, but in 1955 it started to require a high school diploma for employment in the white departments, ostensibly to upgrade the quality and flexibility of the work force. Blacks with high school diplomas were, after 1955, still employed only in the labor department.

Duke Power responded to title VII's enactment by revising its hiring and transfer standards in 1965. A simple test was imposed for entry into the black (labor) department. For initial employment in the previously all-white departments, the passage of two standard industrial tests—the Wonderlic and the Bennett—was superimposed upon the high school diploma requirement. For transfer of incumbents between departments, the company at first required a high school diploma. This requirement kept the black workers without diplomas from crossing into the white departments, but it also prevented some white workers in the least desirable white units from transferring into other white departments.

They protested, and the company then provided that the passage of the two tests, Bennett and Wonderlic, would be sufficient to transfer between departments. Workers in the white departments without high school diplomas were not required to take any tests to retain their jobs or to be promoted within their departments.

When the company had completed its response to title VII in 1965, three classes of blacks could be discerned:

1. Blacks possessing high school diplomas who were in the labor department by virtue of the racial assignment. They had not transferred to previously white units prior to the filing of the complaint with the EEOC.
2. Blacks hired into the labor department before July 2, 1965, who did not have high school diplomas. They had to pass the two tests to transfer into the white departments, whether they were hired before or after the high school diploma requirement was implemented in 1955.
3. Black applicants for new employment after July 2, 1965. To obtain employment in what was previously the black department, they had to pass a simple test. To be employed in a formerly white department, they had to have earned a high school diploma and to pass the two tests. The same standards were applied to white applicants for employment.

As a class action, the *Griggs* litigation involved those black workers who had achieved formal education but had found that it did not help them obtain better jobs, those who did not have as much formal schooling and were locked into the black department, and those black workers in the labor market who had a lower level of formal education and who scored lower on tests than white workers in the labor market. These facts and interests shaped the issues of the case which, in turn, illuminated the fundamental legal question under title VII: how is discrimination defined?

III. WHAT IS DISCRIMINATION?

During the twenty-year period preceding 1965, a time in which some legal effort to eradicate or control racial discrimination in employment had been made, there was little opportunity for the courts or legal scholars to work out carefully a legal definition of discrimination. The term had not acquired a fixed meaning in the context of employment opportunities. . . . The state civil rights agencies tended to concentrate their efforts on achieving "voluntary compliance," which meant that they did not take many cases through the administrative-hearing procedures. . . . Since the state courts would pass on the legal questions concerning discrimination under the state statutes only after the agency process was completed, the nonlitigation approach adopted by the state civil rights agencies meant that courts rarely had to deal with discrimination problems. . . .

The legislators have responded to the tragic social and economic plight of minorities through the enactment of civil rights legislation. They sought to provide a legal solution to a complex social problem and uniformly left many problems, including the definitional problems, to the agencies that must enforce these laws and to the courts. . . .

At the risk of some simplification, we can identify in the law and literature three concepts concerning the nature of discrimination in employment opportunities. In the order of their emergence, they are as follows:

Concept of Discrimination	Interest Protected and Type of Conduct Proscribed	Common Law Parallel
1. Discrimination consists of acts causing economic harm to an individual that are motivated by personal antipathy to the group of which that individual is a member. Proof of discrimination requires evidence of acts, motive (a mens rea), and harm.	Individual economic interest of complainant. Protected against deliberate denials of employment opportunities based on racial prejudice.	Cases involving malice or willful and wanton misconduct. Mens rea in criminal law.
2. Discrimination consists of causing economic harm to an individual by treating members of his minority group in a different and less favorable manner than similarly situated members of the majority group.	Recognition of the individual's interest in securing the same treatment as whites. "Unequal treatment" which may be evidence of racial animus.	Negligence causes in which reasonable man standard has not been adhered to by defendant. Also, constitutional cases involving equal protection, particularly the jury cases.

(continued)

Concept of Discrimination	Interest Protected and Type of Conduct Proscribed	Common Law Parallel
Proof involves evidence of differential treatment and harm. Defense of justification available.		
3. Discrimination consists of conduct that has an adverse effect on minority group members as compared to majority group members. Defense of justification for compelling reasons of business necessity is recognized.	Group interest in seeing that its members are not harmed in employment because of discrimination elsewhere in the society. Individual interest in economic opportunities. Protected against all types of conduct where the injury is foreseeable. Covers all industrial-relations systems because their consequences are foreseeable.	Res ipsa loquitur. Interference with advantageous relations. Strict liability.

Initially, the dominant if not exclusive definition of discrimination was based upon the evil-motive, mens rea, or state-of-mind test. Under this test, it was necessary to establish that respondent was motivated by dislike or hatred of the group to which complainant belonged. This concept produced a series of almost insuperable difficulties, as individual cases became bogged down in the vagaries of fact-finding. The potential law enforcement thrust of the statute was lost in the search for circumstantial evidence that would reveal the employer's state of mind. . . .

Civil rights advocates realized in the 1950's that the state agencies were floundering, and therefore attempted to push legislatures into enacting procedural changes that they thought would free agencies from the bog of individual case-handling. They sought for the agencies the power to initiate "pattern-centered proceedings," which could be commenced on the basis of the agency's analysis of a general situation rather than on the basis of individual complaints. . . . State agencies began to apply the "equal protection" concept of discrimination. This test might be viewed simply as a method of proving the evil motive required under the earlier concept of discrimination. . . . Discrimination required a purpose or motive to harm an individual because of his race, which purpose could be inferred from certain conduct, mainly that denying equal treatment to minorities.

The fundamental question which permeated the activity of the EEOC in its formative days under title VII and which has since consumed much of the energy of lawyers and judges in cases brought under title VII has concerned the concept of discrimination. Respondents have pressed to confine title VII within the mold of the older definitions, while the EEOC, the Departments of Justice and Labor, and plaintiffs' counsel in individual cases have sought to establish . . . an additional dimension to the concept.

This effort was, without doubt, crucial. The traditional definitions of discrimination permitted the employer to translate the unfair treatment of minorities in other segments of society into a limitation on employment opportunities. For example, a much higher proportion of minority group members than of whites are arrested. Therefore, a policy that prohibits employment of persons with arrest records will exclude a higher proportion of minorities, and thus the administration of the criminal law may restrict employment opportunities of minorities. Similarly, if, as in *Griggs,* the employer requires a high school diploma and minorities have a smaller proportion of high school graduates for reasons rooted in their subordination, the diploma requirement spreads the effects of discrimination in education into employment. . . . If an employer with an all-white work force only selects employees referred by his present employees, patterns of social segregation will determine the racial composition of his work force.

These practices were not condemned by either of the traditional definitions of discrimination. An employer could impose such requirements without an intent to exclude minorities, for each of the requirements could be justified on grounds of business convenience. . . . In making these decisions, the employer would not be violating the evil-motive concept of discrimination. In addition, the employer could impose these requirements "equally" on white and black alike, and, as a result, not violate the equal-treatment concept of discrimination either.

The older concepts of discrimination thus permitted the employer to insulate his employment practices from the social and economic problems that had arisen in society as a consequence of the pervasive pattern of discrimination and subordination of minorities. Employers simply did not have to address . . . this problem. Hence, . . . minorities remained at the bottom of seniority lists and at the top of the unemployment statistics. Meanwhile, the industrial-relations system went on its way, leaving the subordinated position of minorities unchanged. Prior to title VII and *Griggs,* employment was not a meaningful avenue of escape from subordination.

Under the pressures of day-to-day decision-making by administrative agencies, with the aid of the private and government attorneys who brought the first litigation under title VII, with some academic assistance and through the initial judicial decisions, the third concept of discrimination was born. It sought to relate the law of discrimination more closely to the social problems that had generated the enactment of the Civil Rights Act of 1964. Under this concept discrimination was measured in terms of the adverse consequences inflicted upon minorities, no matter how achieved. Discrimination became conduct rather than a state of mind—conduct that was illegal unless justifiable under the narrow corridor provided by title VII.

This third concept of discrimination drew heavily on the conceptual framework provided by the law of torts for a legally sound analysis that would make the Civil Rights Act of 1964 viable. . . . The intentional infliction of harm is generally actionable in tort law unless justified. Intention, however, is a legal construct that can connote a range of mental states, from a desire to reach a given result, to the likelihood that a given result will flow from a given action. In the federal statutory context, for example, the concept that the foreseeable results will be viewed as intended is well understood. The concept of interference with advantageous relations, such as contractual relations, is a special case of intentional tort theory. It was devised to deal with the type of interests in economic activity that are similar to those protected under title VII. . . .

A second idea is that of legal protection for group interests. Discrimination of the type prohibited by title VII is a class- or group-oriented phenomenon that challenges the status of every member of the class. Thus the group has an interest in the status of each of its members. The recognition of this group interest takes on both substantive and procedural implications. Substantively, discrimination is established by showing that acts of discrimination have been taken against the class of which plaintiff belongs. Procedurally, plaintiff initiates a class action suit. . . .

A third idea focuses on systems as subjects for legal regulation. This concept has had a full development in labor relations and labor law. The industrial-relations system involves the allocation, functions, conditions, and compensation of employees in large-scale enterprise. It has as one primary purpose the *reduction* of the areas of individual discretion among managers and supervisors. For example, specific hiring procedures may prevent the local manager from hiring his friends and assure distant top management of some quality control over employees. A seniority system, likewise, stops the foreman from playing favorites with promotions by requiring him to give the job to the most senior man who possesses the qualifications for the position. All such systems leave room for individual judgment of managers, but the hiring procedures themselves dictate the initial parameters within which this judgment may be made. . . .

Finally, the principle of liberal construction of the statute is relevant. Title VII of the Civil Rights Act of 1964 was aimed at "all aspects of discrimination,"[1] even though the Senate Committee that issued the report using these words may not have known exactly what they meant. . . . The principle of liberal construction requires an anchor, which for title VII purposes lies in section 703(a)(2). This provision makes it unlawful for an employer to "adversely affect" an individual's employment status because of race, color, religion, sex, or national origin. . . . It suggests that a court's focus of attention should be more on the consequences of actions than on the actor's state of mind.

With these four notions setting the legal background, government attorneys from the EEOC and Departments of Labor and Justice pressed for acceptance of this third definition of discrimination. Gaining acceptance of this definition also became an integral part of the litigation efforts of the NAACP and the Legal

Defense and Education Fund, Inc. Without the devoted and intelligent effort of the many attorneys representing minorities and women, the legal evolution that we are experiencing in this field could not have taken place. . . .

IV. THE EVOLUTION OF THE CONCEPT OF DISCRIMINATION IN GRIGGS

One of Duke Power's black employees who had a high school diploma was promoted after a complaint was filed with the EEOC but before suit was instituted. This may be taken as the extent of "voluntary compliance" under informal legal pressure. After the filing of suit under title VII in the United States District Court for the Middle District of North Carolina, the two other black employees with high school diplomas were promoted. This action must have been taken on advice of counsel who knew what was needed to protect the interests of the company in the litigation. After all, the only explanation for these men being in the black department after July 2, 1965, once vacancies had arisen, was their race. Refusal to transfer or promote them would have perpetuated the deliberate racial assignment. Under the evil-motive test, these acts constituted discrimination.

Duke Power's counsel had correctly anticipated the view of the district court. The district court applied the evil-motive concept of discrimination to the entire case. . . . Since the black high school graduates had been promoted, the court found no discrimination at all. The hiring and testing procedures appeared to the court as rational management techniques for securing the best-qualified employees. Plaintiff's argument that these procedures had to be job-related was dismissed because such a requirement was not, in itself, a part of the statute. . . .

Unlike the district court, the Court of Appeals for the Fourth Circuit applied the second concept of discrimination. Regardless of evil motive, the court held that the company's different treatment of similarly situated black and white employees constituted discrimination. White employees hired before 1955 who had earned no high school diploma had been able during the years to transfer and be promoted into higher paying positions. Black employees had been confined to the labor department. To treat the black employees equally, it was now necessary to permit those hired before 1955 to transfer and be promoted without regard to the high school standard or the testing requirement. Otherwise, the unequal treatment of black and white employees from the pre-1955 period would be perpetuated. . . .

This was the "equal treatment" concept, and, in applying it, the court of appeals indicated . . . that it would remedy the effects of past discrimination. Yet, the only discrimination identified by the equal-treatment test was that involving the racial assignment of blacks to the labor department before 1955. Blacks without high school diplomas who were hired into the labor department *after 1955* were not denied equal treatment because there were no "similarly situated" white employees. All white employees hired after 1955 had high school educations. Since all the black employees with high school diplomas had been promoted, the equal-treatment concept did not help the *Griggs* plaintiffs. In addition, there was no evil-motive discrimination practiced against them after 1965.

Before the Fourth Circuit, plaintiffs again tried to strengthen their case by relying on the Commission guidelines which required tests to be job-related. But the court of appeals majority was unimpressed. Since no discrimination had been found, the EEOC's requirement that tests be job-related appeared to the court as being aimed not at discrimination, but instead at a concern by the EEOC that tests in general be fair. To the majority, the EEOC's position seemed too close to one (concerning testing) that had been rejected by the Congress.[2] Thus, the court concluded that the job-related requirement was beyond the power of the EEOC.

The sole dissenter on the Fourth Circuit, Judge Sobeloff, formulated a definition of discrimination that foreshadowed the unanimous opinion by the Supreme Court in *Griggs*. Relying on the now-famous language of Judge Butzer in *Quarles v. Phillip Morris, Inc.,* that "Congress did not intend to freeze an entire generation of Negro employees into discriminatory patterns that existed before the act" (420 F.2d at 1247). Judge Sobeloff suggested that any practices having this effect are discriminatory. In light of this judgment, his review of the job-relatedness requirement of the EEOC led him to give deference to the agency charged with administering the Act. Moreover, his dissent makes clear his motivation for accepting the third concept of discrimination. In his words, the issue presented by *Griggs* was "whether the Act shall remain a potent tool for equalization of employment opportunity or shall be reduced to mellifluous but hollow rhetoric" (420 F.2d at 1237–38). He concluded:

> This case deals with no mere abstract legal question. It confronts us with one of the most vexing problems touching racial justice and tests the integrity and credibility of the legislative and judicial process. We should approach our task of enforcing Title VII with full realization of what is at stake (420 F.2d at 1248).

The Supreme Court took Judge Sobeloff's point seriously. Chief Justice Burger, recognizing that the case was one of first impression, proceeded to define discrimination as follows:

> The objective of Congress in the enactment of Title VII is plain from the language of the statute. It was to achieve equality of employment opportunities and remove barriers that have operated in the past to favor an identifiable group of white employees over other employees. Under the Act, practices, procedures, or tests neutral on their face, and even neutral in terms of intent, cannot be maintained if they operate to "freeze" the status quo of prior discriminatory employment practices.

The Court of Appeals' opinion, and the partial dissent, agreed that, on the record in the present case, "whites register far better on the Company's alternative requirements" than Negroes. . . . This consequence would appear to be directly traceable to race. Basic intelligence must have the means of articulation to manifest itself fairly in a testing process. Because they are Negroes, petitioners have long received inferior education in segregated schools. . . . Congress did not intend by Title VII, however, to guarantee a job to every person regardless of qualifications. In short, the Act does not command that any person be hired simply because he was formerly the subject of discrimination, or because he is a member of a minority group. Discriminatory preference for any group, minority or majority, is precisely and only what Congress has proscribed. What is required by Congress is the removal of artificial, arbitrary, and unnecessary barriers to employment when the barriers operate invidiously to discriminate on the basis of racial or other impermissible classification. . . .

[T]he [Civil Rights] Act proscribes not only overt discrimination but also practices that are fair in form, but discriminatory in operation. The touchstone is business necessity. If an employment practice which operates to exclude Negroes cannot be shown to be related to job performance, the practice is prohibited.

On the record before us, neither the high school completion requirement nor the general intelligence test is shown to bear a demonstrable relationship to successful performance of the jobs for which it was used. Both were adopted, as the Court of Appeals noted, without meaningful study of their relationship to job-performance ability. . . .

The evidence, however, shows that employees who have not completed high school or taken the tests have continued to perform satisfactorily and make progress in departments for which the high school and test criteria are now used. The promotion record of present employees who would not be able to meet the new criteria thus suggests the possibility that the requirements may not be needed even for the limited purpose of preserving the avowed policy of advancement within the Company. . . .

The Court of Appeals held that the Company had adopted the diploma and test requirements without any "intention to discriminate against Negro employees." . . . We do not suggest that either the District Court or the Court of Appeals erred in examining the employer's intent; but good intent or absence of discriminatory intent does not redeem employment procedures or testing mechanisms that operate as "built-in headwinds" for minority groups and are unrelated to measuring job capability.

The Company's lack of discriminatory intent is suggested by special efforts to help the under-educated employees through the Company financing of two-thirds the cost of tuition for high school training. But Congress directed the thrust of the Act to the consequences of employment practices, not simply the motivation. More than that, Congress has placed on the employer the burden of showing that any given requirement must have a manifest relationship to the employment in question.

The facts of this case demonstrate the inadequacy of broad and general testing devices as well as the infirmity of using diplomas or degrees as fixed measures of capability. History is filled with examples of men and women who rendered highly effective performance without the conventional badges of accomplishment in terms of certificates, diplomas, or degrees. Diplomas and tests are useful servants, but Congress has mandated the common sense proposition that they are not to become masters of reality. (401 U.S. at 429–33)

All of the concepts we have discussed come into play in the Supreme Court's opinion: the objective of achieving equality and the necessity that such equality be real; the need to eliminate barriers unless justified by business necessity and the consequences of failing to meet the business necessity test; the rejection of the evil-motive test and the shift of the burden of proof to the employer once it is found that the consequences of the employer's conduct adversely affect minorities.

The importance of this new concept of discrimination was underscored by the roles in the opinion of the job-relatedness concept, the EEOC guidelines, and the testing provision of title VII. All were viewed quite differently than in the lower courts. There, these factors were considered as part of *plaintiff's* case of *discrimination*. In the Supreme Court's opinion, they were viewed as part of *defendant's* case of *justification* because a prima facie case of discrimination was established without reliance on these factors.

The Supreme Court found discrimination because the diploma and test requirements screened out a higher proportion of minorities than of whites. These facts alone established the prima facie case of discrimination, and there was no need for plaintiffs to rely on the testing guidelines. Having made this finding of discrimination, the Court viewed the testing issue as a matter for the defense. Defendant argued that it was privileged under title VII's testing proviso to use tests for "general ability" that were "professionally developed" without demonstrating any relation to the work in question. . . . The Court, having concluded that discrimination was bounded by the justification of business necessity, viewed the EEOC guidelines as spelling out the details of business necessity in testing situations, and upheld the Commission's interpretation of title VII.

At this point, a review of the effect of the legal process on the situation at Duke Power Company is in order. The statute's passage, without the invocation of any formal procedures, led to a change in the entry level and transfer standards, but no black workers were hired, promoted, or transferred into the more desirable departments or positions. Once the EEOC complaint had been filed, the company upgraded one black worker who had a high school diploma. After the district court proceedings had been commenced, the remaining two black workers with high school diplomas were promoted. The district court therefore concluded that its concept of discrimination (evil-motive) had not been proven.

The court of appeals ordered priority for promotion and transfer of the six black workers who had been hired before 1955. That much was required by its equal-treatment concept of discrimination. The Supreme Court decision extended that priority to all of the remaining black employees, and struck down the high school and test requirements as applied to minority applicants. This reflects the reach of the statute under the Supreme Court's concept of discrimination. It involves a more extensive re-examination of both the conditions of incumbent blacks and the hiring standards than the other two concepts would require.

V. THE SCOPE OF THE BUSINESS NECESSITY DEFENSE

[T]he testing proviso of title VII, as Chief Justice Burger pointed out by the use of italics, has a self-limiting feature, for professionally developed ability tests can be relied upon for personnel decisions only if they are not "designed, intended or *used* to discriminate." Since discrimination is to be measured by effect and since the tests as applied to minorities do have the proscribed effect, the testing proviso appears inapplicable in its own terms.

The EEOC interpretation of the testing proviso was designed to deal with the employer defense that tests measuring "general abilities and aptitudes" that are not related to the particular job or group of jobs for which the minority applicant is being considered may be used, even after title VII's enactment. *Griggs,* however, by upholding the EEOC's conclusion that tests must bear a more intimate relation to the necessities of the work than that provided under the rubric of "general abilities and aptitudes," adequately disposed of this argument. This argument by the employer that a standard of business convenience should govern was too close to the proposition that wrongdoers should be permitted to establish their own standards of conduct, an argument long rejected by the common law of negligence. It is now clear that the standards of necessity under title VII are to be *judicially* established, after a careful scrutiny of the situation, so that conduct having an adverse effect on minorities will not be permitted simply because it would be more convenient for the employer. Often, it was business convenience that created the practices that proved harmful to minorities in the first place. . . .

The language and the legislative history of section 703(e) supports this approach. That section permits conduct otherwise prohibited "in those certain instances where religion, sex, or national origin is a bona fide occupational qualification reasonably necessary to the normal operation of that particular business or enterprise. . . ." On its face, section 703(e) does not extend the occupational qualification privilege to permit racial discrimination, and the legislative reports make clear that the omission of the word "race" from this provision was done purposefully. The bill as reported by the House Judiciary Committee did not include race as a possible bona fide occupational qualification, and Congressman Williams' attempt to amend the bill on the House floor to include race was defeated. . . .

[I]t is clear that the precise issue, whether managerial prerogatives and business convenience would be subordinated to the need to eliminate racial discrimination, was confronted . . . by both houses of Congress. It is therefore simply not a defense under title VII for an employer to argue that conduct that constitutes racial discrimination, as defined in *Griggs,* is justified as reasonably necessary to the normal operations of his business. . . .

[A]s *Griggs* holds, discrimination is conduct which has an adverse effect on minority employees as a class. Yet, at the same time, the Court stated that the law does not provide "that any person be hired simply because . . . he is a member of a minority group. . . . Congress has not commanded that the less qualified be preferred over the better qualified simply because of minority origins" (401 U.S. at 431, 436). . . .

Thus, as the law stands at present, if the minority person is refused employment by an employer who has used a discriminatory recruitment system, the employer may defend on the grounds that the minority person lacks the capacity to perform the work. If the employer wishes to argue that he preferred to have a better-qualified employee, at the least he must bear the burden of proof and show that the employee hired was better qualified by objective standards to do the job. . . .

An alternative line of analysis would conclude that the "hire the best qualified" argument is simply not available while the effects of discrimination persist and while minority applicants have the basic qualifications necessary to do the work. . . . Such an analysis appears at odds with the language quoted from *Griggs* against favoring less-qualified minority applicants. This language can be construed as applicable to situations in which there has not been a finding of discrimination or the effects of past discrimination have been eliminated. It can be argued that only when the headwinds against minorities have dissipated may the employer resort to the best-qualified principle to reject a qualified minority applicant.

. . . .

The phrase used by Chief Justice Burger—"built-in headwinds"—captured the sense of futility and frustration that has confronted minorities in their quest for equality. *Griggs* measured that frustration by gross statistics. The high school diploma test screened out three times as many blacks as whites; the Wonderlic test screened out nine times as many blacks. The Court's prohibition of these requirements will serve to alleviate the impact of discrimination on minorities. But when does the sense of injustice fade? When does the adverse effect dissipate? At what point does discrimination end, or, more precisely, at what point along a continuum is it appropriate to reduce restraints on the employer's practices?

A reduction in legal pressure may be appropriate long before the law gives up jurisdiction. The adverse effect will dissipate before minority groups and women achieve a mathematical proportion of the labor force. *Griggs* does not demand that the work force of each large employer should be a microcosm of the total population or labor force. *Griggs* only requires that the structures responsible for restricting minority opportunity be destroyed. The accomplishment of this objective must be measured by increases in minority or female participation. Therefore, numerical standards are an appropriate tool. But carried to a pseudological conclusion, such standards would structure opportunities on society along lines of race, national origin, and sex. The individualist strain in our traditions stands against that proposition. The moral strength behind the broad definition of discrimination also cuts against a mathematical allocation of job opportunities by group characteristic. Thus, the use of this third concept of discrimination should be decreased, and the range of employer discretion increased, as the crude consequences of minority subordination are eliminated. We will revert back toward evil-motive and equal-treatment concepts of discrimination when the social system operates in a fairer way.

When the adverse effect dissipates is a question of judgment for courts and administrators. . . . There is—and can be—no guarantee that the courts and the administrators will wisely decide whether the adverse effect has been dissipated. The pressure of cases will make them dependent on rules of thumb based on statistics, which may, over time, be incorporated into the law. But we have far to go before this stage is reached. The economic condition of minorities and the continuing lack of employment opportunities suggest that much must be done—and quickly—before serious disagreements over the need to continue such strong remedies will arise.

NOTES

1. S. Rep. No. 867, 88th Cong., 2d Sess. 10 (1964).
2. 420 F.2d at 1233–35.

The testing provision had been written into title VII as a result of the decision in 1964 of the Illinois Fair Employment Practices Commission in Myart v. Motorola, Inc., No. 636-27, reprinted in 110 Cong. Rec. 5662 (1964), *modified sub nom.* Motorola, Inc. v. FEPC, 58 L.R.R.M. 2573 (Ill. Cir. Ct. 1965), *revd.*, 34 Ill. 2d 266, 215 N.E.2d 286 (1966). Many interpreted this decision as banning any test which adversely affected blacks without regard to business need.

9

Redefining Discrimination: "Disparate Impact" and the Institutionalization of Affirmative Action

U.S. Department of Justice
Office of Legal Policy

Sec. 703(a) of Title VII declares it unlawful for an employer:

(1) to fail or refuse to hire or to discharge any individual, or otherwise to discriminate against any individual with respect to his compensation, terms, conditions, or privileges of employment, *because of* such individual's race, color, religion, sex, or national origin; or

(2) to limit, segregate, or classify his employees or applicants for employment in any way which would deprive or tend to deprive any individual of employment opportunities or otherwise adversely affect his status as an employee, *because of* such individual's race, color, religion, sex, or national origin.

42 U.S.C. § 2000e-2(a) (emphasis added). Similar prohibitions are extended to employment agency practices, 42 U.S.C. § 2000e-2(b), labor organization practices 42 U.S.C. § 2000e-2(c), and "employer, labor organization, or joint labor-management committee" apprenticeship and training programs. 42 U.S.C. § 2000e-2(d).

Title VII's prohibitions are framed in terms of the familiar nondiscrimination principle. Distinctions in treatment, *"because of"* of an individual's race, color, national origin, religion, or gender are prohibited. A fortiori, distinctions in treatment of employees based upon non-prohibited criteria fall outside the scope of § 703's terms.

Sec. 703 additionally contains several exempting and clarifying provisions. The latter are distinguishable from the former in that the activity covered is not unlawful under the statute's prohibitory sections and an employer need not bring himself under its terms in order to be in compliance with the law. In contrast, activity which is the subject of an exempting provision would otherwise be

Excerpts reprinted from *Report to the Attorney General*, U.S. Department of Justice, Office of Legal Policy, November 4, 1987.

illegal under the prohibitory sections and an employer must show strict compliance with the exemption's requirements.

Sec. 703(e) exempts religious, gender, and national origin-based selection criteria "in those certain instances where religion, sex, or national origin is a bona fide occupational qualification reasonably necessary to the normal operation of that particular business or enterprise." 42 U.S.C. § 2000e-2(e). Significantly, race and color were not included in this exemption and hence were deemed improper criteria of selection in *all* circumstances.

Sec. 703 contains two clarifying provisions relevant to the topic at hand. Subsection (h) provides that it is permissible "to give and act upon the results of any professionally developed ability test *provided that such test, its administration or action upon the results is not designed, intended, or used to discriminate because of race, color, religion, sex, or national origin.*" 42 U.S.C. § 2000e-2(h) (emphasis added). Subsection (j) provides that nothing in Title VII shall be interpreted to require:

> preferential treatment to any individual or to any group because of the race, color, religion, sex, or national origin of such individual or group on account *of an imbalance which may exist with respect to the total number or percentage of persons of any race, color, religion, sex, or national origin employed by any employer . . . in comparison with the total number or percentage of persons of such race, color, religion, sex, or national origin in any community, State, section, or other area, or in the available work force in any community, State, section or other area.*

42 U.S.C. § 2000e-2(j) (emphasis added).

The foregoing clarifying provisions establish that employers may use ability employee selection tests so long as they are not used to discriminate *because of* the prohibited criteria, and statistical imbalances in a workforce relative to a surrounding area are not grounds for preferential treatment for individuals or groups *because of* their race, color, religion, sex, or national origin.

The most important clarification to § 703 is found in its enforcement provision in § 706(g):

> If the court finds that the respondent has *intentionally* engaged in or is *intentionally* engaging in an unlawful employment practice charged in the complaint, the court may enjoin the respondent from engaging in such unlawful employment practice, and order such affirmative action as may be appropriate, which may include, but is not limited to, reinstatement or hiring of employees, with or without back pay . . . or any other equitable relief as the court deems appropriate.
>
> *   *   *   *   *
>
> No order of the court shall require the admission or reinstatement of an individual as a member of a union, or the hiring, reinstatement, or promotion of an individual as an employee, or the payment to him of any back pay, *if such individual was*

*refused admission, suspended, or expelled, or was refused employment or advance-
ment or was suspended or discharged for any reason other than discrimination on
account of race, color, religion, sex, or national origin or in violation of section
2000e–3(a) of this title.*

42 U.S.C. § 2000e-5(g) (emphasis added). Sec. 706(g) first states that only a
finding of *intentional* discrimination is a sufficient for awarding equitable relief,
and then restates that principle by declaring that no hiring, reinstatement, or
promotion is to be ordered, or backpay awarded, if the plaintiff was disadvantaged for any reason other than discrimination on account of § 703's prohibited
criteria.

In construing § 703(a) of Title VII, the Supreme Court has outlined two
general theories of recovery available to plaintiffs: "disparate treatment" and
"disparate impact." The former is premised upon a showing of discriminatory
intent, while the latter only requires a showing of disproportionate effects upon a
group or class. These theories are considered in turn.

The disparate treatment theory is grounded on § 703(a)(1) of Title VII. *General Electric Co. v. Gilbert,* 429 U.S. 125, 137 (1976). It requires a plaintiff to
establish a *prima facie* case of discrimination on account of one of the proscribed
criteria. A *prima facie* case is established when the plaintiff shows that (i) he
belongs to a protected class; (ii) that he applied for and was qualified for a job for
which the employer was seeking applicants; (iii) that, despite his qualifications,
he was rejected; and (iv) that, after his rejection, the position remained open and
the employer continued to seek applicants from persons of the plaintiff's qualifications. *McDonnell Douglas Corporation v. Green,* 411 U.S. 792, 802 (1973).
However, the facts of Title VII cases obviously vary and the *Green prima facie*
proof scheme is not necessarily applicable to every set of facts. *Id.* In all disparate
treatment cases, though, the plaintiff does bear the "ultimate burden of persuad-
ing the trier of fact that the defendant intentionally discriminated against the
plaintiff." *Texas Dept. of Community Affairs v. Burdine,* 450 U.S. 248, 253
(1981).

In its first occasion to interpret Title VII during its first year of existence, the
EEOC adhered to the common understanding and plain meaning of the statute
and ruled that the differential treatment of individuals based upon educational
qualifications does not violate the Act. Within a few short years, however, the
EEOC would repudiate its own initial interpretation of the statute—to say nothing of the statute itself.

In a revealing article published in the aftermath of the Supreme Court's discov-
ery of the disparate impact doctrine in *Griggs v. Duke Power Co,* Professor
Alfred Blumrosen, head of the EEOC's Office of Conciliations in the late 1960's,
described the federal civil rights bureaucracy's realization that the elimination of
discrimination would not result in a workforce in which every group was proportionately represented, and that a consequent redefinition of discrimination was

necessary, a redefinition that the federal agencies took it upon themselves to carry out.

> The fundamental question which permeated the activity of the EEOC in its formative days under title VII and which has since consumed much of the energy of lawyers and judges in cases brought under title VII has concerned the concept of discrimination. Respondents have pressed to confine title VII within the mold of the older definitions, while the EEOC, the Departments of Justice and Labor, and plaintiffs' counsel in individual cases have sought to establish, in the crucible of administration and litigation, an additional dimension to the concept.

*   *   *   *   *

> Under the pressures of day-to-day decision-making by administrative agencies, with the aid of private and government attorneys who brought the first litigation under title VII, with some academic assistance, and through the initial judicial decisions, the third concept of discrimination was born. It sought to relate the law of discrimination more closely to the social problems that had generated the enactment of the Civil Rights Act of 1964. Under this concept, discrimination was measured in terms of the adverse consequences inflicted upon minorities, no matter how achieved. Discrimination became conduct rather than a state of mind. . . . (Blumrosen 1972, pp. 70–71).

As part of its self-appointed task of redefining discrimination, in 1966 the EEOC—ostensibly pursuant to its authority under § 713 of Title VII to issue procedural regulations—published guidelines for employee selection procedures. Formulated without public comment or consultations with the only federal agency with expertise in the area (the old Civil Service Commission), the guidelines provided, *inter alia,* that the EEOC construed:

> "professionally developed ability tests" [under § 703(h)] to mean a test which fairly measures the knowledge or skills required by the particular job or class of jobs which the applicant seeks, or which fairly affords the employer a chance to measure the applicant's ability to perform a particular job or class of jobs. The fact that a test was prepared by an individual or organization claiming expertise in test preparation does not, without more, justify its use within the meaning of Title VII.[1]

The Labor Department's Office of Federal Contract Compliance (OFCC) followed suit with a similar set of regulations in 1968 in its interpretation of Executive Order 11246.

Griggs v. Duke Power Company: The Judicial Redefinition of Discrimination

In *Griggs,* the plaintiffs were members of a class of present and future black employees of the Duke Power Company in North Carolina who challenged a company policy requiring certain minimum scores on professionally developed ability tests and/or the holding of a high school diploma as a condition of employment or promotion. This policy, applied equally to blacks and whites, had the effect of disproportionately excluding the former as a group, but there was no question that individuals—both black and white—who satisfied these criteria were in fact hired or promoted. The lower courts found that these criteria were used in good faith for legitimate business purposes and without any intention of excluding or disadvantaging minorities. Indeed, the company funded a remedial program for its employees with educational deficiencies. With these findings the Court of Appeals rejected the plaintiffs' Title VII claims. *Griggs v. Duke Power Company,* 420 F.2d 1225 (4th Cir. 1970).

A unanimous Supreme Court reversed. Writing for the Court, Chief Justice Burger announced the disparate impact theory of discrimination for Title VII:

> Congress has now provided that tests or criteria for employment or promotion may not provide equality of opportunity merely in the sense of the fabled offer of milk to the stork and the fox. On the contrary, Congress has now required that the posture and condition of the job-seeker be taken into account. It has—to resort again to the fable—provided that the vessel in which the milk is proffered be one all seekers can use. The Act proscribes not only overt discrimination but also practices that are fair in form, but discriminatory in operation. The touchstone is business necessity. If an employment practice which operates to exclude Negroes cannot be shown to be related to job performance, the practice is prohibited.

401 U.S. at 431. Because the defendant company had not shown that its testing and diploma requirements bore "a demonstrable relationship to successful performance" for the jobs for which they were used, *id.,* the Court ruled that the plaintiffs' showing of a disproportionate exclusionary effect established a violation of Title VII.

The Court accepted the defendant's argument that the diploma and testing requirements represented good faith efforts to improve the overall quality of the workforce, rather than any invidiously discriminatory effort to screen out minorities. Nevertheless, the Court declared:

> [G]ood intent or absence of discriminatory intent does not redeem employment procedures or testing mechanisms that operate as "built-in headwinds" for minority groups and are unrelated to measuring job capability. . . . Congress directed the thrust of the Act to the *consequences* of employment practices, not simply the motivation. More than that, Congress has placed on the employer the burden of showing that any given requirement must have a manifest relationship to the employment in question.

401 U.S. at 432 (emphasis in the original).

The foregoing assertions of the Court are directly at odds with the text of the statute in two ways. First, of course, § 706(g) requires that there be a finding of intentional discrimination before the awarding of relief. Second, § 703(j) bars a court from granting preferential treatment to any group because of a statistical imbalance—yet this is the precise result of giving certain groups standing to challenge neutral selection procedures because they are selected proportionately less than other groups.

Given that the Court's assertions in *Griggs* cannot be squared with the Act's text, an explanation or justification was in order. But as Professor Michael Gold, the author of the definitive scholarly critique of *Griggs,* puts it (1985, pp. 480).

> Instead of citations to legislative history or precedent or even legal theory, one finds only a few undocumented assertions. . . . The Court cited not a line in a committee report, not a colloquy on the floor of either house of Congress, not the testimony of a witness before a committee, not even the report of a journalist in a newspaper.

The reason for these omissions is that no such evidence exists. Indeed, the relevant evidence conclusively reveals a Congressional intent exactly obverse from that which the Court asserted.

According to the Court in *Griggs,* "Congress directed the thrust of the Act to the *consequences* of employment practices, not simply the motivation." 401 U.S. at 844. In reaching this conclusion, the Court simply ignored Title VII's enforcement provision in § 706(g) expressly conditioning the award of relief on a finding of intentional discrimination.

In his celebratory 1972 article in the immediate aftermath of *Griggs,* Professor Blumrosen (1972, p. 62) wrote that:

> *Griggs* redefines discrimination in terms of consequence rather than motive, effect rather than purpose. This definition is new to the field of employment discrimination, in which a subjective test had previously been used.

As we have seen, this redefinition resulted in a concept of discrimination wholly alien to what Congress actually outlawed. Professor Blumrosen (1972, p. 89) predicted that:

> [t]he generating principles in *Griggs*—that discrimination is defined by adverse consequences to minorities as a group and that the right to be free from such discrimination runs to the benefit of members of the group unless the respondent can justify his actions—[would] have ramifications in several directions.

Indeed they would. Among the ramifications that Blumrosen accurately forecast was that in the ultimately vain effort of employers to satisfy the EEOC employee selection standards endorsed by the Supreme Court in *Griggs,* Title VII would "become a full-employment act" for industrial psychologists and lawyers, and that employers would be forced to hire by "numerical standards," i.e., quotas, if they were to retain any objective hiring criteria (1972, pp. 102–106). In short,

"*Griggs* established the critically important concept of discrimination on which affirmative action is based," (Belton 1981, p. 542).

An Engine of Discrimination: The Moral and Economic Toll

The Supreme Court's interpretations of Title VII under *Griggs* and its progeny threaten to expose employers to Title VII liability whenever there is a marked "underrepresentation" of women or minorities in the workforce. Thus, after *Johnson* [*Johnson v. Transportation Agency of Santa Clara*, 107 S. Ct. 1442, 1987], the failure of employers to engage in race- and gender-conscious affirmative action is, in Justice Scalia's words, "economic folly," 107 S. Ct. at 1467, whenever the costs and uncertainties of probable Title VII litigation, or the costs and uncertainities of scientifically questionable efforts at "validating" employee selection and promotion criteria, exceed the costs and predictability of hiring and promoting less capable, albeit minimally "qualified" workers. The result is the transformation of Title VII into "a powerful engine" of discrimination, "not merely permitting intentional race- and sex-based discrimination, but often making it, through operation of the legal system, practically compelled." *Id.*

The moral and social costs of this inversion of Title VII are clear. Ethnic and sexual attributes will become paramount in employer decision-making in the effort to attain statistically representative workforces, and groups will be pitted against groups as individual rights are literally redistributed to ensure proportional representation.

Less obvious than the moral evils of race-based decision-making resulting from *Griggs,* and shielded in *Weber* and *Johnson,* but equally real, will be the economic toll in reduced productivity. Most screening tests in use by employers do not under-predict performance, as learning on the job is the key to performance, and general cognitive ability tests measure learning ability (Hunter 1986).

Even requirements for credentials such as high school diplomas have a legitimate role in filling so-called manual jobs, for as Professor Sowell (1984, pp. 115–16) has written, "job-relatedness" cannot

> be assessed in any mechanical way by the nature of the task. Standards that are *person*-related play the same economic role as standards that are *job*-related. If people who finished high school seem to the employer to work out better than dropouts, third parties who were not there can neither deny its assessment nor demand that it be proved to their uninformed satisfaction. It makes no difference economically whether this was because the specific task relates to what was learned in high school or because those who finish high school differ in outlook from those who drop out. Neither does it matter economically whether those who score higher on certain tests make better workers because of knowing the specific items on those tests or because the kind of people who read enough to do well on

tests tend to differ in outlook from those who spend their time in activities that require no reading.

Various studies have established that the optimal use of employee screening devices has significant implications for productivity, and that the productivity savings from the use of such screening devices can be in the billions of dollars for an employer the size of the federal government. Consequently, the way in which talent is allocated to jobs in our society has enormous implications for national economic productivity (Hunter and Schmidt 1982).

That employee selection standards have been relaxed as a result of disparate-impact driven affirmative action, there is no doubt (Lerner 1979; Abram 1986). Thus, for example, in 1981 the Federal Office of Personnel Management suspended its PACE civil service examinations for some 100 odd entry-level positions because of their disparate impact upon particular groups. The net result is "a marginally less productive workforce" (Maltz 1980, p. 353), with the annual cost to the national economy running in the billions of dollars (Hatch 1980).

The irony, then, is that Title VII—a law plainly intended and plainly written to remove the corrosive criterion of race from employment decision-making—has been turned on its head to require just such decision-making, with all of its attendant moral evils and economic distortions. As Chief Justice Rehnquist aptly noted in his *Weber* dissent, Title VII jurisprudence has come to resemble truth-inversion along the lines of a George Orwell novel.

NOTES

1. *Guidelines on Employment Testing Procedures,* August 24, 1966, *quoted* in Blumrosen, *supra* note 85, at 61 n.7.

REFERENCES

Abram, Morris B. 1986. "Affirmative Action: Fair Shakers and Social Engineers." *Harvard Law Review* 99:1312–1326.

Belton, Robert. 1981. "Discrimination and Affirmative Action: An Analysis of Competing Theories of Equality and Weber." *North Carolina Law Review* 59:531–98.

Blumrosen, Alfred W. 1972. "Strangers in Paradise: *Griggs vs. Duke Power Co.* and the Concept of Employment Discrimination." *Michigan Law Review* 71:59–110.

Gold, Michael Evan. 1985. "Griggs' Folly: An Essay on the Theory, Problems, and Origins of the Adverse Impact Definition of Employment Discrimination, and a Recommendation for Reform." *Industrial Relations Labor Journal* 7:429–598.

Hatch, Orrin. 1980. "Loading the Economy." *Policy Review* 12:23–37.

Hunter, John E., and Frank L. Schmidt. 1982. "Ability Tests: Economic Benefits vs. the Issue of Fairness." *Industrial Relations* 21:293–308.

Lerner, Barbara. 1979. "Employment Discrimination: Adverse Impact, Validity, and Equality." *Supreme Court Review* 1979:17–50.

Sowell, Thomas. 1984. *Civil Rights Rhetoric or Reality?* New York: Morrow.

IV

Economic Consequences of Equal Employment Opportunity Laws

Those who supported EEO legislation hoped and expected that it would dramatically reduce employment discrimination and increase economic opportunities for minorities and women. Some also believed that EEO laws would aid the American economy by encouraging employers to make efficient use of available workers rather than excluding qualified individuals from jobs out of prejudice.

EEO has been the law of the land for a long time now. Have the hopes of its supporters been fulfilled? Have the EEO laws reduced employment discrimination? Are minorities and women doing much better in the labor market than they were thirty years ago because of the EEO laws? Has the American economy benefited?

One might think that after thirty years the answers to these questions would be obvious. But they are not. Some writers and politicians contend that the EEO laws have done a lot of good, others argue they have had little effect, and some even claim that they have done more harm than good. Debates about the economic impact of EEO laws may be said to focus on three issues:

- whether it is theoretically *possible* for EEO laws to benefit minorities, women, and the economy as a whole;
- whether the EEO laws *have* reduced discrimination and improved economic outcomes for minorities and women; and
- whether the EEO laws have helped or hurt business or the economy as a whole, whatever their effects on minorities and women might be.

There are two basic theoretical arguments in favor of EEO laws. Proponents of the first agree with Gary Becker (as described in Paula England's chapter) that competitive markets tend to eliminate discrimination by employers, but claim that EEO laws can speed up this process, hastening the demise of discriminatory employers by increasing the cost of discriminating. Minorities, women, and the economy as a whole all benefit from EEO laws because discrimination is eliminated more rapidly than it would be in the absence of the laws. John Donohue's article "Is Title VII Efficient?" (1986 [excerpted here]) makes this argument.

Proponents of the second theoretical argument for EEO laws make a stronger claim: EEO laws are needed not to speed up normal economic processes, but because much discrimination would never be eliminated by markets. Some types of discrimination may be economically rational, and could therefore continue indefinitely in a competitive market. For example, statistical discrimination may make sense to employers who want to make employment decisions as cheaply as possible; or employers may discriminate because some of their customers dislike dealing with minorities or women in certain jobs (see Lundberg and Startz 1983; Sunstein 1991).

Theoretical arguments against EEO laws are, for the most part, based on Becker's analysis of discrimination. EEO laws are not needed, according to this analysis, because economic competition will bring an end to discrimination. And not only are EEO laws unnecessary, they may actually do harm. To the extent they force employers to act in ways they wouldn't otherwise, they interfere with the free market, and thus must be reducing economic efficiency. Taxpayers are potentially victimized twice by such laws: once when they pay to enforce them, and a second time when the laws reduce the efficiency of the economy. Richard Posner makes these arguments in his response to Donohue, "The Efficiency and Efficacy of Title VII" (1987 [excerpted here]). Taken to an extreme, these views lead to the claim that because EEO laws reduce both freedom (by interfering with the labor market) and economic efficiency, they should be repealed; and this is just what Richard Epstein has recently argued in his book, *Forbidden Grounds: The Case Against Employment Discrimination Laws* (1992).

It should be possible to resolve the debate about the possible consequences of EEO laws by examining their actual consequences. If the laws reduce discrimination and increase efficiency, the case for them would be strengthened; if they fail to reduce discrimination and also decrease efficiency, the case against them would be enhanced.

Unfortunately, it is very difficult to ascertain the impact of the EEO laws, either for minorities and women or for business and the economy as a whole. The most intense controversy about the impact of EEO laws on protected groups focuses on black men, probably because so many supporters of Title VII saw them as its main beneficiaries. The most careful statistical analyses (discussed in Smith and Welch 1989 and Donohue and Heckman 1991 [excerpted here]) show the EEO laws to have had, at best, modest benefits for black men. Smith and Welch claim that "affirmative action" (their term for all EEO law enforcement) produced what they call a "wage bubble," a sharp increase in black men's incomes beginning in 1967 followed by a decline to more traditional levels (relative to whites') after 1972. For them, EEO had little if any long-term effect. Donohue and Heckman see themselves as disagreeing with Smith and Welch, and as claiming that the EEO laws have had a substantial long-term impact; yet even they conclude that a substantial gap remains between black and white men, and that the EEO laws seem to have had no detectable impact since 1975.

We have to be very cautious in reaching any conclusions about the impact of EEO laws because groups other than black men have been the subject of so much less research. Statistical analyses of the impact of EEO laws on women generally lead to conclusions similar to those found in analyses of black men (see Gunderson 1989 [excerpted here]; also see Leonard 1989): Some studies find the laws having no impact, others find a modest, statistically significant impact, and no one claims the laws have come close to eliminating sex discrimination in the labor market. The impact of EEO laws on Hispanics, racial minorities other than blacks, and religious and other minorities is simply unknown (cf. Munafo 1979; Beckley and Burstein 1991 [excerpted in this volume]).

It is possible to reach at least three different conclusions on the basis of the findings we do have. The first is that EEO laws have little impact because they are inherently inefficacious; markets find ways around attempts at interference, employers find ways to evade them (Posner 1986:517–18; cf. Lundberg 1991). The second is that EEO laws may be effective, but have not been because enforcement has been weak (Leonard 1989; cf. Gunderson 1989 [excerpted here]). The third is that the impact of antidiscrimination laws is extremely difficult to gauge through the use of conventional statistical analysis, and that attempts to do so are likely to substantially underestimate their impact. Thus, for example, Smith and Welch attribute part of the increase in blacks' income relative to whites' since 1940 to improvements in the quality of education available to blacks, and view this part of the increase as due to forces entirely separate from EEO legislation. Donohue and Heckman, in response, argue that both EEO legislation and improvements in the education available to blacks were part of a massive set of changes associated with the civil rights movement; viewing educational advance as something separate from EEO enforcement ignores the overwhelming historical forces that led to both. They and Blumrosen (1984:334, 336) argue that attempts to isolate the impact of the EEO laws statistically are sometimes misguided; conventional statistical analyses provide no way to gauge the impact of the pervasive changes in attitudes and institutions of which the EEO laws were a part.

Trying to assess the impact of EEO laws on business and the economy as a whole is equally complex. According to some legal scholars and social scientists, many employers have changed their employment procedures in response to the EEO laws. Alfred Blumrosen argues (1984 [excerpted here]) that forceful advocacy on the part of the EEOC and determined action by the southern U.S. appellate courts led initially recalcitrant employers to change dramatically how they treated black workers. And Lauren Edelman concludes (1992 [excerpted here]) that the EEO laws have led to seemingly permanent changes in the organization of a substantial proportion of American employers; concern about EEO has been institutionalized, so that even when federal enforcement policies are weakened (as they were during the Reagan administration), employers seem to maintain much of their commitment to EEO.

But exactly what kind of impact have the EEO laws had on employers? One possibility, of course, is that they are simply less likely to discriminate than they were previously. Two other, very different possibilities have also been suggested, however. Some observers believe that federal EEO efforts have shifted from mandating equal employment *opportunity* to mandating equal *results,* and that employers, in response, often hire minorities and women to meet numerical quotas rather than on the basis of merit. This is the claim made by Senator Orrin Hatch in his article "Loading the Economy" (1980 [excerpted here]); in line with the theoretical arguments made by Becker, Posner, and Epstein, he argues that the enforcement of affirmative action is not only unfair, but that it produces great economic costs for the economy as well, possibly playing a significant role in the stagnation in American productivity since the mid-1970s.

Another possibility is that rather than demanding too much of employers, federal EEO enforcement demands too little. Those who enforce the EEO laws, Edelman argues, may often be satisfied by changes that are more symbolic than real. Employers may have learned to satisfy the government with a show of "good faith effort" with regard to EEO while actually doing little to improve opportunities for women and minorities (Edelman 1992).

It may be even more difficult to assess the impact of EEO and affirmative on business and the economy than on economic outcomes for women and minorities. As Hatch points out, EEO and affirmative action are just a small part of an extremely complex set of laws and regulations that American business lives with. Economists have a fairly standard set of methods for estimating the impact of EEO legislation and affirmative action on groups' relative incomes, but there seems to be no agreed-upon approach to measuring the impact of EEO and affirmative action on business and the economy. As a result, estimates of their impact vary widely. At one extreme, Peter Brimelow and Leslie Spencer contend (1993:99) in *Forbes* magazine that in 1991 the total cost of EEO and affirmative action, including expenditures for enforcement, compliance, and lost productivity, was 4 percent of the gross national product, "well over $225 billion." Jonathan Leonard, in contrast, cautiously concludes (1986:362) that "direct tests of the impact of governmental antidiscrimination and affirmative regulation on productivity find no significant evidence of a productivity decline," while noting that "the available evidence is not yet strong enough to be compelling on either side of this issue." Donohue calculates (1987) that EEO enforcement imposed on employers (as of the mid-1980s) a cost of seventeen dollars per year for each black they hired. He doubts that this is large enough to have much negative impact; if it did, employers would avoid areas with high percentages of blacks, such as the South, but the South has experienced tremendous economic growth since the EEO laws were adopted. And the strongest contrast with Brimelow and Spencer's conclusion is Nestor Cruz's claim (1980:297) that the economy actually gains more than it loses from EEO, making what he calls a "50 percent return on its investment" in expenditures on EEO enforcement.

If the costs of EEO and affirmative were anywhere near as high as Hatch and Brimelow and Spencer suggest, we would expect business to support major cutbacks in affirmative action programs. That is certainly what the Reagan administration anticipated when it attacked affirmative action in the early 1980s. Much to its surprise, however, as reported by Anne Fisher in *Fortune* magazine (1985 [excerpted here]), much of business by the mid-1980s had come to support affirmative action, so long as that was taken to mean outreach and hiring goals but not quotas (also see "Rethinking Weber: The Business Response to Affirmative Action" 1989). Their behavior may lend credibility to the more modest estimates of the cost of EEO (which are, perhaps not coincidentally, the estimates of economists appearing in academic journals rather than the claims of those less knowledgeable about interpreting economic data).

On balance, it is probably fair to say this: The social changes since World War II that both produced and reflect the activities of the civil rights and women's movements have led to major changes in employer behavior and labor market outcomes for minorities and women. Blacks, other minorities, and women are doing far better economically, compared to white men, in the 1990s, than they were decades ago. Much of this change was produced by a whole collection of factors acting together in ways that are very difficult to disentangle. As a result, there is considerable uncertainty about how much of the gains should be attributed to EEO laws. Nevertheless, the laws seem to have been highly effective at ending the blatantly racist employment practices of the pre-1964 South, and at eliminating many obviously discriminatory barriers to minorities' and women's advance elsewhere in the country as well. The laws are especially effective when strongly enforced. Although there are significant disagreements among the economists who have done most of the empirical work on the impact of EEO laws, most agree that the laws had their greatest impact on blacks in the years just after enactment, and little impact in recent years; no one sees the laws as either having eliminated all discrimination, on the one hand, or as having harmed their intended beneficiaries economically, on the other.

There is much less agreement about the impact of EEO laws on business and the economy. Scholarly work has shown that employers have made some major changes in their employment practices (e.g., Blumrosen 1984; Edelman 1992), but there has been relatively little such work on the economic impact of the changes, either for the employers themselves or for the economy as a whole. As a result, debate on the issue has been pursued largely in policy journals and business magazines, with the reports providing wildly varying estimates of the costs of EEO and of employer attitudes (Hatch 1980; Brimelow and Spencer 1993; Fisher 1985; see also "Race in the Workplace" 1991; Thomas 1990).

Theoretical Issues

10

Is Title VII Efficient?

John J. Donohue III

Title VII of the Civil Rights Act of 1964 is widely regarded as one of the most important pieces of legislation enacted in this century. Whether one views the Act merely as the confirmation of larger events already well underway or as the pivotal event leading to substantial economic progress for blacks and other minorities, it stands as the most visible legislative pronouncement of this country's commitment to equal opportunity for all Americans.

Despite its undoubtedly heroic ambitions and unrivaled legislative prominence, however, the Act is not without its critics. In fact, some view it as the most conspicuous example of a legislative effort to shape private preferences. . . . The neoclassical economic model, which rests so heavily on the desirability of aggregating private preferences expressed in the marketplace, has long provided the theoretical foundation for the argument against this antidiscrimination legislation (Friedman 1962; Posner 1986, pp. 615–25; Landes 1968). Indeed, coupled with the normative principle of wealth maximization, the neoclassical economic model might appear to serve as the basis for unrelenting opposition to any form of government interference in free market outcomes. But, as is now well recognized, legal intervention can also serve to facilitate or enhance the operation of the market, thereby furthering the objective of wealth maximization.

If one looks beyond the traditional static analysis of Title VII and instead evaluates the law in a dynamic context, one finds that the logic of the attack on Title VII is incomplete. As this paper shows, legislation that prohibits employer discrimination may actually enhance rather than impair economic efficiency. . . .

I. THE NEOCLASSICAL MODEL OF THE LABOR MARKET

Consider the market for labor in a nondiscriminatory world. For a given capital stock, firms have a downward sloping demand for laborers, while the supply

Excerpts reprinted with permission from the *University of Pennsylvania Law Review* 1986, vol. 134:1411–1431. Copyright © 1986.

curve for laborers slopes upward.[1] The intersection of these two curves, as shown in Figure 1, determines the equilibrium wage (the vertical axis) and quantity of labor hired (the horizontal axis).

For those unfamiliar with demand and supply curves, it may be helpful to discuss how they are derived and what they represent. The demand curve for labor is predicated on the assumption that capital is fixed in the short run. The first worker hired by a firm will then have a certain capital stock at her disposal, which is used to generate a certain physical product. The value to the employer of the worker's product is represented by the vertical distance from the horizontal axis up to the firm's demand curve and will depend on both the amount of the particular product produced and the price at which the product sells. One can therefore think of the vertical distance to the demand curve as representing the marginal benefit associated with hiring an additional worker.

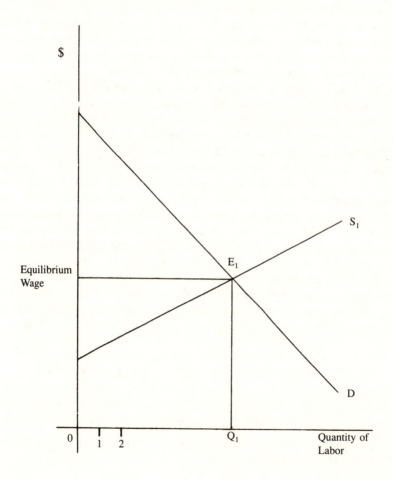

Of course, to obtain this benefit the employer must incur the expense of hiring that worker. The wage that must be paid to hire an additional worker is given by the vertical distance to the supply curve. The supply curve, therefore, represents the cost to society of employing one extra worker. Put differently, it represents the worker's monetary valuation of the cost of working.

Accordingly, so long as the demand curve lies above the supply curve, society will gain by employing an additional worker. This is because the benefit to the employer of the value of the worker's production is greater than the cost to the worker of working—obviously a mutually beneficial transaction. It is important to recognize a central tenet of the neoclassical economic model: in a world without externalities,[2] market-determined private costs and benefits will equal social costs and benefits. It is this assumption that allows one to conclude that, if the *private* benefit to the employer of receiving the worker's output exceeds the worker's *private* cost of toiling, *social* welfare is increased by hiring the worker.[3]

Once the first worker has been hired, the question becomes whether society would benefit by the hiring of a second worker. Again the supply and demand curves provide the answer. Note that in figure 1 the vertical distance to the demand curve associated with hiring the second worker is less than the vertical distance associated with hiring the first worker, a result that follows from the law of diminishing returns.[4] Moreover, if more workers must be hired, one would expect the wage offered to rise because more workers must be lured away from alternative opportunities. As the wage offered rises, more workers will be ready to accept this employment, which generates an upward-sloping supply curve. The demand curve still lies above the supply curve in figure 1 when two workers are hired; thus, social welfare would be increased by putting the second individual to work.

This process can be repeated until the intersection of the supply and demand curves at E_1 is reached—the point of maximum social welfare. If fewer than Q_1 workers are hired, the demand curve lies above the supply curve, which indicates that the benefits of additional hiring are greater than the accompanying social costs. On the other hand, if more than Q_1 workers are hired, the costs will exceed the benefits and social welfare would be reduced. Because E_1 represents the point of maximum social welfare it is, by definition, the economically efficient outcome.

II. INTRODUCING DISCRIMINATION

Thus far, it has been assumed that no discrimination exists in the labor market. Gary S. Becker's pioneering work (1971/57) however, has shown that the neo-classical model can readily be extended to analyze labor market discrimination. Following Becker, discrimination is now introduced in the form of an aversion by employers to certain groups even though all groups of workers are equally productive.

If, for example, employers have an aversion to black workers, the consequence of this discrimination is, in effect, to shift the supply curve for black labor. . . . The benefits derived from hiring additional black workers are still given by the same demand curve, but now there is a cost associated with hiring black workers in addition to the previously specified monetary cost embodied in the wage. Thus, to hire the first worker, a discriminatory employer must pay not only the monetary wage but also a psychic or nonmonetary cost associated with hiring a worker for whom she has personal distaste. The analysis then proceeds exactly as before. Employers will evaluate the benefits of increased production from hiring black workers and will offset them against the total costs, both monetary and nonmonetary, of hiring these workers.

The effect will be to reduce the number of blacks hired from the previous level to a lower level. At the same time, the wage of black workers will fall from the previous level to a lower level. The model therefore generates two plausible predictions: (1) discrimination leads to a reduction in the hiring of black labor, and (2) discrimination causes a decrease in black wages.

The effect of discrimination on the welfare of employers is an important and controversial issue. With capital fixed in the short run, employers are interested in maximizing "profits," which are determined by subtracting the total labor cost from the total value of production. . . .

The introduction of discrimination changes the wage and hiring levels for black workers. Because the number of black workers has declined, total production now falls and the total wage cost falls. But, in addition to the monetary cost imposed by the wage bill, discriminatory employers will also have to bear a nonmonetary cost associated with the hiring of black laborers—a type of "discrimination" tax. . . . As a result, the net profits earned by discriminatory employers fall. . . . Therefore, not only does the black labor force suffer but discriminatory employers are also harmed by the discrimination.

Interestingly, in this partial equilibrium analysis of the black labor market, . . . the *monetary* profits of the discriminatory employers have risen. The reason for this increase in monetary profits is that the reduction in the hiring of black labor has driven the black wage down to such a degree that monetary profits to the discriminators . . . are greater than the profits of the nondiscriminatory firms. . . . Consequently, the uniform pattern of discrimination has caused employers to make more money but to be less profitable in an economic sense.

The implication that employers may earn more money but be less profitable is not as perplexing as it might first appear. This phenomenon occurs in many contexts throughout the economy, because, quite simply, money is not the only thing that people value. For example, consider a professor who applies for a position at Elite University that pays a salary of $30,000 and for a similar position at Podunk University, which offers $40,000. If the professor would prefer to work at Elite in spite of its lower salary, this can be restated in economic terms to say that the difference in prestige is worth more than $10,000 to the professor. If she receives an offer only from Podunk, she will earn more money, but will be less satisfied and less well off in economic terms. Just as the prestige-conscious professor has an incentive not to go to Podunk, the discriminatory employers in the Becker model have an incentive not to hire blacks and thereby bear the associated psychic costs. Therefore, Becker's point is that, even though employers may earn more money because of their discriminatory practices, it is not economic self-interest that prompts employer discrimination.

Consider what would happen if discriminatory employers did not really dislike blacks but merely acted as if they did in the hopes of raising their monetary incomes. At first glance, it would appear that such employers could . . . earn higher monetary profits without suffering any discriminatory cost. But while nondiscriminatory employers would have an economic incentive to restrict the hiring of black workers, . . . they would have no power to do so in a competitive market[5]. . . . [I]n this model, it is the government—which may resort to pernicious legislation such as the apartheid laws in South Africa—not the free market, that stands as the potential enemy of the victims of discriminatory conduct.

III. THE IMPACT OF TITLE VII

Although no one disputes that an unwise or pernicious government can produce socially harmful consequences through interference in labor markets, a more interesting question is whether the government can play a positive role as well. Landes (1968, p. 548) alludes to the traditional view that if one's objective is wealth maximization then the passage of antidiscrimination legislation can only be harmful: "[I]f the benefits [of such legislation] are viewed as the added net (monetary plus psyche) income to the community, then the benefits would be negative, because net income is maximized in the absence of fair employment laws". . . .

Opponents of antidiscrimination legislation urge that government action is not necessary because, in the long run, the operation of the competitive market will return the equilibrium level to E_1. The basic argument is that discriminatory firms are not maximizing profits and therefore eventually will be driven out of the market (see Arrow 1973; Marshall 1974). The short-run analysis had assumed that the level of capital was fixed. In the long run, however, capital will flow to more profitable enterprises, and any employer that has shunned discrimination will earn higher profits. Such a firm would be willing to hire more black workers at the depressed market wage . . . and would be able to expand production and profits beyond the levels of its competitors. As long as there is a single nondiscriminatory employer, all discriminators will be driven out of the market.[6] Therefore, in the long run the nondiscriminatory equilibrium will be restored.

The traditional view thus can be summarized as follows: in the short run, antidiscrimination legislation is harmful because it will reduce total social welfare; in the long run, it is unnecessary because the market will restore the nondiscriminatory equilibrium by disciplining discriminators. Within the framework of the neoclassical economic model, this argument has a certain elegance and logical appeal. Nonetheless, it is incorrect. A more discerning dynamic analysis reveals that there is no a priori basis for assuming that Title VII reduces total social welfare.

IV. A DYNAMIC ANALYSIS OF TITLE VII

The previous discussion has provided only a static analysis of Title VII. . . . It will now be useful to consider explicitly how net social welfare will change over time both with and without antidiscrimination legislation.

First consider the case in which Title VII does not exist. Figure 2 depicts the changing level of net social welfare, beginning at time 0, with SW_2 representing the initial short-run net social welfare associated with the discriminatory equilibrium E_2. As time passes, more and more discriminatory employers will be driven from the market by nondiscriminatory employers, thereby increasing social welfare.[7] Ultimately, when all the discriminatory firms have been driven out, net social welfare will rise to the level of SW_1 associated with equilibrium E_1—where it presumably will remain. The time path of social welfare in the laissez-faire state begins at SW_2 and rises to SW_1 at time 2t. . . .

The dynamic pattern of net social welfare would look different if Title VII were adopted at time 0. Initially . . . net social welfare would be reduced by virtue of the imposition of Title VII. Thus, at time 0, total net social welfare associated with Title VII (labeled SW_3) would be less than the unrestrained market outcome (i.e., $SW_3 < SW_2$).

To dissect the impact of Title VII, however, its effects on the profits of employers as well as on the earnings of black labor must be examined. . . . Imposition of Title VII requires employers to hire units of black labor at the nondiscriminatory wage. The total cost associated with hiring a black worker under the legal constraint of Title VII is . . . the wage cost and . . . the psychic cost of discrimination. Therefore, . . . the net profit to the discriminator under the Title VII regime is . . . less than the profit which is generated in the absence of a legal requirement of nondiscriminatory behavior.[8]

The fact that Title VII causes a reduction in the profits of discriminators has an important implication for the time path of net social welfare: one can assume that discriminators will be driven from the market more rapidly with Title VII than without it. . . . This follows because the full weight of the discriminatory burden, which had previously been shared by both discriminators and victims alike, now is shifted totally onto the discriminators.

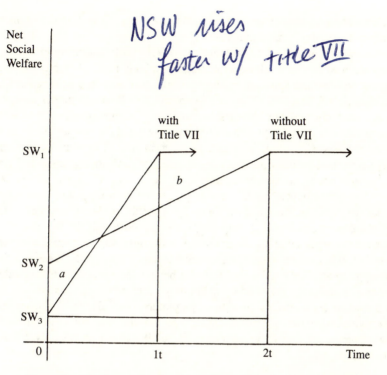

Figure 2. The time path of social welfare with and without Title VII

Burdening discriminatory employers not only promotes arguably normative goals but also has the competitive benefit of more quickly driving discriminators out of the market. In summary, the smaller the sacrifice in initial social welfare . . . and the greater the burden on the discriminator . . . (and therefore the greater the speed with which the discriminators are driven out and social welfare rises to SW_1), then the greater the likelihood that Title VII will be welfare maximizing. . . .

CONCLUSION

This essay demonstrates that the theoretical attack on the efficiency of Title VII is seriously incomplete. Without altering any of the assumptions of the neoclassical model, I have attempted to show that it is impossible to claim, as an a priori matter, that Title VII of the 1964 Civil Rights Act reduces social welfare. It is entirely plausible, although ultimately an empirical question, that Title VII can be understood to represent wealth-maximizing legislation rather than as some tyrannical or misguided attempt to disregard private preferences. Indeed, antidiscrimination legislation may be thought of as a tool to perfect the market response to employer discrimination.

The basic argument is that, although Title VII clearly lowers short-run social welfare it also can be wealth-maximizing in the long run. . . . Some may argue that the neoclassical approach is so impoverished that they would rather forgo this defense of Title VII. They may contend that Becker's model cannot be applied usefully to labor markets or employer discrimination, or that wealth maximization is not an appropriate normative goal, and thereby simply reject this entire analysis. Others, while retaining the principle of wealth maximization, might argue that the discriminatory costs . . . simply are not legitimate and therefore should not be considered as true social costs. . . . Although this argument has strong moral appeal to the opponents of racial discrimination, it necessarily invites the criticism that the decision to disregard the preferences of discriminatory employers constitutes an unprincipled lapse into subjectivism.

I have not argued that the Becker model is the only way, or even the best way, to analyze employment discrimination. But as long as this model is being used as a weapon to attack the Civil Rights Act, I believe it is important to show that a correct application of this model can buttress—rather than undermine—the case for Title VII. Moreover, to the extent one prefers to see the costs of discrimination borne by the discriminators, rather than the victims (who are undoubtedly less affluent), the normative appeal of the civil rights legislation is enhanced commensurately.

ACKNOWLEDGMENTS

I wish to thank George Priest, Ian Ayres, and Peter Siegelman for helpful comments and suggestions on an earlier draft of this paper. I would also like to acknowledge the contribution of Jim Liebeler, whose thoughtful comments inspired the intense reflection that led to this paper.

NOTES

1.   The demand and supply curves are drawn throughout this paper as straight lines for computational ease.

2.   Externalities are said to

arise when the voluntary economic activities of economic agents—in production, consumption, or exchange—affect the interests of other economic agents in a way *not* setting up legally recognized rights of compensation or redress. . . .

. . . .

Externalities, therefore, represent sources of social gain or loss that do not get translated into the [private] market signals that constitute the Invisible Hand. (Hirshleifer 1976, p. 449)

3. For present purposes all of the assumptions of the neoclassical economic model are accepted.

4. The law of diminishing returns applies in this case because, by assumption, there is a fixed supply of capital and an increase in the quantity of labor working with this capital. Because the amount of capital per worker has declined, one would expect the marginal product to decline as well.

5. In a competitive market, employers would be tempted to offer a wage slightly above the prevailing wage in order to attract more workers, because the demand curve (marginal benefit) is considerably higher than the supply curve (marginal cost). The upward pressure on wages would only stop when the equilibrium point was reached.

6. See Arrow 1973; Marshall 1974. A number of points should be made concerning the prediction that discriminators will be driven from the market. First, a single non-discriminating firm will be able to drive out all of the discriminatory firms, given constant returns to scale technology. Constant returns to scale technology implies that the firm can expand as much as it wants without suffering from increasing average costs. If average costs rise with increased production, however, more nondiscriminatory firms might be needed to drive out discriminators.

Second, Arrow, while acknowledging that Becker's model predicts the elimination of discrimination, concludes that because discrimination has persisted for decades, Becker's model "must have some limitation." Arrow, *supra* note 30, at 10. Becker might respond that the persistence of discrimination is probably caused by the obstructions to the free market—government, unions, monopolies—and that where the free market exists the model is correct. . . .

7. Social welfare increases when a discriminatory employer of black labor is replaced by a nondiscriminatory employer because the psychic cost of discrimination is eliminated.

8. This is plausible because Title VII imposes a constraint on the behavior of employers. Because they can achieve any outcome without the constraint that is available with the constraint, one would expect employers to do at least as well or better without the Title VII constraint.

REFERENCES

Arrow, Kenneth. 1973. "The Theory of Discrimination." Pp. 3–33 in *Discrimination in Labor Markets,* edited by Orley Ashenfelter and Albert Rees. Princeton: Princeton University Press.

Becker, Gary. 1971 [originally 1957]. *The Economics of Discrimination.* 2nd edition. Chicago: University of Chicago Press.

Friedman, Milton. 1962. *Capitalism and Freedom.* Chicago: University of Chicago Press.

Landes, William. 1968. "The Economics of Fair Employment Laws." *Journal of Political Economy* 76:507–52.

Marshall, Ray. 1974. "The Economics of Racial Discrimination: A Survey." *Journal of Economic Literature* 12:849–71.

Posner, Richard A. 1986. *Economic Analysis of Law.* third edition. Boston: Little, Brown.

"Race in the Workplace: Is Affirmative Action Working." 1991. *Business Week* (July 8):50–63.

11

The Efficiency and the Efficacy of Title VII

Richard A. Posner

John Donohue argues that Title VII of the Civil Rights Act of 1964, which forbids employment discrimination on racial and other invidious grounds, may well be an efficient intervention in labor markets, even if efficiency is narrowly defined as maximizing social wealth. His argument is of considerable interest. Social welfare legislation, notably including legislation designed to help minority groups, is usually thought to involve a trade-off between equity and efficiency, or between the just distribution of society's wealth and the aggregate amount of that wealth. If Donohue is right and equity and efficiency line up on the same side of the issue, these laws are considerably less problematic than they have seemed to some observers.

Donohue's argument builds on Gary Becker's (1971/57) theory of racial discrimination. For Becker, discrimination by whites against blacks is the result of an aversion that whites have to associating with blacks. This aversion makes it more costly for whites to transact with blacks than with other whites. Becker likens this additional transaction cost to transportation costs in international trade. The higher those transportation costs are, the less international trade there will be. Countries such as Switzerland that are highly dependent on such trade because their internal markets are small will suffer more than countries that, by virtue of the large size of their internal markets, are more nearly self-sufficient. Similarly, blacks will be hurt more than whites by the whites' aversion to associations with them because the white community is more nearly self-sufficient than the black.

Just as there are potential gains from measures that lower transportation costs, so there are potential gains from measures that lower the costs of association between whites and blacks. One of these measures is competition. White employers who are not averse to such associations will have lower labor costs and will therefore tend to gain a competitive advantage over their bigoted competitors.

Excerpts reprinted with permission from the *University of Pennsylvania Law Review* 1987, vol. 136:512–521. Copyright © 1986.

Hence competition should, over time, erode the effects of discrimination, not by changing preferences, to be sure, but by shifting productive resources to firms that are not handicapped by an aversion to associating with blacks.

Donohue's argument is simply that this process can be accelerated by a law against employment discrimination, such as Title VII. By adding a legal penalty to the market penalty for discrimination, Title VII accelerates the movement toward the day when discrimination has been squeezed out of markets and the gains from trade have thereby been maximized. . . .

The obvious objection to Donohue's argument is that he has failed to balance the costs of administering Title VII against the gains from lowering the costs of transacting between blacks and whites. In the year ending June 30, 1986, more than 9,000 suits charging employment discrimination, the vast majority under Title VII, were brought in federal court. The aggregate costs of these cases, and of the many more matters that are settled without litigation, must be considerable. However, I want to emphasize two more subtle points. The first is that, to the extent it is effective, Title VII may generate substantial costs over and above the costs of administering the statute. The second point is that Title VII may not be effective, in which event its administrative costs are a dead weight loss.

I. THE EFFICIENCY OF TITLE VII

An analogy in the international-trade sphere to Donohue's argument would be to advocate passage of a law requiring a nation's industries to increase their exports and imports. Such a law would increase the amount of the nation's international trade, but not by lowering the cost of transportation. It might bring the nation to a level of international trade that it would not otherwise have reached for another fifty years through falling costs of transportation, but there would be no gain in efficiency because those costs had not yet fallen.

In Becker's analysis, the costs to whites of associating with blacks are real costs, and a law requiring such association does not, at least in any obvious way, reduce these costs. Of course, it makes blacks better off, but presumably by less than it makes whites worse off; for if both whites and blacks were made better off, there would be net gains from association and the law would not be necessary. . . . It might be the case that the costs to whites of being forced to associate with blacks are morally unworthy of consideration in the formulation of public policy. . . . But that would not be an *efficiency* justification in the wealth-maximization sense that Donohue employs.

Moreover, it is not altogether plain that a reluctance by white employers to employ blacks *at the same wage as whites* . . . must reflect nothing more than an inexplicable aversion, whether by the employer itself or by its white employees, to associating with blacks. Suppose that, because of past exclusion of blacks from equal educational opportunities or for other reasons, the average black worker is less productive than the average white, and suppose further that it is costly for an employer to determine whether an individual worker deviates from the average for the worker's group. Then an unprejudiced employer might nonetheless decide to pay blacks less than whites. This would be unfair to blacks who were in fact above average, yet might still be an efficient method (in the presence of high information costs) of compensating black workers (Phelps 1972). If Title VII comes along and forbids this method of classifying workers, as it assuredly does, then the employer will either incur additional information costs or, by lumping all workers together regardless of productivity, depart even further from the optimum wage, which is the wage equal to a worker's marginal product. Either way, efficiency will be reduced. . . .

THE EFFICACY OF TITLE VII

I have assumed thus far, as does Donohue, that Title VII is effective—that it improves the employment prospects of black people. If it does not, then its administrative costs yield no gains, either in efficiency or in equity. One's intuition is that a law, which imposes sanctions on employers who discriminate and which is enforceable not only by a federal agency (the Equal Employment Opportunity Commission) but by the victims of discrimination in private suits, *must* improve the employment opportunities of members of a group that, at the time the law was passed, was a frequent target of employment discrimination. But this may be incorrect. . . . Suppose that . . . the market wage rate of blacks is lower than that of whites. Title VII forbids the use of race as a ground for pay differentials. Because this part of the law is difficult to evade,· and because . . . employers find it difficult to measure the marginal product of the individual worker, we can assume that blacks and whites will be paid the same wage by the same employer for the same job. This means, however, that the employer will be paying some or many of its black workers more than their marginal product. The employer will therefore have an economic incentive to employ fewer blacks. The law also forbids making hiring or firing decisions on the basis of race, but this part of the law is very difficult to enforce. To see this, however, it is necessary to get more deeply into the structure of the law than Donohue attempts to do in his article.

There are two basic approaches that plaintiffs can use to make out a case under Title VII. The first, the "disparate treatment" approach, requires proving intentional discrimination. This turns out to be exceptionally difficult in practice. No employer of even moderate sophistication will admit or leave a paper record showing that it has refused to hire, or has fired, a worker because of the worker's race. In the absence of such evidence, the worker may try to eliminate alternative explanations, but this usually is impossible. There are, it is true, some workers who are so superior that no cause other than racial animus could explain a refusal to hire them or a decision to fire them. But even a bigoted employer is unlikely to take out his racial animus against a perfect worker. Most workers are not perfect. As to them, it is usually easy to supply a plausible reason why they were not hired or why they were let go. The plaintiff may try to rebut the reason by showing an overall pattern of racial hiring or firing, but this type of proof is expensive and will rarely be cost-justified when all the plaintiff is seeking is reinstatement or back pay, the most common remedies (along with attorney's fees) under Title VII. . . .

Occasionally, a group of workers will band together in a class action, or the EEOC will bring suit against a company or even an industry on behalf of a large group of workers who have been discriminated against. But there are few such cases relative to the vast labor market in the United States, and the threat of such a suit may not have much deterrent effect because the available sanctions are so mild.

The second basic approach under Title VII is the "disparate impact" approach. If a firm uses a screening device such as an aptitude test or requiring a high-school degree that has the effect of excluding a disproportionate number of blacks, the device is unlawful unless the firm can show a strong business justification for it, even if the device is not intended to keep out blacks. The crux of the problem is identifying disproportionate exclusion. The usual solution is to compare the percentage of blacks employed by the firm with the percentage in the labor pool from which the firm draws. This method of proof makes it more costly for a firm to operate in an area where the labor pool contains a high percentage of blacks, by enlarging the firm's legal exposure. Therefore, when deciding where to locate a new plant or where to expand an existing one, a firm will be attracted (other things being equal) to areas that have only small percentages of blacks in their labor pools.

This incentive exists even if the firm is not worried about disparate-impact suits. Title VII makes it more costly to employ black workers; it also makes it more costly to fire them because the firm may have to incur the expense of defending a Title VII disparate-treatment suit when a black employee is discharged. These costs operate as a tax on employing black workers and give firms an incentive to locate in areas with few blacks.

Thus Title VII can be expected to have several effects: to increase the wages of those blacks who are employed by wiping out racial pay differentials; to eliminate some discrimination in hiring and firing; but, in the case of some employers, to reduce the number of blacks who are employed (see Landes 1968). When the wages of black workers are averaged over all blacks, both those who are employed and those who are not, the average black wage may not have increased (or increased much) as a result of Title VII, and may even have decreased. . . .

Landes (1968) in his study of state fair employment laws, found that the employment and wage effects partially offset each other. Unfortunately, it is difficult to make a parallel study of Title VII. Since Title VII is applicable nationwide, cross-sectional studies are not possible. Time studies are confounded by the number of other developments affecting the wages and employment of blacks since Title VII was enacted in 1964, including changes in welfare benefits (which may affect the incentive to seek employment), changes in the taste for discrimination (besides any such change attributable to Title VII itself), expanded educational opportunities for blacks, the disintegration of the lower-class black family, the shift in jobs from the industrial to the service (including governmental) sector, the increased political clout of blacks, the decline of unions, and a variety of other changes. Disentangling the effects of Title VII from all the other things that have been going on since 1964 and that bear on the wages and employment of blacks seems well-nigh impossible. Even disentangling the effects of all governmental programs to combat racial discrimination from the effects of other developments is extraordinarily difficult and thus far inconclusive. . . . Although some studies find that Title VII has increased both the wages and employment of blacks, and others that the wage and employment effects have cancelled each other out,[1] the most responsible conclusion for the nonspecialist appears to be that the effects of Title VII are unknown.

Of course, Title VII could have indirect effects as well as the direct effects that I have been emphasizing. By putting the government's moral authority behind efforts to eradicate racial discrimination, Title VII may have reduced the aversion of whites to associating with blacks and may have helped blacks overcome the psychological legacy of slavery. . . . Moreover, both the decrease in overt expressions of hostility toward blacks, and the existence of anti-discrimination laws themselves, may reflect the growing political influence and assertiveness of black people and the growing racial tolerance of white people, rather than show that the laws have caused greater tolerance.

To conclude, I am not persuaded by Donohue's argument that Title VII can be defended on strictly economic grounds. . . . Title VII, to the extent effective, ignores, rather than reduces, the costs of undesired associations between whites and blacks. It may be correct on moral grounds to do so, but that is not Donohue's argument. Furthermore, it is an open question whether Title VII has improved the net welfare of black people, directly or indirectly. If it has not, then the costs of administering the law are a dead weight social loss that cannot be justified on grounds of social equity.

ACKNOWLEDGMENTS

I thank John Donohue for his generous comments on a previous draft of this paper, and Lisa Heinzerling and Richard Porter for their comments.

NOTES

1. *Compare* Leonard (1984) *with* Beller (1978).

REFERENCES

Becker, Gary. 1971 [originally 1957]. *The Economics of Discrimination.* 2nd edition. Chicago: University of Chicago Press.

Beller, Andrea H. 1978. "The Economics of Enforcement of an Antidiscrimination Law: Title VII of the Civil Rights Act of 1964." *Journal of Law and Economics* 21(2):359–80.

Landes, William. 1968. "The Economics of Fair Employment Laws." *Journal of Political Economy* 76:507–52.

Leonard, Jonathan. 1984. "Antidiscrimination or Reverse Discrimination: the Impact of Changing Demographics, Title VII, and Affirmative Action on Productivity." *Journal of Human Resources* 19:145–74.

Phelps, Edmund S. 1972. "The Statistical Theory of Racism and Sexism." *American Economic Review* 62:659–71.

Consequences for Workers

12

Black Economic Progress after Myrdal

James P. Smith and Finis R. Welch

I. INTRODUCTION

Forty-five years ago, Gunnar Myrdal published his masterwork on race relations in America, *An American Dilemma*. He began his chapter on the economic situation of blacks with the following summary:

> The economic situation of the Negroes in America is pathological. Except for a small minority enjoying upper or middle class status, the masses of American Negroes, in the rural South and in the segregated slum quarters in Southern cities, are destitute. They own little property; even their household goods are mostly inadequate and dilapidated. Their incomes are not only low but irregular. They thus live from day to day and have scant security for the future. . . . (p. 205)

In the 45 years since Mydral's bleak assessment, this country has undergone a series of dramatic and far-reaching changes—economically, demographically, and politically. These changes have had important implications for the economic status of blacks, especially relative to the status of whites. This essay presents a reassessment of the relative long-term economic progress of black men, focusing on trends over those 45 years and the reasons for them.

The Issues and the Research

During the time period we cover, the American economy grew rapidly. It also shifted from its traditional agricultural and manufacturing base to one that is service and technology oriented. Part of this shift was the elimination of black sharecropping in cotton, which had been the primary economic activity of Southern blacks since the Civil War. This change motivated large numbers of Southern

Excerpts reprinted with permission from the *Journal of Economic Literature* 1989 (June), vol. 27:519–524. Copyright © 1989 by the American Economic Association.

rural blacks to migrate into the inner cities of the North, eventually transforming the black population from predominately rural to largely urban.

During the 1970s, the American economic structure suffered additional shocks. Increased international competition hit the older industrialized sectors of the Northeast and North Central states particularly hard. And these were the areas where blacks had made hard-won advances.

Racial tensions have persisted throughout this forty year period. The civil rights movement achieved stunning judicial and legislative successes in the 1950s and 1960s, partly by appealing to the moral conscience of the nation. The Civil Rights Act of 1964 and subsequent executive orders prohibited employment discrimination on the basis of race. . . .

We take up several issues in this essay. Our most basic concern is whether the economic lot of black men has improved significantly since Myrdal's day.[1] We go beyond that issue by also examining whether economic progress has touched all parts of the black community. Finally, we deal with the thorny problem of isolating the underlying causes of black economic progress. We sought to determine, for example, the extent to which education and its quality, migration to cities and the North, and affirmative action have affected the economic progress of blacks. . . . We use the literature . . . to frame the big questions, and then let the data from the five decennial Censuses speak to these questions. ([T]his project made extensive use of the Public Use Tapes of the decennial Censuses from 1940 to 1980. All data in this article are from these sources unless otherwise indicated.)

Section II describes major trends in black-white male wage ratios from 1940 to 1980 and identifies the distribution of wage gains among important subgroups in the black population. Sections III, IV, and V attempt to isolate some causes of these trends: Section III describes differential racial trends in schooling and the income benefits associated with that schooling. Section IV deals with the influence of two dimensions of geographic location: black migration from the South to the North and the increasing urbanization of the black population.

Section V discusses two historical developments that were not included in our statistical model but that many people believe have played a significant role in recent black economic history: the declining work force participation rates of low-income blacks during the 1970s and affirmative action. The final section discusses changes that have occurred in the 1980s and speculates about future trends in the racial wage gap.

II.   CLOSING THE RACIAL WAGE GAP

Since 1940, black men made a significant and quantitatively large improvement in their economic status relative to the status of white men. . . .

Table 1. Mean Male Income by Race, 1940–80
(In Constant 1987 Dollars)

Census Year	White Men	Black Men
1980	28,212	20,480
1970	28,075	18,078
1960	21,832	12,561
1950	15,677	8,655
1940	11,441	4,956

Note: Yearly incomes are weekly wages multiplied by an assumed workyear of 50 weeks.

Black-White Male Wages 1940–80

Since 1940, the American economy has enjoyed substantial economic growth, and inflation-adjusted incomes of all its citizens have risen dramatically.[2] Table 1 lists yearly incomes of men of both races. To adjust for the sevenfold inflation that has occurred since 1940,[3] all incomes are expressed in constant 1987 dollars.

Real incomes of white men expanded two-and-one-half-fold between 1940 and 1980—but earnings growth was even more rapid among black men. Real incomes of black men more than quadrupled over these 40 years. In 1940, the typical black male employed for a full workyear earned almost $5,000; by 1980 he earned over $20,000.

The standard of living of today's black men has improved not only as measured against earlier black generations, but also relative to their white contemporaries. While incomes of white men were growing at a 2.2 percent rate throughout these 40 years, black men were enjoying an income growth of 3.5 percent per year. Table 2 depicts our estimates of black-white male weekly wage ratios from

Table 2. Black Male Wages as a Percentage of White Male Wages, 1940–80

Years of Market Experience	Census Years				
	1940	1950	1960	1970	1980
1–5	46.7	61.8	60.2	75.1	84.2
6–10	47.5	61.0	59.1	70.1	76.6
11–15	44.4	58.3	59.4	66.2	73.5
16–20	44.4	56.6	58.4	62.8	71.2
21–25	42.3	54.1	57.6	62.7	67.8
26–30	41.7	53.2	56.2	60.6	66.9
31–35	40.2	50.3	53.8	60.0	66.5
36–40	39.8	46.9	55.9	60.3	68.5
All	43.3	55.2	57.5	64.4	72.6

each of the decennial Census tapes[4]. . . . [R]atios are listed for five-year intervals of years of work experience.[5]

Table 2 points to a very impressive rise in the relative economic status of black men over this 40-year time span. . . . In 1940, the typical black male worker earned only 43 percent as much as his white counterpart. By 1980, the average black man in the labor force earned 73 percent as much as the typical white man.

The pace at which blacks were able to narrow the wage gap was far from uniform. The largest improvement occurred during the 1940s, a decade that witnessed a 24 percent expansion in the relative wages of black men.[6] These advances slowed considerably during the 1950s, but the pace picked up again in the years after 1960. During both the 1960s and 1970s, the rise in black wages was more than 10 percent higher than for whites.

Obviously, there has been impressive improvement in the relative economic status of blacks since 1940. . . . However, one must remember that even today black male incomes still lag well behind those of whites. We are left then with a dual message: Considerable progress has been made in narrowing the wage gap between the races—but race is still an important predictor of a man's income.

The Distribution of Black Wage Gains

While average white incomes are well in excess of those achieved by the average black, income distributions of the black and white populations have always overlapped. . . . The overlap between the two income distributions was small in 1940. If income is the measuring rod, black and white men were indeed divided into two separate and unequal societies in 1940. In that year, only one in twelve black men earned more than the average white, and the upper segment of the income distribution resembled an exclusive white club. . . . The view from the other side was equally stark: 70 percent of white men earned more than the top 25 percent of blacks.

While by no means identical, these two income distributions have converged sharply across these 40 years. By 1980, 29 percent of working black men earned more than the median white. Nowhere were these changes more dramatic than in the circles of the economic elite. Even within the upper parts of the income distribution, black men are now more commonplace. Fully 10 percent of black men now rank higher than the white worker whose income puts him among the wealthiest 25 percent. This black penetration into the economic elite has been accomplished largely during the last 20 years. Between 1960 and 1980, the probability that a black man's income would fall in the top 25 percent white income bracket increased tenfold. . . .

As is evident from the last column of Table 3, over the full 40-year period, younger blacks gained more relative to whites than did experienced black workers. However, with the exception of those in the first five years of work,

Table 3. Percentage Growth in Black-White Male Ratios of Weekly Wages

Years of Work Experience	Growth Between				
	1950–40	*1960–50*	*1970–60*	*1980–70*	*1980–40*
1–5	28.1	−2.7	22.1	11.5	58.9
6–10	25.1	−3.2	17.1	8.8	47.8
11–15	27.1	1.9	10.9	10.4	50.3
16–20	24.4	3.1	7.3	12.5	47.3
21–25	24.6	6.3	8.6	7.7	47.2
26–30	24.2	5.6	7.5	9.9	47.2
31–35	22.5	6.6	10.8	10.4	50.3
36–40	16.4	17.5	7.5	12.7	54.2
All experience classes	24.2	4.1	11.3	12.0	51.6

post-1940 relative black wage gains were fairly uniform across experience cells; but between 1960 and 1980, relative black wage gains were largest among younger workers. As a consequence, the cross-sectional decline with experience in black relative wages in Table 2 became steeper in 1980 than it was in 1960. This tilt in favor of younger blacks is an optimistic harbinger of the future. It implies that the pace at which blacks were able to narrow the racial wage gap accelerated over time. . . . Black male wages rose relative to whites between 1940 and 1980 at every schooling level. . . .

Among those with eight or more years of schooling, there exists a distinct pro-skill bias in the rate of black wage improvement. For example, wages of black college graduates grew 45 percent faster than those of whites between 1940 and 1980; in contrast, black wages grew a third more rapidly than whites among men with terminal high school diplomas. This pro-skill bias was especially pronounced between 1950–70. During these 20 years, the relative wage gains of black college graduates were four times larger than those achieved by black high school graduates.

Tracking Black-White Careers

One pattern that characterizes all five Census years in Table 2 is that black-white wage ratios decline with years of work experience. For example, in 1950, among men who had spent 36 to 40 years in the labor market, black wages were 47 percent of white. In the same year, among men in their first five years of work experience, black wages were 62 percent of white. For a long time, the cross-sectional decline in wage ratios with experience was the principal statistical evidence that led to widespread scientific and popular acceptance of a particular theory of labor market discrimination. According to this theory, an important mechanism of discrimination was that blacks were systematically denied access to jobs with more favorable future prospects or larger wage growth. Because of discrimination, blacks tend to be relegated to secondary labor markets and to jobs with little potential for career advancement (see, for example, Paul Osterman 1975; Michael Piore 1971; Michael Reich 1984; and Russell Rumberger and Martin Carnoy 1980).

Such cross-sectional data, however, do not speak directly to life-cycle realities for any group of workers. Men who have more labor market experience in any calendar year belong to older generations. The 47 percent ratio for the 36 to 40 experience interval, for example, may be lower than the 62 percent ratio for the first five years of experience in 1950 because the more experienced workers were born 35 years earlier. Relative to their white contemporaries, these older blacks had less schooling and attended poorer quality schools than their black successors would 35 years later.

Table 4 isolates the actual labor market experiences of labor market cohorts by rearranging the items in Table 2. This rearrangement involved centering the original data by the initial year of labor market entry. For example, men in their first five years of work in 1940 first entered the labor market, on average, in 1938. Among these men, blacks earned 46.7 percent as much as whites. These same men by 1950 had spent 10–15 years in the labor market; blacks in this cohort now earned 58.3 percent as much as whites. By reading across any row in Table

Table 4.   Black Male Wages as a Percentage of White Males by Labor Market Cohort

Median Year of Initial Labor Market Work	Census Year				
	1940	*1950*	*1960*	*1970*	*1980*
1978					84.2
1973					76.6
1968				75.1	73.5
1963				70.1	71.2
1958			60.2	66.2	67.8
1953			59.1	62.8	66.9
1948		61.8	59.4	62.7	66.5
1943		60.0	58.4	60.6	68.5
1938	46.7	58.3	57.6	60.0	
1933	47.5	56.6	56.2	60.3	
1928	44.4	54.1	53.8		
1923	44.4	53.2	55.9		
1918	42.3	50.3			
1913	41.7	46.9			
1908	40.2				
1903	39.8				
All	43.4	55.2	57.5	64.4	72.6

4, we can follow the actual life-cycle path of relative wages of the labor market cohorts indexed in the first column.

The message of Table 4 is unambiguous. In contrast to the cross-sectional implication of deterioration in the relative economic status of blacks across labor market careers, the reality is that . . . black men actually improved their situation relatives to whites. Black men narrowed the gap between their incomes and those of their white contemporaries as their careers evolved in virtually every instance depicted in Table 4. The cross-sectional decline in each Census year that characterized Table 2 is not the result of any increasing life-cycle differentiation by race. Instead, improvement in the quality of black workers relative to white workers across successive birth cohorts accounts for the cross-sectional decline.

[T]he racial gap in men's wages has narrowed considerably over the 40-year period—but why? If blacks are to sustain or increase their economic gains, we need to identify and understand the major reasons for those gains. . . .

III.   CAUSES OF THE CLOSING WAGE GAP: EDUCATION

Causes of the Convergence in Racial Wage Ratios

In this section and the next, we examine reasons for the substantial narrowing of the racial wage gap over time. Our aim here is to quantify how much of the closing was due to gains in education, and in the next section how much should be attributed to migration and the resurgence of the Southern economy. . . . This emphasis on education and location does not imply that they are the only forces at work. Indeed, Section V discusses two more factors that might have some influence: the falling labor force participation rates of black men and affirmative action.

The Statistical Frame

Our results are based on a statistical analysis of male weekly wages in the five micro data files from the 1940 to the 1980 Censuses. Regressions were estimated separately within eight five-year experience intervals, ranging between 1 to 5 and 36 to 40 years of work experience. Separate analyses were conducted for each race and within each of the five decennial Censuses. The dependent variable in each specification was the logarithm of the weekly wage.[7] Explanatory variables fall into five groups: (1) years of schooling; (2) dummy variables indicating residence in the South; (3) standard metropolitan statistical areas (SMSAs);[8] (4) the central cities of these SMSAs, and (5) a set of single-year experience dummies within each experience interval.

Our regression estimates will be used to partition change in the racial wage gap into education and location components. The idea is to quantify the extent to which the narrowing is due to gains in education, and how much should be attributed to migration and the growth of the Southern economy. . . .

Because we have separate estimates for each Census year, the regressions are first run across each of the four pairwise Census comparisons: 1940–50, 1950–60, 1960–70, and 1970–80. Linearity insures that effects over the 40 years can be obtained by summing these 10-year comparisons. The single-decade estimates alongside the 40-year summary help isolate the timing of effects.

The Role of Education

Controversy has always surrounded the prominence that should be assigned to black schools in shaping the economic history of blacks. The early analysis of the 1940 and 1960 Census led many scholars to conclude that the educational route to economic mobility was apparently closed for blacks. . . . Initial microlevel studies . . . painted a consistent picture of low returns to schooling for blacks, as well as a sharp deterioration in relative black economic potential over job careers. . . .

[T]he historical importance of black schooling has been discounted by many scholars (see Orley Ashenfelter 1977 and William A. Darity 1982). They pointed out that blacks' long-term advances in education did not produce any closing of the racial income gap, at least until the mid-1960s. They also pointed to the series of studies cited above showing that blacks derived far less income benefit from their education than did whites.

In short, this consensus of early research implied that even if blacks got more and better education, the racial wage gap would persist. The historical record now strongly challenges this view: It shows that black education has risen relative to white education, that the wage return on black educational investment has risen over time. These factors, together, have significantly narrowed the racial wage gap.

Trends in Educational Differences

The first step in documenting this claim involves tracking racial trends in years of school completed. The number of grades completed is a crude summary index of the amount of learning and skill acquired in American classrooms. But if education plays a significant role in closing the racial wage gap, the most elementary evidence must rely on monitoring the extent to which black educational accomplishments are catching up to those of whites. Table 5 demonstrates that this is happening. . . . [T]he education levels of each new generation of workers

Table 5. Average Years of Schooling for Black and White Men, 1940–80

	Census Year				
	1940	*1950*	*1960*	*1970*	*1980*
White Men					
Ages 26–35	9.89	10.77	11.49	12.36	13.56
Ages 36–45	9.15	9.98	10.93	11.78	13.02
Ages 46–55	8.54	9.20	9.96	11.15	12.20
Ages 56–64	8.07	8.47	9.06	10.16	11.45
Ages 16–64	9.38	9.99	10.65	11.51	12.47
Black Men					
Ages 26–35	5.97	7.60	9.01	10.54	12.15
Ages 36–45	5.40	6.41	7.84	9.49	11.26
Ages 46–55	4.84	5.54	6.51	8.19	9.85
Ages 56–64	4.36	4.92	5.51	6.81	8.48
Ages 16–64	4.70	6.83	8.00	9.47	10.96

increased between 1940 and 1980, but the increase was much greater for black men. Educational differences still persist between the races, but they are far less today than at any time in our history. Between 1940 and 1980, 40 percent of the racial education gap disappeared.

It is easy to forget how little schooling the average black male worker had, even as late as 1960, and how large black-white education differences were in that year. Across the full age distribution, white men had a 2.7 year educational advantage over black men in 1960. . . . The average level of schooling of young black workers in 1960 was about 9 years; the typical older black worker had not even completed the sixth grade. In contrast, the majority of white workers in 1960 still had completed high school, and one in ten were college graduates.

As dismal as these 1960 numbers seem, they represent substantial improvement over those for 1940. In that year, 80 percent of the 1940 black male work force had only elementary schooling and 40 percent had less than five years of education. . . . While the 1940 education credentials of white workers were far less than those of today's workers, white men had a decidedly larger educational advantage over their black contemporaries. In that year, the average white worker completed 9.4 grades, 3.7 more than their black rivals. . . .

An important pattern emerges when we examine trends across age groups within each Census year. Since 1960, the smallest racial difference occurs among the younger workers. . . . This age relation contains important clues about . . . why the rate by which blacks were able to catch up in education has accelerated.

[T]able 6 shows how much black education rose relative to white education over this 40-year period at different experience levels. More experienced black workers narrowed their education disparity by a year or two. In contrast, black men in their first five years of work had narrowed the gap by four years. . . .

Table 6. Black-White Convergence in Average
Schooling: 1940–80

Experience Interval	Decline in Racial Disparity in Years of Schooling
1–5	4.05
6–10	3.17
11–15	2.57
16–20	2.30
21–25	2.09
26–30	1.76
31–35	1.58
36–40	1.10

[T]here has been a substantial narrowing of racial difference in years of school completed. Moreover, this convergence has accelerated as each new cohort arrived in the labor market.

The Wage Gains from Schooling

In examining the role of education, the key issues are (*a*) whether blacks have been able to translate better schooling into higher incomes and (*b*) whether blacks realize the same return as whites on educational investment. Our analyses indicate that education has translated into higher incomes for blacks and has helped narrow the racial wage gap. However, the interracial payoff for education has not been equal until very recently and even then only for younger workers. . . . Black men earned 50 to 55 percent as much as comparably educated whites in 1940. While these racial wage differences narrowed substantially over time, they remained at levels of 70 to 80 percent in 1980. These within-education wage ratios should be contrasted to the aggregate ratios of 43 percent in 1940 and 73 percent in 1980 (see Table 2). The difference informs us that education does play a significant role in explaining the racial wage gap. However, it also warns us that simply equalizing the number of years of schooling alone would leave a sizable racial wage gap.

[C]ontrolling for the number of years of work experience, black-white income ratios in the earlier Censuses decline with years of schooling. This decline is particularly sharp in the high school and college groups and is accentuated among more experienced workers. To illustrate, consider men with 30 to 40 years of work experience in 1940. Black wages average about one-half of white wages for those with 11 years of schooling or less. In contrast, black wages are little more than a third of white wages among high school and college graduates.

However, also note that this pattern of falling black-white wage ratios by education has been eliminated by the latter Censuses among workers in their first 20 years in the work force. This pro-skill bias in black economic gains is documented by the more rapid wage improvement among college graduates between 1940 and 1980. . . .

Estimated Increase in Wages Associated with Increased Schooling

[W]e need to know how much another year of schooling has raised labor market earnings over time. We obtained estimates for each race of schooling coefficients—the proportionate increase in weekly wages associated with an additional year of schooling. . . . [W]e find a persistent narrowing of racial differences in schooling coefficients [not shown].

The end result of this 40-year persistence is that the magnitude of the change eventually became quite large. For example, among those in their first five years of work in 1940, white men's income increased 5 percent more than did black men's for each additional year of school attended. This white advantage declined as each new cohort of workers entered the labor market. In fact, among men who first entered the labor market during the 1970s, the income benefits that blacks received from schooling now exceed those of white men.

Alternative explanations can be offered for this racial convergence in education coefficients. One obvious candidate is the civil rights movement (and its associated legislation) during the 1960s. A number of studies, including our own (for one example, see Smith and Welch 1984), demonstrated that black male college graduates were among the primary beneficiaries of affirmative action pressures. This view is supported by a racial convergence in education coefficients that was twice as large in the 1970s as in the 1960s.

However, this cannot be the whole story nor, for that matter, a very large part of it. . . . The general pattern of rising relative returns to black schooling emerged long before the civil rights activism of the 1960s. The root cause of the improvements in relative black returns apparently lies within long-term improvements across birth cohorts that enabled blacks to translate an incremental year of schooling into more income. The evidence we have accumulated in earlier research clearly points to improving quality of black schools as the most plausible explanation for this cohort improvement. We found dramatic changes in such basic indices as number of days attended, pupil-teacher ratios, the education accomplishments of teachers (Smith, 1984; Welch 1974). . . .

Quantifying Education's Effect on the Racial Wage Gap

[T]he two dimensions that served to close the racial wage gap were the narrowing of education disparity between the races and the improving economic benefits from black schooling. . . .

[T]he wage gap closed by 6 to 36 percent because blacks were more similar to whites in levels of school completion in 1980 than in 1940. This influence of education is clearly largest among younger workers. . . .

In addition to a smaller schooling disparity, blacks also began to experience higher economic benefits of schooling (i.e., race-year effects). Since 1940, there has been a spectacular rise in the income that blacks receive from a year of schooling, a phenomenon we attribute largely to the improving relative quality of black schools. . . .

IV. CAUSES OF THE CLOSING WAGE GAP: GEOGRAPHIC LOCATION

Americans have always tried to improve their economic lot by moving to places where prospects for their economic advancement were better. Since the end of slavery, large numbers of black men exercised their freedom to choose the place where they lived and worked. For many decades, most of this black migration took place within the South. Beginning in 1910, the great black migration northward started, a movement that accelerated after 1940.

While migration has been changing residential patterns, the regional structure of the American economy has also changed—to the point that it bears little resemblance to that of 1940. The agriculture-based economy of the South, for example—characterized by low productivity and little technological advance— was viewed as a drag on black economic progress in 1940. The situation now is far different. Today, the smokestack industries of the North Central and Northeastern states are in decay while the restructured Southern economy is booming.

In this section, we investigate the impact of these changing patterns of regional location on trends in black-white male wage ratios. We will concentrate on the three regional issues that loom most important in the economic literature—the large-scale black South to North migration, the increasing urbanization of the black population, and differential interregional economic growth.

Changing Patterns of Residential Location

Two geographic factors stand out in shaping the economic status of blacks: their concentration in the Southern states and their increasing urbanization. . . . Throughout American history, the economic welfare of blacks has been tied closely to events in the South. Fully nine out of ten blacks were Southerners in 1790, a proportion that changed but little over the next 120 years. Since 1910, the fraction of blacks living in the South has steadily declined. Spurred in part by the cutoff in European immigration, the great Northern black migration spanned the next two decades, 1910–30. . . .

Even so, three-quarters of all blacks still lived in the Southern states in 1940, but with the end of the Depression, the movement North resumed with renewed force. During each decade between 1940 and 1970, a million and a half Southern blacks migrated to the North. The end result was to leave only slightly more than half of all black men Southern residents in 1970. The flow then reversed during the 1970s: As it did for white Americans, the net movement of blacks turned southward. A slightly larger proportion of blacks lived in the South in 1980 than lived there ten years earlier. . . .

The great northern migration had profound effects. The culture, laws, and economy of the South would no longer play so exclusive a role in shaping the economic position of blacks. However, it is also easy to exaggerate the extent of this change. Even today, the majority of blacks remain citizens of the South. . . . Three-quarters of all black men were Southern-born by as late as 1970—another reminder that black roots in the South still run deep.

Besides migration, the geography of black people altered in another fundamental way. After the Civil War, nine of ten blacks lived in rural farm areas, especially in the rural counties of the Southern black belt. This century has witnessed the transition of the black people from largely rural to predominately urban. . . .

Whites were still more urbanized than blacks in 1940. Urbanization affected both races, but blacks far more so than whites. By 1980, four out of every five men of both races lived in urban areas. Today, the principal difference between them is where they live within urban areas: whites in the suburban fringes, blacks in the central cities. Fully 75 percent of all black SMSA residents resided in the central cities, compared with only 38 percent of whites.

Black-White Wage Differences by Geographic Location

Even among men who have the same amount of education and job experience, large geographic wage differentials prevail among regions. . . . Some of these wage disparities may simply reflect cost-of-living differences between regions, or compensating payments for the relative attractiveness or undesirability of locational attributes (e.g., climate, crime, and density). Given the magnitude of the regional wage differentials, it is also likely that they proxy unobserved indices of skill. Finally, the large black-white wage gap in the South may well reflect the historically more intense racial discrimination there. . . . Traditionally, men of either race earned less in the South than in the North. Until the last decade, Southern white men received about 10 percent lower wages than white men located elsewhere; black weekly wages were approximately 30 percent lower in the South than elsewhere. . . . Between 1940 and 1960, there was remarkable stability in these racial wage differences, with a 20 percent larger racial wage gap in the South than in other parts of the country. The southern racial wage disparity narrowed for younger workers between 1960 and 1970, but remained at historical levels among nature male workers. However, the truly dramatic story occurred between 1970 and 1980. A sharp decline occurred during the 1970s as the racial wage gap in the South fell by as much as two-thirds of their 1970 levels.

What accounts for this rapid movement toward the national norm? . . . Two explanations are possible. First, black-white skill differences may have converged in the South as the post–World War II cohorts entered the labor market. To illustrate this point, assume that Southern schools were effectively desegregated in 1960, six years after the Brown decision. The first class of Southern black children who had attended entirely desegregated schools would have first entered the labor market in the early to mid-1970s. Some of the improvement in black incomes during the 1970s may have been due to the skills acquired through this improved schooling. However, that is unlikely to be the whole story because there was a substantial erosion in racial wage disparities even among older workers in the 1970s. A more plausible explanation may well be that racial discrimination is waning in the South. . . .

Quantifying the Role of Location

In this section, we have identified a number of important residential changes that could affect the size of the racial gap. These changes included black migration, the recent erosion of the Southern wage gap, and differential economic growth across regions. What was the relative quantitative significance of these trends? . . .

[T]he data show that migration was important in closing the wage gap. Depending upon the specific experience level considered, migration increased black-white wage ratios by 11 to 19 percent between 1940 and 1980. Overall, these direct wage benefits from migration rival education's role in closing the racial wage gap. Migration and schooling were the two key investments made by black men that drive their economic advances.

[B]lack income gains from migration have declined steadily over time. The largest benefits were concentrated between 1940 and 1960, diminished during the 1960s, and were no longer an important source of black economic improvement during the 1970s.[9]

The second quantitatively important locational influence we identified was the narrowing racial wage gap in the South. Whatever the cause, this change had a significant effect on black relative economic status. The improving situation in the South closed the racial wage gap at the nationwide level by 4 to 10 percent between 1940 and 1980. . . . Virtually all of the change occurred during the 1970s, the only decade where the racial wage disparity declined significantly. . . .

In summary, . . . [m]igration raised black wages 11 to 19 percent between 1940 and 1980; the closing of the Southern wage gap added another 4 to 10 percent. While the decline of central cities had negative consequences for blacks, and the resurgence in the Southern economy positive ones, the overall net effect of these regional developments was small.

V. LABOR FORCE PARTICIPATION AND AFFIRMATIVE ACTION

Our regression analyses focused on those factors that are most likely to have narrowed the racial wage gap. However, other developments may well have affected black wages during the 40 years in question. The most notable among these are the decline in labor force participation rates of less educated and low-income black males between 1970 and 1980 and affirmative action.

The Declining Black Participation in the Labor Force

Trends in wage rates are the primary focus of our essay. But our portrait of the changing economic status of black men is incomplete without a brief summary of parallel trends in employment and unemployment. In spite of the improvement in their labor market opportunities, an increasing number of black men have dropped out of the labor force in the middle of their careers. In addition, rising rates of unemployment, for young blacks especially, raise serious concerns about the labor force young blacks face. . . .

[U]nemployment rates of blacks 16–25 years old were 1.45 times those of whites in 1950. By 1980, the black youth unemployment rate was 22 percent, more than double the rate for young white men.[10] Because conventional labor force statistics give a misleading portrait of activities of young men, we have divided activity status into two groups.[11] SEM (the "good activity") includes schooling, employment, and the military, while UOJ (unemployment, out of the labor force, and jail) are the bad ones.

It may come as a surprise to many that there exists no negative secular trend for black male teenagers. Between 1940 and 1980 roughly one in five black male teenagers was confined to unproductive activities. In fact, the principal secular trend among black male teenagers was within the SEM group, where the fraction in school increased by 35 percent largely at the expense of the fraction at work. Because this is arguably a positive development, there is nothing on the employment side of the labor market that counteracts the positive wage story for black teenagers.

Although the seeds of the problem are certainly sown earlier, the secular deterioration, instead, is concentrated among somewhat older black men. More important, it is confined entirely to the 1970s; 28 percent of 24-year-old black men are in the unproductive group in 1980, a jump of 7 percentage points since 1970. In this age group in 1980, 1 in 9 black men were unemployed, another 1 in

9 were out of the labor force, and 1 in 20 were in jail. Similarly, 1 in 5 black men aged 35–36 are now assigned to our unproductive activities class, with half of them completely absent from the labor market.

[A]mong men 36–45 years old, black participation rates fell by almost 6 percentage points, four times the decline among whites. The drop is even steeper among those 46–54 years old; once again, the fraction of black men who withdrew far exceeds that of white men. Among men 46–54 years old, black participation rates fell by 10 percentage points.

This deterioration in the employment side of the black male labor market raises two critical research questions: (1) What caused the decline in black employment? and (2) What implications does this recent decline in black employment have for the optimistic wage story we have been telling?

Causes of the Decline in Black Employment. In our view, one of the major unsettled research questions on race centers around the reasons for the growing fraction of persistently disengaged black men from the labor market. The competing hypotheses are not new, but a convincing case has not been made on either side. William Wilson (1988) and others have emphasized the demand side, claiming that the substantial restructuring of the economy in the last 15 years eliminated jobs that were disproportionately held by inner-city blacks.

The supply-side counterpoint, Charles Murray (1984), swayed in part by the coincidence in timing, directed attention toward the host of social programs now subsumed under the popular label, the "safety net." It is argued that these programs are an attractive alternative to work for many black men whose market rewards are meager. The political rhetoric surrounding this issue is obviously intense, but it has not yet been matched by scientific precision in settling the question. . . .

Effects of Declining Black Employment on the Wage Series. Fortunately, the other question we posed is more easily answerable, although there is often considerable confusion about precisely what the question is. The question we raise is this: Did the sharp decline in the black LFPRs during the 1970s and early 1980s distort the positive wage story?

[F]or both races, declines in LFPR are far steeper among the less educated. The concentration of these declines among blacks and among the less educated strongly suggests that the men who dropped out of the labor force had lower incomes than those who remained. Because of this correlation with income, these declining participation rates could have important implications for trends in black-white wages during the 1970–80 period. In particular, in an important paper, Richard Butler and James Heckman (1977) have argued that these supply-side reductions in the relative number of working black men were an important cause of the post-1965 rise in the relative income of blacks. . . .

The Butler-Heckman hypothesis rests on compositional changes in the labor force. To assess the practical importance of their argument, 1980 wages were corrected for two compositional changes. The first reflects the more rapid declines in labor force participation among blacks and the less educated. To do this, we substituted observed 1970 labor force participation rates by education level for the 1980 rates.

We also adjusted for the fact that within schooling classes wages of dropouts are typically less than the wages of those who remained in the labor force by 1980. To do this, we use alternative assumptions about the wage of dropouts relative to those who remain in the labor force. . . . Even if we assume that dropouts would earn only half as much as those who remain in the labor force . . . the simulated black-white wage ratios remain similar (within 5 percent) to the observed ratios. Evidently, supply censoring explains at most a minor part of the observed increase in black-white male wages between 1970 and 1980.

Affirmative Action

The next issue we address is affirmative action, which still dominates the debate over government labor-market policy regarding race. . . . Our discussion . . . focuses on two questions: First, has affirmative action significantly altered the types and locations of jobs that blacks can obtain? Second, how has affirmative action affected the incomes of black men?

Employment Effects. To detect discriminatory behavior, EEOC has set up an extensive monitoring system. Since 1966, all firms in the private sector with 100 or more employees, and federal contractors with $50,000 contracts and with 50 or more employees, have been required to report annually on their total employment in each of nine broad occupation categories, reporting separately for each race-sex group. Firms are also required to indicate their federal contractor status on their EEO-1 reports.[12] These reports give enforcement agencies their initial opportunities to detect employment deficiencies.

Because of these reporting requirements, only about half of the nongovernment, noneducation work force is directly covered by affirmative action. Federal contractors employed 35 percent of all nongovernment, noneducational institution workers in 1980, and 70 percent of all EEOC-covered workers.

We test for employment effects by measuring whether affirmative action has altered the location of black employment. If affirmative action is effective and is adequately enforced, minority representation should expand more among firms that are required to report to EEOC than among firms that are not. Because federal contractors have more to lose, the greatest relative gains in employment and wages should occur among those EEO-1–reporting firms that are federal contractors.

While such relocation of black workers should be discernible in total employment figures, the largest minority gains should appear within certain occupation groups. We anticipate that the greatest black gains should occur in professional and managerial jobs for firms that are reporting to EEOC. Once again, these changes should be even larger among those firms that are federal contractors.[13]

Table 7 lists the relative probability that blacks are employed in EEOC-covered employment, and strongly supports the employment-response hypothesis.[14]

The basic test of affirmative action is its effect on employment trends in minority representation over time. On these grounds, the message of Table 7 is unambiguous. Black men were almost 10 percent less likely than white men to work in covered firms in 1966. By 1980, they were 25 percent more likely to work in EEOC-reporting firms. Compared with the 48 percent in 1966, fully 60 percent of all black men worked in covered firms by 1980.

As large as those changes in total employment seem, they pale next to changes within the managerial and professional jobs. Black managers and professionals were half as likely as white managers and professionals to work in covered firms in 1966. By 1980, black managers and professionals were equally likely to be found in covered firms.

The biggest employment changes clearly occurred between 1966 and 1970. . . . Among black men, the trend continued at a diminished pace until 1974, and then apparently stabilized. The growth was greater for black women and persisted throughout the 1970s.

Wage Effects. The economic literature has now reached a consensus that affirmative action significantly altered the industrial location of minority employment. But have these shifts been accompanied by an improvement in the incomes of blacks? Here there exists much less consensus. Early time-series studies by Richard Freeman (1973) and Wayne Vroman (1974) relied on time-series analysis and essentially found a break in the relative wage series when affirmative action laws were enacted. A number of other studies (Charles Link 1975;

Table 7. Representation of Black Men and Women in Covered EEOC Employment Compared with White Men (In Percent)

Occupation	1966	1970	1974	1978	1980
Total Employment					
Black men	91.8	112.5	123.1	128.4	126.4
Black women	91.5	118.7	141.2	144.8	154.4
Officials and Managers					
Black men	53.3	80.0	104.0	101.1	106.8
Black women	61.4	10.5	142.3	178.5	154.4
Professionals and Technical					
Black men	62.8	82.9	137.8	117.2	97.6
Black women	74.5	63.4	84.3	104.3	118.7

Leonard Weiss and Jeffrey Williamson 1973; Joan Haworth, James Gwartney, and Charles Haworth 1975) assign a major role to affirmative action. Unfortunately, the standard practice was to deduce the impact of government as a component of the residual—all changes in black-white images not explained by the explanatory variables.

To avoid exaggerated claims about the wage effects of affirmative action, we need to place them in historical perspective. The Civil Rights Act was passed in 1964 and the powers of two enforcement agencies, EEOC and OFCCP, were slowly put into place during the next decade. As a result, affirmative action is only relevant as an explanation for any post-1965 closing of the racial wage gap.

Table 8 helps illustrate our point. It lists the percentages by which the wage gap for black males narrowed between 1940 and 1960 and between 1960 and 1980. Wage effects attributed to affirmative action must occur in the second 20-year interval.[15] The lesson of Table 8 is clear. While some experience groups were favored in one 20-year period and some in the other, the general pattern reveals that the racial wage gap narrowed as rapidly in the 20 years prior to 1960 (and before affirmative action) as during the 20 years afterward. This suggests that the slowly evolving historical forces we have emphasized in this essay— education and migration—were the primary determinants of the long-term black economic improvement. At best, affirmative action has marginally altered black wage gains around this long-term trend.

Examined with these more limited expectations, affirmative action did alter the pattern of minority wages. These patterns are isolated in Table 9, which lists black-white male wages at key points during affirmative action's existence.

The key impact on wages relates to timing. During the initial phases of affir-

Table 8. Percentage Narrowing of the Racial Wage Gap by Years of Schooling, 1940–80

	Years of Experience				
Period	*1–10*	*11–20*	*21–30*	*31–40*	*All*
16+ Years of Schooling					
1940–60	6.8	31.3	29.0	29.0	21.2
1960–80	23.5	26.3	29.7	31.3	23.5
12 Years of Schooling					
1940–60	3.3	15.7	34.5	53.3	15.8
1960–80	13.1	15.3	13.7	23.1	17.4
8–11 Years of Schooling					
1940–60	3.9	14.0	19.8	24.0	20.6
1960–80	23.4	22.0	15.3	17.5	20.8

Source: Table 5.

Table 9. Weekly Wages of Black Males as a Percentage of White Male Wages, Stratified by Schooling and Experience

Year	*Years of Experience*				
	1–5	*6–10*	*11–20*	*21–30*	*31–40*
All Schooling Classes					
1967–68	69.5	66.1	61.9	59.7	57.7
1971–72	82.1	72.0	66.1	62.5	64.0
1975–76	81.4	74.0	70.2	67.8	68.8
1979	84.2	76.5	72.0	69.3	64.1
16 Years of Schooling					
1967–68	75.7	66.5	59.8	55.3	53.7
1971–72	101.1	84.6	65.3	62.0	69.5
1975–76	89.1	84.1	72.7	67.2	70.9
1979	91.1	87.0	77.9	69.9	64.5
12 Years of Schooling					
1967–68	81.8	76.8	71.2	68.4	68.4
1971–72	90.7	82.3	76.2	71.0	73.8
1975–76	83.1	81.8	77.2	76.7	73.6
1979	84.2	80.4	80.2	78.2	77.8

Source: Yearly Current Population Survey Public Use Tapes for 1967–68, 1971–72, 1975–76. Public Use Tapes of the decennial Census were used for 1979.

mative action, there was a remarkable surge in incomes of young black males. The abrupt jump in relative wages for young black men from 1967–68 to 1971–72, especially for college graduates, is remarkable. According to our estimates, the racial wage gap for young college graduates jumped from 76 percent in 1967–68 to complete wage parity by 1971–72. A similar, but less sharp, surge exists among young high school graduates. In this group, black men earned 82 percent as much as comparable whites in 1967–68; four years later, they earned 91 percent as much.

These black wage gains, however, did not prove to be permanent. By mid-1975–76, the racial wage gap had returned to more normal levels. Wages of young black college graduates were now 89 percent of those of whites, compared with the 1971–72 peak of 101 percent. Similarly, young black high school graduates in 1975–76 earned 83 percent as much as whites, a wage gap little different from the one that prevailed in 1967–68. The timing pattern resembles a wage bubble, with a sharp increase in black male incomes from 1967 to 1972, followed by the bursting of the bubble during the next five years.

In our view, affirmative action is the most plausible cause of this wage bubble. First, the timing of the wage bubble is consistent with the timing of the employment effects. The large shift in black employment was concentrated during the years 1966–70 and was largely completed by 1974. During these early years, EEOC-covered firms rapidly increased their demand for black workers, bidding up their wages. However, once the stock of black workers had reached its new equilibrium, this short-run demand increase was completed and wages returned to their long-run levels.

Two other characteristics of this wage bubble argue that affirmative action was the principal cause. First, most of the new hiring takes place among younger workers, whose skills have not yet been matched closely to specific firms and industries. Consistent with this observation, almost all the black wage increases in Table 9 took place among younger workers. Second, in analyzing employment shifts, we found that the largest changes for black employment took place among the more skilled—in the managerial and professional ranks. Consistent with these employment shifts, the wage bubble was larger among college graduates.

This last observation also points to the final wage effect of affirmative action—its apparent pro-skill bias. The essential purpose of affirmative action is to increase employment of blacks in jobs where they had previously been scarce. Because there are an abundance of blacks in low-skill jobs, the main pressures will be concentrated in the skilled jobs, where blacks had previously been scarce. Thus, if there is a story to be told of effects of affirmative action on relative wages of black men, its main plot must be one of nonneutrality with respect to education, with strong positive effects for college graduates and less strong, not necessarily positive effects at lower educational levels. . . .

VI. GLIMPSES INTO THE FUTURE

Looking back on a 40-year record of black economic progress, we have seen a substantial narrowing of the racial wage gap. The 40 years between 1940 and 1980 have brought a partial American Resolution to Mydral's American Dilemma. But what of the future? Will black progress continue at the pace of the period from 1940 to 1980 or are we entering, instead, an era of black stagnation or even retrogression? Our research provides one perspective on those questions. By identifying the sources of past improvement, we have established the requisites for future progress. The lessons that history teaches give us both optimistic and pessimistic glimpses into black America's future.

The Beginning of the End?

Before our exercise in forecasting, it is helpful to update our story to include the Reagan years. Table 10 lists inflation-adjusted male incomes from 1970 to 1986. In real dollars, incomes of men of either race changed little since 1970. In terms of racial economic progress, the first six years of the Reagan era are perhaps best characterized as treading water. Whether we use incomes of all men

Table 10. Male Incomes by Race: 1970–86 (In 1987 Dollars)

Year	White Men	Black Men	Black-White Ratio
Mean Personal Income			
1970	22,954	13,711	59.7
1975	22,848	13,911	61.2
1980	22,060	13,566	61.6
1982	21,270	13,005	61.1
1984	22,161	13,256	59.8
1986	23,567	14,361	60.9
Mean Personal Income, Full-Time Workers			
1970	31,135	19,830	63.7
1975	31,830	21,521	67.6
1980	30,297	20,838	68.8
1982	29,911	20,596	68.9
1984	30,570	21,076	68.9
1986	32,095	21,873	68.2

Source: Current Population Surveys, Series P-60, various issues.

or only those of full-time workers, the black-white wage gap changed little over these years.

The structure of the racial wage gap, however, was altered during the 1980s in ways that raise real concern about the future. The reasons for concern are illustrated in Table 11, which lists black-white male income ratios by age during the 1980s.[16] The sharp deterioration in racial wage ratios with age that has always characterized cross-sectional data clearly became less pronounced during this decade. The racial wage gap actually widened somewhat from those under age 35, while it continued to narrow for those over 44 years old.

The 1980s represent a sharp departure from the historical record. If anything, that record is one where the expanding wage gap with age became more pronounced with each new decade, a reflection of accelerating across-cohort im-

Table 11. Black-White Male Income Ratios by Age, 1980–85

	Age Group				
Year	20–24	25–34	35–44	45–54	55–64
1985	69.1	69.2	61.9	64.8	55.9
1983	62.9	69.3	62.7	58.7	51.3
1980	76.0	71.2	61.9	56.2	52.3

Source: Current Population Surveys, Series P-60, various issues.

provement in the relative skills of new black workers. If Table 11 signals a permanent shift, this process did not continue into the 1980s. This table does suggest that the wage gains achieved by the black labor market cohorts of the 1950s and 1960s were maintained in the 1980s. As their careers proceeded, black workers in their thirties and forties held on to their wage advances relative to whites. The problem lies instead with young black men, a disturbing harbinger of the future.

Should these recent trends raise serious concerns about future progress? The answer depends on what we see as the underlying causes, a question to which we now turn. There are three critical issues: economic growth, changes in the value of skill, and what is happening in the black schools.

Economic Growth

Across the 40 years between 1940 and 1980, the United States experienced tremendous economic growth that increased the incomes of both races dramatically. . . . How much of the long-term reduction in black poverty was due to post-1940 economic growth and how much reflects the improving relative skills of blacks?

One way of answering this question is to fix the 1980 black earnings ratio at its 1940 level. If that were the case, 46 percent of black working men would be poor in 1980 instead of the actual rate of 24 percent. This disparity indicates that 45 percent of the reduction in black poverty since 1940 was due to economic growth and the remaining 55 percent to the combined effect of improving black labor market skills (relative to whites). . . . The virtual absence of real income growth during the 1970s carried a terrible price in limiting reductions in the ranks of the black poor. Among those aged 26 to 55, the proportion of the black male working poor fell by only 1 percentage point to 24 percent during the 1970s. If the 1970s had duplicated the 1960s in terms of rising incomes, the proportion of black poor would have fallen instead to 19 percent. The disappointing American economic performance during the 1970s had many sorry consequences; one of the cruelest was that the rank of the black poor was 25 percent higher than it would have been if economic growth had continued unabated at the pace of the 1960s.

The Value of Skill

Perhaps the most dramatic change in the wage structure of the labor market in the 1980s was the increased premia to skill. For example, among men 25–34 years old, college graduates earned 24 percent more than high school graduates in 1980. By 1986, college graduates in this age group earned 42 percent more than high school graduates. . . .

While the origins of this labor market change have little to do with race, they have important implications for the racial wage gap. Because of the still significant skill differences between the races, white men benefited more from an increase in the price of skill than black men did. . . .

Black Schooling

In addition to the sustained rapid economic growth between 1940 and 1970, this essay argues that the driving forces behind long-term black economic progress came from the American classroom. In 1940, the typical black male entering the work force finished the sixth grade—four grades less than those new white workers with whom he had to compete. Today, the average new black worker is a high school graduate and trails his white competitor by less than a year of education. And this is only half the story. Dramatic improvements in the quality of black education increased the ability of blacks to translate their schooling into more dollars in the job market. In 1940, whites gained twice as much income as blacks from attending school for another year. Today, there is little racial difference in the economic benefits of schooling for young workers.

This central role of education raises our deepest concerns about future prospects. The remaining racial gap in years of schooling completed is now quite small, so further advances must stem from the far more problematic quality dimension. The historical improvement in the quality of black schooling resulted largely from Southern black migration to the better schools of the North and from the overall rise in the quality of Southern schools. Because these trends have largely run their course, further improvement in black schooling depends critically on what takes place in urban black schools of the North.

Periodic visits to the schools in New York and Chicago's black ghettos are reason enough for skepticism about continued advances in the quality of black education. Such visits would show little evidence of a national commitment and the absence of significant public policy initiatives to improve black schooling. . . .

The Future

Should we be optimistic or pessimistic then about the future? Perhaps the best reason for optimism is the growth of the black middle class, particularly the black elite. A new black economic leadership is emerging that will no longer draw its ranks almost exclusively from the clergy and civil rights organizations. There are real questions about continued racial progress, especially among the black poor. But the continued growth of the black elite is a safe bet, for several good reasons.

First, black college graduates are moving in droves to the private sector. Until recently, they were employed almost exclusively in government jobs. While government work is safe and reliable, it has upper limits on rewards. The real prizes in our economic competition are won in the private sector, and the black elite have now joined the game.

Second, the initial wage gains blacks made right out of college will likely be maintained over their careers. Salary increases and promotions will come at least as rapidly for the new black elite as for their white competitors. Finally, the new black middle class and elite will be able to perpetuate their achievements across future generations. For the first time, many blacks now have the financial ability to secure the American dream for their children.

The expansion in the ranks of the black elite has clearly continued unabated into the 1980s. Through recessions and recoveries alike, the size of the black economic elite has continued to grow. For example, the fraction of men with above middle-class incomes increased from 11.6 percent in 1980 to 14.0 percent in 1983 (the business cycle trough) and 14.2 percent in 1986.[17]

Unfortunately, there are also reasons for concern about the future, especially for the still large black underclass. There was nothing magical about the long-run black progress we document in this essay. It reflected hard-won, underlying achievements that enhanced black market skills, in the context of rapid American economic growth. Take away those underlying achievements and lose that growth, and black progress will stop.

One of the underlying causes, migration, has already lost its clout. With the end of the substantial black wage disparities between the South and the North, the potential for further sizable black wage gains from migration is minute. There are good reasons as well to be concerned about continued improvement in the quality of black inner city Northern schools. The lessons of history assure us that until we deal with the problems of our nation's black schools, and until we restore the growth rates of the 1960s, further long-term improvements in black economic status will not materialize.

ACKNOWLEDGMENTS

The authors would like to thank Joyce Peterson for her help in writing this essay. Financial support was provided by grants from the Sloan, Olin, Russell Sage, and Ford Foundations.

NOTES

1. We limit our focus to black men because including black women and the black family raises a number of issues that, although important, are ancillary to our main thesis.

2. On a national scale, Americans were first surveyed regarding their incomes as part of the 1940 decennial Census.

3. For convenience, we will refer throughout this essay to the year the Census was taken, although all income statistics actually correspond to the calendar year preceding the Census.

4. Our numbers are ratios of arithmetic means of weekly wages. Income is defined as the sum of wages and salary and self-employment income. Weekly wages are calculated as income divided by weeks worked. Our sample consists of men 16 to 64 years old who were U.S. citizens and who did not live in group quarters. A number of additional sample restrictions were imposed. We excluded men (1) who worked less than 50 weeks in the previous year and were attending school; (2) who worked 26 weeks or less in the previous year; (3) who were in the military; (4) who were self-employed or working without pay if they were not employed in agriculture; (5) whose weekly wages put them below the following values: 1940 = $1.50, 1950 = $3.25, 1960 = $6.25, 1970 = $10.00, 1980 = $19.80; (6) whose computed weekly wages put them above the following values: 1940 = $125, 1950 = $250, 1960 = $625, 1970 = $1,250, 1980 = $1,875; (7) who were in the open-ended, upper-income interval and who did not work at least 40 weeks last year. In addition, in the 1950 Census only sample line people (who were asked income questions) were included.

5. Years of market experience is defined as current age minus assumed age at leaving school. The mapping from years of schooling completed and school leaving age is as follows: ed 0–11 = age 17, ed 12 = 18, ed 13–15 = age 20, ed 16 or more = age 23.

6. Throughout this essay, the 1940 statistics include only wage income. . . . As a result, the 1940 sample is not strictly comparable to the other Census years. However, the trends we describe in the text are not affected to any large degree by this limitation. . . .

7. Weeks worked were coded continuously from 1 to 52 weeks in the 1940, 1950, and 1980 Census. In the 1960 and 1970 Census, however, weeks worked were coded into broad intervals. To maintain comparability, the same intervals in all Census years were used. The following within-interval means, as calculated from the 1980 Census, were assigned: 1–13 = 6.50; 14–26 = 21.73; 27–39 = 33.08; 40–47 = 42.67; 48–49 = 48.29; 50–52 = 51.82. We checked this assumption by rerunning the analysis using continuous weeks worked. The differences were trivial.

Each Census contained an open-ended upper-income interval. For each Census year and each open-ended income category (indicated in parentheses next to the Census year), the following values were assigned: 1940 (5,000) = 8,900; 1950 (10,000) = 22,500; 1960 (25,000) = 42,500; 1970 (50,000) = 80,000; 1980 (75,000) = 115,000. These top code values were calculated assuming that the upper part of the income distribution followed an exponential distribution.

8. For reasons of confidentiality in 1960, SMSAs were not reported in a number of low-population states. To maintain comparability, we imposed a similar restriction on the other Census years. Therefore, SMSAs in the following states were not included in our definition: Arizona, Colorado, Delaware, Hawaii, Idaho, Maine, Mississippi, North Dakota, Rhode Island, South Dakota, and Utah. A similar restriction applies for the central city variable.

9. Blacks were essentially transformed from their rural Southern base to a predominately urban group during the 20 years after 1940. As a consequence, the positive black benefits from going to urban places were largely completed by 1960. The wage gains achieved from moving north would last another decade. Then, with the end of the black migration to the North, these migration gains stopped.

10. The causes of this long-term deterioration in black youth unemployment are not well understood. According to John Cogan (1982), most of the decline before 1970 was due to the elimination of agriculture as the primary employer for young blacks. But the reasons for the post-1970 changes remain elusive.

11. For a fuller discussion of this division, see Smith and Welch (1987).

12. In addition to these EEO-1 reports, non-private-sector firms must submit similar reports for their occupation-employment distribution. . . . Because our data files contain only EEO-1 reports, all employment comparisons in the next section eliminate those who are self-employed and employees of the government or educational institutions.

13. Our EEO-1 data were derived from firm EEO-1 reports for 1966, 1970, 1974, 1978, and 1980. For each race-sex group, employers were asked to list the number of employees in nine broad occupation categories. For each sex, the numbers of employees are listed separately by race: white—not of Hispanic origin, black, Hispanic, Asian, and American Indian. Because we could not devise a sensible separation using Census occupational data, we combined two occupations ("professionals" and "technicians").

14. More precisely, these numbers are the share of total black male employment in EEOC-covered employment divided by the share of all white men in covered EEOC employment.

15. This two-way equal division assigns too much weight to affirmative action, because the legislation was not effective in the first five years (1960–65).

16. To smooth this series, three-year averages of income ratios were computed centered on the years listed in the first column. The 1985 entry represents an average of the 1985 and 1986 ratios.

17. We continue to define the elite as men whose income exceeds four-thirds of white male median income in that year.

REFERENCES

Ashenfelter, Orley. "Comment on Smith-Welch, 'Black/White Male Earnings and Employment: 1960–1970'," in *The distribution of economic well-being.* National Bureau of Economic Research, Studies in Income and Wealth, No. 41. Ed.: Thomas Juster. Cambridge, MA: Ballinger, 1977.

Butler, Richard and Heckman, James. "The Impact of Government in the Labor Market Status of Black Americans: A Critical Review of the Literature and Some New Evidence." Unpub. ms., 1977.

Cogan, John F. "The Decline in Black Teenage Employment: 1960–1970," *Amer. Econ. Rev.,* Sept. 1982, 72(4), pp. 621–38.

Darity, William A., Jr. "The Human Capital Approach to Black-White Earnings Inequality: Some Unsettled Questions," *J. Human Res.,* Winter 1982, 17(1), pp. 72–93.

Freeman, Richard B. "Changes in the Labor Market for Black Americans, 1948–1972," *Brookings Pap. Econ. Act.* 1973, 1, pp. 67–120.

Haworth, Joan Gustafson; Gwartney, James and Haworth, Charles. "Earnings, Productivity, and Changes in Employment Discrimination during the 1960's," *Amer. Econ. Rev.,* Mar. 1975, 65(1), pp. 158–68.

Link, Charles. "Black Education, Earnings, and Interregional Migration: A Comment and Some New Evidence," *Amer. Econ. Rev.,* Mar. 1975, 65, pp. 236–40.

Murray, Charles A. *Losing ground—American social policy, 1950–1980.* NY: Basic Books, 1984.

Myrdal, Gunnar. *An American dilemma.* NY: Harper and Brothers, 1944.

Osterman, Paul. "An Empirical Study of Labor Market Segmentation," *Ind. Lab. Relat. Rev.,* July 1975, *28*(4), pp. 508–23.

Piore, Michael J. "The Dual Labor Market," in *Problems in political economy.* Ed.: David M. Gordon. Lexington, MA: D.C. Heath and Co., 1971.

Reich, Michael. "Segmented Labour, Time Series Hypothesis and Evidence," *Cambridge J. Econ.,* Mar. 1984, *8*(1), pp. 63–81.

Rumberger, Russell W. and Carnoy, Martin. "Segmentation in the US Labour Market: Its Effect on the Mobility and Earnings of Whites and Blacks," *Cambridge J. Econ.,* June 1980, *4*(2), pp. 117–32.

Smith, James P. "Race and Human Capital," *Amer. Econ. Rev.,* Sept. 1984, *74*(4), pp. 685–98.

Smith, James P. and Welch, Finis. "Affirmative Action and Labor Markets," *J. Lab. Econ.,* Apr. 1984, *2*(2), pp. 269–302.

———. "Race and Poverty: A Forty-Year Record," *Amer. Econ. Rev.,* May 1987, *77*(2), pp. 152–58.

Vroman, Wayne. "Changes in Black Workers Relative Earnings: Evidence from the Sixties." Unpub. ms., Apr. 1973.

Weiss, Leonard and Williamson, Jeffrey. Black Education, Earnings, and Interregional Migration: Some New Evidence," *Amer. Econ. Rev.,* June 1972, *62*(3), pp. 372–83.

Welch, Finis. "Education and Racial Discrimination," in *Discrimination in labor markets.* Eds.: Orley Ashenfelter and Albert Rees. Princeton: Princeton U. Press, 1974.

Wilson, William J. "Social Policy and Minority Groups." Paper presented at the Institute for Research on Poverty Conference on Minorities and Poverty, Dec. 1988.

13

Continuous Versus Episodic Change:
The Impact of Civil Rights Policy
on the Economic Status
of Blacks

John J. Donohue III and James Heckman

INTRODUCTION

Professional economists are currently divided in their assessment of the contribution of federal civil rights policy to the elevation of black economic status. One group of scholars argues that long-term secular trends in migration and educational attainment largely explain what is viewed as continuous black economic progress. Other scholars focus on the substantial improvement in relative earnings, wages, and occupational status that occurs during the 1960s, and assign a major role to governmental antidiscrimination and affirmative action efforts.[1] The magnitude and timing of this improvement is potentially significant because it coincides with both the effective date of Title VII of the 1964 Civil Rights Act, which forbids discrimination in employment, and the establishment of the Office of Federal Contract Compliance (OFCC), which monitors the antidiscrimination and affirmative action responsibilities of government contractors, as well as the passage of the Voting Rights Act of 1965 and other Federal initiatives designed to eliminate discrimination against blacks.

This essay critically examines the available evidence on the causes of black economic advance in order to assess the contribution of Federal policy. . . . We conclude that the sources of black improvement since 1940 differ among decades: the story of black economic progress is not one of uniform secular advance, but rather of episodic change. Northern migration of blacks out of the low-wage South played a major role until the mid-1960s, but accounts for little of the post-1964 change. There is considerable evidence in the recent literatures in

Excerpts reprinted with permission from the *Journal of Economic Literature* 1991 (December), vol. 29:1603–1643. Copyright © 1991 by the American Economic Association.

sociology and economics that the lack of growth of relative black economic progress since 1975 is due to the decline in the relative wages paid to unskilled versus skilled workers. At issue is what accounts for black progress between 1960 and 1975.

Evidence of sustained improvement in black relative earnings after the introduction of the Federal antidiscrimination effort does not establish that it is due to this policy. But it raises the credibility of that argument. The case for a government policy effect violates two widely held canons of current professional standards. First, it suggests that something other than "basic economic forces" accounts for an important economic phenomenon. The argument is controversial in some circles because it suggests that an *improvement* in black status was due to government policy. Second, the econometric evidence supporting this position is weak in large part because available measures of Federal activity or pressure are weak. Indeed, resort to measures such as the number of employment discrimination cases filed with the Equal Opportunity Commission (EEOC) or in Federal district courts gives rise to the enigma that when the number of cases skyrocketed in the mid-1970s and 1980s, there is little evidence of relative black advance. Yet, in the late 1960s and early 1970s, the period of the greatest black wage and employment gains, policy agency budgets were small, enforcement powers were limited, and the number of private antidiscrimination cases was modest. If the visible indicators of Federal enforcement were weak, how could the effects of Federal activity have been so strong?

Any economic argument with these features has much going against it. At issue is whether the argument has anything going for it. We argue that it does, although, admittedly, the evidence supporting a successful federal intervention is more like that assembled by Sherlock Holmes rather than that routinely published in *Econometrica*.

We contend that the enigma of the apparent temporal mismatch between the intensity of the federal antidiscrimination effort and the period of significant black progress is largely attributable to a misconstruction of Federal civil rights policy. Close scrutiny of Federal activity in the early 1960s reveals a massive attack launched against racial exclusion in Southern employment, voting, and accommodations. . . . Studies that focus solely on the impact of fair employment policy miss the crucial point that it was only one part of a total Federal effort directed against a way of life that previously excluded blacks from many sectors of Southern society. This restricted focus neglects both the size of the entire Federal intervention in the South and the spillovers to employment of successful federal challenges to school segregation and voting exclusion.

Consequently, direct measures of OFCC affirmative action enforcement and of EEOC and private Title VII enforcement understate the full thrust of the Federal activity in that region. Despite difficulties in quantifying the extent of this Federal effort, its existence and well documented success in challenging an entire pattern of racial conduct help to explain how an apparent straw might have broken the back of Southern employment discrimination. Substantial numbers of Southern employers appear to have been willing to gain access to the supply of cheap black labor, but required the excuse of the Federal pressure to defy long-standing community norms regarding employment of blacks. . . . When all aspects of the Federal attack on Southern discrimination are considered, there is significant alignment between the strength of the Federal pressure in the South and the accompanying rise in black economic status there.

The focus on the South serves another important methodological function. One of the most intractable difficulties in assessing the impact of any law is to distinguish the effects of government intervention from those stemming from changes in the underlying attitudes that led to the passage of the legislation in the first place. By noting that black relative improvement was most rapid in the South, we not only make more credible the argument that Federal policy was effective in the period 1965–1975 but also serve to counter the argument that the laws themselves were merely the manifestation of preexisting social change. Federal activity was imposed on the South and had its greatest apparent effect in the region that resisted it the most.

Our focus on labor market and social outcomes that occurred after 1964 should not be interpreted to mean that large scale civil rights activity began in the South in that year. Most scholars of Southern history (C. Vann Woodward 1968) consider 1954 to be the watershed year in which the South was confronted by a direct Federal challenge to its racially discriminatory system. In the *Brown v. Board of Education* decision of that year, the Supreme Court invalidated the "separate but equal" schooling that existed throughout the South. . . .

We focus on the post-1964 period because by then the constitutional prohibition of segregation had been clarified and widely endorsed outside of the South, and the willingness of the executive branch of the U.S. government to enforce the constitutional mandate ending government-sanctioned segregation in the South and of the legislative branch to extend its reach to private behavior had been demonstrated. Our evaluation of the 1964 Civil Rights Act and related legislative and executive acts is really an evaluation of those laws *and* the prior civil rights activity that stimulated them. . . .

Our paper develops in the following way. Section I presents the evidence for sustained improvement in the labor market status of black males beginning in the mid-1960s. Focusing on males because of the wealth of information on that demographic group, we establish the following facts. There is an upward jump in the time series of black earnings and wages relative to white earnings and wages beginning in the mid-1960s. The South was the region of the greatest black economic advance in the period 1960–1970, accounting for at least two-thirds of the increase in black economic status over the decade. There is evidence of substantial desegregation of firms in the South during the crucial 1965–1970 period. This black economic progress following the passage of Title VII coincided with a sharp drop in the outflow of blacks from the South, and even led to black migration into that region between 1970 and 1980.

Section II of the paper documents that during the seventy-year period from 1920–1990, two periods of relative black progress stand out—the period of rebound from the Great Depression brought on by World War II and the 1965–1975 period. The major studies advocating the continuity hypothesis are analyzed, and three conclusions emerge. First, black migration contributed little and relative increases in the quantity of black education contributed modestly to black progress after 1965. Second, the main cause of the observed black relative economic gains during this period are relative black increases in the returns to education. Such increases can be the product of either improvements in schooling quality or changes in the demand for black labor induced by declining racial discrimination, government civil rights policy, or tight labor markets. David Card and Alan Krueger (1991) estimate that roughly 15–20 percent of the black gains in the twenty-year period following 1960 were attributable to relative schooling quality improvements. They find that the narrowing racial gap in years of education completed played virtually no role in elevating black relative wages, while James Smith and Finis Welch (1980) would attribute 20–25 percent of the black relative wage gain to this source. Third, perhaps 10–20 percent of post-1964 black progress is attributable to the selective removal of low-wage blacks from the workforce (James Heckman 1989). Even if one accepts the set of estimates least favorable to the Federal pressure hypothesis, fully 35 percent of the relative black wage gains cannot be explained by any suggested supply-side factor.

Finally, in Section III, we attempt to focus on the possible demand-side influences for the well-documented post-1964 advance in black relative status. There is general agreement in the literature that the Office of Federal Contract Compliance produced a large increase in the employment of blacks in firms required to implement affirmative action programs during the period 1966–1980. Such evidence on employment shifts, however, does not necessarily imply commensurate large-scale wage gains or even an overall boost to black employment. Missing are key parameters—the elasticities of the demand and supply of labor by race to firms and to sectors. A high inter-sectoral supply elasticity could lead to a large shift of black workers into contractor firms without significantly elevating either U.S. aggregate black employment or black wages. The available econometric studies of Title VII and EEOC enforcement activity have reached conflicting conclusions and in general have not received widespread acceptance because of the methodological difficulties in estimating the impact of a law with near uniform applicability. Nonetheless, while the precise mechanism through which Federal pressure was translated into black economic gains is not yet clear, a richer conception of the multifaceted Federal pressure designed primarily to break the racial segregation of the South succeeds in aligning the intensity of government pressure with the period and location of greatest black progress.

I.   THE IMPROVEMENT IN BLACK RELATIVE ECONOMIC STATUS

The simplest depiction of the changes in black relative economic status since 1953 is provided in Figure 1, which presents the time series of the median earnings of full-time black male workers relative to the same measure for white males for the entire country. The graph reveals that significant black progress has occurred. . . . [A] decade of unbroken black progress begins in 1965, followed by a period of decline. Thus, the aggregate black/white earnings ratio rose from .62 in 1964 to .72 by 1975, but then fell with the 1987 figure at .69.

While the existence of the sustained post-1965 growth of the black/white earnings ratio is revealing, its cause is uncertain. Conceivably, the booming economy during the second half of the 1960s or relative improvements in education might help to explain the black economic advance. Richard Freeman (1973) demonstrated, however, that the pattern of post-1964 acceleration in black male relative earnings persists in aggregate Current Population Survey (CPS) data time-series regressions that control for the state of aggregate demand (business cycle effects) and relative educational attainment going back to 1948.[2] Three subsequent analyses that extend the time series forward have confirmed Freeman's original finding: Freeman (1981), Charles Brown (1984), and more recently Wayne Vroman (1989). . . .

But while the evidence for discontinuity is clear using the standards of modern time-series analysis, the reliance on aggregate national data obscures some important features in the improvement of black relative economic status. Figures 2– 5 disaggregate the same time series of relative median earnings of full-time black and white male workers into four Census regions. Underscoring a pattern first noticed in Richard Butler and James Heckman (1977), these figures reveal the importance of the South in accounting for aggregate black progress. The 1965– 1975 growth in the aggregate wage data is a consequence of imposing a Southern upward trend that began in the early 1960s on top of a post-1964 progression in the North Central region that stagnated after 1975.[3] The other regions show little trend in black relative status over much of the period 1953–1987. . . .

Additional micro evidence on this question is given in a recent paper by John Bound and Richard Freeman (1989). Using CPS annual March Demographic Files, they estimated wage equations for males age 20–64 for every year from 1963–1984 controlling for race, region, urban status, age (using separate dummy variables for each year of age), and years of education. Bound and Freeman them computed a time series of estimated racial differentials (the coefficient on a race dummy variable equal to one if a person is black) for both log annual and weekly earnings, . . . and demonstrate that the truly dramatic relative economic gain for blacks came in the South. . . .

Further evidence on the importance of developments in the South in account- ing for black economic progress is presented in Richard Butler, James Heckman and Brook Payner (1989). . . . In a study using Equal Employment Opportunity

Ratio of Non-white to White Total Money Income
of Year-Round Full-time Male Workers, 1955–1989

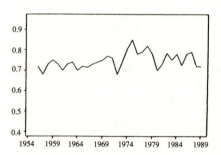

Figure 1. United States

Figure 3. Midwestern region

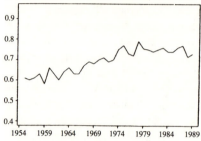

Figure 2. Northeastern region

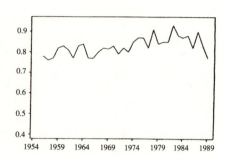

Figure 4. Western region

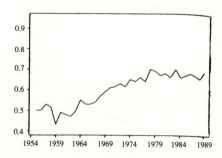

Figure 5. Southern region

Commission data, Orley Ashenfelter and James Heckman (1976) also emphasized the extent of black progress in the South. . . .

II. DO MIGRATION AND INCREASED EDUCATION EXPLAIN POST-1964 BLACK GAINS?

The evidence of episodic as opposed to continuous black economic progress is in apparent conflict with the story of secular black improvement summarized in the following quotation from Smith and Welch:

> The racial wage gap narrowed as rapidly in the 20 years prior to 1960 (and before affirmative action) as during the 20 years afterward. This suggests that the slowly evolving historical forces we have emphasized . . . —education and migration— were the primary determinants of the long-term black economic improvement. At best, affirmative action has marginally altered black wage gains around this long-term trend. (Smith and Welch 1989)

This statement raises two questions: (1) was the post-1964 relative black improvement simply part of a longer historical trend of black progress? and (2) do migration and increased education explain post-1964 black gains? . . .

A.   Was the Post-1964 Relative Black Improvement Simply Part of a Longer Historical Trend of Black Progress?

Donald Dewey (1952, p. 282) notes that in the South:

> In the fifty years before World War II the relative position of Negro workers in Southern industry actually deteriorated; they did not share proportionately in the expansion of urban employment and they were not upgraded as individuals into jobs previously held by whites.

Stability in the racial status quo in the South is the conclusion of Dewey's work. Both Dewey and Gunnar Myrdal (1944) document that blacks were excluded from new industries and occupations in the South over the period 1890–1940. To the extent there was any black advance, it occurred because of migration to the North. Secular trends of improving relative education and advancing industrialization in the South coincided with the stagnant economic status of Southern blacks in the pre-World War II period.

Recent studies of the economic history of South Carolina blacks support the pre-World War II stagnation hypothesis of Dewey and Myrdal as well as the hypothesis of post-1964 sustained advance. . . . Textiles has long been the major manufacturing employer in the state, accounting for 80 percent of all manufacturing employment in 1940 and more than 50 percent in 1970. Through two World Wars, the Great Depression and the Korean War, the share of blacks remained low and stable, despite the fact that the industry was expanding in employment throughout this period. Even when young white men left their manufacturing jobs to fight in World War II, they were replaced not by older black men but by white women. The breakthrough in black employment occurred only after 1964. Black male and female wages (relative to those of white males) accelerated in the industry after that date. The breakthrough in textiles occurred primarily in the nonurban South Atlantic region which is documented by Smith and Welch (1978) to have been the region of the greatest black relative wage gains over the period 1968–1974.

Gavin Wright (1986, 1988) similarly corroborates Myrdal (1944) by documenting the long-term stability in the Southern industrial division of labor by race. The pre-World War II position of blacks was rigidly maintained in the South despite increases in their relative educational levels and the quality of their schooling. Blacks were systematically excluded from new industries during this period. . . . [B]lack progress in South Carolina after World War II occurred in new firms and new sectors of the economy that were not bound by the rigid racial practices of the prewar South.

In summary, . . . blacks failed to gain relative to whites in the 1920s (Smith 1984). In the 1930s, the Great Depression and New Deal acreage restriction policies which encouraged capital intensive agricultural methods in the South had a disproportionately adverse impact on blacks (Myrdal 1944). Blacks rebounded economically in the 1940s with the tight labor markets induced by World War II. Relative stagnation for blacks characterizes the 1950s and 1980s, leaving the periods around World War II and following the passage of the 1964 Civil Rights Act as the only significant spells of relative black progress over the seventy year span from 1920 through 1990. Even though black relative gains were of comparable size in the periods from 1940–1960 and from 1960–1980, this equality does not imply a forty-year trend of unbroken progress. It is questionable whether the 1940 Census provides an appropriate benchmark from which to measure black progress given the extraordinarily poor state of the economy during the 1930s and the immense stimulus to aggregate demand provided by the War. Clearly, black progress in this period was generated far more by demand forces than by schooling effects. Focusing purely on the five Census years of 1939, 1949, 1959, 1969, and 1979 can create the illusion of a stable pattern when a more encompassing effort to correlate periods of improvement with specific causal factors would suggest far more episodic change.

B. The Unimportance of Migration After 1965

The story of black migration between 1940 and 1980 is both dramatic and revealing: 14.6 percent of the black population of the South left during the 1940s,

13.7 percent more departed during the 1950s, and an additional 11.9 percent exited during the 1960s. Such immense population shifts—close to a quarter of young black men left the South *each decade* between 1940 and 1970—are readily explained by the substantial wage disparities across regions. For example, in 1960 Southern black men age 30–40 earned 57 percent less than their white Southern counterparts, while the comparable earnings disadvantage for non-Southern black men was only 32 percent. . . . This Southern outmigration provided a powerful stimulus for black relative economic gain.

The 1970s experienced a reversal of this flow since there was actually net black migration to the South during that decade. But an important fact to note is that the abrupt shift in the pace of migration began in the mid-1960s. Of the net outmigration of 1.4 million blacks from the South during the 1960s, only 15.7 percent left after 1965. In other words, the period of 1960–1965 was one of black migration from the South at a pace considerably higher than the average rates of the 1940s and 1950s, while in the period 1965–1970 migration slowed to a near trickle. This sharp curtailment of black migration further buttresses the thesis of sustained economic advance concentrated in the South because it is quite likely that perceived improvements in economic opportunities would staunch the outflow of Southern blacks.[4]

There is uniform agreement that prior to 1960 black migration out of the low-wage South significantly elevated black relative economic status (Smith and Welch 1986; Farley and Allen 1987). But the timing of the drop in black migration also demonstrates that black migration cannot explain the improvements in black economic status beginning in 1965. The vast bulk of any benefits occurring from migration during the 1960s had already been achieved by 1965. If the long-term historical factors emphasized by Smith and Welch are to explain the sustained improvement in black relative earnings beginning in 1965, the story must rest with relative black educational advance.

C.   The Relative Improvement of Black Education

Smith and Welch (1986) have examined the growth of the years of education for blacks and whites, and changes in the labor market returns to this education, in order to determine the contribution of educational advance to increasing black relative earnings. It is useful, in considering their analysis, to note three factors that would tend to elevate relative black earnings: (1) greater relative increases in the number of years of education accumulated by blacks; (2) greater relative improvements in the quality of schools attended by blacks; and (3) greater relative increases in the labor market valuation of black education.

1. The Modest Impact of Relative Increases in the Quantity of Schooling. Smith and Welch reveal that black relative earnings rose from 18 to 35 percent across experience categories in the period from 1960 through 1980. Particularly for younger cohorts, Smith and Welch contend that education is the over-whelmingly dominant factor in explaining this relative advance. . . . Black eco-nomic progress through education has come more from changes in the *rewards* to black education (compared to that of white education) than from increases in the relative quantity of education. The question left unresolved, though, is the rela-tive importance of increases in the relative quality of black education (the supply side) and of lessening labor market discrimination (the demand side) in generat-ing these changing returns to education. . . .

2. *Improving Relative Schooling Quality or Reduced Discrimination?* Smith and Welch (1986) document the sharp decline in the penalty that blacks incurred by living in the South. In a subsequent paper in 1989, they state that two explanations are possible for the rapid movement toward the national norm in the Southern racial wage gap during the 1970s:

> First, black-white skill differences may have converged in the South as the post-World War II cohorts entered the labor market. To illustrate this point, assume that Southern schools were effectively desegregated in 1960, six years after the Brown decision. The first class of Southern black children who had attended entirely desegregated schools would have first entered the labor market in the early to mid-1970s. Some of the improvement in black incomes during the 1970s may have been due to the skills acquired through this improved schooling. However, that is unlikely to be the whole story because there was a substantial erosion in racial wage disparities even among older workers in the 1970s. . . . *A more plausible explana-tion may well be that racial discrimination is waning in the South.* (1989, p. 543, emphasis added)

As Smith and Welch observe, an explanation for black relative progress based on improvement in the quality of black schooling relative to white schooling must contend with the dramatic black economic advance across all experience groups. Moreover, one ordinarily thinks of changes in schooling quality as occur-ring at a continuous, slowly-evolving pace, with wage gains being experienced only by each graduating cohort. Yet the relative wage improvement that we have documented throughout this paper occurs abruptly and across all age groups.

The potentially attractive feature of the desegregation story, though, is that it appears to offer a basis for a discontinuous advance in schooling quality that could translate into a discontinuous improvement in black economic welfare. It is to this issue that we now turn.

D.   The Schooling Quality Hypothesis

Thus far, we have demonstrated that there is ample evidence of substantial change in black relative status over the period 1965–1975, that this change is concentrated in the South, and that is cannot be explained by migration or the relative black increases in the number of years of education. In addition, we noted that the schooling quality argument could not explain across-the-board increases in black relative earnings for cohorts that had previously finished their education. But it is clear, as Smith and Welch have stressed, that for much of this century there have been substantial relative improvements in the quality of education that blacks have received.[5] Figure 6 is a reproduction of a figure produced by Card and Krueger (1990) showing the rather dramatic black relative improvements in the quality of education as measured by three variables: the student-teacher ratio, the length of the school term, and teacher salaries. The trend is in the direction required to support the increase in the estimated schooling coefficients for successive cohorts (or "vintage" effect) reported by Smith and Welch (1986, 1989). . . . Collectively, these studies suggest that the quality improvement hypothesis must be directly investigated.

By linking schooling quality data by race to microdata on earnings, Card and Krueger (1991) have been able to extend the pioneering work of Smith and Welch. Their ultimate conclusion is that schooling quality improvements do contribute significantly to future earnings growth, and that between 15 and 20 percent of the overall growth in black-white relative earnings between 1960 and 1980 was attributable to these relative schooling quality gains. . . .

One might wonder why the rather dramatic relative improvement in measures of schooling quality documented in Figure 6 would play such a modest role in explaining black gains in the period from 1960–1980. Three factors should be noted. First, the dramatic growth in the ratio of black/white teacher salaries in the 1940s was a consequence of successful teacher salary equalization cases brought by the NAACP that substantially eliminated teacher pay inequities (Henry Bullock 1967). Prior to this NAACP campaign, the disparities in expenditure partly reflected discrimination in salaries, and the rapid elimination of such discrimination may create the illusion of rapidly growing schooling quality. But rather than reflecting a higher average level of black school teachers, the evidence indicates that the existing stock of black school teachers received higher salaries. Any improvement in real teacher quality was likely to have taken considerably more time and been far more gradual in its effects. . . .

Second, the long-term continuous improvement in the relative educational quality enjoyed by blacks is an unlikely source of the secular improvement in black economic welfare that occurred in the decade from 1965–1975.[6] Any claim of improved schooling quality based on the effective desegregation of Southern schools by 1960 is demonstrably false. Despite the *Brown* decision in 1954, virtually no desegregation of schools in the Deep South had occurred by 1960. In 1963 . . . 99 percent of black students in 11 Southern states attended all black schools (U.S. Commission on Civil Rights 1964, Table 2A). Real desegregation began to occur only after the passage of Titles IV and VI of the 1964 Civil Rights Act, which threatened segregated school districts with cutoffs of

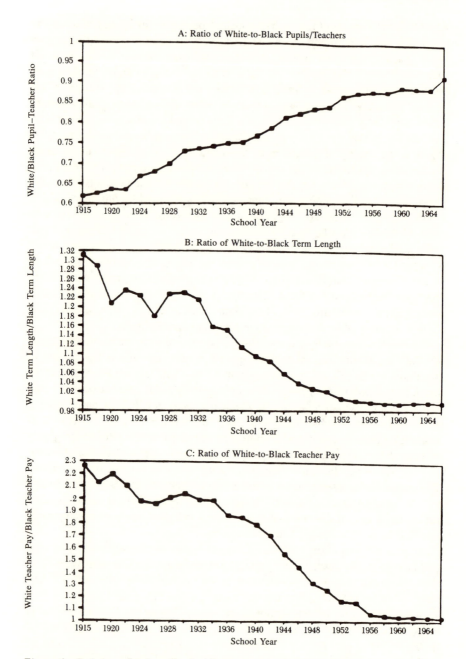

Figure 6. Relative school quality in 18 segregated states, 1915–1966
Source: Card and Krueger 1991, Figure 1.

federal funds and enforcement actions by the Department of Justice. Still, the proportion of blacks in segregated schools had only fallen to 78 percent by 1968. In the landmark decisions of *Green* and *Alexander* in 1968 and 1969, however, the Supreme Court forcefully declared that the command of *Brown* that states must desegregate "with all deliberate speed" finally meant "Now!"[7] The results were dramatic: the number of blacks students attending segregated schools dropped from 78 percent in 1968 to 25 percent in 1972 (Gary Orfield 1983, Table 2; U.S. Commission on Civil Rights 1969, Table 1). Since desegregation in the 11 Southern states occurred roughly ten years after Smith and Welch claimed, any benefits from this desegregation would occur in the early 1980s rather than the early 1970s, as they asserted. Desegregation simply comes too late to explain black economic progress over the decade from 1965–1975.

Finally, it is well documented that the post-*Brown* era (1954–1972) was a period of turmoil in Southern education. Opposition to desegregation led to bombings in Tennessee and riots throughout the South. . . . While there is evidence of greater increases in expenditures for black Southern schools than for white Southern schools between 1953 and 1957, the disruptive effects of Southern opposition to forced desegregation may have been serious enough to offset at least some of the relative schooling quality gains for blacks in the post-1954 era until integration was completed in the late 1960s or early 1970s.

Where does this leave us in our effort to account for black relative advance in the decade following the effective date of Title VII in 1965? We have noted that migration had no effect and increases in the years of education had small effects on black relative progress after 1965. Given Card and Krueger's estimate for the period 1960–1980 of 15–20 percent as the contribution of relative black schooling gains to black relative earnings advances, it would seem that a considerable portion of the black economic progress enjoyed in the post-1964 era cannot be explained by the long-term forces of migration and educational improvement.

We should also note that attachment to the labor force has been dropping faster for blacks than for whites over much of the last three decades. If labor force dropouts tend to be relatively low earners, this selection effect would bias upward the measured growth in black relative earnings. The studies reviewed in Heckman (1989) suggest that the selective attrition of low wage blacks from the labor force likely accounts for 10–20 percent of the black measured wage gains. Conceivably, selective attrition of low-wage blacks could have been concentrated in the South accounting for some of the improvements in the relative wages of Southern blacks over the decade beginning in 1965 and creating the impression of greater economic gains for blacks in the South than in the North. This view receives little support. . . . The relative drop-out rates in the non-South are actually greater than in the South. . . .

If one accepts the Card and Krueger estimates of 15–20 percent as the contribution of relative black schooling gains and the virtually zero role of migration after the mid-1960s, we have perhaps explained between 25 and 40 percent of the measured black gains. Even granting a 25 percent contribution from relative black gains in years of education leaves a sizable unexplained residual. Combining this evidence with the evidence aligning black gains in the South with the focus of the multi-pronged federal assault on racial discrimination in that region lends considerable credence to the argument that government played a considerable role in elevating black economic welfare.

A more expansive conception of Federal action would commensurately increase the proportion of black relative gains attributable to governmental action. For example, at least some of the relative black school quality gains documented in Figure 6 were the product of federal court action in response to NAACP lawsuits seeking to enforce the constitutional mandate of separate but equal in the pre-*Brown* era. Moreover, when educational benefits for black students did come in the form of forced desegregation of Southern schools in the late 1960s and early 1970s, they were the direct product of a massive effort of the legislative, executive, and judicial branches of the Federal government. To a significant degree, the "schooling quality" argument relies on schooling quality engineered by Federal action.

III. DEMAND-SIDE INFLUENCES ON BLACK ECONOMIC PROGRESS

A. Federal Policy Impacts

Most analyses of the impact of Federal civil rights policy on the economic status of black Americans focus on the activities of two Federal agencies: the Equal Employment Opportunity Commission (EEOC) and the Office of Federal Contract Compliance (OFCC). The EEOC was established to monitor compliance with Title VII of the 1964 Civil Rights Act. The law prohibited discrimination in pay, promotion, hiring, termination, and training. Until 1972, the EEOC was limited to merely a passive role: processing complaints, serving as a conciliator, and entering cases as a "friend of the court" only after their initiation by other parties. When the Civil Rights Act was strengthened in 1972, the EEOC was given the authority to initiate litigation on its own.

The OFCC was established in 1965 by Executive Order 11246, which prohibited discrimination by race among Federal contractors above a certain size (with contracts greater than $50,000 and more than 50 employees). Employment in all of a firm's operations were covered, even those unrelated to production for the government. The order was amended to include sex in 1967 (Executive Order 11375). In 1968, the OFCC required Federal government contractors to prepare affirmative action plans that would eliminate any "underutilization" of black workers. Failure to conform with the Executive Order would potentially result in sanctions ranging from disbarment from Federal contracts to fines, backpay awards, and injunctive relief. In 1978, the Office of Federal Contract Compliance Programs (OFCCP) was established to incorporate the OFCC and eleven other compliance agencies into a unified enforcement agency with the Department of Labor.[8]

1. The Contract Compliance Program. Microstudies of the OFCC are summarized in Butler and Heckman (1977), Brown (1982), Jonathan Leonard (1984c), and the U.S. Commission on Civil Rights (1986). . . . The evidence . . . using large national samples reveals the following pattern. Ashenfelter and Heckman (1976) and Leonard (1984c) find that, over the periods 1966–1970 and 1974–1980, the annual rate of relative growth of black male employment in contractor firms was .82 percentage points higher than in noncontractor firms. Using a slightly different specification with the same data set, Leonard (1984b) found that the relative growth of black male employment in contractor firms from 1974–1980 was only .42 percent per year higher than in noncontractor firms. Goldstein and R. Smith estimate a slight decline in black male relative employment in contractor firms in the period 1970–1972. All the studies agree that the added effect of an OFCC compliance review on black male employment is positive and greater in magnitude than the effect of merely being a government contractor.

The effect of contractor status and compliance reviews on the relative occupational position of blacks is in general positive but somewhat less than the impact of these factors on the relative employment of blacks. . . . Because of the absence of wage data in the reports filed with the EEOC, there are no direct estimates of the contribution of the OFCC to black relative wage gains. . . . [A] second set of studies has used wage data from the CPS to assess the impact of the contract compliance program. For the period 1967–1974, Smith and Welch (1977) regress black and white male wages on the standard set of CPS variables already discussed in Section I plus dummy variables for government employment (state, local, and Federal) and the percent of industry output sold to the government for private firms. They find that over their sample period the rate of improvement in black male wages relative to white male wages was most rapid in the noncontracting private sector. They conclude that government contract compliance programs had a negligible impact on aggregate black male wages. Conversely, Leonard (1985) concludes on the basis of cross-section earnings regressions of CPS data for 1973 and 1978 that black males earn higher wages in sectors where affirmative action is prevalent (measured as the proportion of employment in an individual's SMSA and industry that is in Federal contractor establishments). But since Leonard notes that adding industry dummies to his regression equation often eliminates the impact of the "proportion contractor" variable on relative racial wages, it is uncertain whether his results are explained by affirmative action or by some unspecified industry effect.

Neither set of studies provides convincing estimates of the aggregate impact of the OFCC on the relative wages or employment level of black males. Missing is knowledge of key parameters of factor demand and sectoral labor supply elasticities. . . . Because the presence of a governmental effect has been confirmed, although its precise nature is still uncertain, further investigation using better data is now warranted. To obtain a more refined estimate of the impact of the contract compliance program, it will be necessary to employ a general equilibrium model that includes the key ingredients of sectoral supply and demand parameters by race.

2. *Title VII Litigation and the EEOC.*   The available evidence on the impact of Title VII and EEOC enforcement activities is even more meager than that examining the OFCC. Because the entire country is covered by the law (except for firms with fewer than fifteen employees), there is no natural comparison group against which to measure the impact of the law. One is forced to use notoriously fragile aggregate time-series methods to ferret out EEOC effects from numerous other changes that affected the post-1964 American economy. Freeman (1973, 1981) uses cumulative EEOC expenditure—basically a post-1964 time trend—to estimate the impact of this agency using aggregate time-series data. His variable reproduces the aggregate shift already discussed in Section I. . . .

Andrea Beller (1978) explores the effect of discrimination charges filed with the EEOC on both the relative employment and relative wages of black males. She finds that Title VII had only weak effects in the late 1960s, but her study has not been widely accepted because of serious interpretative questions arising from potential reverse causality (Butler and Heckman 1977). The problem is that the frequency of suits in a jurisdiction may be high relative to other jurisdictions either because discrimination is pervasive or because its citizens are more litigious. While Beller recognizes the problem of mutual causation between charges and outcomes and tries to correct for the simultaneous equation bias, her solution—assuming that the presence of a regional EEOC office in a state affects the volume of charges filed in the state and is unrelated to the extent of discrimination—is questionable. The causal link between the number of suits and the presence of an EEOC office may run more strongly in the other direction—the EEOC may locate regional offices where the expected number of claims is high.

Leonard (1984a) offers a more favorable assessment of the impact of Title VII. On the basis of a cross-section study, he reports that the number of Title VII class action lawsuits per corporation is correlated with significantly greater increases in the percentage of black workers over the period from 1966 to 1978.

An indirect argument against strong government policy effects has been advanced by Butler and Heckman (1977) and Smith and Welch (1984). . . . During the crucial period 1965–1975, enforcement budgets were low during the time black advance was so rapid. Few federal contractors lost their contracts because of OFCC actions. Knowledgeable observers such as Phyllis Wallace (1975), James Jones (1976), and Gregory Ahart (1976) write about understaffed EEOC and OFCC offices. Ahart (1976) notes that EEOC and OFCC did not coordinate their enforcement efforts.

From these accounts, the federal effort appears weak during the period in which black breakthroughs in employment and wages took place. As enforcement budgets grew, black relative gains fell off and actually receded in some sectors. These well-documented features of the Federal enforcement effort pose an apparently enigmatic pattern for proponents of the view that federal policy mattered.

B.   A More Refined View of Federal Policy

But the enigma is resolved if one adopts a more refined view of Federal policy that is at once broader in its conception of the Federal tools that were brought to bear in attacking racial discrimination and narrower in its geographic focus concerning the targeting of this Federal action. We have stressed throughout that much of the black improvement in the decade following enactment of Title VII of the 1964 Civil Rights Act came in the South, and it strengthens the case for the importance of the governmental effort to note that most of the Federal activity was directed toward that region. First, Title VII was primarily intended to combat discrimination against blacks in the South—virtually the only area of the country where state laws forbidding racial discrimination had not yet been enacted. . . . Second, a substantial portion of the complaints filed with the EEOC and federal employment discrimination litigation occurred in the South. . . . Roughly half of all charges filed with the Equal Employment Opportunity Commission over the period 1966–1972 originated in the South. Over this same period, more than half of all employment discrimination cases filed in federal court were brought in the South (Peter Siegelman 1990; Jerome Culp 1985, Table 1).

Furthermore, the view that initially enforcement was weak and that it became strong much later is exaggerated. Although . . . the number of employment discrimination cases filed in federal court is very low during the period of considerable black progress and very high during the period of black stagnation, these raw figures create an inaccurate impression of the intensity of civil rights activity for a number of reasons. First, almost all of the growth in employment discrimination cases since the early 1970s has come from cases alleging wrongful discharge, yet it is cases of hiring and wage discrimination, which predominated in the early days of Title VII, that are more likely to generate positive employment and wage effects for blacks (Donohue and Siegelman 1991). Second, the dramatic decline in the number of class action lawsuits at the same time that the number of individual suits rose exponentially once again indicates that the degree of Federal pressure was greater at a time when the number of cases brought was far smaller than the current level.[9] Third, case filings and resolutions probably lag behind effective enforcement, and in general are noisy indicators of enforcement efforts. Employers (even those who are entirely innocent) commonly respond to the threat of litigation or the filing of the lawsuit with some remedial action, thereby obscuring the causal link between the onset or resolution of litigation and favorable employment outcomes for minority workers.

Moreover, the South was the target of Federal civil rights policy in many areas in addition to employment, and it severely understates the magnitude of the Federal effort to focus purely on discrimination in the workplace. The 1954 *Brown v. Board of Education* was an attack on de jure school segregation—a practice that was most prevalent in Southern states and the District of Columbia. The 1962 and 1965 Voting Rights Acts were also focused on the South where blacks had been excluded from political life for over 70 years. In other words, Federal employment discrimination policies were imposed on a pre-existing larger Federal agenda designed to undermine the rigid racial segregation of the South.

There is ample evidence that Federal voting rights and school desegregation policies were effective in the South, especially during the crucial years 1965–1975. . . . There is a sharp jump in black voter registration during the period 1962–1970. . . . Similarly, as we discussed above, the period of greatest desegregation of Southern schools came between 1968 and 1972 as the Federal courts strictly interpreted the mandate of the Constitution and Federal law to call for affirmative integration of Southern schools. Over this short period of time, Southern schools went from being the most segregated to the least segregated in the country. . . .

This evidence indicates the magnitude of the Federal activity on behalf of blacks in the South and reveals its success, at least in the area of school desegregation and voting rights. Even if the South had not been the intended target of Federal legislation and administrative decrees, any rational enforcement strategy would initially have concentrated attention on the South. The wholesale exclusion or segregation of blacks in employment, accommodations, schooling, and voting was easy to document and prove in court cases.

Moreover, in certain ways the South was ripe for change. There is evidence that some Southern employers were eager to employ blacks if given the proper excuse. In their study of the dramatic breakthrough in the employment of blacks in the South Carolina textile industry that began in 1965, Butler, Heckman, and Payner (1989) document that employment of blacks slowed down the growth of labor costs and kept the industry competitive in the period 1965–1975 in the face of rising foreign competition. Integration of geographically isolated textile mills was aided by integration of housing, schooling, and employment, and therefore the results of the multi-pronged Federal effort in all of these areas were mutually reinforcing. Integration occurred rapidly and without major incidents. After 55 years of near total exclusion, blacks became a significant fraction of total industry employment, and black wages rose relative to white wages.

The rapid progress of blacks in the South in the crucial period 1965–1975 is consistent with the multiple equilibria explicit in the tipping models of T. C. Schelling (1971) and George Akerlof (1980). Specifically, Akerlof's model of social custom provides a coherent interpretive framework for the experience of the South in the late 1960s and early 1970s, as an example from the history of Southern school desegregation shows. . . . The firmly entrenched custom of segregation, enforced through pressures from neighbors and employers, made further integration impossible even as the attitudes that gave rise to the custom began to change (Wasby, D'Amato, and Metrailer 1977). Enforcement of the law in the wake of the previously discussed Supreme Court decisions in 1968 and 1969 may have been necessary to break the log jam even when a substantial majority was no longer opposed to desegregation.

Similarly, community norms may have made marginal experimentation in hiring black workers privately costly. (Wright, 1988, reports six such failed attempts in the early history of the textile industry.) Unlike the school desegregation situation, there were monetary benefits to be obtained by employers if they could tap the black workforce without incurring the wrath of their communities. Federal pressure may have tipped the balance and led to a new equilibrium that employers collectively embraced but were individually unable to initiate. In the particular case of the textile industry—where integration of employment mutually reinforced integration of housing and schooling—the multipronged nature of the Federal effort may have been particularly effective.

In sum, the "enigma" of rapid black advance during a period of low Federal enforcement budgets may not be enigmatic at all. The early success of Federal policy occurred because it was targeted toward the South where racial exclusion was blatant. A multipronged Federal effort enlisted willing employers who needed an excuse for doing what they wanted to do anyway. Post-1975 evidence of growing enforcement budgets with weaker employment and wage effects for black workers may largely be a manifestation of the triumph of the initial Southern initiative and diminishing returns to a Federal enforcement effort that turned Northward, and began focusing on sex and age discrimination in addition to racial discrimination.

IV.   CONCLUSION

The debate over the role of Federal civil rights policy in generating black economic progress can be framed as the division between supply and demand explanations and monolithic forces as opposed to episodic change. To be sure, long-term supply factors did generate upward pressure on black earnings and levels of employment over a considerable period of time. But prior to World War II this pressure was ineffective in the South. Much of the significant black economic progress that occurred in the twenty-year period from 1940 to 1960 was the product of migration out of the South. Progress continued over the next twenty years, particularly in the decade from 1965 to 1975, even though Northern migration had ended by that time. We have noted the finding of numerous studies that the overall strength of the economy does not solely explain black relative progress in this period, and that 10–20 percent of measured black relative gains were generated by the selective attrition of blacks from the labor force. In addition, according to Card and Krueger, schooling quality improvements for blacks explain another 15–20 percent of the black relative gains between 1960 and 1980, while the contribution of schooling quantity gains is no larger. Consequently, a considerable portion of the post-1965 black progress would appear to be unexplained by the usual supply-side sources, which may suggest that the role of governmental antidiscrimination efforts was substantial. A major obstacle to attributing the remaining unexplained portion of the post-1964 black progress to Federal civil rights activity is that this position cannot be readily verified or falsified through standard econometric tests because of the difficulties in measuring Federal pressure.

In the introduction to this paper we noted that Federal *judicial* pressure on the South to desegregate began in 1954 with the *Brown* decision by the U.S. Supreme Court. That decision served to invigorate a large-scale private civil rights movement but also provoked widespread white resistance. The result was turmoil in the South over the period 1954–1964. Although white resistance slowed black progress in schooling and may have impeded black labor market advance in the short run, some of this turmoil had a strong effect in generating national support for civil rights legislation. Many southern leaders recognized that change in racial relations was inevitable and integrated workplaces and public facilities. This contributed to black improvement in the region that begins before 1964. The 1964 Civil Rights Acts and related executive orders and legislation presented the South with a unified, vigorous attack on blatant discrimination. It is fair to say that 1964 was the year that effective *legislative* and *executive* pressure was applied to the South. However, it is important to keep in mind that the post-54 civil rights activity laid the foundations for the 1964 laws and orders and brought about social change in its own right. It is inappropriate to attribute all of the impact of Federal policy to civil rights laws passed in 1964, but it is difficult—if not impossible—to parse out the effects of pre-64 from post-64 activity.

However such a division might be made, the nature, location, and timing of black progress in the decade following the passage of the 1964 Civil Rights Act and the creation of the Office of Federal Contract Compliance support a Federal enforcement story. With the greatest relative black improvement coming in the South, which was the target of a comprehensive Federal effort to dismantle segregation in schooling, voting, accommodations, and employment, the inference is buttressed that Federal civil rights policy was the major contributor to the sustained improvement in black economic status that began in 1965. Future work will have to explore more carefully the mechanism by which the Federal antidiscrimination framework translated the command of law into significant black economic advance.

ACKNOWLEDGMENTS

This research was supported by the American Bar Foundation and NSF 87-11845. The authors thank Henry Aaron, Ian Ayres, Gary Becker, David Card, Mark Killingsworth, Alan Krueger, Robert Margo, Dan Ortiz, Len Rubinowitz, George Rutherglen, Stewart Schwab, Peter Siegelman, Rip Verkerke, James Walker, two anonymous referees, and participants in workshops at Princeton University, University of Virginia, and Yale University for their helpful comments on drafts of this paper. The first draft of this paper was prepared in 1989. Sue Holmes and Kirsten Muth provided excellent research assistance.

NOTES

1.   References to "relative" characteristics, such as earnings or years of education, are to the black/white ratio of these characteristics, unless otherwise noted.
2.   The controls for the educational attainments of blacks and whites are based on the number of years of school attended. As we discuss below, however, this measure does not capture any relative gains in the quality of black schooling.
3.   These graphs employ the Census regional definitions. Most critical for our purposes is the expansive definition of the South: Texas, Oklahoma, Arkansas, Louisiana, Mississippi, Alabama, Tennessee, Kentucky, Florida, Georgia, South Carolina, North Carolina, Virginia, West Virginia, Maryland, Delaware, and the District of Columbia.
4.   An effective federal effort to restrain discrimination against Southern blacks could provide the basis for the perception of greater economic opportunity. Conversely, long-term improvements in black schooling quality in the South—whatever their contribution to black progress—cannot explain the abrupt termination of black outmigration in the mid-1960s. If the events most responsible for black economic improvement in the 1960s and 1970s had been schooling gains for Southern blacks in the 1940s and 1950s, why would so many blacks have fled the South during the period 1940–1965, and so few thereafter?
5.   See, for example, Welch (1973), which documents the growth in various measures of black/white relative schooling quality.
6.   Since rural-urban differentials in these indicators of schooling quality were especially pronounced, part of the improvement of these measures of educational inputs may be a consequence of the well-documented migration of blacks from the rural South. This migration reduced the numbers of blacks attending school in rural areas without increasing the schooling inputs available to any rural black student. This may help to explain, in part, the apparent enigma of measured improvements in black schooling quality at a time when blacks were excluded from the political process.
7.   *Green v. Board of Education of New Kent County, Virginia,* 391 U.S. 430 (1968) ended the use of "freedom of choice" plans that were commonly used to forestall desegregation. In *Alexander v. Holmes County,* 396 U.S. 1218 (1969), the Supreme Court held that "continued operation of segregated schools under a standard of allowing 'all deliberate speed' for desegregation is no longer constitutionally permissible." . . .

8. For simplicity, we will not distinguish further between the OFCC and the OFCCP.
9. More than 1,000 class action lawsuits were filed in 1975 and 1976 while by the late 1980s the number had fallen to near zero.

REFERENCES

Ahart, Gregory J. "A Process Evaluation of the Contract Compliance Program in the Nonconstruction Industry," *Ind. Lab. Relat. Rev.,* July 1976, *29*(4), pp. 565–71.

Akerlof, George A. "A Theory of Social Custom, of Which Unemployment May be One Consequence," *Quart. J. Econ,* June 1980, *94,* pp. 749–75.

Ashenfelter, Orley and Heckman, James. "Measuring the Effect of an Antidiscrimination Program," in *Estimating the labor market effects of social programs.* Eds.: Orley Ashenfelter and James Blum. Princeton, NJ: Industrial Relations Section, 1976, Ch. 3, pp. 46–84.

Beller, Andrea H. "The Economics of Enforcement of an Antidiscrimination Law: Title VII of the Civil Rights Act of 1964," *J. Law Econ.,* Oct. 1978, *21*(2), pp. 359–80.

Bound, John and Freeman, Richard. "Black Economic Progress: Erosion of the Post-1965 Gains in the 1980s?" in *The question of discrimination: Racial inequality in the U.S. labor market,* Eds.: Steven Shulman and William Darity. Middletown, CT: Wesleyan U. Press, 1989, Ch. 2, pp. 32–49.

Brown, Charles. "The Federal Attack on Labor Market Discrimination: The Mouse that Roared?" *Research in labor economics,* 1982, *5,* 33–68.

———. "Black-White Earnings Ratios since the Civil Rights Act of 1964: The Importance of Labor Market Dropouts," *Quart. J. Econ.,* Feb. 1984, *99*(1), pp. 31–44.

Bullock, Henry. *A history of negro education in the South.* Cambridge, MA: Harvard U. Press, 1967

Butler, Richard and Heckman, James. "The Government's Impact on the Labor Market Status of Black Americans: A Critical Review," in *Equal rights and industrial relations.* Eds.: Farrell E. Bloch et al. Madison, WI: Industrial Relations Research Association, 1977, ch. 9, pp. 235–81.

Butler, Richard; Heckman, James and Payner, Brook. "The Impact of the Economy and State on the Economic Status of Blacks," in *Markets in history: Economic studies of the past.* Ed.: David W. Galenson. Cambridge, Eng.: Cambridge U. Press, 1989, ch. 6, pp. 231–46.

Card, David and Krueger, Alan. "Does School Quality Matter? Returns to Education and the Characteristics of Public Schools in the United States." 1990.

———. "School Quality and Black/White Relative Earnings: A Direct Assessment." NBER Working Paper N. 3713, May 1991.

Culp, Jerome. "A New Employment Policy for the 1980s: Learning From the Victories and Defeats of Twenty Years of Title VII," *Rutgers Law Review,* 1985 *37*(4), pp. 895–919.

Dewey, Donald, "Negro Employment in Southern Industry," *J. Polit. Econ.,* Aug. 1952, *60* pp. 279–93.

Donohue, John and Siegelman, Peter. "The Changing Nature of Title VII Litigation," *Stanford Law Rev.,* May 1991, *43*(5), pp. 983–1033.

Farley, Reynolds and Allen, Walter. *The color line and the quality of life in America.* NY: Russell Sage Foundation, 1987.

Freeman, Richard B. "Changes in the Labor Market for Black Americans, 1948–1972," *Brookings Pap. Econ. Act.,* 1973, (1), pp. 67–120.

———. "Black Economic Progress after 1964: Who Has Gained and Why?" in *Studies in labor markets.* Ed.: Sherwin Rosen. U. of Chicago Press, 1981, ch. 5, pp. 247–94.

Goldstein, Morris and Smith, Robert S. "The Estimated Impact of the Antidiscrimination Program Aimed at Federal Contractors," *Ind. Lab. Relat. Rev.* July 1976, *29*(4), pp. 523–43.

Heckman, James. "The Impact of Government on the Economic Status of Black Americans," in *The question of discrimination.* Middletown, CT: Wesleyan U. Press, 1989, pp. 50–80.

Heckman, James and Payner, Brook. "Determining the Impact of Federal Antidiscrimination Policy on the Economic Status of Blacks: A Study of South Carolina," *Amer. Econ. Rev.,* Mar. 1989, *79*(1), pp. 138–77.

Jones, James. "Comment," *Ind. Lab. Relat. Rev.,* July 1976, *29*(4), pp. 581–84.

Leonard, Jonathan S. "Employment and Occupational Advance under Affirmative Action," *Rev. Econ. Statist.,* Aug. 1984b, *66*(3), pp. 377–85.

———. "The Impact of Affirmative Action on Employment," *J. Lab. Econ.,* Oct. 1984c, *2*(4), pp. 439–63.

———. "Splitting Blacks?: Affirmative Action and Earnings Inequality Within and Across Races." NBER Working Paper No. 1327, 1985.

Myrdal, Gunnar. *An American dilemma: The Negro problem and modern democracy.* NY: Harper & Row, 1944.

Orfield, Gary. *Public school desegregation in the United States, 1968–1980.* Washington, DC: Joint Center for Political Studies, 1983.

Schelling, T. C. "Dynamic Models of Segregation," *J. Math. Sociology,* July 1971, *1*(2), pp. 143–86.

Siegelman, Peter. "An Economic Analysis of Employment Discrimination Litigation." Ph.D. dissertation, Yale U., 1990.

Smith, James P. "Race and Human Capital," *Amer. Econ. Rev.,* Sept. 1984, *74*(4), pp. 685–98.

Smith, James P. and Welch, Finis. "Black/White Male Earnings and Employment: 1960–1970," in *The distribution of economic well-being.* Ed.: F. T. Juster. Cambridge, MA: NBER 1977, ch. 7.

———. "Race Differences in Earnings: A Survey and New Evidence." Rand Corporation, Santa Monica, CA, 1978.

———. "Closing the Gap." Rand Corporation, Santa Monica, CA, 1986.

———. "Black Economic Progress After Myrdal," *J. Econ. Lit.,* June 1989, *27*(2), pp. 519–64.

U.S. Commission on Civil Rights. *The economic progress of black men in America.* Washington, DC: U.S. GPO, 1986.

———. *Federal enforcement of school desegregation.* Washington, DC: U.S. GPO, 1969.

———. *1964 staff report: public education.* Washington, DC: U.S. GPO, 1964.

Vroman, Wayne. "Industrial Change and Black Men's Relative Earnings." Urban Institute, Washington, DC, 1989.

Wallace, Phyllis. "A Decade of Policy Development in Equal Opportunities in Employment and Housing." Working Paper No. 767–75, Massachusetts Institute of Technology, Jan. 1975.

Wasby, Stephen; D'Amato, Anthony and Metrailer, Rosemary. *Desegregation from Brown to Alexander.* Carbondale, IL: Southern Illinois U. Press, 1977.

Welch, Finis, "Education and Racial Discrimination," in *Discrimination in labor markets.* Eds.: Orley Ashenfelter and Albert Rees. Princeton, NJ: Princeton U. Press, 1973, ch. 2.

Woodward, C. Vann. *The burden of Southern history.* 2d ed. Baton Rouge, LA: Louisiana State U., 1968.

Wright, Gavin. "Segregation and Racial Wage Differentials in the South Before World War II." Working Paper, Stanford U., Dept. of Economics, 1988.

14

Male-Female Wage Differentials and Policy Responses

Morley Gunderson

The single most important development in the labor market over the last 40 years has been the increase in the number of women, especially married women, at work for pay. There have been other periods (e.g., during the two world wars) when women constituted a large fraction of the labor force and assumed jobs once the prerogative of men, but these changes turned out to be largely temporary and after the wars most women gave up their paying jobs. . . . The influx of women into the labor market since the 1950s, however, is showing no signs of being a temporary phenomenon and it is broadly based across virtually all developed countries (Table 1). . . . The increased participation of women in the labor market generally has been accompanied by an increase in their earnings relative to those of men, although a substantial gap remains. In the United States and Canada, the overall gap has remained roughly constant, but there is some evidence that it has narrowed slightly in more recent years[1] especially after controlling for the effects of changes in the skills and attributes of female and male workers.

With the majority of women now participating in the labor force, increased attention has focused on women's earnings and employment opportunities. This attention is reflected in numerous policies initiated since the 1960s designed to raise female earnings and employment opportunities. The rationale for these policies is to counteract the effect of discrimination and, according to some perspectives, to reduce flagrant inequalities in labor market outcomes even if they do not result from discrimination. The efficacy of these policy initiatives has been under considerable scrutiny in part because of the persistence of the overall male-female earnings gap. This has spawned considerable debate on the extent to which the earnings gap reflects discrimination and the extent to which the gap has been affected by various policies.

The purpose of this paper is to (1) discuss the methodological problems in

Excerpts reprinted with permission from the *Journal of Economic Literature* 1989 (March), vol. 27:46–72. Copyright © 1989 by the American Economic Association.

Table 1. Female Participation Rates and Earnings Ratios,
Various Industrialized Countries, 1960 and 1980

Country	Labor Force Participation Rates		Ratio of Women's to Men's Earnings	
	1960	*1980*	*1960*	*1980*
Australia	29.5	55.4	.59	.75
Britain	43.4	62.3	.61	.79
Canada	27.9	50.4	.59	.64
France	44.5	57.0	.64	.71
Germany	46.5	56.2	.65	.72
Italy	35.2	39.9	.73	.83
Japan	47.7	52.7	.46	.54
Sweden	51.0	76.9	.72	.90
United States	37.8	51.3	.66	.66
USSR	77.4	88.2	.70	.70

Source: Adapted from Jacob Mincer (1985, pp. S2, S6). Canadian figures
have been added, based on the Labour Force Survey for participation rates
and from the Census for earnings. Age groups, time periods, and the
definition of earnings differ slightly from country to country.

computing the male-female earnings gap, (2) outline the procedures used to
estimate the components of the male-female earnings gap giving emphasis to
their implications for the potential role of alternative policies, (3) summarize the
empirical evidence on the determinants of the gap, (4) outline the policy responses, and (5) discuss the empirical evidence on the impact of the policy
initiatives.[2]

The emphasis throughout is on the labor market, while recognizing the importance of constraints, attitudes, and policy responses outside of the labor market.
The studies reviewed here pertain mainly to the United States, where most of the
empirical work has been conducted. However, there is some discussion of Canada, Britain, and Australia—other countries where empirical studies exist but the
government policies differ somewhat. This review also contains an expanded
discussion of comparable worth, a policy receiving considerable attention today
but involving procedures not always well understood. . . .

I.   METHODOLOGICAL ISSUES IN COMPUTING
THE EARNINGS GAP

A number of key questions must be addressed before determining what policies, if any, are justified. What is the magnitude of the female-male pay gap?
How much of it can be attributed to discrimination as opposed to differences in

productivity-related factors? To what extent may differences in the productivity-related factors reflect discrimination exercised prior to entry into the labor market? What is the relative importance of different components of the gap—wage discrimination for the same job, discriminatory occupational segregation, different human capital endowments?[3]

The appropriate measure of the earnings gap depends in part on the purpose of the analysis. If the purpose is to obtain a measure of the wage differential attributable to labor market discrimination, then it is necessary to remove the effects of a wide range of wage-determining factors, including those that may reflect discrimination outside of the labor market. Such factors include age, education, training, labor market experience, job-specific seniority, race, union status, health, hours of work, city size, firm size, region, and absenteeism.

Some portion of the differences in productivity-related characteristics and job characteristics themselves may reflect discriminatory pressures from within and outside of the labor market or they may arise as a response on the part of women to wage discrimination and occupational segregation in the labor market.[4] This could be the case for such variables as education, training, general labor market experience, company seniority, absenteeism, and hours of work. For example, women may have higher turnover and absenteeism because they are assigned to low-wage, dead-end jobs or because they bear a disproportionate burden of household responsibility. Or women may not enroll in certain education programs, even if they have an aptitude for them, because they perceive that opportunities to use such training will be closed to them in the labor market (Solomon Polachek 1978). To the extent that these are discriminatory, then it would not be appropriate to control for, or "net out," the effect of such differences in arriving at a measure of the pay gap that reflect *all* such sources of discrimination, and hence that may be amenable to redress through a wide range of policies both within and outside the labor market.

Whether it is appropriate to control for the wage gap arising out of the allocation of men and women to different occupations also depends on the purpose of the analysis. If the focus is on unequal pay for the same work in the same narrowly defined occupation, then it is appropriate to control for differences in the distribution of males and females across narrowly defined occupations. . . . But if the purpose is to obtain a measure of the pay gap that reflects differences in the occupational distribution of females, then it is not appropriate to control for occupation differences.

Most data sets do not contain information on all relevant control variables, thereby giving rise to omitted variable bias when the omitted variables are partially correlated with pay and the included variables. To the extent that females have less general labor market experience, company-specific seniority, or labor market-oriented education than do males, not fully controlling for these differences could erroneously lead to attributing some of their effect to discrimination.

Other variables are measured imprecisely. For example, occupational control variables often include only indicators of broad occupations that mask considerable wage differences within occupations. In such circumstances differences in the broad occupational distribution may not account for much of the overall earnings gap because much of the gap may reflect differences *within* the broad occupations. Similarly, many of the data sets contain only crude controls for hours of work (e.g., full-time versus part-time). Some of the lower annual earnings of females may reflect fewer hours worked within such broad categories.

Some empirical studies (Jacob Mincer and Solomon Polachek (1974) for the United States; Walter Block (1982) and Roberta Robb (1978) for Canada) have restricted their analysis to never-married males and females whose household responsibilities are likely to be more similar than married individuals. In this way a sample is selected that minimizes some differences (e.g., responsibility for care of children) that are often unobserved to the researcher. However, this very selection procedure also introduces new differences that are also conventionally unobserved to the researcher. For example, never-married females may be highly motivated, career oriented, and possess a comparative advantage in labor market work. In such circumstances the wage gap based on never-marrieds may underestimate the wage gap for a random male and female with the same observed characteristics. . . .

II.   METHODS FOR COMPUTING THE EARNINGS GAP

In varying degrees, the following empirical procedures for computing the earnings gap deal with the previously discussed methodological issues.

A.   Narrowly Defined Occupations

One simple procedure to control for many of the variables that could influence the overall earnings gap is to compare male and female wages within narrow occupations, perhaps even within the same establishment. If the occupations are sufficiently narrowly defined, then they will be a surrogate for the human capital and other requirements of the job that otherwise have to be controlled for in the form of independent variables in multiple regression wage equations. In fact, using narrowly defined occupations may even control for some of the differences between men and women that may be important determinants of the earnings gap but that are unobserved by the researcher.

B.   Regression Procedures and Wage Decomposition

The standard procedure to analyze the determinants of the male-female earnings gap is to estimate earnings equations for samples of individual men and women separately. Specifically, the procedure is to fit equation (1) to a sample of male (m) workers and equation (2) to a sample of female (f) workers:

$$W_m = b_m X_m + u_m \qquad (1)$$

$$W_f = b_f X_f + u_f \qquad (2)$$

where W is wages or average hourly earnings, usually measured in logarithmic terms so that the estimated coefficients measure approximately the proportionate effect on wages of changes in the right-hand side variables. X is a vector of measured characteristics of the workers such as education, training, and experience, as well as control variables like race, marital status, and location. The vector of regression coefficients, b, reflects the return that the market yields to a unit change in endowments such as education and experience. The error term, u, reflects measurement error as well as the effect of factors unmeasured or unobserved by the researcher.

The overall average male-female wage gap can be decomposed into two components: One is the portion attributable to differences in the endowments of wage-generating characteristics ($\bar{X}_m - \bar{X}_f$) evaluated at the male returns ($\hat{b}_m$); the other portion is attributable to differences in the returns ($\hat{b}_m - \hat{b}_f$) that males and females get for the same endowment of wage-generating characteristics ($\bar{X}_f$). This latter component is often taken as reflecting wage discrimination.

III.   EVIDENCE ON THE EARNINGS GAP

The diversity of estimates of the male-female earnings gap and its components reflects differences in empirical procedures, data sets, proxy variables, and concepts of what is meant by wage discrimination or occupational segregation. Summaries of the empirical evidence are found in a number of reviews.[5] Donald Treiman and Heidi Hartmann (1981 p. 21) provide a comprehensive list of common control variables: education, age, race, training, labor market experience or its proxy, seniority with a particular employer, marital status, health, hours of work, city size, region, quality of schooling, absenteeism, and number of children.

From the various studies, the following generalizations emerge regarding sex differences in earnings.

1.   The greater the number of variables used to control for differences in productivity-related factors, the smaller the productivity-adjusted wage gap relative to the unadjusted gap.

2.   Even when they use extensive lists of control variables most studies do find *some* residual wage gap that they attribute to discrimination. When the

gap is close to zero that usually results from the inclusion of control variables whose values themselves may reflect discrimination.

3.   Factors originating from outside the labor market (e.g., differences in household responsibilities, *type* of education, career interruptions) are an important source of the overall earnings gap, highlighting the limited scope for policies that focus only on the labor market.

4.   Differences in the occupational distribution of males and females account for a substantial portion of the overall earnings gap. In contrast, pay differences for the same narrowly defined occupation within the same establishment do not account for much of the gap. This finding suggests a greater potential role for equal employment opportunity policies (to break down occupational segregation both within and across firms) and comparable worth policies (to enable comparisons across occupations) than for conventional equal pay policies (which require comparisons within the same job and establishment).

5.   Differences in pay across establishments also account for a substantial component of the earnings gap, thereby limiting the scope of equal pay and comparable worth policies which require comparisons within the same establishment.

6.   The productivity-adjusted earnings gap tends to be smaller in the public than private sector. In the private sector itself, the discriminatory gap tends to be smaller when product markets are competitive.

7.   Being married has a differential effect on the earnings of men versus women. The gap is widest between married men and married women, suggesting that household responsibilities may have an important effect on the earnings gap.

8.   Differences in labor market experience and the continuity of that experience, including the accumulation of company seniority, account for a substantial portion of the earnings gap. As women become more attached to the labor force and accumulate both general labor market experience and company-specific experience and seniority, the gap should diminish.

9.   While women have similar *levels* of education to men, the *type* of education women acquire is often not as oriented toward gaining skills that are rewarded in the labor market. In recent years, however, this has been changing, and this should help reduce the gap in the future.

10.   Differences in preferences for certain types of jobs account for a substantial portion of the earnings gap, although it is difficult if not impossible to determine the extent to which these preferences are shaped by discrimination.

11.   Both the male-female earnings gap and the extent of occupational segregation appear to be declining during the 1970s and 1980s, especially when changes in the skills and attributes of the workers are accounted for.

IV. POLICY INITIATIVES

The main policies to deal with the differential pay and employment opportunities of males and females are equal pay policies (including comparable worth), equal employment opportunity legislation (including affirmative action), and facilitating policies to assist in the adaptation of females to the labor market (e.g., day care, flexible hours, and education policies). . . .

A. Equal Pay and Comparable Worth

Equal pay policies generally require equal pay for the same (or substantially similar) work in the same establishment. Comparable worth (also termed *equal pay for work of equal value,* and *pay equity*) is the latest and strongest form of intervention in the equal pay front. Comparable worth basically differs from equal pay insofar as comparable worth allows comparisons across otherwise dissimilar occupations, usually based upon job evaluation procedures.

The comparable worth procedure typically involves four steps. First, predominantly female and predominantly male jobs within an establishment are compared with each other. The concept of gender predominance itself can differ, albeit an occupation represented by 70 percent or more of one sex is a common cutoff.

Second, a group of "experts" assign job evaluation point scores to the various components (usually skill, effort, responsibility, and working conditions) involved in the job. . . . The point scores for each component are then simply summed to get a total point score for the job.

Third, the total point scores and wages for each of the predominantly male jobs are compared with the total point scores and wages of the predominantly female jobs. This can be done by running a simple regression of pay on total point scores first for the predominantly male jobs and then for predominantly female jobs. The slopes can differ to reflect the possibility that male- and female-dominated jobs may receive different returns to the job evaluation point score. The fourth step involves adjusting female wages to male wages when the job evaluation point scores indicate that the jobs are of equal value.

Typically, the female pay line averages about 80 to 90 percent of the height of the male pay line. Relative to the typical overall unadjusted earnings ratio of approximately 0.60, the job evaluation procedures can be thought of as yielding an adjusted ratio of approximately 0.80 to 0.90 when comparisons are made within the same organization for jobs of the same average productivity and working conditions as measured by job evaluation scores.

The practical problem of job evaluation schemes applied to the comparable worth area have been discussed by both supporters and critics of comparable work (Donald Treiman 1979; Robert Livernash 1980). Gender bias can still prevail if, for example, a larger range of points is allocated for tasks that are performed more often in the predominantly male job, or if compensating points are awarded for dirty work conditions in the predominantly male jobs but not the predominantly female jobs. . . .

A large number of program design features pertaining to the administration of equal value legislation have to be worked out, and they can have a significant influence on the scope and ultimate effect of the legislation. . . . Of more fundamental concern—at least to many economists—is that even if the practical problems can be worked out, the concept of comparable worth is viewed by many to be fundamentally flawed. It is an administrative concept of value that may bear little or no relationship to the economic concept of value. Comparable worth is akin to the notion of "value-in-use" rather than "value-in-exchange." Just as water may have a high "value-in-use" but a low "value-in-exchange" because of its abundance, . . . so some jobs may appear to have a high value-in-use because of the inputs of skill, effort, and responsibility required. However, such jobs need not command a high market wage if there is an abundance of people willing to do them. Value is determined at the *margin* according to basic principles of supply and demand, not according to a job evaluator's concept of the *average* value of the *inputs* required to do the job. . . .

Supporters of comparable worth can argue against these attacks. Job evaluation must have some useful information content, given its survival value in private industry. . . . Supporters of comparable worth also argue that women should not have to leave female-dominated jobs to get higher pay, and this is especially important for older women whose mobility is likely to be severely constrained.

This debate over . . . comparable worth highlights the substantial conceptual divide between the *individual-oriented* pay gap analysis used by most economists and the *job-oriented* analysis used in comparable worth studies. Proponents of comparable worth argue that preferences for different types of work or decisions to acquire certain types of education should not give rise to pay differences across jobs of comparable worth. In short, supporters of comparable worth largely reject the notion that market forces should be the prime determinants of pay. Hence, they often have a normative conflict with economists who tend to emphasize the importance of market forces in reducing discrimination and who stress that individual preferences should be allowed to affect occupational choices providing there is an equality of *opportunity* both within and outside the labor market.

B.   Legislation on Equal Pay and Comparable Worth

In the United States, equal pay legislation was first introduced through the federal Equal Pay Act of 1963 as an amendment to the Fair Labor Standards

Act.[6] The Equal Pay Act requires equal pay for work of equal skill, effort, responsibility, and working conditions. It does not allow comparisons across jobs of different content, and hence it does not entail the comparable worth concept. Compliance is through both complaints and routine investigation.

The principle of equal pay is also a component of Title VII of the Civil Rights Act of 1964. . . . That legislation forbids wage and employment discrimination on the basis of race, color, religion, national origin, and sex. . . . In addition to the federal Equal Pay Act and Title VII, most states have equal pay laws, applying mainly to their public sector employees. As of 1984, 25 states had legislation relating to comparable worth. Of these, 10 had actually implemented or were about to implement comparable worth for their public sector employees, even though in some cases state legislation did not require implementation. . . .

In Canada, where labor matters are largely under provincial jurisdiction, all jurisdictions have a form of equal pay legislation, following the initiative of Ontario in 1951. Canada appears to have gone further than the United States in legislating comparable worth. Such legislation has been in place in Quebec since 1976, in the federal jurisdiction since 1978 (covering approximately 10 percent of the Canadian work force), in Manitoba for its civil servants since 1985, and in Ontario since 1987.[7] The amount of litigation in the area has been scant, however, in part because of the reliance upon a complaints-based system in the federal jurisdiction and Quebec.

In Britain, equal pay for equal work was passed in 1970 but its implementation was delayed until the end of 1975 to allow an adjustment period. . . . Australia is often singled out in the equal value area because federal and state tribunals establish wages by decree for the vast majority of the Australian work force.[8] That system led to the *official* fixing or "markdown" of female wages at 54 percent of male wages for the same job up until 1949 when the ratio was officially raised to 75 percent. In 1969 (to be fully operative by 1972) the principle of equal pay for equal work was adopted in that the official markdown was to be eliminated between males and females in the same job. In 1972 (to be fully operative by 1975) the principle of equal pay for work of equal value was adopted in that the official markdown between predominantly male and female occupations was also eliminated. While this policy has been termed one of comparable worth, it is not comparable worth in the American sense of the awards being based upon a system of formal job evaluation. . . .

C.   Equal Employment Opportunity and Affirmative Action Legislation

Equal employment opportunity legislation is designed to create an equality of opportunity in the various phases of the employment decision such as recruiting, hiring, training, transfers, promotions, and terminations. Affirmative action is concerned with *results* more than opportunities. It involves actions such as the aggressive hiring of females or preferences to females when candidates are otherwise equal.

Affirmative action is designed to compensate for the cumulative effects of a history of inequality and systemic discrimination. The term *systemic* describes discrimination that results as an unintended by-product; in legal parlance it results when an action has a "disparate impact" even if there was not "disparate treatment." For example, it can occur when firms have job requirements that effectively exclude certain groups or that unintentionally place people into positions based upon stereotypes.

Affirmative action programs generally involve the following procedures. First, a data base is established comparing the sex composition of the organization with that of the surrounding *relevant* labor market. Second, targets are set to achieve a representation of the internal female work force that is similar to its representation in the surrounding labor market. Third, a plan and timetable are established for achieving the targets.

In the United States, equal employment opportunity legislation . . . is a component of Title VII. . . . All Canadian jurisdictions have similar laws. . . . In Canada, it was not until 1986 that the federal government initiated affirmative action in the federal jurisdiction (only about 10 percent of the Canadian work force) as well as for federal contractors.

D.   Facilitating Policy

Equal pay and equal employment opportunity legislation have been the main thrust of policy initiatives to deal with sex discrimination, but other initiatives have been followed, generally to facilitate the adaptation of women into the labor market in a manner that would improve their pay and employment opportunities.

Day care policies and flexible work arrangements can be important because women spend a disproportionately large amount of time on household work, even when both spouses work in the labor market. Policies to facilitate divorce, support payments, and the more equitable division of family assets upon divorce have been advocated not only on their own right but because they may enable the labor market decisions of women, especially those related to location and hours, to be less dependent upon the decision of their husband. And to the extent that they lead to more dissolved marriages, the policies may encourage women to invest in skills that are more valuable in the labor market than the increasingly unstable marriage market. Education and training policies can enhance the wages and employment opportunities of women, but it is important that they be free of sex-role stereotyping. Otherwise they may simply lead to women acquiring skills that are not highly valued in the labor market.

V. EXPECTED IMPACT OF POLICIES

In response to equal pay (including comparable worth) legislation, firms should increase female wages so as to avoid the expected penalty associated with not complying. Even firms that do not discriminate may raise female wages so as to reduce the probability of erroneous litigation. . . .

The effect of equal pay laws on the wages of *males* is theoretically indeterminant. On the one hand, employers may seek to comply by lowering male wages, or at least the rate of increase of male wages. On the other hand, the employment and wages of males may increase as they are substituted (perhaps subtly) for the higher-priced female labor; the opposite would occur where they are complements in production. . . .

In contrast to equal pay legislation which fixes wages, equal employment opportunity legislation (including affirmative action) increases the demand for female labor at all phases of the employment decision. This should serve to increase *both* wages and employment. Equal employment opportunity policies, however, may do little to assist women who do not want to change jobs to enhance their earnings.

VI. EVIDENCE ON IMPACT OF POLICIES

[T]he prototype model in most studies is of the form

$$Y = bX + aL + u \tag{9}$$

where Y is a measure of labor market success of females (e.g., earnings, employments, probability of entering a male-dominated occupation), X is a vector of control variables, L is a measure of the legislative initiative, b and a are parameters reflecting, respectively, the impact of the control variables and the legislation and u is the error term. As discussed subsequently, the legislative initiative is usually captured by a variable indicating the time period or jurisdiction where the legislation is in place, or by variables indicating enforcement activity under the legislation. . . .

A. Equal Employment Opportunity Legislation in the United States

[T]itle VII EEO legislation was designed to combat both wage and employment discrimination. Its effects on female earnings, therefore, should be positive, while the effects on employment may be positive (resulting from the equal employment opportunity aspects) or negative (emanating from the equal pay aspects).

Table 2 summarizes the results of studies of the effect of Title VII. Beller (1976) constructs separate enforcement variables reflecting the probability of an investigation (ratio of investigations to number of women) and the probability of a settlement conditional upon an investigation (ratio of successful settlements to attempted settlements) based on data from the compliance files of the EEOC. These enforcement variables are included as regressors in typical earnings equations estimated to a sample of approximately 24,000 individuals from the Public Use Tapes of the Current Population Survey (CPS). A separate equation is estimated for each of 1967 and 1974, years that come before and after the 1972 amendment of Title VII, which provided more effective enforcement by expanding coverage and giving the EEOC the right to sue a respondent. Beller includes the enforcement measures in what she terms the "pre-enforcement cross section" of 1967 to capture the effect of unobserved factors that may be correlated with the enforcement measures. This enables the estimation of a purer enforcement effect by subtracting the enforcement coefficients of the 1967 preamendment cross section equation from the 1974 postamendment equation.[9]

The impact of Title VII has been quantified at more aggregate levels. Leonard (1984a) uses 555 state-by-2-digit-SIC (Standard Industry Classification) industry cells within manufacturing, and regresses the change (between 1966 and 1978) in the percentage of workers who are female on the number of Title VII class action suits per employer as a measure of compliance. Time series regressions have been used to see whether there was a shift in the underlying time pattern after controlling for the effect of the business cycle and any time trend (Oaxaca 1977). . . .

As the last column of Table 2 indicates, the empirical results on the effect of Title VII are somewhat inconclusive. There is some evidence that it has increased female earnings and reduced the earnings gap (Beller 1976, 1979, 1980). However, much of the reduction in the earnings gap occurs because EEO initiatives actually led to a reduction in male earnings (Beller 1979, 1980). Insignificant effects are found in other data sets, based on other methodologies (Oaxaca 1977). The legislation seems to have had some effect on reducing occupational segregation (Beller 1982a), but its effect on female employment has been negative or insignificant (Leonard 1984a). Stricter enforcement procedures led to a larger impact (Beller 1976, 1979, 1980, 1982a). In order to reduce the wage gap, ensuring a successful settlement was less effective than increasing the probability of an investigation (Beller 1976). The opposite was the case for reducing occupational segregation (Beller 1982a).

Clearly, the evidence does *not* unambiguously indicate that the EEO initiatives of Title VII were a resounding success, although there is some evidence of a positive effect on the earnings and occupational position of women. There is also some evidence that the legislation is more effective when it is strictly enforced and when the economy is expanding.

Table 2. Impact of Equal Employment Opportunity Legislation (Title VII of the Civil Rights Act of 1964), United States

Study	Data	Dependent Variable	Impact
Beller (1976)	CPS 1967, 1974	Earnings	Increased female earnings by 4.7 percent over 1967–74 Effect larger after enforcement amendments Increasing probability of an investigation more effective than increasing the probability of a settlement
Beller (1979)	CPS 1967, 1974	Earnings	Reduced gender earnings gap of .68 by .07 between 1967–74 .01 from increased female earnings and .06 from reduced male earnings But statistically insignificant More pronounced in private sector Stricter enforcement leads to larger effects
Beller (1980)	CPS 1968–75	Earnings	Reduced gender gap by .096 between 1968–74 .057 from increased female earnings and .039 from reduced male earnings Enforcement more effective in expanding economy
Beller (1982a)	CPS 1967, 1974	Probability of female entering male-dominated occupation	Reduced sex differential in the probability of being employed in a male-dominated job by .062 between 1967–74 Did so by increasing female probability and reducing male probability Effect larger after enforcement amendments Increasing the probability of a settlement more effective than increasing the probability of an investigation
Leonard (1984a)	EEOC Reports 1966, 1978	Change in employment share	Sometimes negative, generally insignificant
Oaxaca (1977)	Census 1960, 1970	Earnings	No significant change in the discrimination component of the earnings gap between 1960 and 1970 Widened for whites but narrowed for blacks
Oaxaca (1977)	Current Population Reports 1955–71	Earnings	Reduced earnings gap in postlegislative period but statistically insignificant and quantitatively small

B. Affirmative Action Contract Compliance in the United States

A number of empirical studies have examined the effect of affirmative action under the federal contract compliance program based on Executive Order 11246 in the United States. . . . [T]he studies typically regress a measure of success (e.g., the proportion of the establishment's employment that is female) on a number of control variables as well as measures of the policy initiative (e.g., whether the firm has a government contract and hence is subject to contract compliance, and whether the firm underwent a compliance review). . . .

The earlier studies of Morris Goldstein and Robert Smith (1976) and Heckman and Wolpin (1976) found that females, especially white females, were net losers and that males, especially black males, were net gainers. This reflects the early emphasis on race and not sex discrimination. When the emphasis was broadened to sex discrimination, around 1974, the federal contract compliance program seemed to benefit females in several ways: reduced occupational segregation (Beller 1982a; Leonard 1984b), reduced quits (Paul Osterman 1982), and increased employment (Smith and Welch 1984; Leonard 1984c). For example, Leonard (1984c) found that, over the period 1974 to 1980, affirmative action increased the growth of employment by 2.8 percent for white females and 12.3 percent for black females. Aggressive enforcement through increased compliance review (Osterman 1982; Leonard 1984b) or through more stringent targets (Leonard 1985), generally enhanced the effectiveness of the legislation. The legislation appeared to be more effective in expanding firms (Leonard 1984c). . . .

In summary, affirmative action under the federal contract compliance program appears to have improved the labor market position of those groups to which it is directed, with stricter enforcement enhancing effectiveness. . . .

D. Equal Pay Legislation in Canada

Gunderson (1975) estimates the impact of Ontario's equal pay legislation by comparing the male-female wage differential in the same establishments and in the same narrowly defined occupations, in the years before and after the legislation was to be effectively enforced. The legislative effect was captured by a dummy variable for the postlegislative period, in a cross-section regression, based on the years immediately before and after the legislative change. The use of narrowly defined occupations is important because it reduces the need to control for observable or unobservable wage-determining characteristics and it is also the level of aggregation where equal pay comparisons are allowed. Comparisons within the same establishment minimize the need to control for regional or local labor market differences and it is the level of aggregation where equal pay comparisons are allowed. The legislation had no impact on narrowing the male-female wage gap.

It is also possible that the legislation may not show its effect after only one year following its implementation. However, in time series regressions based upon a number of narrowly defined occupations the 1969 legislative change again was found to have no impact in narrowing the male-female wage differential after controlling for the trend and cyclical changes in the gap.

E. British Equal Pay Initiatives

In Britain, the ratio of female to male hourly earnings had been roughly constant throughout the 1950s and 1960s. It increased from 0.58 in 1970 (the year of passage of the Equal Pay Act) to 0.66 in 1975 (the year of implementation) and thereafter remained roughly stable (A. Zabalza and Z. Tzannatos 1985a, 1985b). This increase of 0.08 was generally uniform within occupations, industries, and age groups, suggesting that it was not attributable to compositional changes in the female work force. Zabalza and Tzannatos attribute the substantial increase in female pay largely to the legislation, not to factors such as autonomous shifts in female labor supply, changes in industrial structure, or wage controls. The legislation in large part had its effect through the channels of collective bargaining which cover slightly over 60 percent of the work force. The ratios of female to male job rates (minimum wages specified in the collective agreement for different jobs), which had been relatively stable at around 0.08 to 0.83 from 1950 to 1970, increased to unity by 1976 (Z. Tzannatos and A. Zabalza 1984).[10]

Based upon a time series regression, over a period 1949–75, B. Chiplin, M. Curran, and C. Parsley (1980) also find the postlegislative period to be associated with a statistically significant 8 percentage point increase in the ratio of female to male hourly earnings, after controlling for the effect of the trend and business cycle. . . .

F. Australian Equal Pay Initiatives

The impact of the Australian initiatives in the equal pay area is particularly noteworthy because of the dramatic legislated wage changes. Gregory and Duncan (1981) estimate the employment effect of the Australian legislation by estimating an equation relating the ratio of female to male employment to their relative wages (as affected by the legislation), to a time trend and to the unemployment rate over the period 1948 to 1978. Their analysis indicates the following: by 1977, the ratio of female to male award wages was 0.933, up to 21 percent from the ratio of 0.774 at the time of the equal value awards of 1972, and up 30 percent from the ratio of 0.720 at the time of the equal pay awards of 1969; . . . the increase in the wage ratio . . . was associated with a statistically significant reduction in the growth of female employment relative to male employment; after the legislative change, the average annual growth of female employment was still 3 percentage points greater than male employment; it would have been 4.5 percentage points greater were it not for the relative wage changes associated with the legislation; . . . the substantial female wage gains and moderate reduction in their employment growth led to a substantial increase in their income share.

The analyses and interpretation given by Gregory and Duncan have been challenged by P. A. McGavin (1983) and Killingsworth (1985), who indicate that there is stronger evidence of an adverse effect on *hours* of work of females and that the absence of a substantial *aggregate* adverse employment effect for females can be attributed in part to the sustained growth of female employment in the government sector.

Clearly the Australian experience has led to different interpretations of the behavioral responses to what are indisputably dramatic wage gains on the part of females. Perhaps a balanced conclusion is that there was *some* adverse employment effect but not a substantial one, given the dramatic increase in female relative earnings. . . .

VII.   OVERALL ASSESSMENT

The empirical studies of the effects of the various policies suggest the following conclusions: (1) equal employment opportunity policies and affirmative action policies tend to improve the position of the groups to which they are targeted; (2) stricter enforcement tends to enhance effectiveness; (3) comparable worth, where applied, has raised the wages of females relative to males by 10 to 20 percent, although its economy-wide effect is likely to be severely limited by the fact that it does not enable comparisons across establishments and industries; (4) equal pay legislation is not likely to have an effect if it is limited to a complaints-based system dealing with pay differentials within the same job and establishment, although it can have a substantial effect if it works through the mechanism of collective bargaining (Britain) or wage-fixing tribunals (Australia); (5) although there is not a consensus, the substantial wage increases resulting from many of the policy initiatives do not appear to have led to large adverse employment effects, especially in the public sector.

What are the unresolved and important issues that should constitute the research agenda for the future? First, more evidence is needed on the relative importance of interestablishment, as opposed to intraestablishment, wage differentials as determinants of the earnings gap because equal pay and equal value policies are restricted to comparisons within the same establishment. Second, it is important to get a better picture of the extent to which the earnings gap reflects a compensating wage differential for cost differences associated with differences in such factors as absenteeism, turnover, and pensions—control variables that are often omitted in conventional data sets. Third, new and updated information is needed on the earnings patterns for the more recent cohorts of women who likely have a more permanent attachment to the labor force and who may be entering the new sectors that do not have a legacy of segregation and discriminatory practices. . . .

ACKNOWLEDGMENTS

Without implicating them for any of the contents of the paper, I am grateful to the following for helpful discussions or comments: Andrea Beller (University of Illinois), David Bloom (Harvard and Columbia), Glen Cain (University of Wisconsin), Ron Ehrenberg (Cornell), Victor Fuchs (Stanford), Bob Gregory (Australian National University), Jonathan Leonard (University of California, Berkeley), Roberta Robb (Brock University), and Paul Weiler (Harvard). Financial support of the Humanities and Social Sciences Committee of the Research Board of the University of Toronto is gratefully acknowledged.

NOTES

1.   The earnings data of Table 1 relate to men and women with different skills and attributes. Recent entrants into the labor market have little accumulated experience and, insofar as women are disproportionately represented among the recent entrants, so their earnings will be disproportionately affected. It is important, therefore, to determine the extent to which the relative wages of men and women with the same characteristics have changed. Evidence of the declining earnings gap for persons of the same characteristics is provided in Francine Blau and Andrea Beller (1988), Francine Blau and Marianne Ferber (1987b), June O'Neill (1985), and James Smith and Michael Ward (1984) for the United States; and in Jac-Andre Boulet and Laval Lavallee (1984) for Canada.

2.   By focusing on policies designed to narrow the male-female wage gap, this review differs from a number of related reviews. The emphasis in Glen Cain (1986) is on the theory of discrimination and on the empirical issues pertaining to race and sex discrimination, but not on the effect of government policies. This is also the case with respect to reviews of sex discrimination by Janice Madden (1985), Blau and Ferber (1987b), and Francine Blau (1984), albeit the latter does discuss U.S. studies that attempted to estimate the impact of federal legislation.

3.   The methodological issues associated with estimating discriminatory pay gaps are outlined in more detail in David Bloom and Mark Killingsworth (1982) and Cain (1986).

4.   On the importance of prelabor market discrimination and sex-role socialization, including a review of some of the literature, see Mary Corcoran and Paul Courant (1987). Reuben Gronau (1988) highlights how wage-determining factors like on-the-job training,

turnover, and work intensity are affected by wages, which in turn are determined by these factors.

5. Recent reviews include 21 U.S. studies in Cynthia Lloyd and Beth Neimi (1979, pp. 232–38); 14 U.S. studies in Donald Treiman and Heidi Hartmann (1981, pp. 20, 36); 20 U.S. studies in Janice Madden (1985); 30 U.S. studies in Steven Willborn (1986, pp. 13–15, 20–24); 21 U.S. studies in Cain (1986, pp. 750–52); 22 U.S. studies in Blau and Ferber (1987a); 12 Canadian studies in Gunderson (1985a, p. 229); 9 U.S. studies, 5 Canadian studies, and 4 British studies in Naresh Agarwal (1981, pp. 120–25).

6. Discussions of the legislation and jurisprudence—its evolution, interpretation through the courts, and implementation—is discussed in Aldrich and Buchele (1986), Blau and Ferber (1986), Alice Cook (1985), and Ehrenberg and Smith (1987b) for the United States; Gunderson (1985a) for Canada; and Jennie Farley (1985), Cynthia Goodwin (1984), Eve Landau (1985), and Willborn (1986) for international comparisons.

7. In June 1987, the government of Ontario passed the Pay Equity Act, legislating equal pay for work of equal value for *both* private and public sector employers. The legislation is to be phased in. . . . Rather than relying only on the usual complaints-based system, the Ontario legislation is based upon a "proactive, system-wide" application of comparable worth. This approach requires all employers in the public sector and employers of 100 or more employees in the private sector to utilize bona fide job comparison or evaluation procedures and to make the required wage adjustments. If it turns out to be rigidly enforced, this legislation will be the first major use of comparable worth in the private sector.

8. The Australian situation is discussed in R. Gregory and R. Duncan (1981). It is contrasted with the situation in the United States in R. Gregory and V. Ho (1985).

9. Beller's subsequent studies largely expand upon that methodology in a number of ways: estimates on the effect on male earnings as well as female earnings, and on the government and private sectors separately (Beller 1979); estimates of the effect on the probability of entering a male-dominated occupation (Beller 1982a); estimates for each year between 1968 and 1975 to see whether the effectiveness of enforcement depends upon the state of the economy (Beller 1980); and separate estimates in the periods before and after the passage of Title IX of the Education Amendments in 1972, to determine the additional effect of those amendments (Beller 1982b).

10. Zabalza and Tzannatos (1985a, 1985b) also find that the antidiscrimination initiatives did not have any adverse employment effects for females.

REFERENCES

Agarwal, Naresh. "Pay Discrimination: Evidence, Policies and Issues," in *Equal employment issues: Race and sex discrimination in the United States, Canada and Britain.* Eds.: Harish Jain and Peter Sloane. NY: Praeger Pub., 1981, pp. 118–43.

Aldrich, Mark and Buchele, Robert. *The economics of comparable worth.* Cambridge, MA: Ballinger Pub. Co. 1986.

Beller, Andrea. "EEO Laws and the Earnings of Women," *Industrial Relations Research Association Proceedings.* Madison: U. of Wisconsin, 1976, pp. 190–98.

_____. "The Impact of Equal Employment Opportunity Laws on the Male-Female Earnings Differential," in *Women in the labor market.* Eds.: Cynthia Lloyd, Emily Andrews, and Curtis Gilroy. NY: Columbia U. Press, 1979, pp. 304–30.

————. "The Effect of Economic Conditions on the Success of Equal Employment Opportunity Laws: An Application to the Sex Differential in Earnings," *Rev. Econ. Statist.*, Aug. 1980, *62*(3), pp. 370–87.

————. "Occupational Segregation by Sex: Determinants and Changes," *J. Human Res.*, Summer 1982, *17*(3), pp. 371–92.

Blau, Francine. "Discrimination Against Women: Theory and Evidence," in *Labor economics: Modern views*. Ed.: William Darity, Jr. Boston: Kluwer-Nijhoff, 1984, pp. 53–89.

Blau, Francine and Beller Andrea. "Trends in Earnings Differentials by Gender, 1971–1981," *Ind. Lab. Relat. Rev.*, July 1988, *41*(4), pp. 513–29.

Blau, Francine and Ferber, Marianne. *The economics of women, men and work*. Englewood Cliffs, NJ: Prentice-Hall, 1986.

————. "Occupations and Earnings of Women Workers," in *Working women: Past, present and future*. Eds.: Karen Koziana, Michael Moskow, and Lucretia Tanner. Washington, DC: Bureau of National Affairs, 1987, pp. 37–68.

Bloom, David and Killingsworth, Mark. "Pay Discrimination Research and Litigation: The Use of Regression," *Ind. Relat.*, Fall 1982, *21*(3), pp. 318–39.

Boulet, Jac-Andre and Lavallee, Laval. *The changing economic status of women*. Ottawa: Economic Council of Canada, 1984.

Cain, Glen. "The Economic Analysis of Labour Market Discrimination: A Survey," in *Handbook of labour economics, Volume 1*. Eds.: Orley Ashenfelter and Richard Layard. Amsterdam: Elsevier Science Publishers, 1986, pp. 693–785.

Chiplin, Brian; Curran, M. and Parsley, C. "Relative Female Earnings in Great Britain and Impact of Legislation," in *Women and low pay*. Ed.: Peter Sloane. London: Macmillan, 1980, pp. 57–126.

Cook, Alice. *Comparable worth: A case book of experiences in states and localities*. Hawaii: Industrial Relations Center, U. of Hawaii at Manoa, 1985.

Corcoran, Mary and Courant, Paul. "Sex-Role Socialization and Occupational Segregation: An Exploratory Investigation," *J. Post Keynesian Econ.*, Spring 1987, *9*(3), pp. 330–46.

Ehrenberg, Ronald and Smith, Robert. "Comparable Worth in the Public Sector," in *Public sector payrolls*. Ed.: David Wise. Chicago: U. of Chicago Press, 1987, pp. 243–88.

Farley, Jennie, ed. *Women workers in fifteen countries*. Ithaca, NY: ILR Press, 1985.

Goodwin, Cynthia. *Equal pay legislation and implementation: Selected countries*. Ottawa: Labour Canada, 1984.

Gregory, R. G. and Duncan, R. C. "Segmented Labor Market Theories and the Australian Experience of Equal Pay for Women," *J. Post Keynesian Econ.*, Spring 1981, *3*(3), pp. 403–28.

Gregory, R. and Ho, V. "Equal Pay and Comparable Worth: What Can the U.S. Learn from the Australian Experience?" Discussion Paper No. 123, Centre for Economic Policy Research, Australian National U., July 1985.

Gronau, Reuben. "Sex-related Wage Differentials and Women's Interrupted Labor Careers—the Chicken or the Egg," *J. Lab. Econ.*, July 1988, *6*(3), pp. 277–301.

Gunderson, Morley. "Male-Female Wage Differentials and the Impact of Equal Pay Legislation," *Rev. Econ. Statist.*, Nov. 1975, *57*(4), pp. 462–69.

————. "Discrimination, Equal Pay, and Equal Opportunities in the Labour Market," in *Work and pay; the Canadian labour market.* Ed.: Craig Riddell. Toronto: U. of Toronto Press, 1985a, pp. 219–65.

Killingsworth, Mark. "The Economics of Comparable Worth: Analytical, Empirical, and Policy Questions," in *Comparable worth: New directions for research.* Ed.: Heidi Hartmann. Washington, DC: National Academy Press, 1985, pp. 886–115.

Landau, Eve C. *The rights of working women in the European community.* Luxembourg: Commission of the European Communities, 1985.

Leonard, Jonathan. "Antidiscrimination or Reverse Discrimination: The Impact of Changing Demographics, Title VII, and Affirmative Action on Productivity," *J. Human Res.,* Spring 1984a, *19*(2), pp. 145–74.

————. "Employment and Occupational Advance Under Affirmative Action," *Rev. Econ. Statist.,* Aug. 1984b, *66*(3), pp. 377–85.

————. "The Impact of Affirmative Action on Employment," *J. Lab. Econ.,* Oct. 1984c, *2*(4), pp. 439–63.

————. "Affirmative Action as Earnings Redistribution: The Targeting of Compliance Reviews," *J. Lab. Econ.,* July 1985, *3*(3), pp. 363–84.

Livernash, E. Robert, ed. *Comparable worth: Issues and alternatives.* Washington, DC: Equal Employment Advisory Council, 1980.

Lloyd, Cynthia and Neimi, Beth. *The economics of sex differentials.* NY: Columbia U. Press, 1979.

Madden, Janice. "The Persistence of Pay Differentials: The Economics of Sex Discrimination," in *Women and work: An annual review.* Eds.: Laurie Larwood, Ann Stromberg, and Barbara Gutek. Beverly Hills, CA: Sage, 1985, pp. 76–114.

McGavin, P. A. "Equal Pay for Women: A Re-Assessment of the Australian Experience," *Australian Econ. Pap.,* June 1983, *22*(40), pp. 48–59.

Mincer, Jacob. "Intercountry Comparisons of Labor Force Trends and of Related Developments: An Overview." *J. Lab. Econ.,* Jan. 1985, *3*(1, pt. 2), pp. S1–S32.

Oaxaca, Ronald. "The Persistence of Male-Female Earnings Differentials," in *The distribution of economic well-being.* Ed.: F. Thomas Juster. Cambridge, MA: Ballinger Co., 1977, pp. 303–54.

O'Neill, June. "The Trend in the Male-Female Wage Gap in the United States," *J. Lab. Econ.,* Jan. 1985, *3*(1, pt. 2), pp. S91–S116.

Osterman, Paul. "Affirmative Action and Opportunity: A Study of Female Quit Rates," *Rev. Econ. Statist.,* Nov. 1982, *64*(4), pp. 604–12.

Polachek, Solomon. "Sex Differences in College Major," *Ind. Lab. Relat. Rev.,* July 1978, *31*(4), pp. 498–508.

Smith, James and Ward, Michael. *Women's wages and work in the twentieth century.* Santa Monica, CA: Rand, 1984.

Smith, James and Welch, Finis. "Affirmative Action and Labor Markets," *J. Lab. Econ.,* Apr. 1984, *2*(2), pp. 269–301.

Treiman, Donald. *Job evaluation: An analytic review.* Washington, DC: National Academy of Sciences, 1979.

Treiman, Donald and Hartmann, Heidi, eds. *Women, work and wages: Equal pay for jobs of equal value.* Washington: DC: National Academy Press, 1981.

Willborn, Steven. *A comparable worth primer.* Lexington, MA: D. C. Heath and Co., 1986.

Zabalza, Anton and Tzannatos, Zafiris. "The Effect of Britain's Anti-discriminatory Legislation on Relative Pay and Employment," *Econ. J.,* Sept. 1985a, *95*(379), pp. 679–99.

_____. *Women and equal pay: The effects of legislation on female employment and wages in Britain.* Cambridge, Eng.: Cambridge U. Press, 1985b.

*Consequences for Employers and
the American Economy*

15

The Law Transmission System and the Southern Jurisprudence of Employment Discrimination

Alfred W. Blumrosen

INTRODUCTION

Substantial and significant improvement in minority employment has taken place since 1965. This improvement has resulted from broad interpretations of Title VII of the Civil Rights Act of 1964 which were developed in important part by the southern courts of appeals. Through the operation of the "law transmission system" many employers accepted these interpretations, changing their practices to include minorities in occupations from which they had been excluded. In the 1980s, the Supreme Court narrowed some of these interpretations of the southern courts, relying on the very improvement which the broader interpretations had helped to produce.

By the mid-1970s much of industry had taken affirmative action to increase minority and female participation. The action taken was at least partly in response to the set of policies promulgated and enforced under Title VII and the Executive Order program. The Supreme Court, in *United Steelworkers v. Weber* (443 U.S. 193, 1979) upheld the legality of such race and sex specific programs to improve opportunities for minorities and women. Kaiser Aluminum and the Steelworkers had established a skilled training program which reserved fifty percent of the seats for minorities. The Supreme Court upheld the race-specific feature of the program both because it was consistent with the purpose of Title VII and because it was a result of voluntary action.

The history behind the *Weber* decision illuminates the operation of the law transmission system. The training program in *Weber* was modeled after a massive settlement of discrimination claims in the steel industry.[1] That settlement in turn was a product of a well-developed body of discrimination law which the courts and administrative agencies formed under Title VII. *Weber* protects those who

Excerpts reprinted with permission from the *Industrial Relations Law Journal* 1984, vol. 6 (3):313–352. Copyright © 1984.

take affirmative action from claims of reverse discrimination, thus facilitating voluntary compliance with the regulatory standards set by Congress and the President.

The courts of appeals having jurisdiction over the southern states heavily influenced the development of the body of law that prompted the movement toward self-regulation. In the southern states, overt racial segregation in all areas of life had been the rule before the Civil Rights Act of 1964. The southern courts of appeals approached the problems of employment discrimination with the benefit of hard experience in addressing discrimination in public education, and they used some techniques which had been developed in that area.

In one important development, these courts, followed by other federal courts, held that seniority systems and other practices which perpetuated earlier discrimination against minorities were illegal regardless of the intent of union or employer, and were not protected by the bona fide seniority system provisions in Title VII. Another key development, which occurred in the Fifth Circuit, was the evolution of a presumption that blacks who were denied employment opportunities had been discriminated against and were appropriate class representatives of all black employees and applicants. Title VII could be enforced in across-the-board class actions which reached many employment practices, and afforded relief to victims of discrimination who had not filed individual claims.

These Fifth Circuit interpretations were "transmitted" to employers and unions in the early 1970s. The results were striking. Many major companies changed hiring and promotion practices. Some signed agreements or consent decrees with the EEOC and established affirmative action programs in response to Executive Order (EO) 11,246. The impact on the workplace of this policy transmission is evidenced by the fact that nearly twenty-five percent of the minority labor force in 1980 were in substantially higher level occupations than they would have been under the restrictive patterns of 1965. The improvement in the southeastern states was proportional to the minority labor force located in those states.

Toward the end of the 1970s, the Supreme Court began to reject much of the body of law which had contributed to industry's compliance with Title VII, and had thereby produced these dramatic changes in the occupational status of minorities. This rejection of the "southern jurisprudence" occurred only after long-standing, systematic discriminatory practices had been substantially altered, and blacks had moved in substantial numbers into jobs previously filled only by whites.

This paper first examines . . . the process by which the race-specific program upheld in *Weber* was developed. It then discusses the extent to which anti-discrimination policies have been transmitted and incorporated into industrial relations systems. Finally, the paper assesses the Supreme Court's repudiation of some of the positions which the southern courts of appeals had adopted in interpreting Title VII. The social response to the prohibition on sex discrimination in employment is different from that of race discrimination, and will not be discussed here in detail.

I.   THE LAW TRANSMISSION SYSTEM AND TITLE VII

A.   Formulating Title VII Policies: The Steel Industry and EEOC

Title VII did not take effect until one year after its passage. This "grace period" was designed to allow compliance with the law's requirements. The statute established a five-member Equal Employment Opportunity Commission (EEOC or "Commission") to investigate and conciliate complaints and it provided for civil actions where conciliation failed.

Because the Commissioners were not appointed until May, 1965, the Commission could not, prior to Title VII's effective date, advise the regulated community of its views of the law by guideline or regulation. As a result, employers took little action during that year.

The potential beneficiaries of the new law took the first steps in the operation of the law transmission system. One such group of beneficiaries were black steelworkers in Birmingham, Alabama. . . . Tensions were high over efforts to improve conditions for blacks. These workers faced the risk of violence which ran deep in the history of race and labor relations in the south. . . . Nevertheless, these workers were determined to invoke the Civil Rights Act. These black workers signed complaints of employment discrimination against virtually all of the major employers in the Birmingham area, including U.S. Steel and other firms in heavy industry. . . .

In the fall of 1965 the EEOC began what proved to be nearly ten years of negotiation between the federal government and the steel industry concerning discriminatory seniority practices. At one early meeting, the Steelworkers' initial response to Title VII became apparent. One union attorney declared that *Whitfield v. United Steelworkers of America, Local No. 2708* was controlling.[2] *Whitfield* had held that a discriminatory seniority system was cured if senior black employees were allowed to enter previously "white" jobs as new employees, even though they received no credit for their prior service in "black" jobs. If *Whitfield* applied under Title VII, the outlook for major improvement in black employment opportunities was bleak. Under *Whitfield,* the most senior black employee would be permanently locked in behind the most recently hired white worker.

The steel companies and unions repeatedly urged the EEOC and staff to apply the *Whitfield* doctrine. . . . The EEOC finally decided to seek remedies for discriminatory seniority systems beyond that provided for in *Whitfield.* The Commission articulated its policy in its response to the union-industry arguments concerning a steel facility in Birmingham. EEOC Executive Director Herman Edelsberg authored the Commission's response. . . . Edelsberg insisted that the steel industry both afford black workers "the opportunity to fill vacancies anywhere in the line on the basis of their company seniority," and agree that "company seniority would govern their status in the line for layoff purposes." The EEOC, the toothless tiger of equal employment opportunity law, in a classic low-visibility administrative decision, thus rejected the effort to engraft the *Whitfield* doctrine into Title VII and insisted on greater relief for the senior black employees, including the establishment of training programs.

B.   Implementation of Title VII Policies: Training Programs

The need for training programs to enable black workers to take advantage of newly opened opportunities was recognized in the early days of Title VII. . . . The major success story of 1966 was the Newport News Agreement. This agreement was the first detailed plant-wide revision of industrial relations systems under Title VII and the executive order program. Akin to a collective bargaining agreement in breadth and depth, it specifically provided for enhanced black participation in apprenticeship programs. . . . The Newport News agreement had been negotiated during the suspension of government contracts with the shipyard. . . . [T]he EEOC, the Department of Labor, and the Department of Justice, by the close of 1966, had laid the foundation for those principles which would prove important as the courts began to interpret Title VII. These principles were:

1.   A "fresh start for the future," the *Whitfield* solution, was not a sufficient remedy for seniority discrimination. Senior blacks could not be treated as junior employees in white jobs. Further relief for senior black workers confined to low-paying jobs because of their race was necessary;

2.   Training programs to equip minorities to handle the jobs from which they had been traditionally excluded were an essential part of a major settlement package correcting the historic exclusion of minorities and;

3.   The training opportunities should be allocated by reference to the proportion of blacks and whites in the labor market.

The EEOC pressed these positions in the limited forms which were open to it, including conciliation proposals, publication of sanitized reasonable cause decisions, amicus briefs and guidelines, and speeches by Commissioners and staff. Some employers did not accept the EEOC's broad interpretations of Title VII. Thus, in the late 1960s, the issues moved to the courts.

C. Reinforcing Title VII Policies in the Courts

The principles which the EEOC formulated were asserted in many Title VII class actions brought primarily by private plaintiffs, often supported by the NAACP Legal Defense and Educational Fund, Inc.[3] In defending against these Title VII suits, the steel industry and unions pressed the *Whitfield* argument with some initial success. The Northern District Court of Alabama in *United States v. H. K. Porter* (296 F. Supp. 40, 1968) gave hope to the steel industry and unions by adopting a narrow interpretation of the statutory obligations. These hopes were soon dashed, however, as courts began to take positions which were incompatible with *Whitfield*. In one particularly influential decision, Judge Butzner, in the Eastern District of Virginia, concluded that "Congress did not intend to freeze a generation of Negro employees into discriminatory patterns that existed before the Act," (Quarles v. Phillip Morris, 271 F. Supp. 842, 1967). The Fifth Circuit adopted the view that senior black employees were entitled to advance to their "rightful place" measured by overall length of service; these employees should not remain behind junior white workers, as they would be compelled to do under the *Whitfield* rule. . . .

In *United States v. Bethlehem Steel Corp.* the Second Circuit went further, sweeping away not only the *Whitfield* defense, but also many other legal objections that the steel industry employers and unions had raised to a revision of the seniority system. *Bethlehem Steel* involved a fact pattern of "classic job discrimination in the north" (U.S. v. Bethlehem Steel Corp., 446 F.2d at 655). One issue was whether black employees who transferred into white lines of progression could carry their plant seniority with them for bidding purposes. The court answered the question in the affirmative thus joining the Fifth Circuit in rejecting the *Whitfield* doctrine. . . .

In 1973, two more blows were dealt the steel industry's seniority systems. First, the Secretary of Labor found the system at Bethlehem Steel's Sparrows Point plant in violation of the executive order proscribing discrimination by government contractors. Second, the district court in Birmingham in *United States v. United States Steel Corp.* (371 F. Supp. 1045), . . . found discriminatory the seniority systems of the nine plants of U.S. Steel's Fairfield Works. Judge Pointer's order required revisions in the seniority systems and associated promotional opportunities for *all* employees. . . . His decision was the final event leading to the industry-wide settlement.

D. The Steel Industry Response

After Judge Pointer's decision, steel industry employers and the United Steelworkers sought to settle the seniority discrimination issues being raised throughout the industry. They decided to alter the departmental seniority system and give decisive weight to plant seniority. The modifications would provide long term black employees with seniority credit for time spent in black jobs. . . . This law, uniform throughout the circuits, suggested that the employers and the union would lose many of the discrimination cases which had been filed against them.

After the union and the employers reached this agreement, they sought to negotiate governmental approval. In intricate and exhausting negotiations, the government demanded back pay and increased minority participation in the trade and craft jobs in exchange for its approval. The companies earmarked some thirty million dollars for settlement payments to nearly 50,000 black workers. The union and the employers also agreed to create specific promotional opportunities for minority workers into trade or craft jobs on a 50–50 basis, despite their preference for a color-blind program. The inclusion of craft jobs gave additional opportunities to black employees beyond those provided by the change in the seniority systems while addressing the claim of discrimination in assignment to those jobs. . . .

E. Other Sources of Anti-Discrimination Values: The Executive Order Program and "Plans for Progress"

In the 1960s, the Labor Department attempted to address the virtual exclusion of minorities from some building construction unions. After a series of experiments, the Department established the "Cleveland Plan," which required contractors to agree to meet unspecified minority hiring goals as a condition of obtaining government contracts. After the Comptroller General held this obligation too vague to be enforceable, the Department of Labor decided to adopt more specific standards. It developed a plan for Philadelphia which set specific goals and timetables in those skilled trades where minorities were under-represented. Once again, contractors appealed to the Comptroller General, this time claiming that the specificity which his earlier decision required had produced preferential treatment for minorities, in violation of the Constitution, EO 11,246, and Title VII.

The Comptroller General ruled that the specific goals and timetables were unconstitutional. Both the Department of Labor and the Justice Department viewed this ruling as a usurpation of authority. The Justice Department, supported by the Labor Department, issued an Attorney General's opinion upholding the constitutionality of the "Philadelphia Plan," after which the contractors and unions in Philadelphia sought to enjoin the program. In *Contractors Association v. Secretary of Labor,*[4] a 1971 case, the Third Circuit upheld the goals and timetables aspect of the "Philadelphia Plan."

In 1970, Senator Fannin proposed a rider to an appropriations bill which would have abolished such goals and timetables. The Nixon Administration, prompted by Secretary of Labor Shultz and Assistant Secretary Fletcher, opposed the rider.

The rider was defeated. Thus in the crucible of the construction industry and its history of exclusion of minorities from skilled crafts was born the goals and timetables approach which the Department of Labor, under Order No. 4, expanded to all government contractors in 1970.

The Department of Labor's specific goals and timetables approach was a reaction to an experiment in voluntarism without enforcement. In 1961, EO 10,925, which prohibited discrimination by government contractors, was given teeth. Administrators were authorized to conduct hearings leading to cancellation of government contracts and debarment from future contracts. While the government deliberated whether to take a tough or soft approach to the enforcement of EO 10,925, industry established "Plans for Progress" (PFP); a group of large employers voluntarily dedicated themselves to improving the employment position of minorities. . . . One of the advantages of being a PFP member, however, was relief from even the minimal risk of sanctions under EO 10,925 and, later, EO 11,246.

In early cases under Title VII, some employers argued that "good faith" constituted a defense under Title VII and asserted their PFP membership and activities as evidence of good faith efforts to assist minorities. The EEOC took the position that Title VII was concerned with the results of employment practices, rather than with the state of mind of the employer. Because the results which PFP members achieved appeared unimpressive, the EEOC did battle with PFP on the field of statistics. . . .

In 1968, the EEOC held hearings on white collar employment in New York City. The research report compared the performance of forty-six PFP companies with that of fifty-four nonmembers:

> By almost any measure, we find that those who should be the leaders in this crucial area of local and national concern are, in fact, the laggards. All 100 companies have comparatively large resources which make it possible to recruit with ingenuity on a broad scale; to search with diligence among their existing work forces for the Negro, Puerto Rican, or woman who is employed at a level beneath his or her skills and potentiality; to invest in the company or community-wide training programs necessary to make equal job opportunity meaningful. . . . Such measures as these are known as "affirmative action"—a term which appears in the non-discrimination clause of every Federal government contract and in many of the "Plans for Progress" documents. . . . Among the 100 employers themselves, those who have *not* participated in the Plans for Progress organization have a record of higher minority utilization, in almost every occupational category, than those who have made these pledges. (U.S. EECO 1968)

[A]fter these revelations, PFP was quietly interred, in favor of a new organization called the National Alliance of Businessmen. Before disappearing, however, PFP published, jointly with the National Association of Manufacturers (NAM), recommendations for affirmative action. Included was an outline of a process of self-evaluation, and the establishment of goals and objectives to solve problems which had been identified. The outline stated: "Goals should be specific both for planned results and timetables."

When the Comptroller General's decision concerning the "Cleveland Plan" pressured the Department of Labor to establish specific standards for employers, the PFP-NAM publication literally became the basis of the program, except that compliance with the program was required of, rather than merely recommended to, government contractors. Revised Order No. 4, now in effect, which demands "under-utilization analysis" to identify "deficiencies," and the setting of "goals and timetables" to correct them, is a lineal descendant of this last, and perhaps best, PFP service performed in the cause of equal employment opportunity. By adopting the business-endorsed plan, the Department defused the political pressure which might otherwise have been mounted against this extensive regulation of the industrial relations system.

Thus, by the end of 1971, the Labor Department's program to require specific performance of the affirmative action obligation was in place, and had been upheld by the Third Circuit in the "Philadelphia Plan" case. Major efforts made during the 1972 Congressional review of Title VII to knock out the "Philadelphia Plan" concept of goals and timetables failed. By the time the steel industry and the steelworkers sat down to negotiate their settlement of seniority discrimination issues, the use of specific goals and timetables had been upheld in the courts, and had survived the rigors of Congressional review. . . .

F.   An Increase in Voluntary Compliance

The industrial relations specialists in the aluminum industry were aware of the negotiations in the steel industry. After observing the agonies which the steel industry had endured for nearly a decade, the aluminum industry and the steelworkers decided to improve minority employment opportunities without waiting for the plethora of suits and administrative proceedings which had preoccupied the steel industry. . . . The consent decrees, conciliation agreements, and affirmative action programs, which many other companies in a wide variety of fields had adopted, attest to the degree to which Title VII values had become embedded in American industry. The American Telephone and Telegraph (AT&T) consent decree, for instance, incorporated goals and timetables, training programs, and a "seniority override."

Although one could argue that any action taken in anticipation of possible adverse legal consequences is not "voluntary," such an argument disregards the key role of the law transmission system in modern regulation. Voluntarism in modern regulation does not mean "done of charitable motives from the goodness of the heart." Rather, it means choosing from among options available after considering institutional and legal pressures. Voluntary collective bargaining, for example, means bargaining within the framework of legal and economic pressures which the parties can impose on each other. The concept of voluntarism is best understood as allowing the regulated institutions to exercise options and choices within the framework of law. . . .

In this sense, the course of industrial relations described in this paper represents voluntarism at its most useful. The various institutions involved— employers, unions, administrative agencies, and the courts—all participated to produce a workable result which comported with congressional objectives. . . .

II. THE FIRST FIFTEEN YEARS UNDER TITLE VII

The 1974 steel industry settlement, followed by the AT&T consent decree, signaled that major employers were prepared to take far greater steps to address the problem of minority employment opportunity than they had been willing to take before the enactment of the Civil Rights Acts. The law transmission system had led the employers to the conclusion that their optimum choice was to alter their industrial relations practices. . . .

[W]e cannot help being impressed with the peaceful social revolution through which we have lived and in which we have participated. . . . [T]he law transmission system has been highly successful. One key measure of employment discrimination has been the concentration of minorities in the lower-paying "blue collar" jobs. Table 1 compares the participation rate of minority and white employees in each job category at five-year intervals beginning in 1950. The ratio figure of 100 would mean that the same percentage of the minority work force was employed in the job category as the percentage of the white work force. In 1950, for example, while 11.6% of white employees were officials and

Table 1. Ratio of Minority Worker Employment to White Worker Employment.

Occupation	1950	1955	1960	1965	1970	1975	1980
Officials & Managers	21.5	20.7	21.5	23.4	30.7	39.2	43.3
Professional & Technical	37.5	35.7	36.7	52.3	61.5	73.5	77.0
Sales	17.3	18.8	22.2	26.7	31.3	39.1	42.6
Clerical	25.3	34.5	46.2	50.3	73.3	86.7	98.9
Craftspersons (Skilled)	35.0	36.8	43.0	49.6	60.0	65.7	72.2
Operatives (Semiskilled)	90.2	103.4	113.5	117.0	139.4	136.9	143.7
Labors (Unskilled)	282.0	336.2	306.0	282.0	251.2	193.3	160.5
Services (Excluding Household)	233.3	233.3	213.4	218.3	194.6	184.9	176.1

Note: Ratio $= \dfrac{\text{percentage of minority workers in occupation}}{\text{percentage of white workers in occupation}} \times 100$

managers, only 2.5% of minority employees, were in that category, so that the ratio figure is 21.5.

The percentage of minorities in some of the higher occupational categories (professional and technical, clerical, and craftspersons) has approached the percentage of whites in these categories since 1965. At the other end of the scale, the percentage of minorities workings as unskilled laborers and in service occupations has declined significantly during the same period. . . .

Table 1 also addresses the complex question of "causation" or "attribution" which may be raised whenever social or economic changes are attributed to the legal system. An argument frequently made is that factors and forces other than the legal system are primarily responsible for such results. A comparison of the movement between 1950 and 1960 with that between 1970 and 1980 shows that prior to the passage of Title VII and application of a more stringent executive order, the occupational distribution of minorities did not significantly improve.[5] This at least shifts the burden of demonstrating that the changes are attributable to factors other than the legal system to those who make the argument.

A more fundamental flaw in any claim that factors other than law were responsible for the changes, however, is the assumption that the legal system is somehow separate from and independent of other forces operating in society. This is a false notion in a society where legislation is a reflection of public sentiment. The passage of the Civil Rights Act reflected public notions about the proper treatment of minorities in the labor force as well as the sentiment that regulated institutions were expected to act in accord with those expressed ideas. The actions thereafter taken by the myriad of persons and institutions to comply with the new standard were imbedded in individualized economic, social, and value systems. The effort to separate the force of law from these other factors in connection with millions of personnel decisions is theoretically inappropriate and practically impossible. . . .

III.   THE RISE AND FALL OF "SOUTHERN JURISPRUDENCE" OF TITLE VII

A.   The Emergence of "Southern Jurisprudence"

To understand the role of courts in the transmission of the policies of equal employment opportunity, one must examine the corpus of Title VII law which underlay the steel settlement and its progeny. This body of Title VII law was developed in important part by the circuit courts of appeal for the southern states, and confirmed in a crucial aspect by the Supreme Court in *Griggs v. Duke Power Co.* The key holdings in *Griggs* were (1) that under Title VII, employment practices which had an adverse effect on blacks were illegal unless justified by business necessity, (2) that the "good intent" of the employer was no defense, and (3) that the "present effects of past discrimination" constituted illegal behavior without a "new act" of discrimination.

These holdings confirmed, and thus laid a foundation for the expansion of, a series of southern courts of appeals decisions apparently based on the assumption that a black plaintiff in a Title VII action had probably been discriminated against. In this way, *Griggs* broadened the substance of Title VII beyond previous expectations and provided the legal foundation for the changes in employment practices which followed (Belton 1976; Blumrosen 1971). Numerous important decisions concerning Title VII from circuits other than those located in the south also interpreted the statute sympathetically. The decisions of the Fourth and Fifth Circuits, however, were particularly influential in the overall development of the law, as reflected by extensive citation to them in the opinions of the other circuits. The judges in the other circuits seemed to defer informally to their counterparts in the south who had intimately experienced the relationship between racial prejudice and employment practices. The southeastern states had "open and notorious" job segregation, dual lines of seniority and officially segregated school systems which tended to assure inferior education and employment for minorities. The district judges sitting in those states, with some notable exceptions, were unsympathetic to Title VII. With almost monotonous regularity, they adopted a narrow construction of the statute and made findings of fact in favor of defendants. Thereupon the Fourth and Fifth Circuit Courts of Appeal wrote a remarkable chapter in the history of statutory interpretation. They created a jurisprudence of Title VII which was calculated to simplify the attack on segregated employment systems.

A 1968 Fifth Circuit decision on a procedural point foreshadowed the new jurisprudential approach. The issue in *Oatis v. Crown Zellerbach* was whether the beneficiaries of Title VII were limited to those who had filed charges with the EEOC or whether a class action could include minorities who had not filed charges. The court concluded that a Title VII suit could benefit all such minorities, basing its decision on the premise that "[r]acial discrimination is by definition class discrimination, and to require a multiplicity of separate, identical charges before the EEOC, filed against the same employer, as a prerequisite to relief through resort to the court would tend to frustrate our system of justice and order" (398 F.2d 496, 1968, p. 499). . . .

The southern circuits proceeded to mark out in bold strokes the interpretations which would transform the "faint hope" into legal reality. In *Local 189 Papermaker v. United States,* the Fifth Circuit . . . required the employer and the union to give seniority credit to blacks for time worked in "black jobs" when they competed with whites, until they reached their "rightful place," (416 F.2d 980). . . .

For individual cases of discrimination, the Fifth Circuit developed a presumption of discrimination upon a showing that a vacancy existed, and that the plaintiff had applied, been rejected, and was qualified for the job. After the plaintiff had made such a showing, the employer had to persuade the judge that the rejection had been for nondiscriminatory reasons.[6]. . . .

The knowledge of traditions of racial discrimination shaped the judges' attempt to provide a body of substantive and procedural law that would give a "glimmer of hope" to the intended beneficiaries of Title VII. The premise that discrimination permeated employment patterns in the South lay at the heart of the line of cases discussed above. The way to cut through this fabric of discrimination was to simplify the plaintiff's case while making it difficult for employers to rely on denials of discriminatory intent. These decisions helped prompt both the steel industry consent decree and the nationwide settlement between the EEOC and AT&T.

B. The Repudiation: 1977–1982

In 1977, the Supreme Court rejected the course of decision not only of the Fourth and Fifth circuits but of all the circuits which had subjected previously segregated seniority systems to judicial review. In *International Brotherhood of Teamsters v. United States* (431 U.S. 324, 1977) the Court held that the bona fide seniority systems exemption of Title VII protected seniority systems which perpetuated past discrimination. Concluding that Congress *did* intend to exempt an otherwise "bona fide" seniority system under Title VII even if that system perpetuated pre-Act discrimination, the Court held that such a system was lawful unless it was the product of an intent to discriminate. . . .

The Court has repudiated many of the procedural as well as substantive aspects of the southern jurisprudence. . . . [B]y 1982, the Supreme Court had rejected much of the edifice of Title VII law which the southern courts of appeals had developed around an underlying assumption that a black person denied employment had probably been discriminated against along with all other black prospective employees. Despite its repudiation, this line of cases left its mark on American society, including the south, because of the operation of the law transmission system and the regulated community's of the values represented by this body of law, which the steel industry settlement exemplifies.

C. The Impact of Southern Jurisprudence

The strong medicine of southern jurisprudence profoundly affected southern discrimination in employment. The steel industry settlement had signaled the acceptance by employers and unions of the responsibility for abolishing job segregation. This task had been accomplished to a significant extent before the

Supreme Court repudiated much of the southern jurisprudence. Half of the work force in 1964, the year Congress passed the Civil Rights Act, had retired by 1980, and half of the work force had entered a system which by the mid-1970s no longer reflected the segregation of the past.

The Supreme Court's rejection of the southern jurisprudence does not mean that the practices condemned by Congress are now lawful. It means that the illegality must now be proved; it can no longer be presumed. . . . If Title VII has in fact altered workplace behavior in the last fifteen years, employers may prevail in a greater number of cases because the extent of discrimination has been reduced.

A distinction between first and second generation Title VII cases is important in understanding this conclusion. The first generation cases were based on situations which existed in the late 1960s, where many employment or promotion standards carried forward the previous pattern of explicit segregation and discrimination. Southern judges who had lived with the traditional practices and were committed to implementing the national policy requiring its change deemed proof of the discriminatory legacy unnecessary.

But second generation cases are different. The facts of those cases arose in the 1970s, after employers and unions had implemented changes. The discrimination pattern is no longer so clear. The precise practices which were easily identified as discriminatory in first generation cases are now difficult—or impossible—to locate. Plaintiffs' cases are therefore less substantial, and less winnable under any standard.

Furthermore, the statistics concerning minority employment demonstrate that the presumption of discrimination which southern jurisprudence developed is no longer as valid a social fact in either the south or the nation as a whole. The sharp alteration in patterns of employment over the past fifteen years has made statistically vivid what personal impression suggests. Judges are bound to sense this change just as they once recognized the pervasive quality of discrimination. . . .

In assessing the Supreme Court decisions cutting back on the southern jurisprudence, one should recognize how significant a part of the underlying evil which Title VII addressed has been corrected. The system of seniority in basic steel, the heavy industry of Alabama, and the paper industry, which so heavily dominates Mississippi, has been changed. The pattern of employment in the textile industry in the Carolinas has changed. The segregated systems in the petrochemicals industry in Texas and in Louisiana have been altered.

At this point, the questions become political. How much of a change is "enough" is a basic value judgment which cannot be made through rational processes alone. Considering the improvement in assessing whether the Supreme Court should have continued the presumption of discrimination of the southern jurisprudence is not akin to supporting the repeal of the civil rights law, or the abandonment of affirmative action. The statistics presented suggest that the Court rightly rejected the web of rules which assumed that blacks were usually the victims of discrimination. . . .

Even those who accept the assertion that more than two million minority workers were in improved circumstances in 1980 when measured by 1965 standards, however, may not view this difference as indicating a major improvement in employment opportunity. Minorities are still predominantly employed in the lower blue collar jobs. High unemployment rates and lower income levels persist, and in some instances have worsened. In addition, there is a serious concern that once the Supreme Court has narrowed the scope of Title VII, a resurgence of discrimination could resegregate the work force. This will probably not happen. Any attempt to change back to a segregated system would of course create new acts of intentional discrimination. But there is a deeper reason why the work force will not be resegregated. This lies in the widespread recognition that the "southern pattern" of discrimination was wrong. The new generations of workers, managers and union officials will not seek to revive the old system. The work of legal rules developed by the southern circuits and the passing of the generations have destroyed it.

Some evidence that the changes wrought by the southern jurisprudence are deeply imbedded in our industrial relations system can be gleaned from EEO-1 statistics for the nine southern states in the period after the 1977 *Teamsters* decision. The problem of pre-Act discrimination in seniority systems was most prominent in the southern states with open and notorious segregation practices in the pre-Act period. Therefore, backsliding was an obvious risk in that area. Any significant regression would have manifested itself in two ways: first, the pace of infusion of blacks into white collar and craft jobs would have slowed, and second, the proportion of blacks in the traditional laborer and operative jobs would have increased.

A comparison of the occupational distribution of black workers in 1978 and in 1980 with the distribution which would have occurred if the pattern of 1966 were in place suggests that, in the south, the pattern of discrimination did not reappear in the three years immediately following the *Teamsters* decision. In 1978, 310,000 of 1,386,676 black workers (22.3%) were "better off" in terms of occupational categories than they would have been under the 1966 distribution. In 1980, 355,000 of the 1,480,478 black workers (23.9%) were better off than under the 1966 distribution. These figures indicate that the pattern of continued inclusion of blacks which began under the regime of southern jurisprudence persisted at least to the end of the decade. . . .

Having allowed the southern circuits to dismantle the fabric of segregation which gave rise to Title VII, the Supreme Court decisions which limit the manner in which the law controls employment decisions may have expressed a deeper wisdom: that the law should withdraw when the industrial relations system operates fairly without such extensive judicial or administrative supervision. . . .

CONCLUSION

The *Griggs* decision of 1971 provided authoritative support for the southern jurisprudence which was the bedrock on which the steel industry settlement was founded. This settlement illustrated that unions and employers would give up the "southern way" in employment without the "massive resistance" of school segregation cases. . . . That the Court has now disavowed the southern jurisprudence does not detract from that body of law's achievement. . . .

In the 1980s, the Reagan Administration verbally opposed "goals and timetables" and severely cut back on the number of employees available, particularly in the Labor Department, to enforce anti-discrimination laws. As of the end of 1983, however, the administration had not repealed either the goals and timetables regulations or the affirmative action guidelines of the EEOC which supported this approach; and toward the end of the year, the EEOC and General Motors (GM) entered into a major settlement in which GM agreed to adopt goals and timetables. Thus, while the reduction in administration pressures for affirmative action may have some negative impact on informal decisionmaking by employers, the apparatus of the goals and timetables program remains intact. . . .

The halcyon days of Title VII may be over, however, for reasons beyond the control of either the Court or any particular presidential administration. The extraordinary pace of improvement in occupational status may have slowed because the worst of the pattern of discrimination has been shattered by the law transmission system.

The other two indicators of discrimination, wage disparities and relative unemployment rates, did not improve between 1965 and 1980. The wage disparity issue is only now being litigated under Title VII. The continued high minority unemployment rate may require an approach that is beyond Title VII. . . .

The concept of a law transmission system is central to understanding not only how legal norms are transmuted into social reality, but also where the limits of such norms lie and when alternative methods of achieving social goals should be considered. In our complex and rapidly changing society, the realization of social ideals cannot be channeled for long into any single legal form.

NOTES

1. *See* United States v. Allegheny-Ludlum Industries, Inc., 517 F.2d 826 (5th Cir. 1975), *cert. denied,* 425 U.S. 944 (1976). The agreement is described in 5 U.S. Civil Rights Commission, The Federal Civil Rights Enforcement Effort—1974 556–60 (1975) [hereinafter cited as 1974 CRC Report].

2.   263 F.2d 546 (5th Cir. 1959) . . . Prior to 1956, the Armco Steel Company and the Steelworkers Union had maintained strict job segregation by race at the plant in Houston,

Texas. Jobs were organized in lines of progression, or job ladders. "Black" jobs and black lines of progression were openly acknowledged. Blacks could not obtain any white jobs.

In 1956, the company and the union decided to end their rigid job segregation. Black employees were allowed to enter the previously white line of progression at the bottom as if they were new employees. They were not given seniority credit for their prior service in "black" jobs. . . .

The *Armco* case came before the Fifth Circuit as Whitfield v. Steelworkers, 263 F.2d 546 (5th Cir. 1959). In an opinion by Judge Wisdom, the court upheld the Armco agreement. . . . This opinion limited the legal force of the duty of fair representation in seniority discrimination cases. The maximum relief available to black employees was the opportunity to take a less secure, lower paying job at the bottom of the "white" line. Thus the game was rarely worth the candle. . . .

3. See Belton (1976) for a discussion of the approach of civil rights lawyers to the new law.

4. 442 F.2d 159 (3d Cir. 1971). The construction industry was a major target of civil rights interest through so many years, proceedings, and programs that former Secretary of Labor John Dunlop, perhaps the person who understood it best, had called it a "dismal swamp" for those who would reform its employment practices. Construction work is performed "in public" and some construction work appeared not to require significant skills. In the pre-Civil War South, slaves performed much construction work. They were frozen out of much of that work after the Civil War. These reasons were contributing factors to the focus on the construction industry. Another factor was the energy of the former labor director of the NAACP, Herbert Hill. See H. Hill, Black Labor and the American Legal System (1977). The Supreme Court's willingness in *Weber* to take judicial notice of the pattern of discrimination in that industry flows in important measure from the zeal and perseverance of the NAACP, and the Legal Defense and Educational Fund, Inc.

5. Data for 1950–1965 from U.S. Bureau of the Census, Statistical Abstract of the United States: 1966 at 229; for 1970–1980, from U.S. Bureau of the Census, Statistical Abstract of the United States: 1981 at 400 [hereinafter Statistical Abstract: 1981].

6. *See, e.g.,* Turner v. Texas Instruments, Inc., 555 F.2d 1251, 1255 (5th Cir. 1977); East v. Romine, Inc., 518 F.2d 332, 339–40 (5th Cir. 1975), *overruled,* Texas Dep't of Commerce v. Burdine, 450 U.S. 248 (1981).

REFERENCES

Belton, Robert. 1976. "Title VII of the Civil Rights Act of 1964: A Decade of Private Enforcement and Judicial Developments." *St. Louis University Law Journal* 20:225–307.

Blumrosen, Alfred W. 1972. "Strangers in Paradise: *Griggs vs. Duke Power Co.* and the Concept of Employment Discrimination." *Michigan Law Review* 71:59–110.

Hill, Herbert. 1977. Black Labor and the American Legal System: Race, Work and the Law. Originally published 1927 by the Bureau of National Affairs. Reissued in 1985 by the University of Wisconsin.

United States Equal Employment Opportunity Commission. 1968. "Hearings on Discrimination in White Collar Employment." Washington, DC: Government Printing Office.

16

Legal Ambiguity and Symbolic Structures: Organizational Mediation of Civil Rights Law

Lauren B. Edelman

INTRODUCTION

As laws regulating organizations grow both in number and complexity, the legal environment becomes an increasingly salient determinant of organizational structure and behavior. Studies of law and organizations measure the impact of law, . . . criticize the form and structure of law, . . . and identify factors that motivate compliance and noncompliance. . . . But our understanding of the *process* by which organizations respond to law is very limited. This omission is critical: through the process of response to law, organizations construct the meaning of compliance and thus *mediate* the impact of law on society. . . .

In this article I examine the initial stages of organizational response to and mediation of law; that is, I explore the definition and institutionalization of what constitutes compliance, . . . in the context of equal employment opportunity and affirmative action (EEO/AA) law. . . . Data for the project comes from a nationwide survey of EEO/AA practices in 346 organizations, which I conducted in 1989. . . .

Equal employment opportunity/affirmative action law is perhaps the most important legal encroachment on employers' prerogatives since the labor legislation of the 1930s. It seeks to limit employers' ability to perpetuate social advantage or disadvantage through employment opportunities; in so doing it threatens to constrain traditional managerial prerogatives to choose freely whom to hire, fire, and promote. EEO/AA law consists of a body of antidiscrimination mandates comprising statutes, constitutional mandates,, and presidential executive orders. . . .

This study views compliance with EEO/AA law as a social process that evolves over time as organizations seek to adapt the law to fit their own inter-

Excerpts reprinted with permission from the *American Journal of Sociology* 1992 (May), vol 97 (6):1531–1576. Copyright © 1992 by the University of Chicago Press.

ests. . . . I suggest that organizations, rather than resist law overtly, are motivated by the weaknesses of EEO/AA law and the mechanics of the legal process to construct law in a manner that is minimally disruptive to the status quo. My analysis draws upon institutional theories of organizations, which emphasize organizations' dependence upon and interaction with their normative environments (Meyer and Rowan 1977; Meyer and Scott 1983; DiMaggio and Powell 1983; Edelman 1990). In particular it draws upon the legal environment theory that I have developed as a means of explaining organizational response to general legal norms (Edelman 1990), and it extends that theory to address organizational response to direct legal mandates.

In earlier work (Edelman 1990), I have argued that law creates a "legal environment" that consists not only of law and the sanctions that are built into law, but also of societal norms and culture associated with the law. Organizations that are sensitive to their legal environments develop forms of governance that conform to legal norms in order to achieve legitimacy. Over time, some organizational responses to the legal environment diffuse among organizations and become institutionalized. Thus by influencing organizations' environments, law has an important indirect effect on organizational behavior that goes significantly beyond the direct effect of law and legal sanctions.

EEO/AA LAW AND THE LEGAL ENVIRONMENT

Equal employment opportunity/affirmative action law influences the legal environment by changing public expectations about employees' civil rights and providing a basis for criticizing well-ingrained patterns of governance that favor whites and males. The law bolsters efforts by pressure groups to realize civil rights, and it legitimates employees' claims to those rights. By empowering those who make demands upon organizations, EEO/AA law creates a legal environment that encourages organizations to comply, or appear to comply, with EEO/AA law. But normative pressure from the legal environment does not easily erode long-held managerial prerogatives. Employers resist EEO/AA law not only because it infringes upon managerial discretion but also because employers view EEO/AA law as requiring inefficient and irrational business practices.

The conflict between EEO/AA law and managerial interests poses a dilemma to organizations: they must demonstrate compliance in order to maintain legitimacy and at the same time they must minimize law's encroachment on managerial power. This dilemma motivates a process of response to law in which organizations test, negotiate, and collectively institutionalize forms of compliance that, to the greatest extent possible, maximize both interests; it is through this process that organizations "mediate" the law.

THE CONDITIONS OF ORGANIZATIONAL MEDIATION OF LAW

Equal employment opportunity/affirmative action law is especially open to organizational mediation for three reasons: (1) it is ambiguous with respect to the meaning of compliance; (2) as construed by the courts, it constrains organizational procedures more than the outcome of those procedures; and (3) its enforcement mechanisms are relatively weak. Each of these characteristics broadens the scope of organizational behaviors that may be considered compliant.

Ambiguity

Title VII of the 1964 Civil Rights Act, section 703(a), states that

> It shall be an unlawful employment practice for an employer: (1) to fail or refuse to hire or to discharge any individual, or *otherwise to discriminate* against any individual with respect to his compensation, terms, conditions, or privileges of employment, *because of such individual's race, color, religion, sex, or national origin;* or (2) to limit, segregate, or classify his employees or applicants for employment in any way which would deprive or tend to deprive any individual of employment opportunities or otherwise adversely affect his status as an employee, *because of such individual's race, color, religion, sex, or national origin.* [Emphasis added]

This language is ambiguous both in a legal sense and with respect to organizational policy. The basic ambiguity concerns the meaning of the phrase "to discriminate" together with the fact that the law uses the general terms "race" and "sex" rather than specifically prohibiting discrimination against "racial minorities" and "women."[1] It is interesting that, although Title VII includes definitions for 11 terms, it does not define the term most central to the law: "discrimination."

The ambiguous language of Title VII leaves the law open to at least two interpretations: (1) a procedural interpretation that emphasizes equality of treatment and thus implies that employment practices and procedures should be carried out in a race- and gender-blind manner and (2) a substantive interpretation that emphasizes equality of outcome and thus would require race- and gender-conscious treatment in order to achieve equity in work-force representation (Belton 1981; Fiss 1974; Freeman 1982; Blumrosen 1972; Burstein 1990). This ambiguity has generated significant political debate and been the subject of much EEO/AA litigation over the past 25 years. But, more important, the legal ambiguity of Title VII means that employers have little guidance as to what, other than eliminating overtly discriminatory policies and practices, employers must do in order to comply with Title VII.

The only tangible requirements of Title VII are work-force reporting requirements, which do not in and of themselves necessitate any change in employment policies or practices.[2] While the reporting requirement may encourage organizations to hire more minorities or women to make their numbers look good, it does not help to clarify, or indeed even address, what constitutes compliance.

Executive Order 11246 is even more complex than Title VII because it explicitly refers to "affirmative action," an often-used term that has no clear legal meaning (Jones 1985a). Section 202 of EO 11246 states, "The contractor will take *affirmative action* to ensure that applicants are employed and employees are treated during employment *without regard to their race, color, religion, sex, or national origin*" (emphasis added).

Those who embrace the substantive interpretation of Title VII see the "affirmative action" requirement as basically consistent with the requirement that employees be treated "without regard to their race, color, religion, sex, or national origin" (see, e.g., Fiss 1974; Belton 1981), but those who support the procedural interpretation of Title VII contend that the two requirements are contradictory (e.g., Smith 1978).

Federal employers and contractors had little guidance as to the nature of their obligation under EO 11246 until February 1970, when the Office of Federal Contract Compliance, charged with enforcing EO 11246, issued Order 4 as part of the OFCC Rules and Regulations. The issuance of Order 4 followed a ruling by the Comptroller General that the affirmative action obligation was too vague to meet the legal obligation that minimum contract standards must be clear to the parties. Revised Order 4, which replaced Order 4 in December 1971, requires organizations with 50 or more employees and contracts of $50,000 or more to undertake a "utilization analysis" to determine whether there is an underrepresentation of minorities and women in certain job categories, given their availability in the relevant labor market, and to establish "goals and timetables" to remedy any deficiencies found through the utilization analysis. But Revised Order 4 incorporates, rather than eliminates, the conflict between the affirmative action and nondiscrimination clauses of EO 11246. Section 60-2.12(e) specifies that "*Goals may not be rigid and inflexible quotas which must be met*, but must be targets reasonably attainable by means of applying every good faith effort to make all aspects of the affirmative action program work" (emphasis added), while sections 60-2.12(g) and (h) state that "*Goals, timetables, and affirmative action commitments must be designed to correct any identifiable deficiencies. Where deficiencies exist and where numbers or percentages are relevant in developing corrective action, the contractor shall establish and set forth specific goals and timetables for minorities and women*" (emphasis added).

The meaning of a specific but flexible goal is less than clear. And, like Title VII, although the rules and regulations for compliance with EO 11246 give definitions for 24 other terms, there are no explicit definitions for "discrimination," "affirmative action," or "equal employment opportunity."

Thus the basic ambiguity in EEO/AA law as to what constitutes discrimination and what organizations must (and can) do to comply leaves much open for the courts to interpret. And until judicial clarifications are made, it leaves much for organizations to interpret.

Procedural Emphasis

Laws that constrain procedure more than substance widen the latitude for organizational response because they make it more difficult to detect discrimination that is not blatant. Procedural constraints enhance the potential for organizations to develop forms of compliance that appear to comply with the law but have little substantive effect.

While the Supreme Court has never issued a definitive decision with respect to the conflict between the procedural and substantive interpretations to Title VII, it has—especially since the mid-1970s—been moving closer to the procedural interpretation. In 1971, the Supreme Court appeared to endorse a substantive interpretation of the law in *Griggs v. Duke Power Co.,* when it announced that a finding of discrimination could be based upon the consequences of employer actions rather than the intent underlying them. But since 1976, courts have begun to narrow the applicability of *Griggs.* . . .

Executive Order 11246 seems more result oriented than Title VII since it requires affirmative action (albeit without defining it) and because the rules implementing the order require that contractors establish employment goals for minority and female employment and timetables for achieving those goals. But OFCCP practices and the rules and regulations implementing EO 11246 transform the order into a more procedural constraint by stating explicitly that contractors need not achieve their goals but need only demonstrate a *good faith effort* to do so. . . . Both Title VII and EO 11246, then, leave open the possibility for organizations to create the appearance of compliance without much change to the racial, ethnic, and gender composition of their work forces.

Weak Enforcement Mechanisms

Weak enforcement mechanisms further obscure the boundaries of compliance by providing inadequate and inconsistent feedback on what organizational practices are legal. The major source of weakness in Title VII enforcement is that, although the Equal Employment Opportunity Commission (EEOC) and the Justice Department initiate a small number of lawsuits, the mobilization of EEO/AA law depends primarily upon complaints initiated by individual victims of discrimination. To obtain remedies for discrimination under Title VII, an individual files a complaint with the EEOC or, in some states, the state fair employment agency. The EEOC may try to conciliate, and, if that fails, may (since 1972) bring a lawsuit in federal court. If the agency does not pursue the complaint, the aggrieved employee's only option for redress is to file a lawsuit individually. In either case, the process is lengthy, expensive, and often oppressive, with no guarantees of redress. . . .

Compared to Title VII, the enforcement of EO 11246 is less dependent upon individual mobilization: the OFCCP has authority to enforce the order directly and has a number of sanctions available to it. The order authorizes the OFCCP to delay contract awards, to issue a notice requiring a contactor who appears to have violated the order to show cause why enforcement proceedings should not be instituted, to withhold progress payments, and to bar noncompliant organizations from future contracts.

But contract compliance enforcement has been notoriously weak. The OFCCP (and previously the OFCC) has been repeatedly criticized by the U.S. Commission on Civil Rights (USCCR), the Congress, and studies by independent agencies such as the Brookings Institution for failure to issue guidelines, failure to define "affirmative action," failure to train its staff, and, in particular, failure to use its power to suspend current and bar future government contracts when violations are found (USCCR 1971; House Committee on Education and Labor 1987; Nathan 1969). . . .

The ambiguity and weak enforcement mechanisms of EEO/AA law together with judicial and administrative constructions of law that emphasize fair procedure over fair results weaken the capacity of EEO/AA law to effect change directly. Why, then, do studies of work-force demographics find, fairly consistently, that the status of minorities and women improved significantly between 1964 and 1980, especially among federal contractors? A partial answer lies in the fact that, because of normative pressure from their legal environments, organizations do not simply ignore or circumvent weak law, but rather construct compliance in a way that, at least in part, fits their interest.

THE PROCESS OF MEDIATION OF LAW

Structural Elaboration

Laws that are ambiguous, procedural in emphasis, and difficult to enforce invite symbolic responses—responses designed to create a visible commitment to law, which may, but do not necessarily, reduce employment discrimination. Organizations respond visibly to law by elaborating their formal structures. I use the term "formal structures" to refer to the configuration of offices and positions and the formal linkages between them (the "organization chart") as well as to formal rules, programs, positions, and procedures. By contrast, informal structures refer to the actual communication channels between offices and positions, the actual behaviors of individuals who occupy them, and informal norms and practices. The two are not necessarily coupled: informal practices and norms often deviate from formal procedures and rules.

Organizations' formal structures are more visible to the outside world than their informal structures. As a strategy for achieving legitimacy, organizations adapt their formal structures to conform to institutionalized norms; the structures are symbolic gestures to public opinion, the views of constituents, social norms, or law (Meyer and Rowan 1977). Organizations seek to appear legitimate for a number of reasons: organizations that appear attentive to EEO/AA law are less likely to provoke protest by protected classes of employees within the firm or community members who seek jobs, they are more likely to secure government resources (contracts, grants, etc.), and they are less likely to trigger audits by regulatory agencies. And, if sued, organizations can point to the structural changes as evidence of the nondiscriminatory nature of their policies and practices. While failure to look compliant is unlikely to result in an organization's demise, it does carry an increased risk of legal liability and social disapproval.

Therefore, although EEO/AA law does not specifically require it, organizations respond to law by creating new offices, positions, rules, and procedures (which I will call EEO/AA structures) as visible symbols of their attention to EEO/AA issues and their efforts to comply.[3] To enhance the symbolic value of EEO/AA structures, organizations incorporate the legal language: they create "Affirmative Action offices" or "EEO policies."

The ambiguity, procedural emphasis, and weak enforcement mechanisms of EEO/AA law create the conditions under which EEO/AA structures become a source of legitimacy. In the absence of specific substantive requirements (e.g., a requirement that the racial and ethnic composition of the work force reflect that of the surrounding community or available labor pool), visible symbols of attention to EEO/AA law often suffice as evidence of compliance. . . .

In the arena of EEO/AA law, rules that explicitly prohibit discrimination and offices designed to implement EEO/AA law strongly connote compliance. Given judicial interpretations of EEO/AA law that emphasize fair treatment over fair results, formal policies and procedures that are free of discriminatory language and intent symbolize compliance. Given an enforcement system that depends upon victim mobilization, the effectiveness of these symbols is unlikely to be challenged. And, if challenged, structures that give the appearance of fair treatment make it more difficult for victims of employment discrimination to establish discrimination for legal purposes.

Of course, it is not always the case that structural elaboration is merely symbolic; structural change may be a means of achieving real improvement in minority and female employment status. Nonetheless, structural elaboration does not guarantee change. . . . By creating formal structures that are, or appear to be, mechanisms for implementing legal rules, organizations visibly demonstrate their commitment to comply with EEO/AA law. At the same time, the creation of formal structures can minimize law's intrusion on managerial prerogatives since they do not commit organizations to a particular type or degree of compliance. In some organizations, administrators will expect rules to be enforced and affirmative action offices to work actively and enthusiastically to improve the status of women and minorities within the firm. In others, administrators will create EEO/AA structures as substitutes for compliance, as shams.

Although the quest for legitimacy is a primary motivation for structural elaboration, it is not the only one. Structural elaboration is also a method by which organizations rationalize their legal environments, which is especially important in the face of legal ambiguity. Because judicial interpretations of EEO/AA law are complex and continually changing, employers may consider it rational to hire specialized personnel who can monitor legal changes and, when necessary, modify organizational policy. These EEO/AA structures can also be a means of coordinating compliance efforts and of managing documentation and reporting requirements (although many organizations incorporate such functions into their preexistent structures). It may be efficient, especially for a large organization, to create an affirmative action office to respond to employees' or community members' claims of discrimination. . . .

Organizations create EEO/AA structures, then, largely as gestures to their legal environments; these structures are designed to secure legitimacy and minimize the threat of liability. Although organizations may have rational (efficiency-related) motivations for creating EEO/AA offices, the symbolic value of EEO/AA structures motivates organizations to create them even in the absence of any rational motivation for doing so. Indeed, EEO/AA structures, once in place, may pose new technical problems to organizations. Formal rules, for example, may create problems by providing a basis for employees to challenge managerial actions (Selznick 1969). And new positions and offices may enable people to pose serious challenges to managerial interests, since the personnel in such positions are often more committed to EEO/AA law than the administration that hired them (Edelman et al. 1991). . . .

The Institutionalization of EEO/AA Structures

Legal change engenders a process of institutionalization whereby new forms of compliance are diffused among organizations and gradually become ritualized elements of organizational governance. Whereas organizations that respond to legal change early devise and test ways to demonstrate compliance, organizations that are slower to respond can copy the apparently successful compliance strategies of other organizations. As EEO/AA structures become more prevalent in the population, the structures themselves help to constitute the legal environment. Their visibility as symbols of attention to EEO/AA law increases, making it easier for society to question the commitment of organizations that lack such structures. Thus, over time, organizations become increasingly likely to adopt EEO/AA structures.

The personnel and affirmative action professions play a critical role in the institutionalization process (Edelman 1990; Edelman, Abraham, and Erlanger 1992). Through professional journals, conventions, and workshops, these professionals help to convey interpretations of EEO/AA law and models of compliance. In so doing, they not only shape organizations' response to law and the legal environment, but also managerial conceptions of the rationality of the law. By the early 1970s, two major themes had emerged in the professional personnel literature on EEO/AA law. The first is that the demonstration of good faith is critical to compliance and may be a safer strategy of compliance than quota-based hiring or promotion (e.g., Thorp 1973; Marino 1980). The second theme is that the formalization of EEO/AA policy is propitious to management's interests in efficiency and high productivity (e.g., Garris and Black 1974; Froehlich and Hawver 1974). As employers begin to believe that EEO/AA structures have rational as well as symbolic value, their resistance to those structures begins to fade, which contributes to the general institutionalization of EEO/AA structures.

The courts also reinforce the institutionalization of EEO/AA structures when they treat those structures as evidence of good faith. . . . Judicial support for EEO/AA structures—together with claims in the personnel literature that tend to exaggerate judicial support—help to reinforce the diffusion of EEO/AA structures. . . .

DATA AND METHOD OF ANALYSIS

The data for this analysis come from a nationwide phone and mail survey of organizational EEO/AA practices, which was conducted during the spring of 1989. The survey was administered to a probability sample of 346 organizations, consisting of 248 private firms, 50 colleges and universities (which I will refer to as "colleges"), and 48 government agencies at the federal, state, and local (county and city) levels. I collected retrospective event-history data on changes in EEO/AA practices, structures, and policies from 1964 to 1989. . . .

RESULTS

Patterns of Structural Elaboration over Time

Overall, organizations are clearly more likely to create symbolic structures that require fewer organizational resources and can more easily be decoupled from actual practices[4]. . . . In the survey, "rules" were defined as "a written statement or set of rules about procedures to be used in hiring, firing, promoting, or managing employees to ensure that employees are not subject to discrimination." Respondents were told *not* to include mere statements that the organization is an EEO/AA employer. "Offices" were defined as "a separate department for matters relating to equal employment opportunity or affirmative action." By 1989, 297 of the 346 organizations (86%) in the sample had created rules prohibiting discrimination. By contrast, only 64 organizations (18%) had created EEO/AA offices. The majority of organizations (282) incorporated EEO/AA activities into existent offices (usually personnel) rather than creating a new office. . . .

[T]here is an initial wave of structural response following a change in the legal environment and this wave is followed by a gradual institutionalization of those structural responses over time. . . .

EEO/AA offices. —EEO/AA offices serve as powerful symbols of attention to EEO/AA law because they signify an allocation of resources, space, and personnel and a commitment to compliance. In fact, the offices are generally quite small. Government agencies have the largest EEO/AA offices, with a mean of 7.1 full-time salaried employees, whereas colleges and business organizations have an average of two or fewer full-time salaried employees. In all but four of the 64 organizations that created EEO/AA offices, there was a personnel office previously in place, and EEO/AA offices are almost always smaller than personnel offices.

The data show that organizations most sensitive to the legal environment are far more likely to create such offices. . . . Overall, 19 of the 48 government agencies (39.6%), 15 of the 50 colleges (30.0%), and 30 of the 248 businesses (12.1%) had created EEO/AA offices by 1989. Furthermore, in the early period after the enactment of Title VII, organizations with contractual or administrative linkages to the federal government created EEO/AA offices at almost three times the rate of other organizations, which supports the argument that linkages to the public sphere, as well as sectoral proximity to the public sphere, affect organizations' response to the legal environment. . . .

EEO/AA rules. —In contrast to EEO/AA offices, EEO/AA rules are easy to create and do not require much expenditure of organizational resources; thus the overall formation rate of EEO/AA rules is significantly higher than that of EEO/AA offices. . . . [O]rganizations with personnel departments create rules at almost twice the rate of other organizations. This strong effect supports my argument that these departments act as "windows" to the legal environment and are critical to the institutionalization of structural responses to law. . . .

As an initial response to legal mandates, then, organizations elaborate their structures to demonstrate attention to law. But there are important differences among organizations both in the timing of their responses and in the types of symbolic structures that they create. Organizations most sensitive to their normative environments are the innovators of structural responses and are more likely to create high-investment EEO/AA structures. As societal approval for EEO/AA in employment increases, and as it becomes apparent that EEO/AA structures have some advantages for the governance of employees, these structures help to erode managerial resistance to EEO/AA law. This engenders a second wave of structural elaboration, which is more universal but involves lower-investment EEO/AA structures.

CONCLUSION

This research suggests that, where legal ambiguity, procedural constraints, and weak enforcement mechanisms leave the meaning of compliance open to organizational construction, organizations that are subject to normative pressure from their environment elaborate their formal structures to create visible symbols of their attention to law. Structural elaboration helps to alleviate the conflict between legal norms and managerial interests by helping organizations to secure legitimacy as well as more tangible environmental resources while at the same time allowing administrators to preserve at least some managerial discretion.

Organizations' structural responses to law mediate the impact of law on society by helping to construct the meaning of compliance in a way that accommodates managerial interests. At the level of individual organizations, the construction of compliance becomes a function of internal organizational politics tempered by industry norms and the standards of professional personnel and affirmative action administrators (Edelman et al. 1991). At a broader level, organizations' structural responses to law help to shape legal and societal expectations about what constitutes compliance and good faith efforts to comply. When organizations claim that, by creating EEO/AA structures, they have eliminated discriminatory practices, they force courts, lawmakers, and society to struggle with the question of what constitutes compliance. Courts, for the most part, only legitimate or delegitimate forms of compliance that organizations devise. But it is important to keep in mind that most organizations' constructions of compliance are never examined in court. Thus organizations' collective response to law becomes the de facto construction of compliance; it is shaped only at the margins by formal legal institutions.

The institutionalization process, moreover, appears to render EEO/AA structures somewhat immune from changes in the political environment. It is striking that during the 1980s, 75 EEO/AA rules (31%) and 11 EEO/AA offices (17%) were created, even though the Reagan and Bush administrations significantly reduced pressure to comply with EEO/AA mandates. The continued creation of EEO/AA structures suggests that, over time, pressure shifts from the legal realm to the societal and organizational realms. As EEO/AA structures become institutionalized responses to law, personnel and affirmative action professionals are likely to institute these structures because of their apparent rationality; thus the waning political support has little immediate effect. And as attention to EEO/AA becomes more widespread, local minority and female communities may become more likely to demand change; in some cases, a new affirmative action officer may help to mobilize community or employee demands for change (Edleman et al. 1991).

Internal and societal pressures also mean that waning political support is unlikely to result in significant dismantling of EEO/AA structures. In my sample, only three offices were dismantled during the entire period of observation. Given the symbolic value of EEO/AA structures, to dismantle an EEO/AA office or rule would appear to be a flagrant sign of disdain for civil rights; it would be likely to provoke protest even in a depoliticized environment. I would expect that a reduction in political pressure might lead organizations to cut the budget or staff of an EEO/AA office rather than to dismantle it.

The elaboration of organizational structure is only the initial stage of the compliance process. While I have emphasized the symbolic value of EEO/AA structures, it remains uncertain at this point whether these structures act as a stepping stone toward the achievement of EEO/AA ideals or whether they exist as mere window dressing. . . .

ACKNOWLEDGMENTS

This research was supported by a grant from the National Science Foundation (SES 88-14070). The University of Wisconsin Graduate School provided initial support for designing the project. This article was written while I was a visiting scholar at the Institute of Industrial Relations at the University of California, Berkeley. I gratefully acknowledge support from all three institutions. I would also like to thank Howard S. Erlanger, Alberto Palloni, Glenn Carroll, Jack Tweedy, Vicki Schultz, James E. Jones, Stephen Petterson, Elizabeth Chambliss, and the *AJS* reviewers for their thoughtful comments on an earlier draft of this article; Diane Colasanto for her assistance with the survey design; and Stephen Petterson for his extensive assistance with the data analysis.

NOTES

1.   For the sake of brevity, I use race and sex throughout the paper to refer to all protected categories: race, color, religion, sex, and national origin (which are protected by Title VII) as well as veteran status, age, and other categories that are protected by other laws.

2.   The rules implementing Title VII require organizations with 100 or more employees to report annually to the Equal Employment Opportunity Commission (EEOC), which

is charged with enforcing Title VII. This report consists of a form that summarizes, by race, gender, and ethnicity, the composition of the work force and the composition of applicants to that work force.

3. For federal contractors, EO 11246 does require that some person be appointed director of affirmative action and that a formal *statement* expressing a commitment to EEO/AA be issued. However, the order does not require a formal rule proscribing discrimination within the firm nor does it require that a special office to handle EEO/AA issues be created.

4. The dates of rule creation are missing for 58 organizations because they did not respond to the mail portion of the survey. Therefore, for analyses using dates of rule creation, the sample size was 288, and rules were created in 239 cases. The effect of this missing data on the hazard analyses is to produce more conservative estimates of the rate of rule creation, since all of the omitted cases had created EEO/AA rules.

REFERENCES

Belton, Robert. 1981. "Discrimination and Affirmative Action: An Analysis of Competing Theories of Equality and *Weber.*" *North Carolina Law Review* 59:531–98.

Blumrosen, Alfred W. 1972. "Strangers in Paradise: *Griggs v. Duke Power Co.* and the Concept of Employment Discrimination." *Michigan Law Review* 71:59–110.

Burstein, Paul. 1990. "Intergroup Conflict, Law, and the Concept of Labor Market Discrimination." *Sociological Forum* 5:459–76.

DiMaggio, Paul J., and Walter W. Powell. 1983. "The Iron Cage Revisited: Institutional Isomorphism and Collective Rationality in Organizational Fields." *American Sociological Review* 48:147–60.

Edelman, Lauren B. 1990. "Legal Environments and Organizational Governance: The Expansion of Due Process in the American Workplace." *American Journal of Sociology* 95:1401–40.

Edelman, Lauren B., Steven E. Abraham, and Howard S. Erlanger. 1992. "Professional Construction of Law: The Inflated Threat of Wrongful Discharge." *Law and Society Review,* in press.

Edelman, Lauren B., Stephen Petterson, Elizabeth Chambliss, and Howard S. Erlanger. 1991. "Legal Ambiguity and the Politics of Compliance: Affirmative Action Officers' Dilemma." *Law and Policy* (Spring), in press.

Fiss, Owen M. 1974. "The Fate of an Idea Whose Time Has Come: Antidiscrimination Law in the Second Decade after *Brown v. Board of Education.*" *University of Chicago Law Review* 41:742–73.

Freeman, Alan. 1982. "Legitimating Racial Discrimination through Anti-Discrimination Law: A Critical Review of Supreme Court Doctrine." Pp. 210–35 in *Marxism and Law,* edited by Piers Beirne and Richard Quinney. New York: Wiley.

Froehlich, Herbert P., and Dennis A. Hawver. 1974. "Compliance Spinoff: Better Personnel Systems." *Personnel* (January–February):62–68.

Garris, Steve, and Ann Black. 1974. "Revising Personnel Management Procedures." *Personnel* (November–December):50–58.

House Committee on Education and Labor. 1987. *A Report on the Investigation of the Civil Rights Enforcement Activities of the Office of Federal Contract Compliance Programs, U.S. Department of Labor.* 100th Congress, 1st sess. Serial no. 100-R.

Jones, James E. 1985. "The Genesis and Present Status of Affirmative Action in Employment: Economic, Legal, and Political Realities." *Iowa Law Review* 70:901–44.

Marino, Kenneth E. 1980. "Conducting an Internal Compliance Review of Affirmative Action." *Personnel* (March–April):24–34.

Meyer, John W., and Brian Rowen. 1977. "Institutionalized Organizations: Formal Structure as Myth and Ceremony." *American Journal of Sociology* 83:340–63.

Meyer, John W., and W. Richard Scott, eds. 1983. *Organizational Environments: Ritual and Rationality.* Beverly Hills, Calif.: Sage.

Nathan, Richard P. 1969. *Jobs & Civil Rights: The Role of the Federal Government in Promoting Equal Opportunity in Employment and Training.* Clearinghouse Publication no. 16. Prepared for the U.S. Commission on Civil Rights by the Brookings Institution. Washington, D.C.: Government Printing Office.

Selznick, Philip P. 1969. *Law, Society, and Industrial Justice.* New Brunswick, N.J.: Transaction.

Smith, Arthur B., Jr. 1978. *Employment Discrimination Law.* Indianapolis, Ind.: Bobbs-Merrill.

Stone, Christopher. 1975. *Where the Law Ends: The Social Control of Corporate Behavior.* New York: Harper & Row.

Thorp, Cary D., Jr. 1973. "Fair Employment Practices: The Compliance Jungle." *Personnel Journal* 52:642–49.

U.S. Commission on Civil Rights (USCCR). 1971. *The Federal Civil Rights Enforcement Effort: One Year Later.* Clearinghouse Publication no. 34. Washington, D.C.: Government Printing Office.

17

Loading the Economy

Orrin Hatch

The spread of affirmative action since the passage of the Civil Rights Act in 1964 has been an event without precedent in American history. With astonishing speed, federal and state agencies have asserted the right to impose racial quotas on virtually every area of American life. Even a tiny academic institution like Hillsdale College in Michigan, with a faultless tradition of social progressivism and an established policy of refusing federal monies, is menaced on the ingenious grounds that, since some of its students get veterans' benefits, it is in receipt of federal funds. All of this is in flagrant breach of the letter and the spirit of the Civil Rights Act, as specifically established in congressional debate at the time of its passage. . . .

The legality, or otherwise, of affirmative action will keep lawyers employed for many years. Cultural historians (and possibly psychologists) will make reputations explaining the reluctance of press and politicians to oppose its development, or really to notice that it was going on at all. However, since affirmative action is indeed going on, without benefit of law or legislators, a more immediate concern ought to be what its practical effect is likely to be. Typically, this turns out to be the least studied aspect of all.

Some economists have done work on the effects of affirmative action upon the relevant "protected class.". . . . Intuitively, we might suppose the effect would be similar to tariffs, inducing a local and relative prosperity at the expense of overall welfare. This prosperity would probably be less in absolute terms than might have been the case if the economic system had been permitted to work freely. But a recent survey by the Library of Congress was unable to discover anything substantial from academe on its overall or macroeconomic impact. . . . Given this absence of academic interest, perhaps a U.S. Senator might at least growl in the direction of affirmative action's economic impact, and the questions such a study would raise.

Excerpts reprinted with permission from *Policy Review* 1980 (Spring), vol. 12:23–37. Copyright © 1980 by the Heritage Foundation.

Quotas or Bust

Because most people would rather not think about affirmative action, there is considerable confusion about what it means, not unrelated to the frantic logic-chopping indulged in by its proponents when under pressure. For my present purposes, I want to emphasize that *affirmative action means quotas* or it means nothing. It means discrimination on the basis of race and sex. It does not mean remedial education, special programs for the disadvantaged, or any of the other methods by which we could, and to some extent do, help minorities. It has nothing to do with equal opportunity, although its chief enforcement agency is misleadingly called the Equal Employment Opportunity Commission (EEOC). Affirmative action is about equality of results, statistically measured. Its proponents have made great efforts of casuistry to distinguish between quotas and "goals," "targets," "timetables," and so on. All such distinctions dissolve in practice, particularly when the enforcers are feeling confident about the balance of power on the Supreme Court. . . .

[A]nyone temporarily confused by the affirmative action lobby's shell game should ask himself: Am I supposed to take notice of race, sex, etc.? Or not? He will find the answer (yes, on our terms) nowhere appears in the Civil Rights Act. It is the economic impact of this answer that is the subject of this article.

HOW THE MARKET ERODES DISCRIMINATION

The concept of a free market is valuable not simply as a description of reality, but as an analytical tool. It helps us put discrimination in context. In a system where all actors are free to pursue their own interest, there is an inexorable tendency for everyone to receive the marginal value of his labor. In other words, you will ultimately be paid approximately what your work is worth. The free market undermines all distinctions that are not based on this economic reality. If you belong to some unpopular group, employers may begin paying you less than average, as a matter of tradition. But precisely because they will make more money off you than off more popular but expensive groups, you will come into demand, and your wages will be bid up. Ultimately, you will be paid the average, or even more than that if you happen to be more efficient. The only way this can be prevented is if the state legislates unequal wages or bans you from certain occupations. . . . Private employers cannot effectively do it, because their attempts at collusion are undermined by market forces just as their attempts to form cartels collapse, unless supported by public policy, tariffs or some other constraint on freedom. *Discrimination is costly.* . . .

Two qualifications must be made, however. First, there is no reason why your marginal value should be the same as that of anyone else. Even apart from any question of innate aptitude, different cultures have different attitudes to work and leisure. . . . Secondly, even when your marginal value is the same, it may take time to get paid it. Traditions do not dissolve overnight, although experience in America indicates that where money is concerned, they erode remarkably quickly.

In fact, the American experience is that relying on the market system has been enormously successful in integrating diverse groups, often historically hostile to each other. Groups frequently subjected to majority disapproval, such as Jews and Asians, have nevertheless emerged with incomes significantly above the average. The cash nexus is a noble thing. You don't have to like the man who mends your shoes, but you and he can exchange goods and services to your mutual advantage. . . .

The point of the 1964 Civil Rights Act was merely to hurry this process along, particularly in the area of race, by forbidding certain types of public discrimination. The philosophy behind it was that, once entry to the market was freed of artificial constraints like institutionalized discrimination, it would solve this problem as it had all others.

If you leave people alone, they will tend to employ those who do the best job, and the overall production of wealth will be maximized. But if you don't leave people alone, they cannot do this, and inefficiencies will develop. Wealth will not be maximized. This is exactly the effect of affirmative action.

[T]he U.S. absorbed the great wave of immigration at the end of the last century because the immigrants were employed in the sectors of the economy that needed them—often concentrated at first in the least desirable areas. Under affirmative action, however, the newcomers would be inserted into each area of activity in proportion to their overall numbers, and not because of their skills or because they represent a more efficient use of resources. . . .

Inefficiency in Triplicate

The true nature of affirmative action can be seen in one of the rare reports from the front line, which appeared in the *Washington Star,* albeit in the Business & Finance section:

> Dante DiGaetano's business is so small that he has no office and no secretary— just one carpenter and two laborers.
>
> But the Labor Department has ordered him to take a series of 43 continuing administrative actions which could occupy a sizable office force because, under a recent government contract, 5% of the four laborers working for him and his subcontractors were not women.

As usual, Mr. DiGaetano had signed a conciliation agreement rather than abandon his contract or fight the government in court.

As a result of signing the order, DiGaetano has been ordered to maintain a written equal opportunity policy, appoint an EEO officer with a written job description, include EEO policy in company manuals, maintain records of encouragement of minority and female employees to seek promotion and keep a record of annual reviews by those employees for promotional opportunities.

He must also keep a current listing of recruitment sources for minority and female craft workers, copies of letters to employment groups specifying employment opportunities, files of all responses to these letters and records of contacts with minority and women's community organizations, recruitment sources, schools and training organizations.

On top of this, DiGaetano must submit a monthly "employment utilization report," a quarterly report on minority and female applicants, job offers, new hires, terminations and layoffs and a report stating the date upon which each of the other 42 requirements was met (*Washington Star,* Feb. 21, 1980).

My colleague, Senator Richard S. Schweiker of Pennsylvania, complained to Labor Secretary F. Ray Marshall about this situation. Mr. Marshall replied that Mr. DiGaetano had only himself to blame. He hadn't submitted his "monthly Employment Utilization Reports, Form CC257." Mr. Marshall added that although this case was unusual, it was too difficult on administrative grounds for his agents to take note of the size of their victims.

A society which allows this sort of harassment is, in an important sense, no longer free. Beyond that, it is not even efficient. Obviously, the heightened threshold of fixed costs is going to exclude smaller contractors from such fields. But the impact on the major contractors is perhaps worse. They survive, but waste much of their assets on bookkeeping, and other compliance activities. Additionally, they are no longer dedicated to the pursuit of profit, with its continuous, systematic pressure against waste and error. This is partly because they are now staffed by people who, by definition, are not the ones who would have been selected had the principle of merit been applied. . . .

AN ECONOMIC IMPACT STATEMENT

[T]he EEOC has sometimes been credited with opening up new pools of labor that corporations somehow contrived to ignore, and occasionally with hastening the breakdown of traditional barriers to labor mobility. But in the context of the market's endless search for efficiency, these anomalies would have been eliminated anyway, leaving only the question of whether they were worth the expenditure compelled by law. Affirmative action is a net cost to the economy. On the whole, its advocates have defended their policies in terms of social justice. And this is a more reasonable position. No one, after all, expects the state to profit from the money it expends on looking after the aged.

Measuring the costs of regulation is not an easy task. In the case of Dante DiGaetano, for example, it is possible to quantify the incremental expenditures he is now forced to make—hiring an EEO officer, secretaries, posting letters, and so on. It is more difficult to assess the changes in his way of working—including the time he himself must divert from other activities. And the true dynamic effects—the opportunity cost of all this expense and effort, the diminution of competition, inefficiencies due to the employment and promotion of marginal labor and the consequent demoralization of good workers—can only be a matter of conjecture, although they are clearly the most important of all. No measurement can be made, for example, of the cost to the entire economy of a decision not to terminate a bad worker because he or she belongs to some category required to satisfy government inspectors, a near-universal phenomenon in contemporary America. It is safe to say, however, that the dynamic effects of affirmative action are some considerable multiple of the static costs.

UNEARNED INCREMENTS

The Arthur Andersen (1979) study resolved this problem by counting only such incremental costs as could be exhaustively documented. Under this minimal definition, the 48 companies which were examined proved to have spent some $217 million to comply with EEO regulations in 1977. The greater proportion of these, some 96%, were operating and administrative costs which recur annually. The companies noted that the full impact of treating the handicapped as a "protected class" had not yet been felt in 1977.

Since these 48 companies represent only 5% of the U.S. workforce, excluding military, government and agricultural employees, it would be logical to conclude that costs across the entire sector are $217 million $\times$ 20 = $4.34 billion. Any shortfall resulting from the crudeness of this measure is amply compensated by the fact that it does not include the effect of state and local government demands, or specialized federal activities such as the fair housing laws. . . .

The federal government's estimate of its 1979 expenditures on overseeing and complying with its own equal opportunity regulations was $170.4 million, with an additional $39.7 million for military equal opportunity. The figures for 1981 are expected to be $194.9 million and $42.9 million (U.S. Office of Management and Budget 1981).

This is substantially less than the estimate of affirmative action costs that the Congressional Research Service (1976) arrived at by polling selected government agencies—$367 million. These, of course, by now would be substantially higher. The reason for the discrepancy probably lies in accounting definitions, with the government now taking a far more restrictive view than did the individual agencies. . . .

The costs of affirmative action to state and local governments remain an unexplored continent. In 1976, the Congressional Research Service's intrepid analyst attempted to estimate the costs of federally-mandated programs in this area by asking selected states directly. Unsurprisingly, the results were rudimentary, but they suggested nationwide 1976 costs of approximately $185 million. . . .

There seems to have been no estimate of the costs to colleges and universities since the American Council on Education (1976) published one for six selected institutions. It said the cost was $1,800,000. Extrapolating across the 250 colleges and universities that, according to HEW, had affirmative action programs in April of 1975, the Congressional Research Service concluded that the total 1974–5 cost had been $75 million. In 1979, the federal government estimated that it had spent $14.8 million on "equal educational opportunity," which includes oversight of employment policies. Interestingly, this sum will rise to an estimated $40.7 million in 1981.

This still leaves areas of the economy unassessed. Perhaps the most notable is that of primary and secondary education. . . . Still, what we have is enough for a consciously-low estimate:

Private sector—Arthur Andersen/Hatch, 1977	$4.3 billion
Federal govt.—Actual 1979	.35 billion
State and Local govt.—CRS estimate, 1976	.18 billion
Universities, Colleges—CRS/ACE estimate 1974	.08 billion

Considering the partial and dated nature of these figures, the fact that inflation in the four years of President Carter's Administration seems likely to average nine percent a year and the dramatic proliferation of programs of affirmative action in recent years, its incremental cost must be clearly in excess of $5 billion—perhaps as much as $7.5 billion. It is essential to remember at this point that *$5–$7.5 billion is only the tip of the iceberg.* It is just the incremental cost of compliance. . . .

Affirmative action is yet another wedge driven between the American worker and the fruits of his labor. The most obvious wedge is that proportion of the fruits commandeered in the shape of direct and indirect taxes. Affirmative action certainly contributes to this because of the expensive oversight apparatus that accompanies it. But a less obvious wedge is the inefficiency it induces in the productive base. . . .

Since 1973 particularly, there has been a drop in American productivity growth that cannot be explained in terms of the changing combination of capital and labor input. In real terms, national income per person employed in the first half of 1979 was below that of 1973. The most obvious culprit is the distortion and misallocation effect caused by complying with federal regulations. Affirmative action is only a small part of this—Murray Weidenbaum (1979) estimates that total incremental cost of oversight and compliance was some $102.7 billion.

But since it has such a personal impact on the labor force, its dynamic economic impact is probably out of proportion. One can work happily designing a pollution filter, but not if passed over for a promotion on the grounds of race. In any event, affirmative action is a symbol and a symptom of the regulatory socialism which, sprouting with the New Deal, has grown like a kudu vine until our institutions and their classical liberal inspiration are on the point of vanishing from sight. . . .

18

Businessmen Like to Hire by the Numbers

Anne B. Fisher

If the Reagan Administration warriors taking shots at affirmative action think business is on their side, they are in for unpleasant surprises. Some corporate managements, no doubt, push affirmative action only because government pushes them. But persuasive evidence indicates that most large American corporations want to retain their affirmative action programs, numerical goals and all.

The Administration's position is that employers can achieve true fairness in hiring standards only by ignoring race and sex altogether—not by favoring women, blacks, and Hispanics over white male applicants. Clarence Thomas, chairman of the Equal Employment Opportunity Commission in the Reagan Administration, has been outspoken in his belief that companies should not be held to statistical standards to prove that they are hiring enough minorities and women. Taking account of race and sex in hiring, he says, violated Title VII of the 1964 Civil Rights Act—the section that prohibits discrimination in employment. "Title VII says you can't consider race or sex in hiring decisions, period." notes Thomas. "It doesn't say *which* race or sex it's okay to favor."

So far, in spite of the Administration's rumblings, nothing much has happened that affects the way companies run their affirmative action programs. The Labor Department's Office of Federal Contract Compliance Programs, which enforces equal opportunity in companies that do business with the federal government, has gone right on enforcing the rules. But in mid-August the Administration sent up a strong signal—a proposed presidential executive order that would put an end to mandatory goals and timetables in affirmative action programs. Whether it was a rocket or a trial balloon remains to be seen.

The requirement that government contractors adopt goals and timetables was a legacy of the Nixon Administration. It was issued by the Labor Department in the early 1970s. The authority for the Labor Department's action derived from Executive Order 11246, signed in 1965 by President Lyndon Johnson. Among other things, that order created the Office of Federal Contract Compliance Programs to

Excerpts reprinted with permission from *Fortune* Magazine, September 16, 1985. Copyright © by Time-Warner Inc.

see that government contractors (which include most large American corporations) obeyed government rules against discrimination.

As drafted, the Reagan order would give mandatory goals and timetables both barrels. "The Secretary of Labor," it runs, "shall immediately revoke all regulations and guidelines promulgated pursuant to Executive Order No. 11246" if they require companies doing business with the government "to use numerical quotas, goals, ratios, or objectives." In effect, that would make numerical goals and timetables voluntary.

But the draft went a great deal further, with this incendiary language: "Nothing in this executive order shall be interpreted to require or provide a legal basis for a government contractor or subcontractor to utilize any numerical quota, goal, or ratio, or otherwise to discriminate against, or grant any preference to, any individual or group on the basis of race, color, religion, sex, or national origin with respect to any aspect of employment . . . " These words would not make company goals and timetables illegal—that would take an act of Congress or a ruling by a court. But they would weaken the legal basis for such programs, possibly exposing employers to a blizzard of suits by white male employees or job applicants claiming that affirmative action had discriminated against them. . . .

The floating of the draft order stirred predictable outcries to the effect that it would destroy affirmative action. It wouldn't. If Reagan signs, some companies will back off, but most large corporations will maintain their programs as before—though perhaps proceeding more warily in view of that White House language weakening the "legal basis" of the programs.

Many chief executives of large American companies would agree with a comment by John L. Hulck, chairman of Merck, after the text of the proposed Reagan order floated forth. "We will continue goals and timetables no matter what the government does," Hulck said. "They are part of our culture and corporate procedures." John M. Stafford, president and C.E.O. of Pillsbury, was of the same mind: "It has become clear to us that an aggressive affirmative action program makes a lot of sense. So if the executive order is issued, it wouldn't affect us."

Strong evidence regarding the breadth of the corporate commitment to affirmative action comes from a survey conducted late last year by Organization Resources Counselors, a consulting firm headquartered in New York. The respondents were chief executive officers of large corporations, most of them on the FORTUNE 500. More than 90% of the C.E.O.s—116 out of 127 who responded to the question—said that the "numerical objectives" in their company's affirmative action program were established partly to satisfy "corporate objectives unrelated to government regulations." Even more impressive was the response to this question: "Do you plan to continue to use numerical objectives to track the progress of women and minorities in your corporation, regardless of government requirements?" Of the 128 who replied, 122 said yes—a bit better than 95%.

Opponents of affirmative action sometimes argue that in effect goals and timetables amount to quotas, but much of corporate America disagrees. If any high executive of any large American company favors quotas in employment, he is being very quiet about it. A report commissioned by the Ford Foundation and published in 1983 surveyed 49 government contractors with affirmative action programs. "None see the goals and timetables element in their affirmative action plans as requiring the use of quotas," the report concluded. "Without exception those interviewed were opposed to quotas on the basis of race or sex."

Last May the directors of the National Association of Manufacturers adopted a policy statement supporting affirmative action as "good business policy," adding a caution that "goals, not quotas, are the standards to be followed in the implementation of such programs." William S. McEwen, director of equal opportunity affairs at Monsanto and chairman of the NAM's human resources committee, recently told a congressional subcommittee that the NAM, despite its support of affirmative action, does "not endorse quotas in whatever form manifested." But McEwen defends goals and timetables. "Business," he says, "sets goals and timetables for every aspect of its operations—profits, capital investment, productivity increases. Setting goals and timetables for minority and female participation is simply a way of measuring progress."

At some companies, no doubt, the commitment to affirmative action reflects idealism on the part of the C.E.O. or other top executives. By now, moreover, most large companies have an entrenched affirmative action bureaucracy in the personnel department. But companies also have practical reasons to support affirmative action and to preserve their goals and timetables even if the government says they don't have to.

Once a company has an affirmative action program in operation, it cannot stop or even retreat noticeably without stirring grievances and impairing morale among women and minorities on the payroll. On the positive side, affirmative action can enlarge the pool of talent for companies to draw on. Some people in management, especially but not only affirmative action officers, maintain that this helps productivity. Hard evidence is lacking, but the claim has some plausibility. . . .

Affirmative action can also have practical business value in customer relations, especially for makers of consumer goods or providers of consumer services. Peggy Sieghardt, division manager of human resources at AT&T, puts it this way: "Everyone is a potential customer of AT&T, and they look at us. Why would someone want to be a customer of an all-white male company?"

Avon sells about 20% of its cosmetics to minorities, and nearly all of its sales are to women. In early 1984 the company brought in Phillip Davis—a former director of the Labor Department's Office of Federal Contract Compliance Programs—to set up an aggressive program. Avon has only one division that is a government contractor, and so isn't required to have corporate goals and timetables, but Davis has put them in anyway. He has also tied managers' compensation to their affirmative action performance and started special training programs for talented women and minority employees. "When affirmative action started, the aim was to bring in victims of past discrimination," says Davis. "Now that minorities have come in the door, the job of affirmative action is to oversee the upward mobility of these people. That is the focus in the 1980s."

Clearly, most large corporations will keep their goals and timetables programs even if the Administration rules that they no longer have to. But making numerical measures voluntary could still bring trouble for companies. Employees are likely to be less patient with a voluntary program than a program operating under government rules and scrutiny. If the Labor Department no longer has the power to hold companies to goals and timetables, employers could be dragged through a new round of Title VII cases brought by employees, including white males, who consider themselves discriminated against. Says a labor attorney who represents besieged employers in affirmative action cases: "Getting rid of the Johnson executive order would turn the corporation into a battlefield. Again."

Judith Vladeck, a senior partner in the New York labor law firm Vladeck Waldman Elias & Engelhard, agrees: "Without the Labor Department involvement, employees with grievances would have fewer options, and they'd be a lot more confrontational. The number of lawsuits, which has been declining, would probably shoot up again."

In the Administration draft floated in mid-August, the unstated but unmistakable message was that the authors want to go beyond making goals and timetables voluntary and make them illegal. This would be a much more radical and disruptive outcome. If it comes about, the immediate effects will include badly impaired morale among women, blacks, and Hispanics. The longer-term effects will almost certainly include a big increase in litigation as employees who consider themselves discriminated against turn to the famous Title VII. Under Title VII, preference is legal as a remedy for a person who has been discriminated against as an individual.

The essential reason affirmative action makes things more peaceful is that a person can benefit from preference without having to prove discrimination. But that is precisely why affirmative action with goals and timetables is controversial. Discrimination in favor of some people entails discrimination against others. That is what the Administration wants to stop.

The Administration is pursuing its campaign in federal courts, arguing that preference of any kind is illegal except for people who have been discriminated against as individuals. The argument is based upon a sweeping interpretation of a 1984 Supreme Court decision. In *Firefighters Local Union 1784* v. *Stotts,* the court ruled that racial quotas don't supersede seniority as a basis for deciding who gets laid off. The Justice Department interpreted the decision to mean that in hiring or layoffs any preference based on race or sex is illegal. The department has used that reading in efforts to change court decrees upholding quotas in states, municipalities, and school districts around the country. So far, however, six courts of appeals have rejected the broad interpretation of *Stotts* that Justice is relying on.

The decisive battles, however, will be fought in the Supreme Court. . . . However it decides the pending cases, the Supreme Court is unlikely to forbid the voluntary use of numerical goals in affirmative action. On that matter, the Court has already spoken. In an opinion handed down in 1979, it said that making all race-conscious affirmative action illegal would "diminish traditional management prerogatives" and "limit traditional business freedoms." This does not mean affirmative action will come through the round of cases now on the docket without any nicks. But in momentous matters, the Supreme Court usually tries to avoid making big waves. Banning goals and timetables would make angry waves indeed.

V

EEO in a Diverse Society: Dealing with Difference

As discussed in Section III ("Legal Definitions of Discrimination"), when Title VII was adopted the definition of discrimination seemed obvious to most people: treating someone worse than others because of his or her race, gender, religion, national origin, or other ascribed characteristics (see, for example, Gold 1985; U.S. Department of Justice 1987; Glazer 1978; cf. Fiss 1971; Gordon 1981; Burstein 1990). Nondiscrimination meant ignoring such characteristics and, in the employment context, making decisions on the basis of merit or productivity. When Title VII forced workers, employers, and policymakers to confront the complexities of labor markets, however, they discovered that what seems fair in the abstract sometimes leads to what some see as unfair on the job.

This has become especially apparent when employers and unions encounter the diversity of American society. Differences among workers in terms of race, religion, and gender, along with historical differences in how the various groups have been treated by the larger society, lead to situations in which seemingly equal treatment harms some groups. Confronting these harms has led to three similar but historically distinct attacks on the traditional definition of discrimination and to demands that differences between groups be accommodated by employers and unions, even if the result is not strict equality of treatment.

The first and best-known attack on the principle of ignoring group differences—known as the principle of "color blindness" because the doctrine was first developed in cases involving race (Fiss 1971; Pole 1978:ch. 7)—came in the case of *Griggs v. Duke Power Co.* already discussed. By the time the case was brought, Duke Power was formally treating black and white job applicants equally, requiring the same educational credentials and test scores of both. Part of the black plaintiffs' argument was, in essence, that although this seemed fair—and nondiscriminatory—it was not. Because of the history of race relations in the South, blacks had been deprived of educational opportunities, so relatively few of them (compared to whites) were able to meet Duke Power's standards. Intentionally or not, therefore, Duke Power's employment criteria had the effect of perpetuating the effects of prior racial discrimination. If the criteria were really related to productivity, the plaintiffs argued, Duke Power could continue to use them. But if the criteria were not related to productivity, and were in effect simply an impediment to blacks' economic opportunity, then they should be viewed as discriminatory even though they were applied to blacks and whites equally.

The Supreme Court, as we know, adopted the plaintiffs' view, to the satisfaction of some and the dismay of others. By doing so, the Court essentially said that sometimes history must be taken into account, so that disadvantages imposed by the larger society—inferior, segregated education, for example—do not become the basis for seemingly legitimate disabilities imposed by employers. The implicit message was that although blacks are inherently equal to whites, the harms they have suffered must be taken into account in antidiscrimination law; sometimes equal opportunity requires acknowledging group differences, even if only temporarily.

The argument that fairness sometimes means taking group differences into account and that, legally, not doing so may be considered discriminatory next arose in the context of religion. In many ways, American legal doctrine in the 1960s regarding religion resembled that regarding race. While the doctrine of color blindness demanded that government ignore race in its decision-making, the doctrine of "strict separationism" called for the separation of church and state and opposed the legal recognition of religious differences (Laycock 1986). Thus, the basic assumption underlying Title VII's ban on religious discrimination was the same as the assumption behind its ban on racial discrimination: Religion should be ignored in employment decisions.

Right from the start, many believed that there should be some exceptions to this general rule. Sometimes religion could be relevant to job performance, most obviously with regard to the clergy and to teaching in religious institutions; exemptions permitting employers to take the religion of job applicants into account in specified circumstances were included in Title VII as adopted in 1964. But soon another, potentially more challenging problem emerged: Because different religions impose different behavioral requirements on their adherents, at times the requirement that adherents of all religions be treated alike could harm some of them. For example, if some religions forbid adherents from working on Saturdays, employers who require all employees to work on Saturdays may be simultaneously treating all employees the same and harming members of the religious minority group.

Confronted with this issue, Congress amended Title VII in 1972 to require employers and unions to "reasonably accommodate" employees' religious practices. This doctrine of reasonable accommodation is both similar to the doctrine of adverse impact propounded by the Supreme Court in its *Griggs* decision and different from it. The similarity is fairly plain: The law requires employers to take group differences into account when their treating all workers the same would disproportionately harm—have an adverse impact on—members of some groups. This undercuts the notion that nondiscrimination—legally, at least—means treating everyone the same way.

The difference between the adverse impact doctrine developed in the context of racial discrimination and the reasonable accommodation approach to religious discrimination is less obvious but is nevertheless important. Initially, at least, blacks suffered adverse impact from particular employment criteria because they had been the victims of pervasive discrimination, both in and out of the labor market, in the past. As changing attitudes, antidiscrimination laws, and their own efforts enabled blacks to do better economically, much of the adverse impact of employment criteria should disappear (this idea may be inferred from a reading of Blumrosen 1984). In the long run, most people have assumed, blacks and whites will be equally qualified and do equally well, and at that point it will be possible for the law to be color-blind.

Religious differences are different, in that they are assumed to be permanent. Although individuals can, of course, change religious affiliations (unlike their race), in the late twentieth-century United States it would be considered unfair to expect them to do so as the price of economic success; and for the most part people are seen as having a right to observe the practices of their religions. Thus, the need for accommodation, however great it might prove to be in practice, cannot be expected to disappear. Consequently there is likely to be continuing concern about the circumstances in which treating different people the same way could be viewed as discriminatory.

The third attack on the notion that nondiscrimination means strict equality of treatment is the product of concern about sex discrimination. Historically, women have been seen as different from men in so many different ways— biologically, socially, mentally, emotionally, intellectually, and so on—that it has often seemed unclear even to many proponents of women's rights how they should be treated in the law and in labor markets (see, e.g., Pole 1978; Harrison 1988; Goldstein 1989; Rothman 1978; Lehrer 1987). While some favored equal treatment in all areas of life, others believed that women required special protection from the harshness of the labor market, and supported laws limiting women's hours of work and their access to jobs deemed excessively dangerous or physically taxing.

Some of the differences between men and women are clearly permanent— only women have children—some are the product of how men and women have been treated, and the status of others is uncertain (Epstein 1988). Might EEO law require employers and unions to take some gender differences into account, as it has racial and religious differences? Can strictly equal treatment of men and women sometimes be seen as discriminatory?

Again the answer has been affirmative. The courts have, for example, defined as discriminatory the use of height, weight, and physical agility requirements for jobs, when the requirements disproportionately excluded women and could not be shown to be job-related (Schlei and Grossman 1983: 417–21).

It is concerns about sex discrimination that have led to the most serious questioning of conventional ideas about nondiscrimination and equal treatment.

Feminist scholars have claimed that the labor market is structured to men's advantage in a vast variety of ways, from the assumption that workers are available for long (and potentially variable) hours because they have someone (that is, a wife) at home to take care of children and domestic obligations, to the way equipment is designed (airplane cockpits are designed for tall pilots rather than short ones), to taken-for-granted beliefs (often built in to hiring criteria) about the personality types suited for particular jobs (those selling major appliances must be "aggressive"). Many employment criteria, in other words, meet men's needs (as traditionally defined) but not women's, and applying them equally to all workers disadvantages women. Truly equal opportunity would require rethinking much of what is normally taken for granted about how labor markets operate (Eichner 1988).

What all three lines of attack on the notion of nondiscrimination as equal treatment suggest is that many employment criteria, customarily described as necessary for business efficiency, were developed in part for the benefit of the dominant groups, whether dominance be defined in terms of race, religion, or gender (see Baron [excerpted here]). The criteria may contribute to efficiency, but it is often difficult to show that they do (Burstein and Pitchford 1990), and others might do just as well without disadvantaging minorities or women. No malice need be involved (though it sometimes has been); those setting standards for hiring just naturally adopt those which serve their convenience.

This view meets a great deal of resistance. We have already seen the antagonism aroused by the adverse impact definition of discrimination in race cases (and will return to it when dealing with affirmative action in later chapters). Accommodation to the needs of religious minorities has been described as discrimination against the majority by Justice White (in *Hardison v. Trans World Airlines,* 14 FEP Cases 1706, 1977), and women have had relatively little success in getting the courts to accept the idea that many conventional job requirements systematically disadvantage women (Eichner 1988).

The controversy between those who see some conventional employment practices as discriminatory, even if not adopted with the goal of harming minorities or women, and those who seem them as unobjectionable business practices, calls to mind a long-standing debate about what would happen to the United States as it absorbed immigrants from Europe (Gordon 1964; 1981). Many Americans wanted the result to be what has been called "Anglo-conformity," in which all the groups adopted norms established by the dominant group of English Protestant ancestry; others foresaw a "melting pot" in which a new American culture, uniform but absorbing elements from many groups, would be created; and some anticipated that the result would be "cultural pluralism," in which groups would maintain some communal institutions and traditions while generally integrating into the broader society. A key question in the debate has always been, Whose standards of behavior would be applied in which domains of social life? Would everyone have to adopt the standards of the dominant group? Would new standards be developed out of the interaction between groups? And might there be uniform standards in some areas of life but not others? As the federal government has come to regulate a wider domain, these questions become more central to federal policymaking (even if only implicit). As the work force becomes more diverse and more groups organize on behalf of their interests, the question of whose criteria for employment will dominate becomes important. Debates over what constitutes discrimination when groups with different needs, backgrounds, and demands confront each other in the labor force become central to analyses of EEO.

How Congress and the courts have dealt with religious and gender diversity are the subjects of the articles by Gloria Beckley and myself (1991 [excerpted here]) and by Eichner (1988). Congress and the courts show both a willingness to view equal treatment as discriminatory if it harms some groups, and an unwillingness to expand the concept too far. There are two competing forces at work in determining how EEO law will respond to issues of diversity. On the one hand, the American work force is becoming more diverse, incorporating not only American blacks, women, and European immigrants, but peoples from around the world, bringing an ever-increasing variety of national and religious backgrounds to the United States. Virtually nothing is known about the use these groups make of EEO law (Munafo 1979; Burstein 1991), but it is easy to imagine a rising chorus of demands that employment practices that disadvantage them be defined as discriminatory. On the other hand, there is a strong reluctance on the part of lawmakers and the courts to go very far beyond the notion that nondiscrimination means equal treatment, and nothing more. They went beyond the conventional definition with regard to race, probably out of a sense of the profound injustices experienced by blacks (and provoked intense opposition), but they have clearly not been willing to go so far with regard to religious minorities or women. The chapters in this section provide an introduction to issues likely to be increasingly important as the United States moves toward the twenty-first century.

19

Religious Pluralism, Equal Opportunity, and the State

Gloria T. Beckley and Paul Burstein

Americans have historically enjoyed considerable freedom of religious belief (or nonbelief) and worship. Yet their freedom to pursue their religious tenets has been constrained in at least two ways. First, Americans have often been hostile to religious minorities. Adherents of minority religions often felt that if they wanted to gain access to educational opportunities or desirable jobs or housing, they should hide (or change) their beliefs and denominational memberships, and minimize the expression of distinctive religious practices.

Second, American law has long distinguished between religious belief and religious practice. "When . . . one's religious beliefs encompassed consequences for one's daily secular life, then freedom of religious often has been problematic," note Way and Burt (1983: 652); ". . . the freedom to act on the basis of one's religious beliefs may be narrowly circumscribed by public opinion and the law."

However, changes in American society during the last several decades may have significantly reduced both the legal and socioeconomic constraints experienced by religious minorities. Not only has prejudice against religious minorities declined, but legal doctrine has been altered as well. Way and Burt (1983) argue that changes in judicial interpretations of the free exercise clause beginning in the 1960s produced a "more generous and accepting spirit" toward the religious practices of marginal religions. . . . Furthermore, in a dramatic break with the past, government has gone beyond simply allowing free exercise (up to a point) to actively intervening in social and economic life to ensure that Americans are not deprived of access to jobs, public accommodations, education, or housing because of the religious prejudices of their fellow citizens. The Civil Rights Act of 1964 and other major civil rights laws prohibit discrimination on the basis of religion as well as race, national origin, and, in some areas, sex. . . .

But what is the nature of the equality mandated by the civil rights laws? Do such laws require—in line with the earlier, more restrictive readings of the free exercise clause—only that individuals not be penalized for religious affiliation and belief? Or might the concept of equality be expanded—as interpretations of the free exercise clause have broadened—to include the notion that society should accommodate, to some degree, the religious practices of adherents to minority religions?

As the scope of federal government activity has extended to the regulation of employment practices, it has had to address this issue and to confront two competing views of what constitutes fair treatment for religious minorities in the labor market. One—the "assimilationist" view (Post 1988: 103)—argues that nondiscrimination means forbidding employers to distinguish among employees on the basis of religious affiliation or belief. If employees' religious practices interfere with standard business practices, however—if, for example, some employees want special days off for religious reasons—the employer has no obligation to accommodate them, and the government has no reason to prevent the employees from being penalized. The competing—or "cultural pluralist" (Post 1988: 106)—view claims that it is important to accommodate religious practices as well as beliefs. Full acceptance of religious minorities would mean going beyond treating members of all religions identically; true nondiscrimination means granting legitimacy to minority religious practices as well as beliefs (see also Galanter 1966).

This paper examines the state's posture toward religious diversity in the labor market. It considers the extent to which the notion of equality has been expanded to not only prohibit discrimination based on religious beliefs or affiliation, but also to require the accommodation, to some degree, of minority religious practices. . . .

The paper tests two hypotheses. . . . The first is that the principle of accommodation in American law has increasingly played an important role in litigation involving religious discrimination in the labor market. Accommodation has redefined what constitutes religious discrimination in the labor market and provided new opportunities for legal redress to religious minorities. Accommodation promises not only the right to believe but also the right to act on beliefs. The second is that accommodation of minority religious practices has been limited by restrictive court interpretations: as proposals to accommodate religious differences are . . . implemented, resistance . . . increases, and religious plaintiffs will be increasingly likely to lose their cases. Cultural pluralism may have made some headway against the doctrine of uniform treatment, but it may also still be true that when judges, administrators, and members of Congress find the two in conflict, accommodations to minorities remain limited. . . .

RELIGIOUS DISCRIMINATION IN EMPLOYMENT

American society is more tolerant of religious minorities than it used to be, and religious discrimination in employment is much less common than it was as recently as the 1950s (see Aronson 1950: 99; 1952; Burstein 1985; Leskes 1954; Lieberson 1980; U.S. Congress 1978; U.S. Equal Employment Opportunity Commission 1978). But it has not disappeared. Over 40,000 complaints of religious discrimination have been filed with the U.S. Equal Employment Opportunity Commission (EEOC) since Title VII of the Civil Rights Act of 1964, the most important EEO law, went into effect. The number of charges has actually risen fairly steadily, from 169 in fiscal year 1967 to 1,176 in 1972 and 3,417 in 1984 (the last year for which data are available).

The number is smaller than might have been expected on the basis of testimony presented to Congress in the early 1960s, amounting to about 2.4 percent of the total number complaining of discrimination on the basis of race, religion, national origin, and sex; the 243 federal court decisions in EEO religious discrimination cases published through early 1987 is even a slightly lower percentage. Many more persons, however, surely felt they had been discriminated against but did nothing or complained through less official channels—the National Jewish Commission on Law and Public Affairs receives a thousand complaints a year of discrimination against Jews on the basis of Sabbath observance alone (U.S. EEOC 1978: 106). . . . Yet the court cases may be critical to these religious groups to use as leverage with employers and unions. The cases can send a message to potential plaintiffs and defendants about how sympathetic the courts—and the administrative agencies that follow their lead—will be to complaints of religious discrimination. Thus, the judicial decisions have considerable practical as well as symbolic significance.

Which groups see themselves most often as victims of religious discrimination? The EEOC does not gather information on the religions of those charging religious discrimination, so the only data available are those compiled from the judicial decisions. Jews and Seventh-Day Adventists bring the most cases (Table 1), each accounting for almost a quarter of the total; other Sabbatarians (including the Worldwide Church of God) bring a sixth, and many other religious groups divide the rest.

PLURALISM AND THE CONCEPT OF RELIGIOUS DISCRIMINATION

Americans have been dealing with the problem of cultural diversity since colonial times. According to Milton Gordon (1964; cf. Higham 1984), we have developed three contradictory solutions: "Anglo-conformity," demanding that all immigrants conform to norms established by the dominant group of English Protestant ancestry; the "melting pot," in which groups contribute to the creation of a new American culture; and "cultural pluralism," which imagines immigrant groups maintaining some communal institutions and traditions within a general pattern of integration into the broader society. A central question has been how political and social institutions should treat people who continue to differ in

Table 1. Plaintiff's Religion in Discrimination Cases

Religion	Number	Percent
Jewish	49	24
(Of these, Orthodox	7	3)
Adventists	49	24
Other sabbatarians	35	17
Roman Catholics	14	7
Mainstream Protestants	9	4
(Episcopal, Presbyterian, Lutheran, Methodist)		
Other Christians	24	12
(Baptist, European Free Church, Pentecostal, Mormon, Holiness, other)		
Eastern religions, Muslim	16	8
(not Black Muslim)		
Black Muslim	6	3
Other	5	2

Note: Percent does not add to 100 due to rounding. Information was available for 207 cases; for 36, no information on plaintiff religion was available, or the plaintiff was an organization, such as the EEOC, and no information on the religion of those on whose behalf it was acting was available.

religion, language, and other ways. One possible answer is to treat people uniformly and ignore their differences. This answer is consistent with both the Anglo-conformity and melting-pot approaches, but not with pluralism. It is also the answer that has dominated American history.

The push toward uniformity manifests itself most clearly in the doctrine of "color blindness," the dominant American approach to redressing racial discrimination: racial differences are to be considered irrelevant to whatever decisions are being made and are therefore to be ignored (see Fiss 1971). But a similar principle has been central to the federal government's stance toward religion as well—the principle of "strict separationism," which opposes the legal recognition of religious differences (Laycock 1986). . . .

The pluralist approach, in contrast, attempts to accommodate diversity; laws based on pluralist precepts, Post has written (1988: 106), try to "create ground rules by which diverse and potentially competitive groups can retain their distinctive identities" and a climate in which "diversity is to be safeguarded." The idea of formally accommodating religious differences in American law was first introduced by Justice William O. Douglas, when he suggested in the early 1950s that the separation of Church and State did not mean that public institutions could not ". . . accommodate the religious needs of the people" (*Zorach v. Clauson,* 343 U.S. 315, 1952). Support for accommodation has increased in recent years. Chief

Justice Burger argued, for example, that the ". . . Constitution . . . affirmatively mandates accommodation, not merely tolerance of all religions, and forbids hostility toward any" (*Lynch v. Donnelly,* 104 S. Ct. 1359, 1984). . . .

Possible tensions between uniform treatment and accommodation were barely addressed in the congressional debate over Title VII. Because of the power of the metaphor of color blindness, the overwhelming need and desire of blacks to be treated as well as whites, and the general American inclination toward uniform treatment, Title VII equated nondiscrimination with ignoring group membership. . . .

The general thrust toward uniform treatment was modified, however, albeit slightly, by the realization that totally ignoring religious differences would raise some problems. Some members of Congress suggested that at times religion might be relevant to job performance. Should not a Baptist college be permitted to prefer Baptists for teaching positions? Congress concluded that it sometimes made sense to let employers take religion into account. Yet Congress did not want to loosen the requirement of uniform treatment so much that religious minorities could be harmed by differential treatment. Congress finally decided that under Title VII religious organizations would be permitted to hire people of a particular religion for religious or educational purposes; in addition, employers in general were permitted to use religion, national origin, and sex as employment criteria when they were "bona fide occupational qualifications" necessary for running a business.

These exemptions gave employers the right to take religion into account when it was relevant to job performance. But another problem emerged: the require-ment that adherents of all religions be treated alike (with a few exceptions) could harm adherents of some religions. If an employer requires all employees to work on Saturdays—treating them alike—those who refuse to work on Saturdays for religious reasons (including Christian Sabbatarians and Orthodox and Conserva-tive Jews) may be fired. Should EEO laws define nondiscrimination only in terms of uniform treatment, with very narrow exceptions? Or should religious diversity be accommodated when uniform treatment harms some groups?

When this issue first arose, the EEOC responded in a way consistent with its general view (applied to race, sex, and national origin as well as religion) that policies requiring uniform treatment ("facially neutral" policies) should be viewed as violating Title VII if they adversely affected protected groups. Its 1966 "Guidelines on Discrimination Because of Religion" required employers not only to refrain from discriminating but also to affirmatively "accommodate to the reasonable religious needs of employees . . . where such accommodation can be made without serious inconvenience to the conduct of business" (Schlei and Grossman 1983: 210). Complaints from Sabbatarians led it to strengthen the guidelines in 1967, stating that employers should make reasonable accommoda-tion to religious needs of employees "where such accommodation can be made without undue hardship on the conduct of the employer's business" (see U.S. Commission on Civil Rights 1983: 43).

Employers soon challenged the guidelines, however, and in 1970 their challenge was upheld by the Sixth Circuit Court of Appeals, which ruled that the guidelines lacked any statutory basis (*Dewey* v. *Reynolds Metals Co.,* 2 FEP Cases 687, upheld in 1971 by an equally divided Supreme Court). Congress responded by amending Title VII to define the term "religion" in a way intended to require employers to accommodate employees' religious needs. "The term 'religion'," section 701 (j) now reads, "includes all aspects of religious observance and practice, as well as belief, unless an employer demonstrates that he is unable to reasonably accommodate to an employee's or prospective employee's religious observance or practice without undue hardship on the conduct of the employer's business."

This amendment had two significant implications. First, it redefined the concept of "discrimination," departing significantly from what had been thought of as a common-sense definition. The law requires not that adherents of all religions be treated alike but that employers provide special treatment—"reasonable accommodation"—for those with special religious needs, unless doing so would be an undue hardship. In fact, if an employer fails to accommodate, equal treatment can be adjudged discriminatory. Thus, in the eyes of the law there are now two types of religious discrimination in employment—"disparate treatment" (Schlei and Grossman 1983: ch. 7), which involves treating adherents of some religions worse than others, and "failure to accommodate" the special needs of members of a particular religion.

Second, the reasonable accommodation amendment explicitly attacked the longstanding distinction between religious belief, which had constitutional protection, and religious practice, which had been subject to considerable constraint (Way and Burt 1983). At least in the employment context, Congress had not only mandated that the federal government accommodate religious diversity, but that private employers, labor unions, employment agencies, and state and local governments covered by Title VII do so as well—provided that the accommodation did not cause "undue hardship." This amendment, which occasioned little debate and was passed 55–0 by the Senate (there was no recorded vote in the House of Representatives), could be seen as a significant breakthrough for the pluralist view of American society.

The reasonable accommodation amendment has been very important for adherents of minority religions who believe themselves the victims of employment discrimination—58 percent of the court cases involved claims of failure to accommodate (of the 222 cases for which data are available). The most common dispute—in a third of all cases, and 57 percent of accommodation cases—was over Sabbath observance, with employees (or union members) claiming that their employers (or unions) demanded they work on a day their religion forbade them to work. Nearly all these cases were brought by workers observing the Sabbath from sundown Friday to sundown Saturday, mostly Seventh-Day Adventists and other Christian Sabbatarians. . . .

Other accommodation cases involved refusal to pay union dues for religious reasons (the basis of 7 percent of the cases), often by Seventh-Day Adventists; personal appearance, including claims of having been penalized for wearing yarmulkes or turbans (6 percent), and time off for religious holidays other than the Sabbath (3 percent); and other issues.

Adherents of different religions make different types of claims. Roman Catholics, non-Orthodox Jews, Muslims, and members of Eastern religions most often believe themselves the victims of disparate treatment. In contrast, non-Catholic Christians (particularly Sabbatarians) and Orthodox Jews are most likely to complain of failure to accommodate. . . .

Thus, the fight against religious discrimination, as that term is now defined in Title VII, is being pursued along two fronts. For some groups, the right to equal treatment is still the major issue. Others, however, seek the right to be different. What has been the response to these claims?

HOW MUCH RELIGIOUS ACCOMMODATION?

Way and Burt argue that there is greater official and unofficial acceptance of the practices of what they call "marginal" religions than there used to be; in fact, they propose in their central thesis that "official legitimacy for marginal religions," implying "governmental acceptance of religiously motivated conduct," is "a function of their marginality" (1983: 652–53). Their argument is that adherents of marginal religions, defined in part as those requiring their adherents to act in many areas of life according to religious dictates, are more likely than adherents of mainstream religions to find their religiously mandated conduct burdened by secular regulations. Until the 1960s, they had little legal recourse, because longstanding Supreme Court doctrine held that the Free Exercise Clause did not protect religious conduct. The judicial approach changed, however, with *Sherbert* v. *Verner* (374 U.S. 398) in 1963 and *Wisconsin* v. *Yoder* (406 U.S. 205) in 1972; under these cases, if members of marginal religions can show that a law or regulation imposes a significant burden on their religion, the government has to show that it has a compelling interest in the law or regulation which is more important than the burden placed on religious conduct.

Way and Burt claim that this change in judicial doctrine has provided significant advantages to marginal religions, encouraging their members to bring more suits and enabling them to win more often than before. Nevertheless, the Free Exercise litigants whom Way and Burt study still lose a majority of their cases. Why might this be the case? . . .

[A]mericans tend to favor equality (or equal rights) in the abstract, but are often reluctant to put egalitarian ideals into practice (Karst 1989; Myrdal 1962; Pole 1978). In addition, though social diversity is sometimes praised as an

American value, the pressures toward Anglo-conformity have always been extremely strong (Gordon 1964; 1981; Galanter 1966). Thus, it could make sense to modify Way and Burt's thesis and conclusions: official willingness to grant legitimacy to unconventional religious practices, or to accommodate them, may increase up to the point that mainstream groups believe themselves notably inconvenienced; then, there will be no further increase in legitimacy or accommodation. . . .

JUDICIAL DECISIONS AND DOCTRINE

How sympathetic are the federal courts to claims of religious discrimination? Not very. EEO plaintiffs claiming religious discrimination lose 64 percent of their cases. . . . In a study comparable to this one (though dealing with appellate cases only), religion plaintiffs lost 13 percent more often than women or blacks. There are probably many reasons for this, including the fact that religion plaintiffs are less well organized and get less help from the federal government than plaintiffs in race and sex cases (Burstein 1991). But developments in legal doctrine seem extremely important as well.

What is the relationship between the rationale used for deciding a case and its outcome? Table 2 shows what the judges said was controlling in their decisions in the religious discrimination cases. The possibilities include:

Table 2. Plaintiffs' Victories by Justification for Decision

Percentage of Cases Won by Side Claiming Discrimination		
Justification for Decision is:	*Total*	
Title VII disparate treatment analysis	18%	(39)
Free Exercise Clause *and* non-constitutional rationale	67	(12)
Establishment Clause *and* non-constitutional rationale	79	(14)
Free Exercise Clause	33	(21)
Establishment Clause	0	(2)
Reasonable accommodation analysis, based on interpretation of statute, or, before 1972, EEOC guidelines	44	(27)
Hardison or *Philbrook* decisions	22	(46)
Disparate treatment *and* reasonable accommodation	0	(3)
Other (procedural, case turns on facts, etc.)	31	(78)
Total	33	(242)
	p = .004	

Note: Hardison is *Hardison* v. *Trans World Airlines, Inc.* 432 U.S. 63 (1977); *Philbrook* is *Ansonia Board of Education v. Philbrook,* 55 USLW 4019 (1986).

- standard Title VII disparate treatment analysis, in which the case revolves around whether adherents of one religion were treated differently than others, with the order and allocation of proof established according to criteria laid down in *McDonnell Douglas Corp. v. Green* (411 U.S. 792, 1973) and related cases (see Schlei and Grossman 1983: ch. 2);
- constitutional decisions based on the Free Exercise or Establishment Clauses of the First Amendment;
- combination of constitutional and statutory interpretation;
- analysis of whether a requested accommodation of a religious practice is reasonable, according to the court's reading of Title VII, or, before Title VII was amended in 1972 to define "reasonable accommodation," the court's interpretation of the EEOC's 1967 definition of that term;
- application of the precedents established by the Supreme Court in the *Hardison* (1977) or *Philbrook* (1986) cases, the leading cases defining how much accommodation to religious needs is required of employers and unions;
- combination of disparate treatment and reasonable accommodation analyses; and
- "other," including cases decided on procedural grounds, cases turning on the facts in ways not a part of the analyses listed above, cases decided under statutory exemptions for religious institutions, don't know, etc.

There are three striking patterns in the case outcomes: plaintiffs do badly in disparate treatment cases, especially well in cases which combine constitutional and statutory considerations, and much worse in reasonable accommodation cases decided after the 1977 *Hardison* decision than before. . . . Religion plaintiffs win just 18 percent of their disparate treatment cases, they win 67 percent of cases in which the judges invoked the Free Exercise Clause and a statute, and 79 percent of those in which they relied on the Establishment Clause and a statute. How can such a striking difference be explained?

As it turns out, the Constitution-and-statute victories, though real, are also limited. Religious discrimination cases are distinguished from others in statutory terms by the requirement in Title VII that employers try to accommodate the religious practices of employees. In ten of the 14 cases involving the Establishment Clause and a statute, however, employers and unions argued that this provision is unconstitutional because it grants special benefits to religious employees and thereby violates the Establishment Clause. The courts rejected this argument in nine of the cases (including all those decided by Courts of Appeals[1]. . . . These victories were important, but also . . . fundamentally defensive; the courts generally said only that the Constitution permitted Congress to require some accommodation to religious practices.

The cases involving the Free Exercise clause and a statute do not fall into a clear pattern, but several are consistent with the Establishment-Clause-and-statute cases, with the courts cautiously suggesting that there may be some free exercise rights in the workplace under certain circumstances—that is, one cannot rule out having to take religious practices into account, under the Free Exercise Clause.[2]

Thus, the most common issue in cases involving the First Amendment and a statute is whether there can be *any* constitutional right to the protection of religious differences in the workplace. Plaintiffs' victories suggest that there can. Two important issues remain open, however. First is what will ultimately be decided about the constitutionality of the reasonable accommodation provision; although it has consistently been upheld at the appellate level, it has never been ruled on by the Supreme Court. And second is how much religious difference will be protected. It is here that judicial decisions about what "accommodation" is "reasonable" and what constitutes "undue hardship" become critical.

As long as the courts relied on the 1966 or 1967 EEOC guidelines or directly on their own reading of the reasonable accommodation amendment to Title VII, they were relatively sympathetic to employees' pleas for accommodation. . . . This situation changed dramatically with the Supreme Court's *Hardison* decision in 1977, however. In *Hardison,* the Court held that accommodations imposing more than a "*de minimus*" cost on an employer constituted an undue hardship and need not be adopted. In the Hardison case itself, this meant that employers need not deny the shift and job preferences of some employees in order to accommodate the religious needs of others; nor need the employer pay extra wages to another employee who might substitute for Hardison so that he could have his Sabbath off. In fact, Justice White, writing for the Court, saw reasonable accommodation not as a way to safeguard minorities, but as discriminatory itself, stating that "we will not readily construe the statute to require an employer to discriminate against some employees [by making them work Saturdays] in order to enable others to observe their Sabbath" (14 FEP Cases 1706, 1977).

Hardison immediately raised fears among Jews, Seventh-Day Adventists, and others that not only would employers cease offering new accommodations to employees, but that they might withdraw existing accommodations. And the fears were justified; the proportion of reasonable accommodation cases won by plaintiffs fell by half. . . . The Supreme Court's second reasonable accommodation decision, *Ansonia Board of Education* v. *Philbrook* (55 USLW 4019 [1986]), seems likely to exacerbate this trend; it narrows the provision further, stating that once an employer has offered a reasonable accommodation, it has fulfilled its obligation, even if it rejects other accommodations less disadvantageous to the employee (Kandel 1987).

In principle, minority religious practices are entitled to some protection in the workplace; but the principle has been interpreted so narrowly that in practice the accommodation may be minimal. The most immediate result of these decisions has been the defeat . . . of religious minorities. The longer term implications depend not only on the cases, but on how Congress responds as well.

CONGRESS AND THE POLITICS OF DIVERSITY

Until the reasonable accommodation amendment was adopted in early 1972, there was little debate between the assimilationist and pluralist views. . . . Once the requirement of reasonable accommodation became law, however, employers began to challenge it as an unconstitutional establishment of religion. A seemingly simple attempt to help minorities was thus transformed into a constitutional issue and stimulated much more thought about how much diversity Americans were willing to accommodate. The result has not generally been openness to diversity.

Hardison was a member of the Worldwide Church of God, but the accommodation case leading to the most intense legislative debate involved a Jew. Simcha Goldman, an Orthodox rabbi serving in a secular capacity as a clinical psychologist in the U.S. Air Force, was forced from active duty when the Air Force decided that its dress requirements forbade Goldman to wear his yarmulke and Goldman refused to cease wearing it. In a decision based on the Free Exercise Clause, the Supreme Court decided, 5–4, that the Air Force had the right to do as it had (*Goldman* v. *Weinberger,* 40 FEP Cases 543, 1986). . . . The decision outraged many members of Congress, and they began trying to get Congress to mandate flexibility in the armed services' dress codes to permit accommodation to religious needs.

Their first proposal was narrowly defeated in the Senate in 1986. Reintroduced . . . in late 1987, it occasioned much greater controversy than the reasonable accommodation provision of Title VII ever had, even though it applied only to military uniforms and not more broadly to accommodation in the civilian labor force. Opposition was substantial. In a letter to the Senate, Secretary of Defense Weinberger both reiterated the importance of the issue and opposed the amendment, writing that "the uniforms of the Armed Forces are cherished symbols of Service pride, history, and traditions. Authorizing individual members to modify the uniform would clearly operate to the detriment of order and discipline by fostering resentment and divisiveness among members" (U.S. Congressional Record 1987: S12797). . . .

American diversity was a major focus of the debate. Senator John Chaffee of Rhode Island argued that ". . . the United States is made up of all sorts of people from diverse backgrounds and of diverse religious faiths, and that has been one of our great strengths" (U.S. Congressional Record 1987: 12793). . . . [H]owever, he went on to say that "one of our other strengths has been that in this country we have not permitted diversity to breed divisiveness," and voted against the amendment. It was adopted anyway, and is now law, but the 42 senators who voted against it contrast strikingly with the number voting against the 1972 reasonable accommodation amendment—none. When judges and legislators begin to think seriously about accommodating diversity, many switch with only modest prompting from the notion that "diversity is a source of strength" to the conclusion that "diversity breeds divisiveness"—and they do not like divisiveness.

CONCLUSIONS

Where does the pursuit of equality lead for minority groups in the United States? Historically, the answer has been that the essence of what Karst (1989: 242) calls "equal citizenship" was the right to uniform treatment—to be treated exactly the same way as the majority.

This view has, at times, failed to satisfy members of some minority groups who wanted to preserve their distinctive identities and ways of life. They developed a pluralist vision of American society, in which it would be possible for government and private institutions to accommodate their needs.

The end of mass immigration in the 1920s and the subsequent assimilation of the children of immigrants reduced the tension between the assimilationist and pluralist approaches. The possibility of tension increased after the New Deal, however, as the expansion of government led to its regulation of activities which had been seen as purely private, and increased the number of decisions made by Congress and the courts about how to deal with minority demands for recognition and rights.

One new focus of federal government activity was its attempt to ensure EEO for minorities and women. The basic approach adopted in Title VII of the Civil Rights Act of 1964 was to equate equal opportunity with uniform treatment; the essence of nondiscrimination is to treat members of all groups the same. When considering discrimination on the basis of religion, however, Congress, the EEOC, and the courts soon identified problems stemming from the fact that individuals differ not only in religious affiliation and belief, but also in religious practices that may affect their needs or behavior on the job. And the government responded by trying to accommodate these differences. . . .

The promise of accommodation proved important, as over half the EEO religion cases involved claims of failure to accommodate. When the promise led to significant conflict over how much accommodation would be reasonable, however, Congress and the court had second thoughts. . . . The principle of accommodating minority religious practices has been accepted, but in practice the willingness to accommodate does not go very far.

EEO legislation has been one way the United States has responded in recent years to the tension between assimilationist and pluralist views of American society. Title VII is most obviously, in some ways, a pluralist achievement, recognizing that the society is made up of many groups and requiring that they all be treated with equal respect. Yet there is an assimilationist core to it—all workers are assumed to be so much alike, regardless of race, religion, national origin, or sex, that no special attention need be paid to differences among them. This assimilationist core has, in turn, been modified by some attempt to recognize and even accommodate differences between religious groups. But the modifications turn out to be very modest; when minorities seek to turn the promise of accommodation into reality, resistance increases, and concessions to diversity tend to be small.

Why has pluralism made so little headway in the EEO context, particularly for religious minorities? There are at least five reasons.

First, majorities have little reason to support pluralism because in a democracy they get what they want without it; concessions to minorities simply dilute their power (Galanter 1966). . . .

Second, although minorities (or relatively powerless majorities, such as women) will favor pluralism because of their special needs, their enthusiasm is likely to be tempered by their marginality. Many immigrants want to maintain traditional ways, for example, but short-term economic needs impel them to seek to be treated like members of established groups. . . .

A third reason for the weakness of pluralism in the EEO context may be that some minorities can do well without recourse to law. Small groups have often found satisfactory niches for themselves in the American economy, so long as they were not especially visible targets of hostility (Lieberson 1980).

Fourth, with regard to employment specifically, pluralism is limited by business interests. Tensions between the state's role as protector of the market and its role as supporter of cultural diversity is usually resolved in favor of business's desire to minimize regulation. The section of Title VII requiring reasonable accommodation draws the line at "undue hardship" to an employer's business, and under pressure from defendants, the courts have steadily lowered the threshold for establishing "hardship."

Finally, there is little social base for pluralist thought on religious issues. Those fighting for religious freedom have often seen their goal as separation of church and state, not pluralism, and have had little interest in what rights religious minorities might acquire as members of distinctive religious communities. . . .

Overall, religious minorities have both gained and lost from recent developments. The gains from uniform treatment are obvious. Beginning with the prohibition of religious tests for public office in Article VI of the Constitution, and the

Free Exercise and Establishment Clauses of the First Amendment, religious minorities have benefited from standing in the same relationship to the state as everyone else. The extension of guarantees of uniform treatment to the private sphere, through Title VII and other laws, has been a further sign of acceptance and legitimacy.

To some extent, though, the recent gains come at the expense of a pluralist vision. The pressure toward uniform treatment—often ardently desired by minority group members themselves—has made it difficult to take diversity into account. As Justice Marshall, writing in dissent, said of the *Hardison* decision, "one of this Nation's pillars of strength—our hospitality to religious diversity—has been seriously eroded. All Americans will be a little poorer until today's decision is erased" (14 FEP Cases 1711, 1977).

ACKNOWLEDGMENT

Revision of a paper presented to the annual meeting of the American Sociological Association, San Francisco, California, August 13, 1989. The work was made possible by grants from the American Jewish Committee and the National Science Foundation (SES-8509055), and is based in part on a report to the Committee. For helpful advice and comments we would like to thank David Singer, Lawrence Grossman, Calvin Goldscheider, Sam Rabinove, Alfred Blumrosen, Arval Morris, Cornelius Peck, Marvin Stern, Florence Katz, Lisa Cubbins, Marshall George, Terence C. Halliday, Judy Howard, Satoshi Kanazawa, Satomi Kurosu, Ken Pike, Xinhua Ren, Stuart Scheingold, Gi-Wook Shin, Edie Simpson, Beth Weinstein, and Siok-Cheng Yeoh.

NOTES

1. *Protos* v. *Volkswagen of America,* 41 FEP Cases 598 (1986), Third Circuit; *Machinists* v. *Boeing Co.,* 42 FEP *Cases* 732 (1986), Western District of Washington; *Gibson* v. *Missouri Pacific R.R.,* 39 FEP Cases 369 (1985), Eastern District of Arkansas; *Anderson* v. *General Dynamics,* 26 FEP Cases 101 (1981), Ninth Circuit; *Tooley* v. *Martin-Marietta Corp.,* 26 FEP Cases 95 (1981), Ninth Circuit; *Gavin* v. *Peoples Natural Gas Co.,* 21 FEP Cases 1186 (1980), Third Circuit; *McDaniel* v. *Essex International, Inc.* 30 FEP Cases 831 (1982), Sixth Circuit; *Nottelson* v. *Smith Steel Workers,* 25 FEP Cases 281 (1981), Seventh Circuit; *EEOC* v. *E.I. Dupont de Nemours & Co.,* 623 F. Supp. 15 (1985), Eastern District of North Carolina.

2. See *Weitkenaut* v. *Goodyear Tire & Rubber Co.,* 10 FEP Cases 513 (1974); *Lutcher* v. *Musicians Local 47,* 24 FEP Cases 859 (1980); *McCormich* v. *Bd. of Ed. of Belvidere,* 32 FEP Cases 504 (1983); *McGinnis* v. *U.S. Postal Service,* 24 FEP Cases 999 (1980).

REFERENCES

Aronson, Arnold. 1950. "Employment." *American Jewish Yearbook* 51:99–109.

———. 1952. "Employment." *American Jewish Yearbook* 53:93–106.

Burstein, Paul. 1985. *Discrimination, Jobs, and Politics.* Chicago: University of Chicago Press.

Fiss, Owen. 1971. "A Theory of Fair Employment Laws." *University of Chicago Law Review* 38:235–314.

Galanter, Marc. 1966. "Religious Freedoms in the United States: A Turning Point?" *Wisconsin Law Review* 1966:217–96.

Gordon, Milton. 1964. *Assimilation in American Life.* New York: Oxford.

———. 1981. "Models of Pluralism: the New American Dilemma." *Annals of the American Academy of Political and Social Science* 454:178–88.

Higham, John. 1984. *Send These to Me: Immigrants in Urban America,* rev. ed. Baltimore. Johns Hopkins University Press.

Kandel, William L. 1987. "Religious Discrimination after *Philbrook:* De Minimus Reduced." *Employee Relations Law Journal* 12:690–97.

Karst, Kenneth L. 1989. *Belonging to America.* New Haven: Yale University Press.

Laycock, Douglas. 1986. "'Nonpreferential' Aid to Religion: a False Claim about Original Intent." *William and Mary Law Review* 27:875–923.

Leskes, Theodore. 1954. "Discrimination in Employment." *American Jewish Yearbook* 55:27–41.

Lieberson, Stanley. 1980. *A Piece of the Pie.* Berkeley: University of California Press.

Myrdal, Gunnar. 1962 [originally 1944]. *An American Dilemma.* New York: Harper and Row.

Pole, J. R. 1978. *The Pursuit of Equality in American History.* Berkeley: University of California Press.

Post, Robert C. 1988. "Cultural Heterogeneity and the Law." *California Law Review* 76:101–39.

Rae, Douglas. 1981. *Equalities.* Cambridge: Harvard University Press.

Schlei, Barbara Lindemann, and Paul Grossman. 1983. *Employment Discrimination Law,* 2nd ed. Washington, DC: Bureau of National Affairs.

U.S. Commission on Civil Rights. 1983. *Religion in the Constitution: A Delicate Balance.* Washington, DC: Clearinghouse Publication No. 80.

U.S. Congress. 1972, 1987. *Congressional Record.* Washington, DC: Government Printing Office.

U.S. Congress, House Subcommittee on Compensation and Employee Benefits of the Committee on Post Office and Civil Service. 1978. *Hearing: Leave Time for Observing Religious Holidays.* Washington, DC: Government Printing Office.

U.S. Equal Employment Opportunity Commission. various years. *Annual Report.* Washington, DC.

U.S. Equal Employment Opportunity Commission. 1978. *Hearings on Religious Accommodation.* Washington, DC: Government Printing Office.

Way, Frank, and Barbara J. Burt. 1983. Religious Marginality and the Free Exercise Clause. *American Political Science Review* 77:652–65.

20

Getting Women Work That Isn't Women's Work: Challenging Gender Biases in the Workplace Under Title VII

Maxine N. Eichner

Although title VII of the Civil Rights Act of 1964 has prohibited discrimination in employment for almost a quarter of a century, the labor market remains overwhelmingly segregated by sex. Almost half of all employed women work in occupations that are at least eighty percent female, and over half of employed men work in occupations that are at least eighty percent male (Reskin and Hartman 1986; Rytina 1981). This sex segregation limits women to fewer types of jobs,[1] restricts their opportunities for career advancement, and ensures that they receive considerably less pay than men.[2]

Attempts to rid the work place of intentional discrimination have allowed women to make considerable progress toward equality, yet women's current confinement to the "pink collar" sphere of the labor market does not result solely from intentional discrimination by employers. Instead, job descriptions and structures that have been adapted to male incumbents continue to bar women from those sectors of the labor market from which they were once historically excluded by intentional discrimination.[3] Demands of physical strength beyond that which most women possess, scheduling that conforms to typically male life patterns, job descriptions calling for stereotypically masculine traits, and myriad other requirements modeled on male characteristics perpetuate women's exclusion from traditionally male jobs. These employment standards assume men to be the norm and relegate women who diverge from this norm to second class status in the labor market. If sexual equality is to be achieved, women's exclusion from traditionally male jobs must be recognized for what it is—not the natural product of women's differences from men, but the product of the social (de)valuation of women that isolates these differences and thereby ensures that women remain economically subordinated. As a growing literature of feminist jurisprudence

Excerpts reprinted with permission from *The Yale Law Review* 1988, vol 97:1397–1417. Copyright © 1988 by The Yale Law Review Company.

argues, achieving sexual equality requires recognition that standards that disadvantage women are neither necessary nor unbiased, but are, in fact, discriminatory in a society composed of both men and women.[4]

Despite title VII's commitment to equality in the workplace, courts have not used either of its two frameworks of analysis, disparate treatment or disparate impact, to confront entrenched conceptions of job performance that exclude women. Disparate treatment doctrine, which prohibits practices motivated by discriminatory intent, is inherently unsuited to the task of identifying these biases because it guarantees similar treatment only for the similarly situated. Women, when they cannot or will not conform to male patterns of behavior, remain outside the scope of its protection. Disparate impact doctrine, which prohibits employment practices that have a discriminatory effect, could in theory challenge entrenched assumptions regarding job performance. This method of analysis has the potential to isolate and eliminate biased practices that exclude women. Yet in practice, courts have limited its effectiveness by wrongly accepting entrenched biases as essential to the job's performance and therefore as exempt from title VII's ban on practices that exclude women.

This essay argues that title VII's ban on sex discrimination in employment compels courts to alter radically judicial analysis of challenges to jobs from which women are excluded in order to eliminate "male-biased" job standards. Part I argues that pervasive perceptions that jobs must be performed according to standards unnecessarily biased toward men deny women traditionally male jobs on the basis of their real and perceived differences from men. It suggests that these entrenched conceptions of job performance do not derive from requirements integral to jobs themselves, but instead reflect the gender of current job holders; women's historical exclusion from the labor market thereby causes and perpetuates these biases. Part II argues that courts refuse to challenge male-biased requirements because they tacitly accept these job standards as necessary and normal. Part III proposes a reformulation of disparate impact doctrine that challenges entrenched assumptions about job structures that are based on the image of the male worker.

I. MALE BIASES IN THE LABOR MARKET: JOB REQUIREMENTS THAT DISADVANTAGE WOMEN

Many jobs in today's labor market require traits and life patterns generally associated with men. Although such job demands typically are perceived as necessary for optimal job performance, often they are unconnected to the actual needs of the job itself. Instead, these requirements are based on the faulty supposition that the job must be performed as it has always been performed by past employees. This assumption severely disadvantages women; because of women's historical exclusion from large sectors of the labor market, past employees of well-paying positions in our society are almost exclusively male. These beliefs about job performance may involve "mischaracterizing" the job (insofar as employers wrongly perceive that the job requires "masculine" traits) or "misstructuring" the job (insofar as employers unnecessarily construct the job in ways that do, in fact, make it more appropriate for men).

Large numbers of traditionally male jobs in our society are mischaracterized as requiring traits predominantly associated with men. As sociologists have long recognized, however, sex-typed traits commonly associated with a job often have little inherent connection with performance; instead, the perception that a job requires masculine traits typically derives from associating the job with its incumbents (see, e.g., Cohn 1985; Epstein 1970; Oppenheimer 1970). For example, physicians in this country have traditionally been male, and good doctors have long been thought to exhibit traits associated with men, including detachment and rationality. In the Soviet Union, however, where seventy-five percent of physicians are women, medicine has long been considered an occupation requiring such qualities as nurturing and caring. Similarly, before the Civil War, the position of primary schoolteacher was seen as an intellectually grueling "male" occupation for which women lacked the requisite mental stamina. When the shortage of men during the Civil War necessitated the recruitment of female teachers, however, women moved into the profession, and schoolteaching was soon considered a nurturing activity which demanded a mothering presence.

In addition to their association with male stereotypes, jobs also possess structures adapted overwhelmingly to the lifestyles and characteristics of men. This "misstructuring" of jobs may take several forms. For example, many jobs historically held by men demand typically male physical characteristics because machinery used on these jobs has been adapted to the physique of its incumbents. Smaller women may not be able to use equipment designed for the male physique as efficiently or as safely as men and will therefore be deemed unsuitable for these jobs.[6] Other job requirements reflect the family roles and work schedules that men have traditionally adopted. For example, many occupations in our society require frequent travel, night hours, or overtime work at little notice. Such schedules require the employee to subordinate family responsibilities to work requirements. Women, who still assume the greater burden of caring for children, other dependents, and the home, even while employed, cannot effectively compete against men for these jobs.

The link that is widely thought to exist between "male" characteristics and traditionally male jobs creates a vicious cycle for many women. Because these jobs are associated with the traits and lifestyles of men, employers fail to hire women who cannot or will not adopt "male" standards of behavior. Men therefore continue to dominate these positions, which, in turn, continue to be viewed as male and adapted to men. Women, meanwhile, remain trapped in the "pink collar" ghetto of the labor market.

II.   THE LIMITS OF CURRENT JUDICIAL TREATMENT:
TITLE VII AND MALE-BIASED JOBS

Although title VII prohibits discrimination in employment on the basis of sex, courts often fail fully to enforce this prohibition when male-biased standards are at issue. Courts either limit their inquiry to disparate treatment doctrine, which can neither identify nor eliminate these biases, or they apply disparate impact doctrine and defer to the employer's characterization of the job. In neither case do courts challenge the legitimacy of the job's requirements themselves.

A.   Disparate Treatment Analysis: Differences
as Justification for Exclusion

Courts have decided the majority of title VII sex discrimination claims by using disparate treatment doctrine, which prohibits employment practices motivated by discriminatory intent. Yet, as this doctrine has been developed by courts, the prohibition on disparate treatment applies only to situations in which women are the same as men with respect to hiring criteria. Where women are different or perceived to be different from men on the basis of hiring criteria, disparate treatment doctrine's guarantee of "similar treatment for the similarly situated" lacks the power to identify and remedy male-biased requirements.

EEOC v. Sears, Roebuck & Co.   (628 F. Supp. 1264, 1986) illustrates the limitations of disparate treatment challenges to male-biased hiring standards. In that case, the Equal Employment Opportunity Commission (EEOC) argued that Sears, Roebuck Department Stores had discriminated on the basis of sex in hiring for its highly paid commission sales positions. The EEOC demonstrated that although most of the applicants for sales positions were women, the department store selected far greater numbers of men to fill commission sales vacancies. In response to the EEOC's claim, Sears argued that a nondiscriminatory explanation for the disparities existed: Women were less interested in and less qualified for these positions than men. According to the defendant, although it sought women for commission sales positions, most women disliked the "dog-eat-dog" competition associated with these jobs, were uncomfortable with the evening hour demands which might conflict with family obligations, and were less familiar than men with the products sold on commission, including hardware, men's clothing, and automotive equipment.

In analyzing the EEOC's claim of discrimination, the court applied disparate treatment analysis. As the court framed the issue under this analysis, the charge of discrimination turned on the adequacy of Sears' supposedly nondiscriminatory explanation—whether women were, in fact, different from men with respect to the stated hiring requirements. The court eventually found many women were genuinely less suited to and less interested in these jobs than men under these standards, and consequently held that Sears' hiring practices were non-discriminatory. In reaching this decision, however, the focus of disparate treatment analysis on the issue of difference obscured the real problem in the *Sears* case: the stores' demand that commission salespersons display those characteristics largely possessed or perceived to be possessed by men.

As the court's description of Sears' hiring practices makes clear, Sears' hiring criteria for commission sales jobs were closely modeled on traits associated with men. The job description found by the judge to better apply to men demanded "aggressiveness or assertiveness, competitiveness, . . . persuasiveness, an outgoing . . . or extraverted personality, self-confidence, personal dominance, [and] a strong desire to earn a substantial income. . . ." (628 F. Supp. 1290, 1986). It therefore almost perfectly captured the stereotypical American man. The tests used to screen applicants for these qualities also reflected a male bias. A questionnaire for the "vigor" Sears deemed necessary for the job sought affirmative answers to such questions as: "Do you have a low pitched voice?" "Do you swear often?" "Have you participated in wrestling?" "Have you played on a football team?" (*Sears* brief at 34). In addition, the qualities sought by interviewers were those found successful in past commission salespersons—almost all of whom were men. The commission sales job structure also favored men. Sears required that commission sales employees be available to work at night; as the court found, the requirement posed a particular hardship for women, who assume more responsibility for child care than men in our society. Moreover, as recognized by the court, most commission sales items, which included sporting goods, technical goods, automotive equipment, and men's clothing, fall into traditionally male areas of interest.

Nonetheless, disparate treatment analysis did not call these job requirements into question. Were Sears' job characterization and structure actually necessary for successful sales? Did salespersons have to be aggressive to sell merchandise successfully? Could Sears structure the commission sales department differently to decrease the competition that many women found disturbing, perhaps by pooling commissions? Must all employees necessarily be available for evening work? Why was men's clothing sold on commission when women's was not? Under current disparate treatment doctrine, which limits the guarantee of sexual equality to situations in which women are similarly situated to men with respect to hiring requirements, such questions about job structures are never answered because they are never asked.

B.   Disparate Impact Analysis: Limitations on *Griggs* and Title VII's Equality Guarantee

Disparate impact scrutiny, the other avenue of relief open to plaintiffs under title VII, can in theory reach entrenched biases like those in *Sears*. As established by the Supreme Court in *Griggs v. Duke Power Co.,* facially neutral employment practices that have significant adverse effects on protected groups may violate title VII, whether or not these procedures are motivated by discriminatory intent. . . .

The Supreme Court's construction of disparate impact doctrine properly encompasses male-biased job practices in the doctrine's ban. As with other prohibited practices, male-biased job requirements are "fair in form, but discriminatory in operation." Moreover, such practices function as "artificial, arbitrary, and unnecessary barriers to [women's] employment" which have "operated in the past to favor an identifiable group of . . . employees over other employees," (401 U.S. 430–31 1971). . . . To implement the equality of opportunity guaranteed specifically by *Griggs* and more generally by title VII, jobs must be more than open to women in name alone—they must be accommodated to women as well as to men.

Courts, however, have typically failed to fulfill the promise of *Griggs* in their evaluation of male-biased job requirements. Rather than giving the careful scrutiny to these requirements that disparate impact analysis supposedly guarantees, courts have tended simply to assume that requirements that exclude women are inevitable features of the work place and thus uphold them with little scrutiny. The primary error in judicial use of disparate impact doctrine lies with the concept of "business necessity," which ensures that no employment practice with an adverse impact will be upheld under title VII unless the employer can show both that it is job related and that no less discriminatory substitute can be found. In investigating the necessity of employment practices that exclude women, however, courts typically seek to determine only that selection practices effectively screen in an unbiased manner for the qualities and structures deemed necessary for the job by the employer. They fail to recognize that the employer's conceptions of necessary job qualities and job structures may themselves contain entrenched discriminatory biases.[7] In addition, courts consider in-depth scrutiny of a job's characterization and structure to be an inappropriate invasion of the province of the employer.

Levin v. Delta Air Lines (730 F2d 994, 1984) illustrates courts' "hands off" approach to existing job characterizations and structures. In that case, the Fifth Circuit found that the employer airline did not discriminate against pregnant flight attendants by compelling them to stop work during the full term of their pregnancy rather than reassigning them to available ground duties. According to the court, once the employer demonstrated the job-relatedness of a practice, the practice would be considered nondiscriminatory unless an alternative practice accorded amenably "with the employer's customary practices," (730 F.2d 1001, 1984). The court ignored the possibility that the employer's customary practices might themselves be discriminatory in excluding women; by doing so, the court allowed the biased underlying job structure to justify the continued exclusion of women.

III. REVISING THE DISPARATE IMPACT INQUIRY: USING TITLE VII TO ERADICATE MALE-BIASED JOB STRUCTURES

Job stereotypes and structures that unnecessarily exclude women violate title VII's guarantee of protection for women's employment opportunities. If the *Griggs* promise of equal opportunity is to have meaning for women, requirements that assume women must be exactly like men to perform jobs well must be rethought. This Note suggests a reformulation of disparate impact doctrine which will allow courts to better evaluate whether male-biased employment practices are truly related to optimal job performance. . . . Because conceptions of optimal job performance are currently so mired in male-biased assumptions that disentangling them will take time, this proposal aims to encourage courts and employers carefully to rethink male-biased assumptions rather than attempt to determine in advance in which cases courts should order remedies.

A. Adverse Impact

At the first stage of a disparate impact case, the standards of statistical proof currently used by courts to establish that a challenged requirement has an adverse impact on protected groups should suffice to identify male-biased employment practices. Courts should, however, carefully avoid using stereotyped notions of job performance to define the pool against which the adverse impact of the requirements is measured, as defining the pool in this way could make it unnecessarily male and thereby obscure the practice's adverse impact.[8] Thus, the employer should be required to show the business necessity of controversial requirements used to limit the relevant pool.

B. The Business Necessity Defense

At the second stage of disparate impact scrutiny, employers must establish the business necessity of the challenged requirements. When evaluating requirements for a male bias, courts should use a two-part test to ensure that they do not accept stereotyped assumptions regarding job performance as business necessities. They should first ask whether the challenged requirement is essential to the core function of the job. If the answer is affirmative, courts should then consider whether the selection process screens for that requirement in an unbiased manner.

The core function test would require courts to look beyond stereotyped notions of how the job should be performed to the basic function of the job itself. This test would enable courts to determine whether the requirement and the job itself are actually closely linked. . . . Where a clear-cut determination of the job's core function is difficult, as might be the case, for example, in many professional positions, judicial scrutiny should focus on the extent of the employer's effort to rethink the necessity of the job's requirements in light of their discriminatory impact. For these purposes, the employer, at the very least, should have analyzed the job to determine the qualities essential to effective job performance. Such an analysis should persuasively demonstrate that the requirements are truly necessary to perform the job well, rather than are simply a description of the traits needed to perform the job in the same way as the job is currently performed.[9]

In addition to demonstrating that the traits that employers require are essential to the core function of the job, employers should demonstrate that selection procedures which screen for these traits are free of stereotypes. At this stage, procedures commonly used by courts to assess disparate impact claims can be employed to determine whether the screening procedure is biased. When the screening process involves the subjective assessment of applicants—as, for example, when a plaintiff contends that an interviewer sought to determine vigor in a way reflecting masculine stereotypes—determining bias becomes somewhat more difficult. In such cases, courts should require that subjective hiring systems set out standards of evaluation with enough specificity to limit the potential for discrimination.

C.   Available Alternatives

If an employer proves that the contested practices are a business necessity, at the third stage of the disparate impact case the court must still determine whether the employer could use alternative employment devices of comparable business utility that have a less discriminatory impact. At this stage, employers should be required to show that they have considered alternative means of performing the job and that these alternatives have proven unsatisfactory. For example, where positions exclude women on the basis of demands for extensive overtime, employers should be required to show they have explored alternative ways that the jobs could be structured that would better accommodate family responsibilities. Employers might therefore be obligated to explore such options as job sharing, schedules with flexible hours, and systems in which employees receive compensatory time off if they have to work overtime. Plaintiffs should have an opportunity to rebut the employers' claims with their own studies or with evidence that other employers have found it feasible to structure similar jobs in ways more inclusive of women.

Employers should also be required to show that job requirements do not disadvantage women by undervaluing their strengths. For instance, employers should demonstrate that job descriptions that demand only physical characteristics commonly associated with men, such as strength and speed, do not ignore the importance of attributes associated with women, such as flexibility, balance, endurance, and agility.[10] If the latter characteristics are found appropriate for the job's performance, courts should require their incorporation into the job description. A court might thus have insisted that Sears justify its commission sales description's omission of qualities traditionally associated with women that might improve commission sales prowess, such as the ability to listen well to the needs of customers.

D. Cost

Whether a practice is a business necessity and whether alternative practices are feasible will frequently turn on the issue of cost. Most jobs that require significant overtime, for example, could have their work divided among more employees—it might simply cost the employer more to do so. Similarly, equipment designed for the male physique could be replaced with equipment better suited to women—for a price.

When evaluating claims based on costs, courts should not simply assume that alternative practices will necessarily be more costly than current practices. Re-characterizing and restructuring male-biased jobs will in many instances lower, rather than raise, costs. Demands for characteristics and life patterns not truly necessary for a job narrows the applicant pool by eliminating suitable candidates. Similarly, failure to require "non-masculine" traits that are useful for the job precludes selection of optimal candidates.

If a case arises in which values of cost and equality do compete, where a court draws the line between the two will necessarily depend upon the facts of that specific case. However, claims of cost should never be treated as determinative; title VII does not allow discrimination merely because it is profitable. Thus, courts should impose a strict standard of necessity on employers who present cost claims by, for example, requiring them to show substantial harm to the business. This relatively high standard for business necessity recognizes that cost to an employer should not justify forcing women to subsidize a discriminatory business by working at lower-paying jobs elsewhere, or not at all. . . .

IV.   CONCLUSION

This [essay] calls for judicial recognition that job standards that exclude women do not do so because women are *inherently* unfit to perform these jobs. Rather, such job standards reflect biased assumptions about the way that work must be performed that are derived from the *social* valuation of the relative worth of men and women. Courts must use title VII to challenge these biased notions regarding optimal job performance if women are truly to receive the equality of opportunity in employment promised by the statute. It is time to recognize that jobs modeled on the male image are neither necessary nor appropriate in a society composed of both women and men, and to adapt such jobs to both sexes.

NOTES

1. Despite women's movement during the last decades into some sectors of the labor force traditionally occupied by men, the overwhelming majority of women remain in traditionally female occupations. In 1987, women represented 80% of all administrative support (including clerical) workers, but only 9% of all precision production, craft, and repair workers. Moreover, in that year, women constituted only 6.4% of apprentices. *Id.* Overall, one quarter of all employed women work in three basic job categories—they type, sell retail goods, or prepare and serve food. Norwood (1985).

2. Approximately 35–40% of the discrepancy between men's and women's salaries can be traced to the fact that "female" jobs pay considerably less than do "male" jobs. Women, Work, and Wages: Equal Pay for Jobs of Equal Value 33, 321 (Treiman & Hartmann 1981). . . .

3. Women's exclusion from the work force dates back to the early 19th century, when production moved from the home to the workplace as a result of industrialization (Cott 1977). For the next century and a half, women were openly discriminated against by private employers, many of whom explicitly refused to hire women; even those who did hire women refused to hire married women or women with young children. . . . Women's second class status in the labor market was reinforced by state regulations that restricted the hours women could work and the occupations they could perform (Kessler-Harris 1982; Reskin and Hartman 1986). The federal judiciary encouraged exclusionary policies against women. For example, in the now-infamous case of Bradwell v. Illinois, 83 U.S. (16 Wall.) 130, 141–42 (1872), the Supreme Court upheld women's exclusion from the Illinois bar. . . .

4. Debating such issues as pregnancy leave over the last decade, the feminist movement has split regarding how best to achieve sex equality. Advocates of the "equal treatment" position argue that women should strive for sex-neutral standards that deemphasize differences between the sexes; according to these advocates, women will be more successful in moving towards equality if simply allowed to compete against men under facially neutral standards. *See, e.g.,* Williams (1985) . . . They would therefore support a law requiring pregnancy leave only when it is part of a disability leave program available to both sexes.

"Special treatment" proponents, on the other hand, believe that the equal treatment position inadequately protects women when they differ from men. . . . Rather than treating women equally only when they are situated similarly to men, "special treatment" advocates would support gender-specific classifications that benefit women when there are real differences between the sexes. They would thus accept a law requiring a pregnancy leave policy even where no general disability policy exists for workers of both sexes. . . .

An emerging group of feminists has begun to express dissatisfaction with the limited terms of this debate, however. Attention to whether women are treated similarly or differently under existing standards, they argue, ignores the real problem: the legitimacy of standards constructed on the basis of a male norm. . . . Sex equality efforts, these scholars contend, should move beyond a focus on similarity and difference to challenge the male-biased standards themselves and the social valuation of sexual difference. *See, e.g.,* MacKinnon (1979); Finley (1986); Scales (1986). This Note is predicated on that view. Sexual equality, it posits, concerns neither women's similarities with, nor their differences from, men. Instead, it concerns the relative power and social status of the sexes. In this view, women's similarities or differences from men are relevant only insofar as they are used as vehicles to perpetuate hierarchy.

6. In the experience of American Telephone & Telegraph, for example, women in outdoor jobs had higher accident rates than men while using equipment ordered when only men worked in the field. After the introduction of lighter-weight and more mobile equipment, however, women performed their jobs as safely as men (Reskin and Hartmann 1986). . . .

7. In Zahorik v. Cornell University, 729 F.2d 85 (2d Cir. 1984), for example, the court denied the plaintiffs' claim that the university's tenure selection process was discriminatory under disparate impact doctrine, despite the fact that 65% of men and only 42% of women received tenure. The court upheld the university's selection criteria on the ground that the criteria were "obviously" relevant to employment in tenured professorships. Even the fact that the decisionmaking process was decentralized and it was therefore impossible to discern how fairly the criteria were applied was of no moment to the court, because the process was "based on generations of almost universal tradition."

Similarly, in Boyd v. Ozark Air Lines, 419 F. Supp. 1061 (E.D. Mo. 1976), *aff'd,* 568 F.2d 50 (8th Cir. 1977), the court failed to challenge a height requirement for pilots despite its disproportionate impact on women, because the planes used by the airline were designed on the scale of the male physique. Refusing to question the purchase of the planes or to demand that, even prospectively, the airline purchase planes more accommodating to women's height, the court simply accepted the height restriction. . . .

8. *See* Bartholet (1982). For example, in Wheeler v. Armco Steel Corp., 471 F. Supp. 1050 (1979), the court confined the relevant labor pool for a non-entry level position to employees within the company rather than the metropolitan area labor market. In doing so, the court allowed any discriminatory criteria used to select entry-level employees to be passed along to the challenged position. . . .

9. *See* Bartholet (1982). . . . Bartholet's discussion reveals the problem with the approach used in cases such as Contreras v. City of Los Angeles, 656 F.2d 1267 (9th Cir. 1981), *cert. denied,* 455 U.S. 1021 (1982), in which the court accepted a job description produced by having incumbents determine the qualities they believed essential to job performance.

Courts should require job analyses to be recent to avoid exclusion of women that is not justified on the basis of current circumstances. Under this standard, Sears' job description, developed in 1953, would have been presumptively invalid. Similarly, employers must rethink height, weight, and strength requirements in light of new technology. In addition, industry-wide use of particular requirements would not be a valid defense to a discrimination claim because male-biased job requirements often pervade an entire industry.

10. *See* Berkman v. City of New York, 626 F. Supp. 591, 599 (E.D.N.Y. 1985), *aff'd in part, rev'd in part,* 812 F.2d 52 (2d Cir.) (criticizing firefighting test that deemphasizes endurance in favor of strength and speed as "invidiously discriminat[ing] against women"). . . .

REFERENCES

Bartholet, Elizabeth. 1982. "Applications of Title VII to Jobs in High Places." *Harvard Law Review* 95:947–1027.

Cohn, Samuel. 1985. *The Process of Occupational Sex-Typing.* Philadelphia: Temple University Press.

Cott, Nancy. 1977. *The Bonds of Womanhood*. New Haven: Yale University Press.

Epstein, Cynthia Fuchs. 1970. *Woman's Place*. Berkeley: University of California Press.

Finley, Lucinda M. 1986. "Transcending Equality Theory." *Columbia Law Review* 86:1118–82.

Kessler-Harris, Alice. 1982. *Out to Work: A History of Wage Earning Women in the United States*. New York: Oxford University Press.

MacKinnon, Catherine. 1979. *Sexual Harassment of Working Women*. New Haven: Yale University Press.

Oppenheimer, Valerie. 1970. *The Female Labor Force in the United States*. Population Monograph Series, no. 5. Berkeley: University of California Press.

Reskin, Barbara, and Heidi Hartmann, editors. 1986. *Women's Work, Men's Work: Sex Segregation on the Job*. Washington, DC: National Academy Press.

Rytina, Nancy F. 1981. "Occupational Segregation and Earnings Differences by Sex." *Monthly Labor Review* 104 (January):49–53.

Scales, Ann D. 1986. "The Emergence of Feminist Jurisprudence." *Yale Law Journal* 95:1373–1403.

Treiman, Donald, and Heidi Hartmann, editors. 1981. *Women, Work, and Wages*. Washington, DC: National Academy of Sciences Press.

Williams, Wendy W. 1985. "Equality's Riddle: Pregnancy and the Equal Treatment/Special Treatment Debate." *New York University Review of Law and Social Change* 13:325–80.

VI

Equal Employment Opportunity in Other Countries

Labor market discrimination is hardly confined to the United States. Discrimination on the basis of race and ethnicity seems to occur in almost all racially and ethnically diverse countries; religious discrimination is common in some countries; and what most Americans would see as sex discrimination appears to be virtually universal.

There is great variation in how nations deal with racial, ethnic, religious, and gender differences. In some, women have yet to attain the most basic rights of citizenship, and racial, religious, and ethnic antagonisms often turn murderous. At the same time, however, many Western governments and some others (including the Japanese), responding partly to movements within their own countries and partly to pressure from international organizations, have prohibited labor market discrimination on the basis of race, ethnicity, religion, and/or sex (see Thomas et al. 1987 on international trends in the rights of citizenship).

Some aspects of the laws in other countries are very similar to American EEO law (in ways going beyond the general notion of prohibiting discrimination); some national legislatures have even drawn on the American experience when writing their own laws. The British 1976 Race Relations Act, for example, incorporates two concepts of discrimination: *direct discrimination* and *indirect discrimination*. Direct discrimination is what would be called disparate treatment in American law, conforming to the traditional definition of discrimination as involving the intentional treatment of one person less favorably than another on the basis of race; it was first banned in the original British law against employment discrimination, adopted in 1968. Indirect discrimination is essentially the same as adverse impact, the newer concept of discrimination enunciated by the U.S. Supreme Court in *Griggs v. Duke Power Co.* in 1971 and discussed in the chapters by Blumrosen and the U.S. Department of Justice; its addition to British law, John Solomos has written (1989:44), "was partly based on the American experience of affirmative action against institutionalised forms of racism" (see also Tolley 1991).

Often, however, antidiscrimination law in other countries differs significantly from American law. For example, the Japanese Equal Employment Opportunity Act, which prohibits discrimination against women, is considerably more vague about what it prohibits than Title VII is (even considering Title VII's vagueness about the definition of discrimination, discussed above), and provides no real sanctions against employers who discriminate (see Bergeson and Oba 1986 [excerpted here]). In addition, exceptions to the general prohibition of discrimination have been interpreted far more broadly in Japan than in the United States, apparently making it easier to justify differential treatment there [compare Bergeson and Oba (1986) with Schlei and Grossman (1983:340–60), on sex as a "bona fide occupational qualification"]. Enforcement procedures vary significantly across countries as well. Some governments play a far more active role than the U.S. government in setting wages to overcome unequal pay by gender; some assign a significant enforcement role to unions in cooperation with management, and others rely almost entirely on mediation and conciliation (see Gunderson 1989 [excerpted here]; Wainwright 1979; Bergeson and Oba 1986; Jenkins and Solomos 1989).

Gauging the consequences of EEO laws is, of course, no easier with regard to other countries than it is for the United States. There is certainly some evidence that such laws can improve economic outcomes for the groups they are supposed to benefit. In his review of work on laws prohibiting sex discrimination, Gunderson (1989 [excerpted here]) concludes that "equal employment opportunity policies and affirmative action policies tend to improve the position of the groups to which they are targeted [and] stricter enforcement tends to enhance effectiveness." Most readily available studies focus on the Anglo-American countries, however, so we do not know how effective the laws are on the European continent; it would be particularly interesting to learn the extent to which attitudes about gender roles might reduce the effectiveness of laws against sex discrimination (outside Scandinavia), both directly and by undermining pressures for enforcement.

One interesting possibility raised by research on EEO laws is that they are more effective against sex discrimination than against racial discrimination. Because individual researchers seem to be interested primarily in sex discrimination or race discrimination, but not both, most studies focus on one or the other. As a result, it is difficult to find studies of the two similar enough to permit comparison of the consequences of EEO laws for minorities and women. For example, studies of Great Britain argue that EEO laws have substantially improved economic outcomes for women (Zabalza and Tzannatos 1985 [excerpted here]) but not for racial minorities (Brown and Gay 1985 [excerpted here]; Jenkins and Solomos 1989); unfortunately, the methods used to study race discrimination differ from those used to study sex discrimination, so we cannot be sure that the results are comparable. One study of American EEO laws did use identical methods to gauge the impact of EEO laws on women and blacks, and found that women arguably gained more (with minority women gaining the most by some measures; Burstein 1985:ch. 6). As it is, we really know very little about which groups benefit most from EEO laws—whether they help ethnic or racial minorities more under some circumstances rather than others, for example, and whether women are more likely to benefit than minorities (with minority women raising interesting issues in their own right).

The chapters that follow analyze discrimination and EEO laws in two countries relatively similar to the United States in level of economic development. One, Great Britain, is included because it is normally seen as quite similar to the United States culturally and politically, and the other, Japan, is included because it is seen as quite different.

Great Britain is the subject of two chapters, one focusing on race discrimination and the other on sex. Brown and Gay adopt a technique for studying race discrimination rarely used in analyses of employment discrimination in the United States. Most quantitative analyses of discrimination estimate its impact indirectly, by statistically comparing different groups and arguing that differences in labor market outcomes not the result of differential qualifications are due to discrimination (see, for example, the chapters by Goldin and Gunderson). Brown and Gay, in contrast, conduct an experiment to estimate directly how common one type of discrimination is; they have members of different racial groups begin the process of applying for jobs by letter and telephone, and then determine how employers responded to applications identical in every way except for the race of the applicant. Comparing their results to those of previous, similar studies, they conclude both that race discrimination remains pervasive in Great Britain and that the Race Relations Act seems to have had little impact: Discrimination had not declined in the ten years between studies. Similar experimental studies have been conducted in Australia (Riach and Rich 1991) and the United States (Turner, Fix, and Struyk 1991); all find discrimination against minorities to be fairly common.

Zabalza and Tzannatos use more a more conventional statistical approach to estimate the impact of Great Britain's Equal Pay Act (adopted in 1970 but put into effect in 1975) and its Sex Discrimination Act (adopted in 1975) on the relative pay of women. The effect of the laws appears to have been almost immediate (as Title VII apparently was for American blacks; see Smith and Welch 1989 [excerpted here]; Donohue and Heckman 1991 [excerpted here]). It appears to have been permanent and substantial as well; Zabalza and Tzannatos estimate that it eliminated between half and three-quarters of prevailing discrimination against women. (In contrast, Title VII seems to have had less impact, and researchers disagree about its permanence.)

This does not mean that eliminating sex discrimination is easy or that other nations have more effective ways to do so than the United States. Mary Brinton's work on Japan shows how pervasive some forms of sex discrimination are there. Although Japanese women participate in the labor force at rates comparable to the rates in some Western nations, the wage gap between men and women is higher there and women's representation in management jobs lower. Japan has an EEO law prohibiting sex discrimination, but—Bergeson and Oba argue—it is not likely to be effective. Many Japanese see the law as having been forced upon them by outside pressures; it really only urges voluntary change in employment practices, and imposes no penalties upon employers who continue to discriminate; and the legal and social environment remains unsympathetic in many ways to women seeking equality.

One should not conclude from this that the Japanese law will do no good, or that EEO laws can do little unless the whole society is in sympathy with their aims. The American ban on sex discrimination was added rather unexpectedly to an EEO bill originally directed only at discrimination on the basis of race, religion, and national origin. Many (including, initially, the EEOC) did not take it seriously and few had given much thought to what such a ban implied. But enforcement of the law provided a focus for the newly resurgent women's movement, and the organizational and legal developments prompted by efforts to strengthen enforcement proved a catalyst for social change (Harrison 1988).

Comparative work on EEO and EEO law helps us understand what we both do and do not know about ending discrimination in labor markets. Even though many economists remain dubious, evidence is mounting that EEO laws can be effective without disrupting labor markets or indirectly doing more harm than good. But we know very little about the circumstances under which they are most efficacious. Gunderson's conclusion that they have greater impact when strongly enforced seems reasonable, but what that means is rather unclear. Strong judicial enforcement, perhaps combined with economic incentives for change, seems to have played a crucial role in eliminating at least blatant forms of racial discrimination in the American South (Donohue and Heckman 1991 [excerpted here]; Heckman and Payner 1989; Blumrosen 1984 [excerpted here]), but it is not at all clear what differences in enforcement had to do with the apparently greater impact of British laws on sex discrimination than on race discrimination. Work on the systematic cross-national studies needed to understand the limits and possibilities of EEO laws has not even begun.

Great Britain

21

Racial Discrimination: 17 Years after the Act

Colin Brown and Pat Gay

I. INTRODUCTION

Racial Discrimination in Employment

In 1968 the British Parliament passed legislation that for the first time made it unlawful for employers to discriminate between job applicants on grounds of racial origin. . . . The law was consolidated and extended in the 1976 Race Relations Act. Racial discrimination in recruitment has therefore been outlawed in this country for nearly 17 years.

The main aims of this report are to give a minimum estimate of how extensive discrimination is today and, by making comparisons with previous research, to show trends in the extent of discrimination over the past ten years.

The following extracts from the 1976 Race Relations Act set out the basic legal obligation of employers to deal fairly with applicants from different racial backgrounds:

'A person discriminates against another in any circumstances relevant for the purposes of any provision of this Act if-

(a) on racial grounds he treats that other less favourably than he treats or would treat other persons; or

(b) he applies to that other a requirement or condition which he applies or would apply equally to persons not of the same racial group as that other but-

(i) which is such that the proportion of persons of the same racial group as that other who can comply with it is considerably smaller than the proportion of persons not of that racial group who can comply with it; and

    (ii)   which he cannot show to be justifiable irrespective of the colour, race, nationality or ethnic or national origins of the person to whom it is applied; and

   (iii)   which is to the detriment of that other because he cannot comply with it. . .'

'. . . It is unlawful for a person, in relation to employment by him at an establishment in Great Britain, to discriminate against another-

    (a)   in the arrangements he makes for the purpose of determining who should be offered that employment; or

    (b)   in the terms on which he offers him that employment; or

    (c)   by refusing or deliberately omitting to offer him that employment.'

It is important to understand that the law makes a distinction between those acts of <u>direct</u> discrimination where a job applicant is selected or rejected by an employer simply and deliberately on the basis of his or her racial origin, and those acts best described as <u>indirect</u> discrimination, where practices and policies racially bias the recruitment process, regardless of the way they are formulated and regardless of the employer's motive. The research described in this report provides a measure of the extent of direct discrimination only; it provides no measure of the extent to which black people are further disadvantaged in the job market by indirect discrimination.

A Minimum Measure

The method used to estimate the level of direct discrimination faced by black job applicants is one used by different researchers in several countries over the past 19 years. The essence of the 'discrimination test' . . . is the recording of the responses of individuals and organisations advertising job vacancies when approached by applicants of differing ethnic origins. This is done experimentally by employing actors or by making bogus written applications; the individuals and organisations under study have no knowledge of the experiment. Applications are taken no further than an initial request for an interview, and, whilst the experiments reveal the extent of direct discrimination at this first contact, no information is obtained on any discrimination that might occur at later stages of the recruitment process. This is why we refer to the result of the tests as a minimum measure of the extent of discrimination; when genuine applicants for jobs surmount the first obstacle of obtaining an interview, they may still be treated unfairly on the grounds of race at the interview or during the actual selection of the successful applicant. It is therefore likely that the actual level of direct discrimination faced by black job applicants is greater than is reported here.

Previous Measurements of Discrimination

The first research of this type was published in 1967 by one of PSI's predecessor institutes, Political and Economic Planning (PEP). Since then the method has been used several times in Britain, and there have been similar studies in the USA, the Netherlands, France and Australia. . . .

The PEP study comprised a series of tests in six towns and cities in England to assess the discrimination faced by people of West Indian, Indian, Pakistani, Italian and Greek origins when trying to obtain jobs, buy houses and obtain private tenancies (McIntosh and Smith 1974). The applications were made personally or by letter, as appropriate. The employment tests covered a broad range of jobs from unskilled manual work to accountancy, and revealed that there was considerable discrimination against the black applicants. For each job a pair of applications were made, one by a white person and one by someone of a different ethnic origin. One third of the employers rejected the black applicants while offering to take the white applications further. Part of the research design was a comparison of the effect of being an immigrant and the effect of being black: the much lower level of discrimination faced by the Greek and Italian applicants (about one case in ten) showed that discrimination was more related to race than to overseas origin. Comparisons between the results of the tests using West Indian, Indian and Pakistani applicants showed that there was no significant difference between the levels of discrimination faced by the various black groups.

In Nottingham between 1977 and 1979 the local Community Relations Council (CRC) conducted a similar set of tests for nonmanual jobs advertised in that city. For each vacancy three written applications were made, one by a white person, one by a person of West Indian origin and one by a person of Asian origin. The results showed that the level of discrimination faced by blacks in Nottingham was even higher than that found in the PEP study: over forty percent of employers rejected the black applicants while offering the white applicant an interview (Hubbock and Carter 1980).

II. THE TESTS

At the heart of the discrimination test method is the experimental comparison of an employer's reactions to applicants with different ethnic origins but with equivalent qualifications for the job. Although the principle is simple, the need to control those factors that could bias the results does make the execution of the tests fairly complicated. In the next few pages we explain in some detail the way in which the tests were carried out.

The Three-Applicant Test

The two studies described earlier did not share exactly the same research methods. The PEP tests employed a pair of applicants for each job, one of whom was white and the other of a different ethnic origin. The Nottingham CRC tests employed three applicants for each job: one white, one of West Indian origin and one of Asian origin. Although the three-applicant test is correspondingly more expensive to administer for each vacancy, it is more valuable than the two-applicant test because it gives an indication of any tendency on the part of individual employers to treat Asian and West Indian applicants differently. For this reason it was decided to use three-applicant tests in the present study. . . .

Valid and Invalid Tests

Where one or more applicant is invited by the employer to take their application further the results are, for our purposes, fairly easy to classify: the employer treats the applicants equally favourably or one is favoured above another. However, in cases where all of the applicants are rejected, things are not so simple. In a sense they have all been treated equally, but in fact we have no evidence as to whether discrimination has taken place. The applications may have been turned down for a number of reasons: an earlier applicant may have got the job, or there may have been a better-qualified applicant, or the researcher's assessment of the kinds of qualifications required may have been wrong. Had each of the test applicants been better qualified, or had they applied sooner, then the employer would have had the opportunity to discriminate. There is a logical asymmetry between the equal treatment of success and the equal treatment of failure. For this reason we accepted as valid only the tests where one or more applicant received a positive response; where all three applicants were rejected, the test was treated as invalid. This is the practice adopted by the PEP and Nottingham CRC studies. . . .

The Three Areas

The tests were carried out in London, Birmingham and Manchester, with roughly a third of the work in each area. It was agreed to concentrate on these three cities for several reasons.

First, it was not possible to cover a sample of vacancies that would be nationally representative (as, for instance, in the case of a national interview survey) because of the costs that would have been involved. The three urban areas around the cities chosen contain some 60 percent of Britain's black population, and are therefore the areas that give the best coverage of the geographical labour markets in which black workers find themselves. Secondly, within the size of the project, statistically reliable results can be derived for each of the areas separately: the project involved tests with over a hundred employers in each area. . . . Thirdly, the areas chosen have different types of labour market, and in particular have different levels of unemployment. This gives a good spread of conditions in which to carry out the tests in order to avoid the possibility that the estimated extent of racial discrimination was peculiar to a single set of circumstances. . . .

Practical considerations meant that we had to choose *parts* of London, rather than the Greater London area as a whole, in which to carry out the tests. We chose Croydon, central London, and Islington as representing a range of local job markets. In Birmingham and Manchester the much smaller geographical size of the cities meant that we were able to apply for any jobs advertised in the local papers, with the proviso that they were not completely unreasonable travelling distances from the applicants' addresses. The test applicants had addresses near to each other, to ensure that differences in travel-to-work distances did not affect the employer's view of their suitability for the job.

The Types of Job

The research aimed to cover a range of jobs in the non-manual and skilled manual fields, with an even spread between sets of male and female applicants, and a good balance between jobs for people about 30 years old and for people 18 to 20 years old. There was also some value in choosing job categories that had been used for the PEP and the Nottingham CRC tests. There were also practical considerations in the choice of jobs—vacancies had to exist in such numbers as to enable the researchers to organise sufficient applications during the lifetime of the project. Only private-sector jobs were included in the study.

After a series of pilot tests and a period of checking the vacancies advertised in the newspapers, the following types of job were selected:

For tests by letter application

Sales representative, age about 30 (male applicants)

Secretary, age about 30 (female applicants)

Clerical worker, age about 30 (female applicants)

Junior sales representative, age 18–20 (male applicants)

Office junior, age 18–20 (female applicants)

Office junior, age 18–20 (male applicants)

For tests by telephone application

Skilled manual worker, age about 30 (male applicants)

In the event there were few advertised jobs in the younger age group that male applicants could write in for. . . . We had expected these junior vacancies to be less common than the others, but were unprepared to find that this part of the job market was almost non-existent, at least as regards newspaper advertisements. . . .

The Letter Tests

Applications for the non-manual vacancies were prepared by the PSI researchers, but the addresses used for the 'applicants' were those of volunteers. In each area all three were located in districts that were known to have relatively large numbers of black residents. The volunteers received the replies and sent them on to PSI after cancelling any interviews that were offered by the employers. All of the applicants' names were fictitious.

The ethnic origin of the West Indian applicant was indicated by stating that their early education was in Jamaica, and with a distinctive name; the Asian applicant had a distinctive Hindu name.

Every effort was made to ensure that the three applicants had equivalent experience and qualifications and that the employer would see them as independent applications. . . .

Evaluation of the replies was made according to a simple set of rules. A *positive* response was recorded when the employer replied offering an interview. . . . A negative response was recorded where the employer replied but rejected the application, or when there was no reply at all.

The Telephone Tests

In each city three volunteers agreed to make telephone applications for the skilled manual vacancies, which are mostly advertised with telephone numbers rather than addresses. One volunteer was white, one was of West Indian origin and one was of Asian origin. Both black volunteers had ethnically distinctive accents but spoke good English and all the volunteers had a competent telephone manner. Again, precautions were taken to ensure the tests were unbiased . . . .

Evaluation of the responses was again made by simple rules. A positive response was recorded when the employer offered the job, offered an interview, or asked the applicant to telephone later for a discussion of the work involved. A negative response was recorded when the applicant was rejected or told to telephone later because there was no-one there to deal with the enquiry. When the testers were asked to phone back for this reason, the recall was attempted if the time given was within the test session (usually an afternoon), and in these cases it was only recorded as a negative response once the second attempt had been made.

For the letter tests, the numbers of invalid tests (those with all-negative results) could be accurately recorded, because it was always clear when all the applications received negative responses. For the telephone tests, however, it was hard to make a firm distinction between invalid tests and some of the tests abandoned for reasons of non-contact or because the applicants found themselves speaking to different people or different departments. We have therefore not calculated an exact figure for the proportion of invalid telephone tests.

Timing

The tests began in February 1984 and the majority were completed by the end of March 1985. Over 90 percent were carried out in 1984.

III. THE RESULTS

The final tally of tests is shown below. Sets of postal applications were sent to over 450 employers, and from these over 250 valid discrimination tests were obtained. Over 100 employers were telephoned by the volunteer 'applicants' and from these nearly 70 valid discrimination tests were obtained.

Overall Outcome of the Tests

[I]n nearly half of the cases all three applicants received positive responses— that is to say they were offered interviews or sent application forms. In nearly a quarter of all the tests two applicants received positive responses while the third was rejected—although in only four percent of all cases was this the white applicant, compared with ten percent for the West Indian applicant and ten percent for the Asian applicant. Nearly a third of all employers rejected two applicants although, again, the rejections were not evenly distributed between the three applicants. Most of them were rejections of both black applicants, rather than rejection of one white and one black applicant. This general pattern can be seen to be repeated for every one of the job types, with some minor variations.

This is evidence of substantial racial discrimination against both the Asian applicant and the West Indian applicant for each type of job. It also shows that although a small group of employers discriminate against black applicants of Asian origin but not against those of West Indian origin, and a further group vice-versa, the total impact of discrimination on the two black applicants is the same. . . . Taking all the valid tests together, . . . 90 percent of the white applications were successful, compared with 63 percent of the Asian applications and the West Indian applications. . . .

[T]o ensure that the variations in the success rate of the three applicants could not be the result of these random variations we applied the chi-squared test of statistical significance. The test shows that there is less than one chance in a thousand that the differences between the success rates of the white and the West

Indian, or between those of the white and the Asian, are the results of random variations in the responses to their applications.

When we apply the same test to the small difference between the success rates of the two black applicants, however, we find that it is not statistically significant: in other words it is within the degree of random variation you would expect to find within these test results.

How Widespread is Racial Discrimination?

So far we have analysed the test results in terms of the individual success rates of the three applicants; we have seen that black applicants for jobs are less likely to be successful than equally-qualified white applicants, but although this gives some idea of the overall impact of discrimination on black job-seekers it does not show the frequency with which acts of racial discrimination are taking place. For an impression of how widespread racial discrimination is we need an estimate of the proportion of employers actually committing acts of racial discrimination. . . . We can say confidently that a minimum of one in five of the employers in these job categories in these areas discriminate against both Asian and West Indian job applicants and at least a further one in eight discriminate against either Asian or West Indian applicants; in total at least a third of all the employers discriminate against one or both groups of black applicants.

Comparisons of the Results for the Different Jobs

For every job type the comparison of the success rates of the black applicants shows a substantial level of racial discrimination, and the chi-squared tests show the differences are statistically significant at the 0.01 level in every case except one. This case is the comparison of the white and Asian success rates for the female clerical jobs (84 percent and 58 percent respectively) and the test gives a chi-squared value with a probability less than 0.05. None of the comparisons of the Asian and West Indian success rates are statistically significant at the 0.05 level. . . .

[T]here is little difference between the results for men and women; in both cases there is a substantial level of discrimination against the black applicants and although this is slightly worse for the women the sex difference is not statistically significant. The results for younger and older applicants are also very close together and although discrimination for the younger applicants is a little worse, the gap between the age groups is not statistically significant. . . . [W]e look at the results for the three geographical areas of the study. The first and most important point to note is that in all three the level of discrimination against the black applicants is substantial and the difference between the success rates of the black and white applicants is significant at the 0.01 probability level. . . .

[F]inally, therefore, it is not possible to conclude from these tests that racial discrimination varies in any systematic way between different geographical labour markets in Britain.

IV. TRENDS OVER THE LAST DECADE

An important aim of the study was to obtain an estimate of the extent of racial discrimination in employment recruitment that could be compared with those of the 1973/4 PEP study and the 1977/9 Nottingham CRC study. For this reason there is some continuity in the selection of the job types covered in our project and these earlier ones. The results provide no evidence to suggest that the level of racial discrimination has decreased since 1973.

The Paired-Test Model

The present study and the Nottingham CRC study both used three-applicant tests, while the 1973/4 PEP study used two-applicant tests, and the results are therefore of a slightly different form. . . . We cannot directly compare the two sets of results. However, we can treat each three-applicant test as a pair of two-applicant tests: that is to say the Asian-white element of the test and the West Indian-white element are treated as separate tests. We refer to this as the 'paired-test' model, and it gives us two results for each employer; obviously, it does not double-up the scale of our study in terms of statistical reliability since it is still based on the same number of employers. . . .

Comparisons of the Same Jobs

[F]or all three studies the level of apparent discrimination against the white applicant is around seven percent. The proportion of employers discriminating against the black applicant, however, varies considerably. For the comparison group of jobs, the level is 30 percent for the PEP study in 1973/4, 49 percent for the Nottingham CRC study in 1977/9, and 37 percent in the 1984/5 study.

It is important to remember that the date is not the only difference between the three studies: the PEP work covered six towns and cities (London, the West Midlands and the North West region were, however, all represented among them), the CRC study was confined to Nottingham, while our latest project covered only London, Birmingham and Manchester. There were also differences of detail in the execution of the tests. . . . We should not, therefore, attempt a detailed speculative explanation for the fact that the overall level of discrimination found in this study is lower than that found in 1977/9 while it is higher than that found in 1973/4. However, we can be sure that there is no evidence here to suggest that racial discrimination in job recruitment has fallen over the period covered by these studies. . . .

[F]or the secretary and the female junior clerk the level of discrimination found in this study and in the 1977/9 study are remarkably similar, and are higher than those found in 1973/4. For the sales representative, the level found in the present study is somewhat higher than in 1973/4, but much lower than in the intervening study. For the skilled manual jobs—for which there were no corresponding tests in Nottingham—the level of discrimination is again slightly higher now than in 1973/4. Overall, the increase in the level of discrimination between 1973/4 and 1984/5 is not statistically significant—in other words it could be the result of random variations within the tests.

The Changed Job Market

It is important to remember that since the 1973/4 study there has been a massive change in the job market in this country. Unemployment has risen and finding work has become more difficult. Since 1974 the official unemployment rate has grown from less than 3 percent to more than 13 percent. The burden has fallen more heavily on black people than on white people: results from the 1984 Labour Force Survey show that among blacks the proportion of economically active people who are unemployed is almost twice as high as it is among whites.

The recession has had a particularly hard impact on minority racial groups for a number of reasons. Black workers are disproportionately represented in the geographical areas and industrial sectors that have experienced the worst effects of the economic contraction. But also, as this study confirms, black people who are already suffering the consequences of these economic disadvantages face a further block to getting a job: substantial racial discrimination.

On average there are now many more job-seekers competing for each vacancy, and in this harsher job market one might expect that racial discrimination would have become more common. When recruiting staff an employer now has more opportunity to discriminate because the number of white applicants from which to choose is greater, and some employers might also be more inclined to discriminate during a job shortage because they hold the racialist view that white applicants are more 'deserving' than black applicants. The fact that there has been no change in the level of discrimination could therefore be seen as an encouraging sign; in other words, it could be argued that things mights have been worse. But . . . . it would be small comfort to black British job-seekers, already having to contend with constricted job markets, to be advised that racial discrimination is only as bad as it used to be. The brutal fact is that, despite the law, direct discrimination persists as an additional and powerful impediment to any economic progress by blacks.

V. CONCLUSIONS

Last year PSI published the report of its most recent survey of the circumstances of the British black population (Brown 1984). In it we described in some detail the position that workers of Asian and West Indian ethnic origin occupy in the labour market, and how that has changed over the 1970s and early 1980s. Based on a nationwide interview survey of 5000 black adults and 2300 white adults in 1982, the report showed that both Asians and West Indians are found in jobs that are lower down the occupational ladder than whites, and are also more likely to be unemployed. . . . The study also showed that there had been very little change over the period 1974–1982 in the types of jobs in which blacks were found: this was demonstrated by reference to PSI's previous national survey and by examining the job histories of those interviewed in 1982. . . .

The results of the tests reported here show that racial discrimination has indeed continued to have a great impact on the employment opportunities of black people. We can summarise the findings in the following way:

1. In every job category and in all three cities we find substantial discrimination against the black applicants. . . . At least a third of the employers recruiting people to the jobs covered in this study discriminate against Asian applicants or West Indian applicants or both. We should emphasize here that this study aims to provide a *minimum* estimate of the extent of discrimination: the actual level is likely to be higher than that reported here.

2. There are no systematic differences between the overall levels of discrimination faced by Asian and West Indian applicants; this is also the case within each job category. . . .

3. [W]e cannot point to any of the job types or areas as significant exceptions to the general findings on the level of discrimination.

4. Comparisons between this and previous studies show no evidence of a decrease in the extent of racial discrimination over the past decade. . . .

The Annual Extent of Discrimination

We have shown the results of these tests as proportions of applicants meeting discrimination and proportions of employers discriminating. Each time an employer makes an unfair choice because of the race of the applicant, he or she is breaking the law. How often does this happen every year in Britain? The answer to that question is impossible to give in exact terms, partly because our test results are very likely to be underestimates of the true extent of discrimination, but also because we do not have the necessary information about the number of vacancies for which black applicants compete with whites annually. But even a conservative estimate would put the figure at tens of thousands of acts of racial discrimination in job recruitment every year.

It should be noted that in the normal course of events a black applicant who is discriminated against would have no evidence to suggest that it had happened. In the majority of cases of discrimination in our tests a polite letter of refusal was sent to the victim, often 'explaining' that other applicants were better qualified and even in some cases wishing the applicant well in his or her search for a job. The applicant would have no reason to suspect he or she was a victim of racial discrimination and even if there was such a suspicion, there would be no immediately available evidence to support it. The individual illegal act of discrimination is often invisible to the victim.

Racial Discrimination and the Law

A major reason for the persistence of discrimination must be that an individual employer is very unlikely to be caught doing it. It seems that a proportion of decision-makers have a propensity to discriminate when selecting employees, either because of their own racialist attitudes or because they see it as expedient for the business. For many of them the fact that discrimination is illegal does not make the avoidance of discrimination a moral imperative. They continue to discriminate because there is only a minimal risk of detection. The legislation may originally have had an effect as a moral declaration but by now it can have no additional effect of that kind.

The law can be criticised for 'having few teeth' when dealing with cases that do come to light, and for the difficulties that face individual victims when pursuing their cases through the Tribunals or Courts; yet the heart of the problem is that employers know that cases rarely get as far as legal action because the victim is very unlikely to be aware that he or she has been discriminated against. . . .

Individual court actions are not the only available method of enforcement of the law against racial discrimination. The Commission of Racial Equality has powers to mount investigations into the policies and practices of employers (and other organisations) to determine whether they have discriminated on racial grounds; with such systematic investigations it is possible to see what the individual victim cannot see—the employer's recruitment practice as a whole, and its consequences. This more strategic approach might therefore be justifiably expected to have a more powerful deterrent effect, if it were pursued on a sufficient scale. If an employer is (or has been) discriminating, this fact is unlikely to escape the close scrutiny that is possible under these provisions of the Race Relations Act. But scale is, of course, the problem. With the resources of the CRE at their present level the annual number of these investigations is bound to be small, so they are unlikely to have much of an impact on an employer's impression that discrimination is easy to get away with.

This argument leads us to conclude that if the law against racial discrimination is to have an increased impact on the actual extent of discrimination, then it must be through the deterrent effect of systematic and strategic investigations on a greater scale than at present and of legal actions stemming from them.

We have a law against racial discrimination not only to condemn but also to try to eradicate it. We can see from the research reported here that there has been no reduction in the extent of discrimination over the last decade. . . . The choice is therefore plain: we can keep the Race Relations Act as a fine expression of what is right and what is wrong, while a substantial proportion of employers continue to hire people on the basis of their skin colour; or we can use the Act to try to stop discrimination, by a legal strategy that involves scrutinising a sufficient number of employers to make it a real deterrent.

ACKNOWLEDGEMENTS

This research project was conducted by the Policy Studies Institute in collaboration with the Commission for Racial Equality. The funding for the work was provided by the Commission for Racial Equality.

Jim Hubbuck at the Commission for Racial Equality was a joint manager of the project and gave us valuable help at all stages of the work. David Smith at PSI also gave us advice and help throughout the study.

The pilot fieldwork for the project was carried out by Sheila Benson and Stephen Small at PSI; they established many of the detailed procedures on which the main fieldwork was based.

The study would have been impossible without the goodwill and hard work of many people who typed letters, forwarded letters, made phone calls, and helped us to contact the right people at the right times. In London, our personal thanks go to Dhirendra, Jheni, Pam, Raj, Ray, Safder, Stephanie and Thelma; in Birmingham, to Alison, Dean, Geoff, Joy, Leroy, Mohammed Javed, Nassim, Pat, Raghib, Ron, Satnam and Steve; in Manchester, to Angela, Brian, Carol, Fiona (and her colleagues), Jack, Kaleem, Pat, Si, Suchi and Winston.

REFERENCES

Brown, Colin *Black and White Britain: the third PSI Survey,* Heinemann Educational Books (London: 1984).

Hubbuck, Jim and Simon Carter, *Half a Chance? A report on job discrimination against young blacks in Nottingham,* Commission for Racial Equality, (London: 1980).

McIntosh, Neil and David J. Smith, *The Extent of Racial Discrimination,* PEP Broadsheet No. 547, (London: PEP, 1974).

22

The Effect of Britain's Anti-Discriminatory Legislation on Relative Pay and Employment

A. Zabalza and Z. Tzannatos

Between 1970 and 1980 female relative hourly earnings rose by 14.8% and the increase affected all occupations and industries quite similarly. There was also a remarkable similarity in the timing of this increase. In practically all sectors, most of the gains in female pay were achieved in the period 1974 to 1976. It is certainly tempting to attribute this increase to the anti-discriminatory legislation enacted in Britain around precisely that time. The Equal Pay Act, requiring equal pay for the same or like work by men and women, was passed in 1970 but its application was delayed until the end of 1975 to allow employers time to adjust to the new set of conditions on pay. The end of 1975 was also the time at which the Sex Discrimination Act, requiring equal employment opportunities for men and women, became law. Thus there is a very clear coincidence between the increase in relative pay and the application of this legislation.

A coincidence, however, is not sufficient to establish that the anti-discriminatory legislation was the main contributory factor behind the increase in female relative pay. There are other factors, which also changed during this period, and which could be the cause of this increase quite independently of legislation. One such factor, which has been put forward by some authors (see Chiplin *et al.* 1980) as a possible cause of the increase in female relative pay, is the effect of the various incomes policies applied in Britain during the 1970s. Some of them had flat rate provisions which could have benefited women to a larger extent than men. Another factor which could possibly explain the rise in female relative pay would be an autonomous decrease in the supply of female labour. Here, however, the evidence does not seem too corroborative. Overall, there has been an impressive increase in the number of women in the labour force during the 1970s. Between 1970 and 1980, female relative employment increased by 18.3%, and female relative hours by 17.6%.

Excerpts reprinted with permission from *The Economic Journal* 1985 (September), vol. 95:679–699.
Copyright © 1985 by Basil Blackwell Ltd.

In this paper we attempt an evaluation of the possible effects of anti-discriminatory legislation by considering the labour market as a whole, taking into account not only relative employment but also other factors that, through their influence on demand and supply, may have affected relative pay. The prima facie evidence in favour of the effectiveness of this legislation is very strong, and we want to see if this evidence is maintained after considering all these additional factors and their interaction within the context of the labour market. . . .

I. THE FACTS

The main facts that we want to explain in this paper are shown in Fig. 1, where we plot relative pay (W_f/W_m) from 1950 to 1981. Relative pay is defined as relative hourly earnings of all manual and non-manual employees. . . . The evolution of relative pay shown in this figure can be divided into three clearly differentiated periods. First, a twenty-year period of stability with a very mild downward trend, that lowered female relative wages from 0.596 in 1950 to 0.580 in 1970 (an overall 2.7% fall). Then a period of seven years in which relative pay rose dramatically from 0.580 in 1970 to 0.685 in 1977 (an overall 18.1% increase). And finally a last period in which relative pay appears to have stabilised itself around the level reached in 1975. In 1980, the last year used in the econometric analysis below, relative pay was 14.8% higher than in 1970.

Did employers respond to this substantial rise in the cost of one type of labour by hiring less of it? Nothing of the sort occurred. If we look at the number of women relative to the number of men employed in the whole economy (F/M),

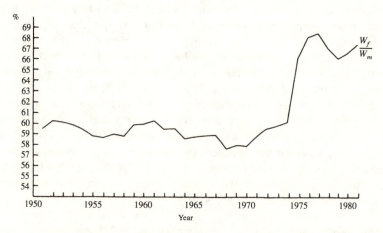

Figure 1.   Relative hourly earnings of all employees in Great Britain. *Source:* Annexe.

we see that the rising trend that was already in evidence before 1970 has persisted during the last ten years. . . . Even after taking part-time work into account, it cannot be concluded that female work has fallen. Relative to men's, the number of hours worked by women has increased by 17.6% between 1970 and 1980, which represents an average annual rate of growth of 1.6%, and the tendency appears to have been accentuated in 1981. . . . It is remarkable that relative female employment continued to grow, even after the substantial increases in the relative cost of female labour documented above. . . .

So, we have on the one hand a dramatic increase in female relative pay, which coincides both with the period over which the anti-discriminatory legislation was being applied, and with income policies which, due to their flat rate provisions, could also have contributed to the observed rise in pay. On the other hand, we have a fairly steady rise in female relative work, even after taking into account the substantial upsurge of part-time employment. The rise is mostly concentrated in the public sector, and it has been checked somewhat after 1975. But neither in the economy as a whole, nor in the private sector, has the rise in female relative pay resulted in any important fall in the relative amount of hours they have been able to work. We now turn to a possible explanation of these facts.

II. A MODEL OF RELATIVE PAY AND EMPLOYMENT

Previous studies on the effect of anti-discriminatory legislation have tended to follow Becker's model of discrimination, and have concentrated mostly on the impact of racial anti-discriminatory measures in the United States. . . . In the context of this model the effect of anti-discriminatory legislation is to make it more costly for employers to indulge in discriminatory practices. After the legislation is passed, therefore, we should observe fewer discriminating employers than previously, and possibly a smaller degree of discrimination among those who still violate the law. The end result would be an increase in relative female wages at any given level of relative female employment, and therefore an increase in the overall demand for female relative to male labour.

Financial penalties for breaking anti-discriminatory legislation are not as important in the United Kingdom as they are in the United States, and it is doubtful that they have played any important role in changing employers behaviour in this country. Tzannatos and Zabalza (1984) argue that the machinery of collective agreements may have been much more effective in actually raising female relative pay than fear of prosecution. The Equal Pay Act explicitly provided for the removal of discrimination (by abolishing differentiated female rates) in the pay structures determined by collective agreements and statutory Wage Orders, and the wide degree of coverage must have meant a rise in the relative price of female labour for many employers. If, for any reason, employers did not respond to this increase by reducing female employment (that is, if they were prepared to hire the same number of women at higher relative wages), then the result of the legislation would have been again an increase in the relative demand for female labour. It is difficult to explain why employers would not react otherwise, but the existence of sizeable turnover costs (i.e. fixed expenses related to hiring and firing), the likely deterioration of labour force morale that large employment adjustments would entail, and the possible threat of union reprisals, are all reasons that may be significant enough to prevent employers from undertaking large adjustments in the composition of their labour force.

[T]he empirical model represents the anti-discriminatory legislation by means of a dummy variable (D) affecting the position of the demand relationship and treats both relative employment and relative wages as endogenous variables. Although the only aim of this exercise is to estimate the demand curve, the endogeneity of employment and wages means that we must also specify the variables that, in addition to relative wages, determine relative supply.

The relative wage variable is defined as relative hourly earnings of manual and non-manual employees. The relative employment variable is defined as total woman-hours divided by total man-hours for manual and non-manual employees, and includes female part-time employment. . . .

The demand function that we want to estimate is an aggregate relationship and compositional changes could affect the relative level of female employment quite independently of any price influence. For instance, during the period in question due to autonomous changes (e.g. change in tastes, external demand, technical innovations) some sectors could have expanded more than others. If the sectors that have expanded more are intensive in the employment of female labour, then we would observe an increase in the relative amount of female labour employed, only on account of this change in the structure of the economy. Ideally we would like to isolate the effect that changes in relative wages have on relative employment for a given industrial structure, and we can do this by holding constant the distribution of male employment over the period. We call this index of industrial structure, I, and we define it as

$$I_t = \sum_{i=1}^{n} A_i \frac{M_{it}}{M_t},$$

where M_{it} is the employment of male workers in sector i in year t, M_t is total employment in year t, n is the number of sectors considered and the A's are time invariant weights. These weights are obtained as the average of the female-male wage bill ratio during the period 1970–1980, although an alternative definition using only 1980 data gave practically identical results.

Demand for female relative to male labour is likely to increase during upturns in economic activity. Due to its relative short attachment to the labour force, female labour is likely to have less specific training than male labour and thus to experience more employment fluctuations over the cycle. This view, first explicitly stated by Becker (1964), implies that a variable measuring the cycle should also be included as an argument of the demand function. We represent this variable by a measure of vacancy rates adjusted for the increase in the coverage of the Job Centres, and we call it V.

The theoretical arguments considered above to generate the demand relationship are valid if men and women have equal productivity (otherwise there would not be much point in talking of discrimination). Thus, if there are differences in productivity by sex, these should be taken into account in specifying the demand equation. One way of standardising for this would be to enter relative levels of education as a proxy of relative levels of productivity; but the problem here is that it is difficult to obtain a long enough series of annual data. Nevertheless, temporal changes in this variable have been smooth and its influence (plus that of other unidentified factors) is likely to be captured well by a simple time trend, which we denote by T.

As discussed above, British anti-discriminatory legislation consists of two Acts (Equal Pay and Sex Discrimination) both of which became law the last day of 1975. The Equal Pay Act, however, had been passed five years earlier, and the interim period was conceded to allow employers to make the necessary changes in pay practices in a uniform and gradual manner. Thus, rather than only specifying the anti-discriminatory legislation dummy as one variable taking the value 0 up to 1975 and 1 afterwards, we allowed also several other specifications which could capture a more gradual effect. After some experimentation, the specification that best fitted the data was a set of four dummy variables which measure the *cumulative* effect of the legislation during the years 1971, 1972, 1974, and 1975. The dummy corresponding to the year 1971, D71, takes the value 0 up to 1970 and the value 1 afterwards. D72 takes the value 0 up to 1971 and the value 1 afterwards, and so on.

Another variable that must be included in the demand function is a dummy for incomes policies. To the extent that incomes policies have been equalising (through their flat rate provisions, in those cases in which such provisions have been present), they may have contributed to the increase of female relative wages. If Chiplin *et al.* (1980) are correct, this dummy should be more important in explaining shifts in the demand curve than the dummy representing anti-discriminatory legislation. We call this variable *IP*.

We initially tried two alternative incomes policies dummies. The first took the value 1 during all the periods in which there has been a compulsory incomes policy in effect, whatever its type, and the value 0 otherwise. This gives a value 1 for the year 1967 to 1969 (both inclusive), the year 1973 and the years 1976 to 1978 (both inclusive). But this formulation brings in together incomes policies which were of a proportional type and therefore ought not to have any equalising effect, and incomes policies with flat rate provisions which had potentially equalising effects. Since the latter are the ones that may have had an effect on female relative earnings, the specification finally used in the empirical analysis takes the value 1 only during 1973 and 1976 to 1978 (both inclusive). As we would expect the latter specification performs better than the first one in all cases.

Taking all these variables into account, the demand equation that will be estimated is

$$\ln (W_f/W_m) = \alpha_0 + \alpha_1 \ln (FH/MH) + \alpha_2 \ln (I)$$
$$+ \alpha_3 V + \alpha_4 T + \alpha_5 D + \alpha_6 IP + u \qquad (1)$$

where the α's are the parameters to be estimated, $\ln (\cdot)$ is the logarithmic function, FH/MH is woman-hours relative to man-hours and u is a random error.

To estimate (1) when both relative employment and relative wages are considered endogenous we must also take into account those factors that determine these two dependent variables via the supply function, and use them as additional instruments in the estimation of the demand relationships.

The economic variables most frequently considered in cross-sectional studies of female participation are own female wages and other income. In the case of married women, most of 'other income' is made up of husband's earnings, which in our case is already captured by the presence of W_m and need not be explicitly considered. But we use as an instrument aggregate disposable non-labour real income (Y) to detect any additional effect coming from dividend income or interest on savings. The second variable that we consider is a fertility index (FI); the number and age of children are the most important determinants of female participation in cross-sectional studies, and should also be important in a time-series context. Here we define this index as the number of live births in the last five years per thousand women. Finally, we use as an instrument the rate of male unemployment (U), which appears to have a significant influence in time-series studies of female participation, through what are known as the 'added and discouraged worker effects' (Mincer, 1966).

III. RESULTS

Table 1 shows the results of estimating the demand function. In the first column, the dummy variables are not included and the results are quite unsatisfactory. The relationship between relative employment and relative pay is positive and significant, which is contrary to what we would expect on theoretical grounds. Additionally, we see that the Durbin Watson statistic is very low, thus suggesting that the equation may be mis-specified. Things do not improve much when we add the incomes policy dummy IP in column 2; if anything, the significance of the positive relationship between earnings and employment is

Table 1. Instrumental estimates of the demand relationship for the whole economy (1950–1980)
(Dependent variable ln (relative hourly earnings), mean dependent variable $= -0.4991$)

Explanatory variables	Equation number			
	1	2	3	4
Constant	−0.1966	−0.6485	−0.1319	−0.0568
	(0.28)	(0.95)	(0.40)	(0.19)
ln (FH/MH)	0.7725	0.7544	−0.1422	−0.2467
	(4.98)	(5.29)	(0.79)	(1.90)
ln (I)	−0.3442	−0.6465	0.2605	0.3801
	(0.64)	(1.25)	(0.88)	(1.52)
V	−1.4425	−1.5714	−0.2585	—
	(2.94)	(3.44)	(1.00)	
T	−0.0002	−0.0013	−0.0033	−0.0038
	(0.07)	(0.44)	(1.90)	(2.54)
D71	—	—	0.0138	0.0221
			(0.93)	(2.00)
D72	—	—	0.0128	0.0112
			(1.18)	(1.06)
D74	—	—	0.0514	0.0564
			(2.98)	(3.59)
D75	—	—	0.0800	0.0873
			(5.78)	(7.63)
IP	—	0.0363	0.0178	0.0151
		(2.29)	(2.61)	(2.53)
DW	0.6230	0.6483	2.2032	2.2816
Standard error of the regression	0.0251	0.0231	0.0083	0.0080

Notes: (1) The additional instruments used were a fertility index, male unemployment and nonlabour-income.
(2) Figures in parentheses are absolute t statistics.

reinforced. But when we include the set of anti-discriminatory legislation dummies in column 3 the results change substantially. First the relationship between relative pay and relative employment turns negative as we would expect and also is statistically significant. Second, the Durbin Watson statistic takes a much more satisfactory value and the fit of the regression improves substantially (the standard error of the regression goes down from 0.0251 to 0.0083, with a mean value of the dependent variable equal to −0.4991). Finally, the added legislation dummies all take the expected value and most of the effect is concentrated on the years 1974 and 1975.

In the specification shown in column 3 all variables take the expected sign except vacancies. We would have expected V to have a positive coefficient, reflecting a higher relative demand for female labour in the upturn of the cycle, but the estimate obtained is negative, although insignificant. This would be suggesting the absence of cyclical effects on relative wages, but the result could also be due to the fact that labour heterogeneity has not been fully taken into account. As the level of economic activity increases, more women with below average pay may enter the labour force, and this would push down female relative earnings.

In column 4 we exclude this variable and although the overall effect of the legislation dummies remains the same, the estimates of the other variables appear better determined than in the previous specification. Relative employment is negatively related to relative pay and significant at the 10% level. The result suggests a fairly elastic demand curve, with a wage elasticity equal to -4.05, which in turn implies the existence of a relatively small degree of variation in discrimination tastes and/or a high degree of substitution between male and female labour. The coefficient on the industrial index takes a positive sign and is large and significant, suggesting that the change in the industrial structure has had an important effect on the rise of female over male employment. The considerable expansion of service relative to manufacturing sectors that has taken place over the period is consistent with this result.

The legislation dummies show a positive and significant effect, even after the time trend, which has a small negative coefficient, and all other variables are taken into account. The results on these dummies suggest that the legislation began to have an influence quite early in the transitional period and that most of the effect took place precisely during this period, particularly during the last two years. We tried a set of dummies covering the whole decade, but the only significant ones tended to be those included in the equation. It is interesting to compare these results with the plot of relative wages in Fig. 1 above. There, without taking into account the joint influence of other variables, we see that the most substantial gains in female relative earnings occurred in the years 1975 and 1976, with marginal improvements in 1974 and 1977. Here, on the other hand, we conclude that most of the increases in 1976 and 1977 were due to the effect of income policies, and that the anti-discriminatory legislation had its largest influence in the years 1974 and 1975.

The overall effect of legislation, as measured in column 4 of Table 1, has been to increase relative female earnings by 19.4%, if the non-significant effect of 1972 is taken into account, or by 18.0% if that effect is ignored. . . . The 19.4% increase in relative female earnings as a result of anti-discriminatory legislation is a *ceteris paribus* effect. That is, it tells us by how much female relative earnings would have risen if everything else had remained constant. . . . However, other things have not remained constant and, in particular, there has been a substantial increase in the level of relative employment, which has meant a final increase in relative earnings somewhat below the 19.4% level mentioned above. . . . The actual increase in relative wages between 1970 and 1980 was 14.8%, while the predicted increase is 15.0%.

It could be argued that we have been able to isolate a positive effect of the legislation on the relative demand for female labour due to the fact that our analysis has included both the private and the public sector. Public employers are not necessarily cost-minimisers and could have been the ones responsible for most of the huge rise in female employment, despite the substantial increase in female wages. This would imply that the anti-discriminatory legislation had operated only through a rather narrow channel, with little effect among private employers. It is therefore important to repeat the exercise above, excluding this time the public sector.

Ideally we would have liked to define for the private sector all the variables used in the previous estimation. But due to data difficulties it is not possible to obtain these variables for the whole of the period considered. So we repeat the exercise in Table 1 redefining only the relative employment variable and the industrial structure index, which are obtained as above but excluding the following industries: Mining, Transport, Utilities (Gas, Electricity and Water), Professional and Scientific Services and Public Administration. This is not totally satisfactory, because there are some private employers among the excluded industries and some public employers among those that remain. Nevertheless this new variable is likely to pick up reasonably well the evolution of female relative employment in the private sector during the period considered. Relative wages, on the other hand, could not be obtained for the private sector alone, and we must conform ourselves with the previously defined variable. Thus, the results of this exercise cannot be taken as conclusive, but they are useful in that they can indicate whether there are any important difference in the effects of the legislation between private and public sectors.

The estimates of this exercise suggest quite clearly that, on the basis of these data it is not possible to detect any dramatic divergency in the effect of the legislation between the private and public sectors. Despite the fact that relative employment in the private sector behaves quite differently from that in the public sector, the effect of the legislation dummies is very similar in its timing and somewhat larger in magnitude. The *ceteris paribus* effect of the legislation is now 19.8%, as compared to 19.4% when the public sector was also included. . . .

IV. SUMMARY AND CONCLUSIONS

[W]e find that even after taking into account the concomitant change of other variables, together with their inter-relations within the labour market, anti-discriminatory legislation has had a positive and significant effect on both relative earnings and relative employment of women. . . . Thus, these results cannot reject the hypothesis that, as a consequence of the legislation and of its implementation by collective agreements, employers were faced with a higher price for female labour and overall did not take any action to reduce female employment. . . .

The estimated timing of the effects is also interesting. We have found that the effect of the legislation on relative pay was beginning to be felt as early as 1971, which is consistent with the information we have on actions directed at the implementation of Equal Pay by collective agreements. The main thrust, however, was concentrated in the years 1974 and 1975. It is important to emphasise that these are permanent effects. . . . From 1970 to 1975 Equal Pay legislation helps to lift female wages up to around two-thirds of male wages. . . .

We have measured the effect of Equal Pay legislation to be a 19% increase in female relative pay. How large is this gain? To put this figure in perspective, it is convenient to use the results obtained in Zabalza and Arrufat (1983) on the extent of discrimination. They estimate that the complete elimination of discrimination, as seen from the year 1975, would involve an increase of the relative wage for married women from 0.623 to between 0.670 and 0.731. That is, a percentage increase in average relative pay of between 7.5 and 17.3%. These results refer to married women only, but since (as shown by these authors) the extent of discrimination between married and single women is about the same, we can use them as representative of the whole female population. Now, as we have seen above, by 1975 most of the effect of the anti-discriminatory legislation had already taken place. So it is reasonable to assume that the above figures, which correspond to the year 1975, already incorporate the gain resulting from this legislation. We have measured this gain to be a 19.4 percentage increase of the average relative pay. We have then, that, as compared with the pre-legislation situation (that is, as compared with 1970), the total potential increase in relative pay needed to eliminate discrimination would be between 26.9 and 36.7%. Of this, the legislation has achieved an increase of 19.4%, which represents between 52.9 and 72.1% of the total potential increase. That is, it has achieved between one half and three quarters of the total possible gains needed to eliminate discrimination completely. Thus, we think it is reasonable to conclude that women in Britain have benefited from Equal Pay. Anti-discriminatory legislation in Britain has had an effect on female pay, and this effect is large relative to the total needed to eliminate discrimination. . . .

ACKNOWLEDGMENTS

We would like to thank J. L. Arrufat, G. Chowdhury, R. Layard, J. Muellbauer, W. Narendranathan, two anonymous referees and an Associate Editor of this JOURNAL for useful comments and suggestions.

REFERENCES

Becker, G. S. (1964). *Human Capital: A Theoretical and Empirical Analysis, With Special Reference to Education,* National Bureau of Economic Research, New York: Columbia University Press.

Chiplin, B., Curran, M. M. and Parsley, C. J. (1980). 'Relative female earnings in Great Britain and the impact of legislation.' In *Women and Low Pay* (ed. P. J. Sloane). London: Macmillan.

Mincer, J. (1966). 'Labour force participation and unemployment: a review of recent evidence.' In *Prosperity and Unemployment* (ed. R. A. Gordon and M. S. Gordon). New York: John Wiley.

Tzannatos, Z. and Zabalza, A. (1984). 'The anatomy of the rise in British female relative wages in the 1970s: evidence from the New Earnings Survey.' *British Journal of Industrial Relations,* vol. 22 (July), pp. 177–94.

Zabalza, A. and Arrufat, J. L. (1983). 'Wage differentials between married men and married women in Great Britain: the depreciation effect of non-participation.' London School of Economics, Centre for Labour Economics Discussion Paper No. 151.

Japan

23

Gender Stratification in Contemporary Urban Japan

Mary C. Brinton

INTRODUCTION

The rate of female labor force participation in Japan roughly parallels that of Western industrial nations, yet the role played by women in the economy remains largely uninvestigated. Researchers routinely cite the low status of women in the Japanese workplace (Clark 1979; Cole 1979; Rohlen 1974) and link it inferentially to the permanent employment system. The permanent employment system refers to the internal labor market structure of the large firms in the economy, where workers are hired directly upon graduation from school and move up career ladders through principles of seniority and merit. Observers of the Japanese economy allege that women do not have access to these career ladders, and case studies of work organizations support this view. But organizational case studies leave a number of questions unresolved.

First, we do not know what proportions of women enter large firms. Second, we have no estimates of the number of women who gain access to career ladders in these firms. Thus it is unclear whether Japanese women are excluded from the large-firm sector of the economy or, alternatively, participate heavily in this sector but are in non-career-track roles. Third, we do not know the extent to which exclusion from career ladders is based on human capital considerations (e.g., sex differences in education and ability) or on other considerations such as discriminatory hiring and job assignment practices. This paper investigates these questions. . . .

JAPANESE WOMEN'S PARTICIPATION IN THE ECONOMY

As shown in Table 1, Japanese women exhibit a labor force participation rate similar to that of women in Western industrial nations. With 49 percent of adult

Excerpts reprinted with permission from the *American Sociological Review* 1989 (August) vol. 54:549–564. Copyright © 1989 by the American Sociological Association.

Table 1.   Female Labor Force Participation Rate in
                    Industrial Economies

Japan	48.6
United States	52.7
Canada	54.3
West Germany (1984)	41.1
England (1984)	37.4
France (1984)	43.1
Norway	59.8
Sweden	68.1
Denmark	59.0
Australia	46.2

Notes: (*a*) All figures are for 1985, except where indicated.
(*b*) Figures are calculated as (total number of women in the
labor force/total female population age 15 and above) ×
100, with the following exceptions: For England, the de-
nominator is the total female population (thus rendering the
figure relatively low); for Norway and Sweden, the denomi-
nator is the total female population age 16 and above.
Source: International Labor Organization (1986); Japanese
Ministry of Labor (1987).

females in the labor force, Japan stands between the high rates of North America
and Scandinavia and the somewhat lower rates of Western Europe. However, an
examination of the relative patterns of men's and women's participation in the
economy shows Japan to be an outlier among industrial economies.

Among industrial economies, Japanese women make up the lowest proportion
(36 percent) of paid workers relative to men. . . . The sex distribution of the self-
employed is fairly even in Japan; but 20 percent of women work as family
enterprise workers as opposed to only 3 percent of men. In short, the compara-
tively low rate (67 percent) at which Japanese women work as employees in
complemented by the high rate of unpaid family enterprise workers in small
family-run businesses or farms. . . .

The proportion of the Japanese female labor force who work as employees is
highest at young ages (20–24) and declines monotonically except for a slight
increase in the age-group 40–44, when women's childcare responsibilities typically decrease. In short, even among working women, the proportion of paid
employees decreases sharply with marriage and childbearing in the late 20s and
early 30s and does not again approach the earlier level. . . . [T]his is largely an
age rather than a cohort effect. While the proportion of employed women in each
age-group who work as employees has increased over time, the shape of the
curve remains the same: large numbers of women move from employee to
nonemployee status after age 25. These data may reflect conflict between wom-
en's family responsibilities and the demands of paid labor, or reflect employer

discrimination as women reach marriageable age. . . . Both explanations likely come into play. . . .

[Y]oung men and women employees (ages 20–24), who have generally just left school and entered the labor market, have very similar rates of entrance to work organizations of different sizes. . . . But men's and women's representation in firms of different sizes changes dramatically in the older age-groups. By age 45–49, women's participation rate in small firms in one and a half times that of men. . . . Conversely, women age 45–49 participate in large firms at a rate approximately three-fifths that of men. . . .

These trends could be produced either by an age (life cycle) effect or by a cohort effect. That is, the data could be indicating that employed women move out of large firms and into small firms later in life (an age effect), or that older employed women are overrepresented in small firms because they started out in small firms (a cohort effect). In order to assess these two explanations, similar tables were constructed for 1972 (the first year such data are available), 1975, and 1980. The same age pattern also appeared in these former periods: women employees began to work in large firms at a rate somewhat higher than men, but the firm size pattern by sex reversed at older ages. This suggests a life cycle interpretation whereby women employees leave the large firms they initially entered, either dropping out of the labor force or shifting to smaller firms. Whichever of these two courses they pursue, it is clear that women are not moving up in career ladders in the internal labor markets of large firms.

Managerial and wage data support this view of limited female participation in career ladders. International comparability of both occupational and wage data is limited, but a few illustrative figures may be given. The ratio of Japanese female to male employees in managerial ranks is only 13 percent, compared to 68 percent in the United States, 63 percent in Canada, and 41 percent in West Germany (International Labor Organization 1986). The overall female/male wage ratio for full-time workers in 1983 ranged in Western industrial nations from a low of 66.5 (weekly rate) in the United States to highs in the 84–89 percent range (hourly) in France and Northern Europe. Wages in Japan are typically reported as monthly rates, and the female/male ratio in 1983 was 55.5, substantially lower than in any other industrial country (Japanese Ministry of Labor 1987).

Attitude survey data and ethnographic data supplement these aggregate labor force figures. A national opinion poll of 3000 people conducted by the *Yomiuri* newspaper in Japan in April 1984 indicated a widespread perception of sex discrimination in Japanese workplaces: 80 percent of respondents believed that women are treated in a "disadvantageous" way in regard to hiring, and 84 percent felt that this situation also applies to job rotation and promotion.

Young Japanese women and their parents take note of the restrictive recruitment policies for women. Especially marked is the perception of low returns to university-educated women in the labor market. People interviewed during my fieldwork in 1984 indicated that education for a daughter was well and good to a point; once that point was reached, education didn't help and could actually hurt a young women's chances of getting a job. . . .

Japanese employers have customarily asked women during the job interview whether they plan to quit when they marry.[1] Many young women reported in my fieldwork interviews that previous job seekers advised them to state an intention to quit, because this would heighten their chances of being hired. By quitting in their mid- to late 20s, Japanese women provide employers a cushion against too many "permanent" employees. Yet at the same time that employers encourage this behavior, many claim that they do not give equivalent training and promotion opportunities to men and women because they fear women will get married and leave the labor force. The employer's returns from the investment in women workers' training will then be lost. This constitutes one of the contradictions of female employment in Japan, a link in the vicious circle of strongly gender-defined expectations on the employer side and conforming behavior on the labor supply side.

Japanese employers are strongly motivated to hire employees who plan to remain with the firm over a long period, so that the costs of on-the-job training will not be wasted. Past experience has taught them that women are more likely to quit and that investment in women's training is therefore riskier than investment in men's. In this way, the pervasiveness of the internal labor market structure and accompanying firm-specific training constitutes an institutional barrier to women. And as poignantly illustrated in the ethnographic material above, employer expectations and behaviors feed back to young women's attitudes and behavior as well as to their parents. . . .

ENTRANCE INTO LARGE FIRMS AND CAREER LADDERS

Descriptive Predictions

I make two descriptive predictions concerning labor market entrance of men and women.

(1) Japanese men and women will have roughly equal probabilities of initially being hired into large firms upon school graduation; women's probability may be slightly higher.

Why? Japanese employers in large firms have only a limited number of career-ladder positions to offer; career lines represent "packages of training and jobs" (Miyahara 1988, p. 41). Hiring women over men into *non*-career-track positions in the firm represents savings in wage costs for employers, for these women will "retire" in a few years and be replaced by new school graduates at starting wages.

If this is true, we should expect to see large numbers of women entering large firms, but we should expect to see them entering different *slots* than men. This leads to the second prediction:

(2) Significantly more men than women will enter career-track positions on their first job.

Causal Predictions

I make several predictions about the process of entering large firms and career tracks, and differences in the process for men and women. A number of factors can be hypothesized to be important: (1) the individual's educational attainment and the quality of education; (2) ability; (3) labor force attachment (relevant for women); (4) the historical timing of labor force entry, represented by cohort; and (5) family background variables (father's employment status and mother's labor force participation). . . .

Educational Level and Quality. Educational attainment is typically used as a measure of human capital in the prediction of job placement. The hierarchical structure of the Japanese educational system and the strong link between schools and work organizations (Miyahara 1988; Rohlen 1983) suggest that "quality" of schooling in addition to level is an important predictor.[2] Further, the effects of educational level and quality may differ for males and females. Specifically:

> Educational attainment should be positively related to entrance into a large firm and into a career track for males. . . .
>
> A linear relation is expected between females' educational attainment and probability of entering a large firm, with only a slight gain for women with a university education. For entrance into a career-track position, education will be significantly less helpful to women than to men. Further, only the most highly educated women (graduating from top universities) will have any chance of entering a career-track position.
>
> *Ability.* Ability is hypothesized to be a predictor of placement in both large firms and career positions for men and women.
>
> *Work plans.* No relationship is predicted between women's work plans and placement in a large firm, but a positive relationship is expected between women's placement in career-track positions and plans to work across the life cycle.

Japanese employers frequently claim that it is not economically rational to place women in career-track positions and on-the-job training programs because of their high propensity to quit upon marriage or childbirth. This is difficult to test without a longitudinal study, but an indirect approach is to examine the relationship between first job and women's retrospective report of their adolescent plans for future work life. If the claim of Japanese employers is correct, we would expect to find an association between women's plans for continuous work and their placement in a career-track position. And if the arguments in this paper are correct, we would also expect that women's plans for continuous work do not have anything to do with placement in a large firm per se, because it is likely that they will be in positions that neither require nor encourage long-term employment.

Control Variables

Cohort. It is predicted that members of the older cohort (40–44 years of age) in the sample experienced greater opportunities initially to enter career-track positions than members of the younger cohort (25–29 years of age).

The sample includes two cohorts. Members of one (40–44) entered the labor market in the early 1960s during a period of rapid economic growth, and members of the other (25–29) entered in the late 1970s, a recessionary period. Some scholars have suggested that Japanese women are the first to be affected by economic downturns, as employers attempt to protect the core male workers who are permanent employees (Rohlen 1979). If this is correct, then female members of the younger cohort would have been particularly subject to exclusion from career-track positions.

Father's employment status. Father's employment status is a control variable and is not expected to directly influence labor force entry, except that children of self-employed fathers may be less likely to work in large firms or in career-track positions because their labor is valued in the family business.

Mother's labor force participation. In the highly sex-discriminatory environment of Japan, mothers' participation in the paid labor force may exert a discouraging effect on daughters' career-track entrance because daughters witness their mothers' difficulties. . . .

DATA AND METHODS

Data for the following analysis come from a survey (the "Survey on Work Patterns") I conducted in three urban locations in Japan during 1984: Sapporo, Kodaira (a suburb of Tokyo), and Toyohashi. . . . Questions in the mail survey include extensive information on natal family, educational, marital, and work histories, as well as educational aspirations and behaviors towards respondents' own children. A stratified random sampling procedure was followed, with random samples of men and women in two cohorts (25–29 years and 40–44 years). . . . A 13-page questionnaire was mailed to the sample, with an overall response rate of 50.1 percent for the three cities. This response rate, while respectable for a mail survey, nevertheless may entail biases that could affect the statistical results. Therefore, a number of checks were carried out to assess the degree of response bias. . . .

Measurement of the variables is described in Table 2, and means and standard deviations are shown in Table 3. (Means for dummy variables are proportions of

Table 2. Measurement of Variables

Cohort	Dummy variable (representing historical timing of respondent's entry into the labor market); 0 = respondent 25–29 years of age, 1 = respondent 40–44 years of age.
Father's employment	Series of dummy variables for father's employment status when respondent was 15 years of age: unemployed or absent, self-employed or farm, blue-collar, white-collar (omitted category).
Mother's employment	Dummy variable for mother's employment status outside home when respondent was 15 years of age: 0 = mother was full-time housewife, family worker, or worked in a home handicraft job; 1 = mother was employed part-time or full-time outside the home.
Ability	Respondent's class rank in senior year of high school, by decile, scored 1–5. (If respondent did not attend high school, class rank in final year of junior high school is substituted.)
Education	Series of dummy variables for respondent's educational level and, for university, educational quality: junior high school (omitted category), high school, junior college/ vocational school, low-ranking university, medium-/high- ranking university.[a]
Work plans	Dummy variable representing women's reported plans in adolescence to work continuously across the life cycle.[b]
Large-firm placement	Dummy variable representing initial job placement in the government sector or in a firm employing 1000 + employees.
Career-ladder placement	Dummy variable representing initial job placement in a career ladder (see text for details on measurement).

[a] The scale of university quality was constructed with the cooperation of Professor Keiko Nakayama Watanabe, a member of the Social Stratification and Mobility (SSM) project in Tokyo. Universities were ranked into three groups: the former seven Imperial Universities, Tokyo Institute of Technology, and Hitotsubashi University (Group 1), a larger group of public and private universities (Group 2), and lower-ranked private universities (Group 3). A complete listing of universities and their rankings is available from the author.

[b] The survey question was phrased in the following way: "When you were about 18 years old, what combination of work and family life did you most hope to have in the future?" The proportion of women reporting the expectation of working continuously throughout the life cycle was only 15.9 percent; this category was combined with the category of women who expected that they would quit work temporarily with childbirth and later reenter the work force. The combined category represents 39.6 percent of women.

Table 3.   Means and Standard Deviations of Variables

	Males (N = 424)		Females (N = 651)	
	Mean	*S.D.*	*Mean*	*S.D.*
Cohort	.587	.493	.570	.495
Father's employment				
Unemployed or absent	.083	.276	.077	.266
Self-employed	.425	.495	.421	.494
Blue-collar	.252	.435	.258	.438
White-collar	.241	.428	.244	.430
Mother's employment				
outside home	.217	.408	.241	.421
Ability	3.234	1.018	3.315	.899
Education				
Junior high	.160	.367	.137	.344
High school	.373	.484	.471	.500
Junior college/				
vocational school	.090	.286	.252	.434
Low-ranking				
university	.226	.419	.094	.292
Medium-/high-				
ranking University	.151	.358	.046	.210
Work plans				
(in adolescence)	—	—	.396	.490
Large-firm placement	.307	.462	.300	.458
Career-ladder placement	.219	.414	.069	.254

respondents who scored "1" on those variables.) A dummy variable was created to measure initial placement in a large firm, with large firm considered to be one what employs at least 1000 people, or the government sector. This measure is in accord with Hashimoto and Raisian's (1983) conceptualization and is consistent with classic studies of the Japanese economy such as Cole's (1979) and with published government statistics on firm size.

The variable measuring initial career-track position was constructed as a composite of several indicators. . . . Individuals were classified as starting their work life in a career ladder if they (1) started as full-time employees or managers in a firm (not an individual establishment) of 1000 or more employees or in the government sector, (2) reported having perceived some possibility for promotion (to section chief or any category above), (3) were neither in an agricultural occupation nor in an "assistant clerical" position, and (4) were not working in primary industry (agriculture, mining, or fishing).

The principal unconventionalities in the construction of the career ladder variable are the use of perceived promotional possibilities and the limited use of occupation and industry. . . . Positions in large Japanese work organizations are arranged in vertical tiers, each corresponding to a span of control: (1) supervisor or foreman (*kakaricho*), generally in charge of up to 5 subordinates, (2) section chief (*kacho*), heading a section of approximately 10 subordinates, (3) department head (*bucho*), supervising a department (typically consisting of three or four section), and (4) the highest level administrative positions, above department head. This structure is common in large firms across industries, and it represents both the factory and office systems of titles and statuses. . . .

The survey question that addressed the issue of position/status was as follows: "At the workplace where you held your first job (after leaving school), what was the highest promotional possibility for you and for others doing the same type of work as you?" The question was phrased in such a way as to inquire about the promotional possibilities inherent in the *position* rather than for the specific respondent. All those who reported having promotion possibilities to the second level (*kacho*) or above were considered as fulfilling this measurement criterion for career track.

Occupation and Industry. Occupational and industrial classifications were used in only a limited fashion to construct the career ladder variable because both occupations and industries are quite heterogeneous. Blue- as well as white-collar jobs may be structured in career ladders . . . and this is particularly true in Japan. . . . When promotional possibilities are cross-classified with occupational categories, the occupations that emerge as having very low promotional possibilities are agricultural activities and the assistant clerical category. Other occupational categories such as sales work, general office work, and services demonstrate a wider distribution across promotional categories. Only two occupational categories were therefore used to sort respondents into career ladders: people in the combined category including agriculture, fishing, and mining, or in the category of assistant clerical work were classified as non-career-position incumbents. . . .

Industrial classification was used only as a check to classify people whose work lives began in primary industries (agriculture, fishing, mining) in the non-career-ladder category and to include government sector employees in the career-ladder category (if they fulfilled the other qualifying criteria listed above). . . .

RESULTS

Virtually equal proportions of men and women (30.7 percent vs. 30.0 percent) in the sample entered a large firm upon leaving school (see Table 3). . . . But the proportions of men and women whose first job was a career-track position in a large firm are significantly different: 22 percent of men and only 7 percent of women started their work lives in a career ladder. Stated differently, fully 71 percent of men who started out in large firms were in career-track positions, in contrast to 23 percent of their female counterparts. This is brought into sharp relief when we consider the fact that 60 percent of the women who entered a large firm when they left school entered as clerical workers. Among these, three-quarters were "assistant clerical" positions. In contrast, one-third of the men who entered large firms were placed in clerical jobs and only 7 percent of these (one-tenth the proportion of women) were "assistant clerical" positions. . . .

The process of entering a large firm is similar for males and females. Ability and education are positively associated with entering a large firm for both sexes, and family background variables do not exert significant effects. High school education is worth more than junior college/vocational school or low-ranking university for males, whereas progressively higher educational attainments increase women's probability of entering a large firm. For women, mother's labor force participation is not related to entrance into a large firm. Nor are work plans. . . . These findings are as predicted.

When . . . men and women are compared, high-ability men are significantly more likely than high-ability women to enter large firms. Male high school graduates are also significantly more likely to start out in large firms than are female high school graduates.

Further sex differences emerge when the process of entrance into career-track positions is examined. Human capital variables significant for men's placement in a career ladder are ability and attendance at a medium-/high-ranking university (Table 4). The coefficients for education suggest a monotonic effect of educational attainment, but the only educational credential that *significantly* affects probability of placement in a career ladder is graduation from a medium-/high-ranking university. . . .

Ability exerts a strong effect on women's probability of placement in a career ladder and the coefficients for educational attainment suggest a linear effect for education, but the similarities in the process of placement in a career ladder for the two sexes end there. Graduation from a medium-/high-ranking university has a positive but insignificant effect on women's probability of entering a career track, and graduation from junior college has a *negative,* though insignificant, effect. Graduation from a low-ranking university has a positive insignificant effect. The pattern of these coefficients shows that university graduation does not substantially increase women's chances of entering a career-track position; junior college graduation may actually *damage* those chances. . . .

Family background variables also exert some play in determining women's probability of entering a career ladder. Having a self-employed father depresses a woman's probability of entering a career track, and having a mother in the paid labor force dampens the probability.

Women's adolescent plans for labor force participation exert a predicted strong positive effect on probability of entrance into a career track (whereas there was no effect on the probability of entrance into a large firm). Causal interpretation of

Table 4. Logit Coefficients Describing the Effects of Individual
Characteristics on Entrance into a Career Track
after Leaving School

	Males	Females
Constant	−2.769**	−5.297**
	(.540)	(.870)
Cohort	−.005	.738*
	(.274)	(.393)
Father's employment		
Unemployed or absent	−.312	−.860
	(.522)	(.694)
Self-employed	−.644*	−1.013**
	(.338)	(.412)
Blue-collar	−.278	−.059
	(.348)	(.429)
White-collar	—	—
Mother's employment outside home	−.080	−1.325*
	(.315)	(.595)
Ability	.453**	.713**
	(.133)	(.194)
Education		
Junior high/high school	—	—
Junior college/vocational school	.134	−.338
	(.500)	(.444)
Low-ranking university	.353	.088
	(.327)	(.580)
Medium-/high-ranking university	1.176**	.384
	(.354)	(.562)
Work plans in adolescence	—	.758*
		(.333)
Maximum likelihood χ^2	399.62	284.32
D.F.	414	640

Note: All significance tests are one-tailed; $*p<.05$, $**p<.01$.

this variable must be somewhat tentative because of its retrospective nature.
Nevertheless, the importance of the variable . . . offers support for the notion
that there is a strong fit between women's entrance into career ladders and their
intention to work continuously across the life cycle. But other significant coefficients in the model remain stable when the variable measuring work expectations
is added, indicating that work motivation is not the *mechanism* through which
those variables operate.

Finally, cohort exerts a significant effect on women's, but not men's, probability of entering a career ladder. Women in the older cohort had significantly
higher chances of initially entering a career track upon leaving school than
women in the younger cohort. Between 1973 and 1978, when most of the younger cohort in our sample entered the labor market, Japan experienced its worst

recession in the post-World War II period. While permanent employment for men was largely preserved, large numbers of women exited from the labor force and employers' willingness to allocate career-track slots to women became even slighter than in the era of high economic growth (Rohlen 1979). . . .

Despite the differences in independent variables' effects for men and women, the only coefficient that differs significantly for the sexes is that for mother's labor force participation (a predicted effect). . . .

CONCLUSION

Japanese women participate in the labor force at rates similar to women in other industrial nations but are less likely to work as employees. And among the employee labor force, the male-female wage gap is greater in Japan and women's representation in managerial ranks is lower. As women move across the life cycle, they are more likely to work in family businesses; older women who are employees are also more likely than younger women to work in small firms. These findings from aggregate government statistics coupled with ethnographic evidence suggest that very few Japanese women find their way into career ladders at the start of their work lives. Rather, they are apt to work as temporary employees in low-level clerical positions.

[W]hile about 30 percent of each sex enter large firms when they initially start working, women are much less likely to enter career ladders (the Japanese "permanent employment system") than men: 22 percent of men and only 7 percent of women have such an experience. Among the population entering large firms, twice as many women as men enter as clerical workers, and the majority of these women are in low-level "assistant clerical" positions.

Although not always statistically different for men and women, the effect of human capital variables (ability and education) on men's entrance into large firms and career-track positions is generally stronger than for women. . . .

The paper demonstrates that the strong gender stratification patterns in the Japanese economy are already apparent at the beginning of individuals' work lives. But we would not have seen this were our focus only on the distribution of men and women in the large- and small-firm sectors of the economy when they start working, for this sex distribution is even. This points to the importance of attempting to measure career-ladder position and constructing such a measure in a culturally appropriate fashion. . . .

On a more upbeat note, the Japanese Diet ratified an Equal Employment Opportunity Law in spring 1985, after years of debate within the Labor Ministry, employers' groups, labor unions, and women's associations. The law prohibits sex discrimination in all phases of the employment process from recruitment to retirement, but no penalties are imposed on employers who do not conform. A recent check of classified advertisements in Japanese newspapers shows that some employers continue to recruit on the basis of sex as well as age. The effectiveness of the law will depend heavily on the degree to which local administrative units set up by the Japanese government monitor businesses, and the degree to which firms find it in their interest to gradually move away from a statistical discrimination rule that reserves the great majority of career positions for men. Future research on gender stratification in Japan will need to address this new exogenous influence on the operation of labor markets.

ACKNOWLEDGMENTS

Data collection for the research reported in this paper was supported in part by grant #SES84-07208 from the National Science Foundation. Support from the Social Science Divisional Research fund at The University of Chicago, the Japan Foundation, the Social Science Research Council, and the National Academy of Education is also gratefully acknowledged. I received valuable suggestions on the paper from participants in the Fall 1987 Organizations Colloquium at Stanford University, the Demography Workshop of The University of Chicago, Mary Jean Bowman, and anonymous ASR reviewers.

NOTES

1. Such questioning is now formally illegal as a result of the Japanese Diet's passage of an Equal Employment Opportunity Law in 1985.
2. In Japan, both high schools and universities are hierarchically ranked, with entrance to each level regulated by a highly competitive examination system.

REFERENCES

Clark, Rodney. 1979. *The Japanese Company*. New Haven: Yale University Press.
Cole, Robert E. 1979. *Work, Mobility, and Participation: A Comparative Study of American and Japanese Industry*. Berkeley: University of California Press.
Hashimoto, Masanori and John Raisian. 1983. "Employment Tenure and Earnings Profiles in Japan and the United States." *American Economic Review* 75:721–35.
International Labor Organization. 1986. *Yearbook of Labor Statistics*. Geneva: International Labor Organization.
Japanese Ministry of Labor. 1987. *Fujin Rodo no Jitsujo* (Status of Women Workers). Tokyo: Government Printing Office.
Rohlen, Thomas. 1974. *For Harmony and Strength*. Berkeley: University of California Press.
———. 1979. "'Permanent Employment' Faces Recession, Slow Growth, and an Aging Work Force." *Journal of Japanese Studies* 5:235–72.

24

Japan's New Equal Employment Opportunity Law: Real Weapon or Heirloom Sword?

Jan M. Bergeson and Kaoru Yamamoto Oba

Scholars sometimes compare law in Japan to an heirloom sword that is no more than an ornament or a prestige symbol used to make Japan appear respectable in Western eyes; it is taken out and shown to outsiders but is rarely, if ever, used.[1] This analogy accurately reflects Japan's inability to legally prevent sexual discrimination. Although the Japanese Constitution[2] specifically prohibits governmental sex discrimination, and other laws require equal pay for equal work,[3] serious discrimination continues in Japan.

Various groups have tried to enact anti-discrimination legislation, but have failed for one reason or another. However, the Japanese legislature recently passed the Equal Employment Opportunity Act (EEOA),[4] which calls for equality in job recruitment, training and promotion, and provides for equal working hours and equal access to fringe benefits provided by employers. This comment first examines the EEOA in light of the traditional Japanese attitudes towards law and women, and the existing labor laws which it supplements and amends. It next examines the EEOA amendments to these laws, and the probable effect these amendments will have on Japanese society. The comment concludes that although the EEOA seems to introduce significant changes, the new law will probably not have great practical effect; the role of formal law in Japan and traditional Japanese attitudes towards law and women may well frustrate its implementation. . . .

I. BACKGROUND: OVERVIEW OF JAPANESE CULTURE

Like most Japanese statutes, the EEOA can only be fully understood in the context of Japanese culture. One of the important initial aspects of that culture is

Excerpts reprinted with permission from the *Brigham Young University Law Review* 1986:865–883. Copyright © 1986.

that the "Japanese do not like law" (Noda 1976, p. 160). Except for lawyers and those possessing some refined knowledge of law, Japanese generally view law as an instrument of state-imposed constraint. Law is thus synonymous with pain or penalty.

In addition, the legal codes of other countries have heavily influenced Japanese law. Several of these foreign laws were adopted wholesale without adapting them to Japanese society. Thus, a disparity developed between the laws as written in the books and the normal practices of Japanese society. A key to understanding the role of Japanese law lies in understanding this disparity, which is best described in the Japanese notions of *tatemae* and *honne: tatemae* is "the desired appearance of things," and *honne* is the "actual condition, the real thoughts, the motives that one has." The inevitable disparity between these two concepts does not trouble the Japanese, although they do try to satisfy the *honne* without compromising—at least on the surface—the *tatemae*. . . .

This discrepancy between law and reality is at least partially responsible for the Japanese preference for conciliation (or mediation) as a method of dispute resolution. . . . This preference for mediation also results from the Japanese concept of harmony. Japanese culture is built on the spirit of *wa* (harmony or accord), and the resolution of a dispute requires the restoration of *wa* and mutual understanding. . . . Japanese behavior does not readily conform to formal laws which are not in accordance with the realities of society. Therefore, any anti-discrimination law which is not founded in the realities of Japanese society will be likely to fail in application and merely provide Japanese society with an unreal appearance of modernity. This seeming aversion to formal law coupled with the Japanese need to achieve harmony results in the popularity of mediation as a method of dispute resolution. It is in light of these preferences that this comment will next examine the labor laws which preceded the EEOA and the EEOA amendments to that law.

II. PRE-EEOA LAW

The EEOA consists primarily of amendments to the already-existing Labor Standards Act (LSA) and the Working Women's Welfare Law (WWWL). In order to understand the impact of these amendments, a familiarity with some of the provisions of the pre-existing laws is necessary. Previous laws dealing with sex discrimination include the Kenpō (Japanese Constitution), the LSA, the WWWL and Article 90 of the Civil Code.

A. The Constitution

Unlike the United States Constitution, the Japanese Constitution explicitly prohibits discrimination on the basis of sex. . . . This provision, largely a product of General MacArthur's influence after World War II, introduced the concept of sexual equality into the Japanese legal system. But the provision is an example of *tatemae:* it maintains a respectable facade for Western eyes, but the Japanese seldom use it to combat discrimination.

Judicial construction of the clause has significantly weakened its potential impact. In *Moriaki v. Chief of Tateyama Ward,*[5] the Supreme Court held that this provision "is to be construed as prohibiting differentiation *without reasonable grounds therefor.* It does not prohibit some differential treatment in view of the nature of the matter." Thus, instead of prohibiting discrimination, the constitution has been judicially construed to permit "reasonable" discrimination.

B. The Labor Standards Act

1. Article 4

Chapter VI of the Labor Standards Act (LSA) contains regulations of women's working conditions, most notably a provision mandating equal pay for equal work. Like the EEOA, Article 4 of the LSA was promulgated in response to an international treaty.[6] The Japanese government cites this provision to support claims that it is trying to improve the situation of working women.

The Ministry of Labor claims that "[g]uidance and inspection are carried out to ensure the strict observance of equal pay for equal work,"[7] but Japan still ranks lowest among the industrialized nations in the ratio of women's to men's wages. The primary reason is that women are prevented from ever reaching an "equal" position meriting equal pay.

2. Protective Provisions

The LSA also contains several provisions limiting women's work in various ways. For example, these provisions limit women's holiday or overtime hours. Also, women are not usually allowed to work underground or in what are termed "dangerous and harmful jobs."

Proponents of these restrictions argue that they are necessary for the "protection" of women and of maternity. Opponents maintain that the restrictions are just a thinly veiled means of legally discriminating against women, and are no longer necessary.

C. Working Women's Welfare Law

The purpose of the Working Women's Welfare Law (WWWL) of 1972 was to "further the welfare and improve the status of working women."[8] The WWWL focuses on eliminating discriminatory employment practices and improving women's vocational abilities through counseling, vocational guidance and training. Amendments to those provisions constitute a significant part of the new EEOA.

D.   Civil Code Article 90

Article 90 of the Minpō (Civil Code) does not expressly prohibit sex discrimination, but it has been the primary legal weapon in the battle for equal opportunity employment. It provides that "[a] juristic act which has for its object such
matters as are contrary to public policy or good morals is null and void."[9]
Japanese courts have used it to strike down discriminatory employment contracts
requiring women to retire upon marriage or pregnancy. . . .

Article 90 analysis focuses on the reasonableness of discriminatory conduct. If
discrimination is unreasonable then it is "contrary to public policy" and thus
void. However, Article 90 may leave too much discretion to the courts. Japanese
courts are not bound by prior factual determinations of reasonableness, so a
plaintiff cannot rely absolutely on courts to follow earlier decisions. Furthermore,
Article 90 is not capable of reaching beyond explicit sex-based policies to more
subtle areas of discrimination such as job assignment, layoffs, on-the-job training
and promotion. Nonetheless, Article 90 has been the most successful legal means
of fighting discrimination in Japan.

Thus, even before the passage of the EEOA, Japanese law supposedly barred
sexual discrimination, required equal pay for equal work, and refused to enforce
discriminatory "juridical acts" which contravened public policy. However, these
safeguards against discrimination are easily sidestepped. . . . A statutory provision such as the EEOA would seem to be the best way to deal with these
problems, but the EEOA stops short of being an effective weapon in the fight
against discrimination.

III.   THE EEOA PROVISIONS

The EEOA is based upon a U.N. resolution calling on signatory countries to
undertake "all appropriate measures, including legislation, to modify or abolish
existing laws, regulations, customs and practices which constitute discrimination
against women."[10] The Japanese government felt both domestic and international
pressure to sign the resolution and to then ratify it by enacting similar provisions
in Japanese law.

A.   Amendments to the Working Women's Welfare Law

The original Working Women's Welfare Law suggested various ways to improve the position of the female worker, but rarely imposed more than a "duty"
upon employers not to discriminate. The strongest measure requires only that an
employer "shall endeavor" to follow the provisions. The EEOA's amendments to
the WWWL provide two different standards to be applied to discriminatory

activity by employers. Similar to the WWWL, the first standard provides that in recruiting, hiring, assigning and promoting workers, employers "*should endeavor*" to treat female workers "on an equal footing with male workers."[11] Second, the EEOA amendments require that when providing training and fringe benefits, and in establishing mandatory retirement guidelines, employers "*shall not* treat female workers discriminatory [sic] from male workers on the ground that they are women." Although it would appear that the EEOA prohibits employer discrimination in training, fringe benefits and non-discriminatory retirement provisions, in reality neither of the two standards is likely to have much effect.

1. The "Should Endeavor" Provisions

The major weakness in the "should endeavor" provisions is that the victim of discrimination has no real remedy. The provision "does not provide a legal basis to demand damages,"[12] and the EEOA's mediation process does not extend to violations of the recruitment and hiring provisions.[13] Additionally, the "should endeavor" language is vague and is open to varying interpretations. For example, in the recruiting context the language might not even prohibit the common practice of advertising jobs "for males only," or "for females only." Employers could argue that they are "endeavoring" to give equal opportunity, but that changes must be gradual and consensual.

Discrimination in job assignment and promotion, more than in hiring, poses serious problems to female workers in Japan. Japanese men oppose placing women in business positions equal or superior to those of men. A Mitsubishi spokesman explained why his company placed all ninety female college graduates hired in 1982 in secretarial or clerical positions: "They were hired under the category of secretarial work. We cannot go ahead with a higher-ranking recruitment at a time when many people find it improper for women to be at business negotiations."[14] . . . Women are not given the opportunity to break into higher, more prestigious jobs, especially if they are classified as "part-time" workers, who receive lower wages and fewer benefits, rather than as "regular" or "full-time" workers.[15] This distinction is significant because women comprise more than eighty percent of all part-time workers in Japan.

The big Japanese companies employ large numbers of part-time workers. Directors of those companies actively resist the enactment of any law requiring more pay for women because resultant increased costs could eliminate some of their competitive advantage. It is largely due to the influence of these big companies that the EEOA contains only a duty to "endeavor" to avoid discrimination instead of an express prohibition against discrimination.

2. The "Shall Not Discriminate" Provisions

The EEOA amendments also provide that employers shall not discriminate against women when providing on-the-job training, fringe benefits to employees, or in establishing mandatory retirement guidelines. These provisions, even though expressly prohibiting discrimination, do not provide for penal sanctions for their violation. As with discrimination in job assignment and promotions, discrimination can be very difficult to prove because companies can usually provide some non-sex-based reason for the discrimination. And even if the discrimination were clear, many Japanese women may not dare demand equal benefits for equal work because they fear they will upset their employers or lose their jobs. . . .

[A]ccording to the Ministry of Labor, the strength of a company's opposition to the new law directly correlates to the extent that company uses women as short-term, supplementary labor.[16] . . . Companies benefit from . . . high turn-over in women employees because it continually brings in new young workers who, under Japan's tenure-based wage system, can be paid much lower wages. . . .

Thus, the EEOA amendments to the Working Women's Welfare Law do not have much legal significance—they still do not provide an independent basis for legal action. The Ministry of Labor has indicated that an employee could bring suit if the provisions for equal treatment in training, fringe benefits and retirement are violated, but that the court's decision would still be based on the Article 90 consideration of whether the discrimination was "unreasonable" or contrary to public policy.

B.   Amendments to the Labor Standards Act

The EEOA's amendments to the Labor Standards Act are much more specific than the amendments to the Working Women's Welfare Law. The new LSA amendments abolish what have traditionally been considered "protective" laws. The amendments abolish several prohibitions on female labor and allow women to work underground, to work overtime and on holidays and, in certain circumstances, to work at night.

Because these amendments are specific and unambiguous, their effect will likely be more immediate and tangible than that of the amendments to the WWWL. . . .

C.   Alternatives to Formal Legal Processes

The strongest criticism of the EEOA is that it does not punish violators. But the lack of sanctions is not unusual, given the traditional Japanese aversion to formal law and the strict exaction of legal penalties. Instead of sanctions, the EEOA provides for informal methods of resolving discrimination problems. . . .

1.   Administrative Guidance

The EEOA authorizes the Minister of Labor, when he deems necessary, to issue "guidelines" for employers to follow with respect to recruitment, hiring, job assignment and promotion. Such guidelines would not be "laws" per se, but would be more in the nature of *gyōsei shidō* ("administrative guidance"), which is a "common Japanese regulatory technique that, although generally nonbinding in a strictly legal sense, seeks to conform (by pressure or coercion) the behavior of regulated parties to broad administrative goals."[17]

Administrative guidance has proven to be an effective way of regulating behavior on an informal level. However, this technique may have little effect on sexual discrimination. The success of administrative guidance in introducing reform depends on the extent to which the Ministry of Labor considers equal employment an important administrative goal. . . .

2. Conciliation through Mediation Commissions

Japanese people prefer conciliation and mediation as opposed to litigation to achieve social control or dispute settlement. The EEOA's mediation provisions clearly reflect this preference. . . . The EEOA also provides that a female employee and her employer should first try to settle any employment discrimination dispute between themselves. The parties may also seek advice, counsel or recommendations from the Director of the Prefectural Women's and Young Worker's Office.

Additionally, the EEOA establishes an "Equal Employment Opportunity Mediation Commission" to which the parties may apply for mediation. The Commission is empowered to formulate a mediation plan, but, as with all mediation or conciliation in Japan, the Commission can only recommend and encourage that the parties accept the plan. The parties are under no legal obligation to follow the commission's recommendation. . . .

3. Potential Problems with the Mediation Process

Although mediation and conciliation have been successful in resolving disputes and maintaining social order in Japan, problems still exist with the mediation process in the context of sexual discrimination. Because of its informal nature, the typical mediation process would seem to be more *honne* than *tatemae.* . . . There is no assurance that the commissioners will consider the law, even if just as a guideline, in making their decisions. . . .

The danger of the mediation commission becoming no more than a facade is especially real in sexual discrimination cases. If mediation commissioners disregard the law (the EEOA), their decisions will probably rest upon the customs and mores of Japanese society which have traditionally treated women as belonging in the home (or, if in the labor force, as being only supplementary labor). In addition, mediation commissioners are typically chosen from among the more prominent members of the community (usually men), and their decisions or mediation plans tend to favor traditional institutions and reflect conservative values. Therefore, even the process of conciliation, which is often used successfully in other areas, may not help women in the Japanese labor market achieve equality.

IV. CONCLUSION

The EEOA in its final form managed to please almost no one. It represents a compromise between women's groups, who wanted the law to expressly prohibit discrimination and to provide penalties for violation, and employers' groups, who wanted to block passage of the law entirely. Nevertheless, the EEOA is a step towards equality. . . .

The EEOA is a step in the right direction, but it may not immediately become an effective legal weapon in fighting discrimination. Like the heirloom sword, the law may become one more example of tatemae. Even the EEOA's informal conciliation procedure may not help women achieve equality until Japan's traditional attitudes about women change. A group of prominent employers maintains that business practices "reflect the views of society" and that government "simply cannot legislate away mores and customs that are ingrained in the culture."[18]

NOTES

1. *E.g.,* T. Kawashima, Nihonjin No Hoishiki (Japanese Legal Consciousness) 47 (1967); Stevens, *Japanese Legal Systems and Traditions,* in Current Legal Aspects of Doing Business in the Far East 13 (R. Allison ed. 1972).

2. Japan's present constitution, promulgated in 1946, was heavily influenced by General Douglas MacArthur and the Occupation Forces. It reflects not only the idea of equal rights for women, but also the concept of human rights as a whole, both of which are concepts foreign to traditional Japanese thought. Y. Noda, Introduction to Japanese Law 190, 195 (A. Angelo trans. 1976).

3. "The employer shall not discriminate women against men concerning wages by reason of the worker being a woman." Rōdō Kijun Hō (Labor Standards Act [hereinafter LSA]) art. 4, Law No. 49 of April 7, 1947; *see infra* notes 23–27 and accompanying text.

4. This new law was passed by the Japanese legislature on May 17, 1985, with an effective date of April 1, 1986. . . .

5. 18 Sai-han Minshū 676, 678 (May 27, 1964).

6. International Labor Organization Treaty No. 100 (Equal Remuneration).

7. Ministry of Labor, Official English Summary of the EEOA 1 (1984).

8. Japan Ministry of Labor, The Status of Women in Japan 22 (1983).

9. Minpō (Civil Code) art. 90, Law no. 89 of 1896 and Law No. 9 of 1898.

10. United Nations Convention Concerning the Elimination of All Forms of Discrimination Against Women, G.A. Res. 34/180, 34 U.N. GAOR Supp. (No. 46) (107th plen. mtg.) art. 2(f), at 193, 195, U.N. Doc. A/34/830 (1979) [hereinafter U.N. Convention].

11. EEOA, supra note 6, at art. 7. (emphasis added). In comparison, the U.N. Resolu-

tion calls for measures to ensure "the right to free choice of profession and employment, the right to promotion [and] job security." U.N. Convention, supra note 36, art. 11(1)(c), at 195.

12.   Interview with the Chief Guidance Clerk, Policy Planning Divisions, Women's Bureau, Ministry of Labor, in Tokyo, Japan (June 17, 1985).

13.   Labor ministry officials explain that the EEOA's mediation process does not extend to recruitment and hiring violations because "there would be too many cases." Id.

14.   O'Reilly, *Women: A Separate Sphere,* Time, Aug. 1, 1983, at 68–69.

15.   These designations are deceptive because part-time employees often work essentially the same number of hours that full-time workers are on the job. The primary difference is that full-time workers are hired with the intent that they be with the company for life and are thus given extensive on-the-job training. On the other hand, part-time workers are not hired with such intentions and seldom receive extensive training.

16.   Nihon Keizai Shimbun (Japan Economic Journal) Oct. 13, 1984, at 3, col. 1. The Ministry of Labor noted that this correlation is most obviously present in steel, aluminum and petrochemical companies.

17.   Young, *Judicial Review of Administrative Guidance: Governmentally Encouraged Consensual Dispute Resolution in Japan,* 84 Colum. L. Rev. 923, 926 (1984).

18.   *New York Times,* Feb. 24, 1985, at C1, col. 2. Inayama, the chairman of the powerful *Keidanren* (Japan Federation of Economic Organizations), a leading organization of the country's most powerful companies, insisted that the new law was not necessary because "a woman's place is in the home raising children." *Nihon Keizai Shimbun,* (Japan Economic Journal) March 13, 1984, at 5, col. 3. The chairman of the *Nikkeiren* rejected the EEOA's provisions, insisting that "just because they do these things in other countries, that alone is not enough reason to do it here." *Id.,* June 13, 1983, at 3, col. 1.

Although mores and customs cannot be legislated away, the EEOA is an important step in the process of change. The Japanese firmly believe that change should be made gradually and with the consensus of all. This concept of gradual change is referred to as nemawashi (the practice of transplantation), and is one of the most distinct characteristics of Japanese decision-making methods. *Nemawashi* involves digging around a tree a few years before it is actually transplanted and wrapping the roots repeatedly so that the roots are preserved and ready to grow in different ground. Figuratively, *nemawashi* refers to the ground work to enlist support or to secure informal consent from the people concerned. Japanese Business Glossary 28 (1983).

VII

The Politics of EEO and Affirmative Action

Affirmative action is probably the most controversial aspect of the struggle over EEO. Like discrimination, its definition is the subject of controversy. Unlike discrimination, however, affirmative action has no "traditional" definition; its "exact meaning," Russell Nieli has written (1991:ix) has been "highly fluid and often elusive."

The most widely accepted sense of the term is that it involves something "extra" beyond EEO, taking group membership into account to help minorities and women. How much extra is implied by the term, and how much, if anything, should be done, are the questions seemingly crucial to the debate. The law itself is of little help. The legal basis for affirmative action is found in Title VII, which states that when a federal court has found discrimination, it may order the discriminator to pursue "such affirmative action as may be appropriate" (sec. 706[g]), and in Executive Order 11246, which requires federal contractors to take affirmative action in their treatment of applicants and employees. Neither Title VII nor the executive order spells out what affirmative action means, however, leaving the path to controversy open.

Some analysts (e.g., Glazer 1978) distinguish between "good" affirmative action, which ensures that minorities and women are informed about job opportunities and perhaps provided training, and "bad" affirmative action (which Glazer calls "affirmative discrimination"), which involves preferential treatment or quotas (see also U.S. Office of Management and Budget 1985:J-3). Others insist, along with Senator Orrin Hatch (1980 [excerpted here]), that "affirmative action means quotas or it means nothing," and oppose vehemently the notion that there can be any such thing as "good" affirmative action.

The intensity of the conflict over affirmative action stems in part from an increasing divergence between two views of what it takes to achieve equal opportunity. As Kluegel (1990 [excerpted here]) points out, most Americans take an "individualistic" view of black-white differences in labor market outcomes (and of other labor market outcomes as well); they believe that the differences are due mainly to racial differences in motivation or innate ability, rather than to differences in opportunities or to discrimination. Once blatant forms of discrimination—which the vast majority of whites oppose, at least in principle—

have been eliminated, labor market outcomes are seen as simply the product of individual skill and effort. Those who adopt this view, Kluegel shows, see little need for policies providing special assistance for blacks.

The competing view, which has been adopted by an increasing number of those involved in analyzing labor markets since the 1960s, is that much of what happens to minorities and women in the labor market is the product of neither individual ability and effort nor blatant discrimination. Instead, economic progress for minorities and women is hindered by many traditional organizational practices that harm minorities and women without contributing to efficiency (as suggested by the *Griggs* decision and discussed in England, Baron, Eichner, and Blumrosen 1972 [excerpted here]), and by the ease with which employers can achieve the appearance of fairness while continuing to discriminate (see discussions in Ashenfelter and Oaxaca 1987; Posner 1987 [excerpted here]; Lundberg 1991). Some of those adopting this point of view (but not all, e.g., Posner 1987) conclude that the attainment of equal opportunity requires not only eliminating blatant forms of discrimination, but also rethinking many traditional employment practices and changing some of them in ways that will lead to more favorable outcomes for minorities and women.

To the extent that the proponents of this second view are successful in winning Congress, the courts, and administrative agencies over to their way of thinking, the public will see traditional employment practices being changed in ways intended to improve labor market outcomes for women and minorities. Because most people do not see such practices as discriminatory, they will often see the changes not as attacks on discrimination, but as preferential treatment for minorities and women. Thus, two different understandings of the nature of discrimination and the causes of group differences in labor market outcomes lead to different conclusions about many of the changes in organizational practices mandated by EEO policies.

The conflict over affirmative action achieves its intensity not only because people disagree about how to achieve equal opportunity (which is an empirical question in many respects) but because of a more philosophical disagreement as well: a disagreement over the goal of the civil rights movement and the means to be used to achieve it.

For many (perhaps most) Americans, including many participants in the civil rights movement, the "overarching political goal," as Abram (1986:1312) has written, "was equality—an equality to be reached by the elimination of discriminatory barriers that denied the individual the opportunity to exercise his franchise effectively, to compete for housing and employment, and to use public accommodations." The "first principles" of the civil rights movement, Abram argues, were "zealous regard for equal opportunity and the promotion of color-blind law and social policy," with government completely ignoring the race, sex, and ethnic origin of citizens. The government's job, from this perspective, is to make sure that no one impedes another's opportunities on the basis of race, sex, or ethnic origin; once barriers have been removed, government's job is done.

The competing view is that the fundamental goal of the civil rights movement was not to end *discrimination,* but to end racial *subjugation,* to help blacks overcome the consequences of centuries of oppression. For a time, Randall Kennedy (1986 [excerpted here]) has written, "it seemed that racial subjugation could be overcome by mandating the application of race-blind law." But that has not turned out to be the case, and, Kennedy says, many have now concluded that "the concept of race-blindness was simply a proxy for the fundamental demand that racial subjugation be eradicated" (see also Fiss 1971:313). Opponents of affirmative action, Kennedy suggests, confuse the goal of the civil rights movement with one of the means used to try to achieve it. The true goal of the movement was to improve the lot of blacks. The principle of antidiscrimination, or color blindness, was to be a crucial means for reaching this goal, but was not the goal itself. If color blindness proves inadequate to the task, then affirmative action is called for.

There are also two other sources of opposition to affirmative action. One is economic theory, as interpreted by some economists and lawyers who have adopted an economic approach to legal scholarship. They argue that affirmative action programs are morally repugnant because they are coercive, and economically inefficient because they force employers and workers into employment contracts they would avoid in a free market. Posner (1987, excerpted here) and Richard Epstein (1992) are forceful advocates of this view; in his recent book *Forbidden Grounds,* Epstein carries it to its logical conclusion and proposes that all EEO laws be repealed.

An additional source of opposition includes those characterized by what Randall Kennedy has called (1987:1344) "an impulse to protect the prerogatives of whites at the least hint of encroachment by claims of racial justice." It is a sign of how far race relations in this country have come that few "respectable" politicians and academics make overtly racist arguments against equal opportunity. Nevertheless, Kennedy points out, racism has been so central to American history that its role in the affirmative action debate cannot be ignored.

The very fact that affirmative action is so often portrayed as a racial issue shows the importance of racial antipathy in the debate. Principled arguments against affirmative action apply to affirmative action on any basis, and it is almost surely the case that its main beneficiaries are women. Yet the most vehement attacks on affirmative action are usually directed at programs benefiting blacks (see, e.g., U.S. Office of Management and Budget 1985:J-1–29).

The struggle over affirmative action acquires some of its intensity, finally, from the very fact that the term has no traditional meaning. Because federal EEO laws and policies permit, and at times require, affirmative action, what the term means is obviously important to those—employers, unions, and workers—directly affected by it. In addition, the definition can affect the political debate; in this as in many other areas of political conflict, those involved in the debate devote a great deal of effort to defining its terms in ways likely to benefit them (Gamson and Modigliani 1987 [excerpted here], 1989).

Since the 1960s, Gamson and Modigliani write, three views of affirmative action have competed for acceptance: a *remedial-action* view, whose proponents argue that affirmative action is the use of race-conscious policies to redress the continuing effects of past racial discrimination; a *delicate-balance* view, whose proponents contend that affirmative action involves helping minorities without adopting quotas that harm the majority; and a *no-preferential-treatment* view, whose proponents see affirmative action as inevitably granting unfair preferences to minorities, most often by requiring reverse discrimination. The remedial action view dominated discussions of affirmative action in the mass media in the late 1960s and 1970s, but since the mid-1980s, the no-preferential-treatment view has predominated; affirmative action has come to be presented as linked to reverse discrimination.

The competition among definitions is important because Americans are somewhat sympathetic to remedial action but hostile to preferential treatment. If proponents of the no-preferential-treatment view succeed in convincing most Americans that affirmative action means quotas, then they will have gone a long way toward eliminating anything labeled affirmative action as a viable policy option.

The intensity of the controversy over affirmative action has tended to peak, as might be expected, when especially important policy decisions are made (including Supreme Court decisions) and during election campaigns (see Gamson and Modigliani). This occurred most recently during debate of the bill that became the Civil Rights Act of 1991. The main purpose of the act was to overrule a number of Supreme Court decisions seen as weakening enforcement of the laws against employment discrimination, including *Wards Cove v. Atonio* (109 S. Ct. 2115, 1989), in which the Court substantially undermined the view of discrimination it promulgated in *Griggs v. Duke Power Co.* (Belton 1990). Debate over the bill became the occasion for heated rhetoric about preferential treatment, affirmative action, and quotas, and in fact President Bush twice vetoed earlier versions of the bill, claiming that it was a "quota bill," sure to force employers to adopt quotas for hiring and promoting minorities and women in order to avoid the risk of lawsuits. As adopted, the bill did prohibit (sec. 201) what had been seen by many as an especially blatant form of preferential treatment: the practice of "race norming," whereby rankings on standardized written tests were calculated separately for blacks, Hispanics, and non-Hispanic whites so that minorities would be competing only with each other in the rankings, and not with non-Hispanic whites whose average scores were often higher. The fact that it was nevertheless attacked as a quota bill shows the importance of concerns about preferential treatment as a political issue.

The readings in this section describe the political and social context in which the debate about affirmative action takes place and present the views of two prominent participants in the debate. William Gamson and Andre Modigliani describe the struggle over what affirmative action means, while James Kluegel shows how Americans' beliefs about discrimination and labor market outcomes affect their attitudes toward public policies intended to help blacks. Morris Abram and Randall Kennedy, in their debate in the *Harvard Law Review,* show how two individuals strongly committed to equal rights for all groups can nevertheless be strongly opposed on the issue of affirmative action. Taken together, the readings show that the debate over affirmative action is likely to remain intense for a long time to come (also see Burstein 1992, 1993).

25

The Changing Culture of Affirmative Action

William A. Gamson and Andre Modigliani

AFFIRMATIVE ACTION EVENTS

In 1965, President Lyndon Johnson issued an executive order (#11246), requiring all federal contractors to take "affirmative action." The context was the Civil Rights Act of 1964 and the continuing struggle for equal employment opportunity. In the past two decades, the term "affirmative action" has been used to mean many things—a symbol in a contest over the language and definition of the underlying issues.

In this paper, we define the affirmative action issue as: what use should be made, if any, of racial and ethnic classifications to promote the hiring and admission of blacks and other minorities?[1] The 1965 executive order saw affirmative action as a device for insuring "that employees are treated . . . without regard to their race, creed, color, or national origin." But contractors were also directed to consider race in several areas including recruitment, selection for training and apprenticeships, upgrading, and rate of pay. The drafters of this executive order apparently found no tension between the idea of paying attention to race in hiring and promotion and the idea of color-blindness.

By 1969, the conflict over affirmative action centered in the construction industry. Major demonstrations had taken place in several cities by black workers demanding entry into the building trades, and these stimulated counter-demonstrations by white workers in Chicago and Pittsburgh. The spectre of racial violence loomed again. Furthermore, there were labor shortages in the industry at a time when an economic boom was anticipated. A housing shortage existed with an estimated 26 million housing units needed in the next decade.

For complex political reasons, the new Nixon Administration sided with the advocates of affirmative action. . . . The major vehicle for affirmative action was the "Philadelphia Plan," named for the first city in which a Labor Department

Excerpts reprinted with permission from *Research in Political Sociology*, Richard Braumgart, ed., vol. 3, 1987 pp. 137–177. Copyright © 1987 by JAI Press Inc.

agreement with federal contractors had been reached. The plan set specific numerical goals for each of the building and construction trades, based on the extent of current minority employment and the availability pool. Labor Department officials announced that "because of the deplorably low rate of employment among members of minority groups" in the industry, they would set up similar plans in other major cities.

The Philadelphia Plan, unlike the earlier executive order on which it was based, stimulated considerable opposition. The plan, it was charged, embodied "quotas"—an important code word in the battle over language. Not so, explained Secretary of Labor George P. Schultz. "A quota system is a system which keeps people out. What we are seeking are objectives to get people in." Opponents were not convinced. . . .

By 1972, the Nixon Administration had shifted its rhetoric. As the Presidential campaign moved into high gear, both Nixon and Agnew found opportunities to express their opposition to quotas. . . . "Dividing Americans into quotas is totally alien to American tradition," Nixon told the Republican convention in his acceptance speech. . . . For the next few years, the Nixon-Ford Administration was too preoccupied with other matters to say much about affirmative action. With the advent of the Carter Administration in 1977, affirmative action again took on a higher priority. . . . During this period, a number of legal challenges to affirmative action were wending their way through the court system. . . . Some of these challenges were upheld in lower courts but, pending action by the Supreme Court, affirmative action remained in a kind of limbo.

This state of limbo was only partially removed by the Supreme Court in 1978 with the first of its major affirmative action decisions. A white medical school applicant named Allan Bakke challenged an affirmative action program at the University of California at Davis. The program involved the setting aside of a specific number of slots for deprived minorities. Bakke claimed that he would have been accepted for medical school had there not been places in the entering class closed to him because of his race. This, he contended, was racial discrimination, prohibited by the Civil Rights Act.

No five justices on the Court were able to agree on a single opinion in the case. The separate opinions involved two different coalitions, with Justice Lewis Powell providing the swing vote. Powell joined four justices in finding that Bakke had been illegally excluded from medical school, although he did not share their basis of judgment. He also joined the other four justices in upholding the use of race as a legitimate consideration in admissions, suggesting that affirmative action programs that did not employ a specific quota were legal. Paradoxically, Powell's opinion became the opinion of the Court even though his reasoning was not shared in full by *any* of the other eight justices. The complexity of the decision allowed ample room for different interpretations and emphases. The Carter administration chose to emphasize that part of the decision that upheld the legality of race-conscious programs. . . .

A year later, the Court decided a second case that gave unequivocal encouragement to the proponents of affirmative action. In 1974, the Kaiser Aluminum and Chemical Company, in an agreement with the United Steelworkers Union, had instituted a program to correct a racial imbalance among craft workers in a Gramercy, Louisiana plant. Blacks were to be given half the openings in a training program until the imbalance was corrected. The result of this program was that some blacks were accepted who had less seniority than several white applicants who were rejected. One of these white applicants, Brian Weber, claimed that his exclusion constituted illegal racial discrimination prohibited by the Civil Rights Act.

This time, the Court managed a more clear-cut decision with only two dissenters. The Civil Rights Act, the majority argued, did not prohibit voluntary private efforts to overcome racial imbalance. "It would be ironic indeed," Justice Brennan wrote for the majority, "if a law triggered by a nation's concern over centuries of racial injustice and intended to improve the lot of those who had been excluded from the American dream for so long, constituted the first legislative prohibition of all voluntary, private, race conscious efforts to abolish traditional patterns of racial segregation" (*Newsweek,* July 9, 1979:77). . . .

Under the Reagan Administration, affirmative action clearly had a low priority, but in the early years, there was little adoption of the rhetoric of opposition. . . . Internal differences within the Reagan Administration apparently prevented full backing of the efforts of Senator Orrin Hatch and others to ban all "color-conscious" public policies, including any which permit "quotas, timetables, goals, ratios, or numerical objectives on the basis of race, color, sex or national origin" (*In These Times,* September 28, 1983:8). . . .

In December, 1983, this internal dispute was temporarily resolved . . . when the Justice Department challenged the Detroit Police Plan. This plan, in effect since 1974, called for the promotion of white and black officers in equal numbers from separate lists until racial balance was achieved. Acknowledging that the Detroit plan was a "response to undeniable past discrimination against blacks," the Administration's brief to the Supreme Court argued that nevertheless all such race-conscious programs are illegal and unconstitutional. . . .

The affirmative action contest is not over. At this writing, many affirmative action programs continue to function, albeit some with considerable languor, and additional legal challenges are still wending their way through the courts. Unresolved internal battles on the issue continue within the Reagan Administration. But in the 20-year strip of events described above, there have been many dramatic shifts in the nature of public and official commentary on the issue.

In this paper, we analyze the language and symbolism on affirmative action as it has appeared in a systematic sample of mass media commentary. How were these events framed and interpreted? How has political discourse on affirmative action changed and evolved in this period, and what accounts for these changes? And, finally, to what extent can this analysis of public commentary on affirmative action lead us toward a more general theory of political discourse? To address these questions, we briefly present the working assumptions about discourse on which our analysis is based.

THE NATURE OF ISSUE CULTURES

Every policy issue is contested in a symbolic arena. Advocates of one or another persuasion attempt to give their own meaning to the issue and to events that may affect its outcome. Their weapons are metaphors, catch-phrases, and other condensing symbols that frame the issue in a particular fashion. This is not to deny the clashes of material interests that may underlie the struggle but simply to highlight another, complementary level of analysis.

Every issue has its own special language and phrases, its characteristic arguments, metaphors, and the like. When events occur that affect policy outcomes, commentary about them draws on culturally available idea elements and symbols. The ideas in this cultural catalogue are organized and clustered; we encounter them not as individual items but as packages. Frequently it is possible to suggest the package as a whole by the use of a prominent element—for example, a succinct catch-phrase such as "reverse discrimination." One can think of the complete *set* of packages that are available for talking about the issue as its "culture."

At the core of a package is its *frame*. A frame is a central organizing idea or story line that provides meaning to an unfolding strip of events, weaving a connection among them. The frame suggests what the controversy is about, the essence of the issue. . . .

A frame generally implies a policy direction or implicit answer to what should be done about the issue. Sometimes more than one concrete policy *position* is consistent with a single frame. Hence, it is more useful to think of a package as specifying a range of positions rather than a single one. Many policy debates take for granted a common frame; indeed, it is characteristic of frames that they are the least accessible part of a package, typically implied rather than articulated directly.

In public commentary, packages are usually displayed through *signature* elements that imply the core frame and invoke the whole with handy condensing symbols. By examining the relative frequency of these signature elements over time, we can trace the ebb and flow of different packages. Each package has a career. Some packages may be prominent in the beginning and gradually decline; others may rise to prominence out of nowhere; still others may languish throughout their careers. . . .

Affirmative Action Packages

Before we can explain the changing issue culture of affirmative action, we first must chart it. How do we identify the packages whose careers will concern us? If we were to rely on our mass media samples for this task, we would run the risk of missing packages that, although culturally available, have extremely low prominence in public discourse. But the absence of certain packages can be at least as significant as relative changes in the standing of major contenders.

We define a package as culturally available if there is any organization or advocacy network within the society that sponsors it. Our initial source, then, is not the mass media but more specialized publications by individual and organized sponsors, public and private. We take particular care to include the publications of challengers since it is here, we hypothesize, that we will be most likely to discover candidates with little or no media prominence.

For affirmative action, we examined the opinions of the Supreme Court justices in the Bakke and Weber cases as well as various speeches and statements by government officials. For members, we examined many of the 155 *amicus curiae* briefs filed in the Bakke Case by established organizations, making particular use of the one filed by the Anti-Defamation League of B'nai B'rith. We examined the writings of neoconservatives on affirmative action appearing in *Commentary, The Public Interest, Public Opinion,* and *Policy Review* plus important books such as Nathan Glazer's *Affirmative Discrimination* (1975). The major challengers on the affirmative action issue are on the right. The Ku Klux Klan, John Birch Society, and other like-minded groups offered their views in publications such as *The Crusader, National Vanguard,* and *American Opinion. . . .*

It is difficult to be fair in the statement of a package that is not one's own. An adequate statement should meet the fundamental ground rule that it is accepted as fair by an advocate. We attempt to satisfy this rule below by relying on the exact language of advocates and sponsors, quoting directly as much as possible.

1. Remedial Action. The core issue, in this package, is whether race-conscious programs should be used to redress the continuing effects of a history of racial discrimination. "In order to get beyond racism, we must first take into account race. There is no other way. And in order to treat some persons equally, we must treat them differently" (Justice Harry Blackmun, opinion in Bakke case, 1978). . . . Affirmative action is the present phase of a long struggle to achieve genuine equality of opportunity and to overcome chronic minority underrepresentation and institutional racism. . . .

"Reverse discrimination" (for this package) is simply the latest battle cry of a long tradition of historical resistance to efforts to bring blacks into the mainstream of American life. . . .

2. Delicate Balance.   The core issue is how to maintain a proper balance, helping old victims of discrimination without creating new ones. We need to strive for racial equality while at the same time upholding the right of individuals to be protected from discrimination on the basis of race. Providing opportunities to those who have been denied them is fine, but this should not become preferential treatment. . . .

It is fine to consider race as a factor in admission and hiring, but not as *the* factor. The difference between a quota and a goal is subtle but real. Quotas cross the line between striving to include more members of a minority group and actually excluding other individuals on the basis of race. . . .

3. No Preferential Treatment.   The consideration of race or ethnicity, however benignly motivated, is not the American way. Race-conscious policies inevitably lead to preferential treatment and unfair advantages for some at the expense of others. . . . The core concept of justice should be equal opportunity for individuals, not statistical parity for government-approved groups.

Between quotas and goals, there is a distinction without a difference. Goals are quotas in covert form, and institutions will inevitably be forced to treat them as quotas to avoid being charged with discrimination. . . . Public policy should be exercised without distinction of race or national origin.

Within this general package, there are four somewhat different subpackages whose careers are worth tracing separately. While sharing the general *no preferential treatment* frame, each has its characteristic emphasis.

3.1 Reverse discrimination.   The emphasis here is on how affirmative action programs exclude individuals on the grounds of race and, hence, violate the right to be judged as an individual. . . . When affirmative action comes to mean statistical requirements based on race or ethnicity, this abandons the "first principle of a liberal society, that the individual and the individual's interest and good and welfare are the test of a good society" (Glazer, 1975:220). . . .

3.2 Undeserving advantage.   The emphasis here shifts from who is excluded to the unfair advantage of those who benefit from affirmative action. Affirmative action gives minorities something they have not earned and do not deserve. Whatever happened in the past is over; this is now. Other groups had handicaps to overcome and did not get any special treatment. There should be no "special Americans"; the same rules should apply to all. . . .

One variation of this package emphasizes the hypocrisy and arrogance of affirmative action bureaucrats and the unholy alliance between the liberal establishment and black militants. The cost of affirmative action is carried by white, middle Americans, the silent majority. . . .

3.3 Blacks hurt.   The emphasis here is on the injury to the minorities who are the supposed beneficiary. Special programs reinforce common stereotypes since they imply that certain groups need special help to succeed in life. Affirmative action stigmatizes the minorities it is supposed to help. . . . Affirmative action deprives minorities of credit for their genuine achievements. . . .

3.4 Divide and conquer. The emphasis in this "populist" sub-package is on the centrality of class or economic disadvantage rather than race or ethnicity. Poor whites are a "minority" too. "Just because you're white, that doesn't mean that you've had it made in America the last 200 years" (Leonard Walentynowicz, spokesman for the Polish-American Congress, *U.S. News and World Report,* July 9, 1979:71). A mind is a terrible thing to waste whether it is a black mind or a white one. Affirmative action divides those who have a common interest. . . .

Note that we distinguish three main packages: *remedial action* (RA), *delicate balance* (DB), and *no preferential treatment* (NPT). Within the last main package, we further distinguish four variations or sub-packages: *reverse discrimination, undeserved advantage, blacks hurt,* and *divide and conquer. . . .*

MEASURING PACKAGE CAREERS

[W]e chose to sample five time periods, and four different types of mass media commentary. Our time sampling exploits the fact that events make the culture of an issue visible. They stimulate commentary in the mass media by sponsors and journalists. Indeed, with continuing stories such as affirmative action, journalists look for "pegs"—topical events that provide an opportunity to present broader, more timeless coverage and commentary. These pegs provide us with a way of identifying those time periods in which issue packages are especially likely to be displayed. . . .

By sampling commentary at the time of specific stimulus events, we end up with a small series of snapshots of the issue culture at irregular intervals, instead of the movie that we would prefer. Furthermore, the stimulus events are not all of the same type. While they never speak for themselves and can be interpreted in multiple ways, they affect the nature of the commentary and must be incorporated in our explanation of cultural change. In effect, our measurement strategy best reflects a model in which change occurs in sporadic bursts rather than gradually and incrementally.

Our earlier account of the affirmative action issue helps to identify three relevant strips of events: the controversy over the Philadelphia Plan, the 1972 Presidential campaign, and the continuing series of court decisions. We used these to identify events that produced sufficient commentary during a two-week period to allow us to measure the relative prominence of different packages. After considerable preliminary investigation, we were able to discover only five such points:

1. The introduction of the Philadelphia Plan (September 23 to September 29, 1969);
2. Presidential campaign and reevaluation of the Philadelphia Plan (September 4 to September 10 and December 19 to December 25, 1972);
3. The Supreme Court Bakke decision (June 27 to July 10, 1978);
4. The Supreme Court Weber decision (June 27 to July 10, 1979);
5. The Supreme Court Memphis Firefighters decision (June 12 to June 25, 1984).

Several factors influenced our choice of what media to sample. Although this paper does not address the issue, our longer term research aims at illuminating the connection between public commentary in the mass media and popular political thinking on the same set of issues. For this, we need a pure measure of media prominence, uncontaminated by any a priori assumptions about influence or impact. It would not do, for example, to look only at the most prestigious publications and news organizations, that is, those presumed to be influential.

At the same time, we wished our sample to transcend differences between media and to represent the universe of public commentary within each. To do this, we chose well-defined populations of commentary in different media, recording everything that met our criteria of relevance during the time period examined. By picking media that address the broadest and most inclusive audience possible, we buttress our claim to reflect the general issue culture. Four different media samples were used. These included: (1) television: the early evening national newscast of the three major networks; (2) newsmagazines: all opinion columns, special boxes, interviews, and cartoons from *Newsweek, Time Magazine,* and *U.S. News and World Report;* (3) editorial cartoons: all relevant cartoons from the newsmagazines and from a regionally stratified sample of 50 metropolitan daily newspapers; and (4) syndicated opinion columns: all relevant opinion columns from the sample of 50 metropolitan daily newspapers[2]. . . .

RESULTS

There are subtle qualitative changes as well as quantitative ones in public commentary, and we will present both kinds, constructing the general issue culture by first examining each medium separately.

Television

This medium, with its simultaneous words and images, is complicated by the fact that audio and video are not always in harmony. Words shape and define the visual images for the viewer but, if we are to allow for mixed messages, we must analyze audio and visual portions independently. The audio part of television can be treated in the same manner as a print medium. Here we find the signature elements by which we identify that one or another package has been displayed and how often. Figure 1 summarizes the television audio careers of the main packages for the three time points with sufficient data.

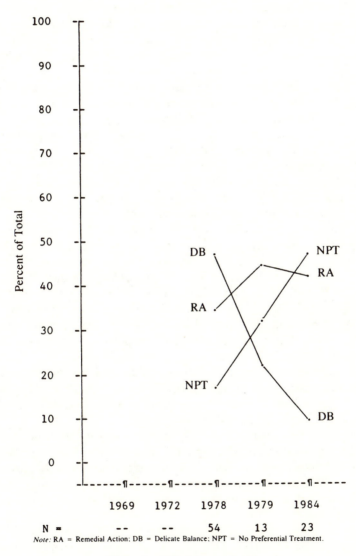

Figure 1.   Television packages.

Figure 1 shows a dramatic decline for *delicate balance* after Bakke. It was represented in 1979 mainly through one quote from Justice Brennan in which he emphasized the acceptability of the Kaiser plan because it was both temporary and did not exclude whites. By 1984, this package had declined still further. *Remedial action* enjoyed a better than 2-1 edge over *no preferential treatment* in 1978 but had fallen behind by 1984. . . .

Figure 1 groups and includes all forms of *no preferential treatment,* but perhaps the most interesting result here is the dominance of one particular sub-package, *reverse discrimination,* over other versions of the parent package. There were, in all, 24 displays of *no preferential treatment,* but only once (4 percent) was there a display of any alternative to the *reverse discrimination* variation. . . . After 1978, *reverse discrimination* had the field to itself.

As many have testified, a television news producer begins by asking what are the possible visuals for a story. Affirmative action clearly presented some problems since it did not lend itself readily to action footage. . . . But there were some recurrent visual images of relevance. Most symbols have multiple levels of meaning, and we do not mean to imply that a given image will be interpreted by all viewers in the same way. Our focus is on how images are encoded by the sender rather than decoded by the receiver. We ask, in effect, what images a camera crew and editor would be most likely to include if they were operating within a given, taken-for-granted organizing frame?

Initially, the story is visually linked to the civil rights movement. In 1978, all three networks showed footage of a demonstration by women and minorities in San Francisco, protesting the Bakke decision. There were shots of pickets and marchers, of signs and banners saying "Fight Racism, Overturn Bakke" and "*Abajo con Bakke*" (Down with Bakke). Heroes and heroines of the civil rights movement such as Julian Bond, Jesse Jackson, and Coretta Scott King were interviewed along with spokespersons for the NAACP, Urban League, Southern Christian Leadership Conference (SCLC), and the Congressional Black Caucus. . . .

This visual message was still used in 1979, although it was more muted. . . . By 1984, this message was still more muted if, indeed, it could be said to exist at all. No pickets or marchers appeared or any other symbol of social movement activity, nor any icons of the civil rights movement. . . .

An emphasis on affirmative action as a legacy of the civil rights movement and a continuation of the historical struggle for racial equality is an integral part of the *remedial action* package. Hence, we submit that these images provided it with once strong, but now fading, visual support. Visually, the story is about group conflict, especially between white workers and blacks. The viewer saw many hard hats. . . .

This group conflict message does not seem to us to support any particular package. All packages acknowledge conflict and compete in their interpretation of what it is about. But, as we will argue below, this particular dramatic form reinforces the tendency to reduce an issue to two opposing packages. . . .

In sum, there were visual messages that supported *remedial action,* but they have sharply diminished. *No preferential treatment,* at best, received some ambiguous support through possible images of discrimination as a vestige of the past. Finally, there were no consistent images that lent support to *delicate balance,* even in its 1978 heyday.

Newsmagazines

The sheer volume of words, compared to television, gave newsmagazines many more opportunities for displays of packages. Figure 2 shows some similarities and some differences with television prominence.

Delicate balance peaked in 1978 and fell off after that although less dramatically than for television. . . . By 1984, it was expressed particularly as a balance between making special efforts in recruiting combined with color-blindness in allocation—but it remained infrequent.

Remedial action and *no preferential treatment* were much more in balance than for television, although two discrepancies require some comment. In 1969, *no preferential treatment* appeared to be much more prominent than *remedial action,* but this difference was largely an artifact. During the time period sampled, *Newsweek* (October 6, 1969) ran a special feature on "Middle Americans." While this article did not focus on the Philadelphia Plan or affirmative action, it included many relevant quotes. Fully 75 percent of the *no preferential treatment* displays came in this one article and most of these featured the *undeserving advantage* variation. Aside from this one article, *remedial action* had more than twice as many displays as *no preferential treatment* in 1969.

In 1979, all three newsmagazines had more *remedial action* displays, and *Newsweek,* in particular, provided five displays of this package and none of any other. As with television, the edge had swung the other way by 1984.

Reverse discrimination clearly became the dominant variation of *no preferential treatment* after the early years. In 1969, newsmagazines quoted opponents of affirmative action who were overtly racist. . . . The package displayed is *undeserving advantage,* but the underlying message is the racism of affirmative action opponents, a *remedial action* theme.

By 1978 there had been a dramatic swing toward the *reverse discrimination* version (58 percent) with even *blacks hurt* receiving more prominence (8 percent) than *undeserving advantage* (4 percent) or *divide and conquer* (0 percent).[3] Compared to the early years, anti-affirmative action rhetoric in newsmagazines no longer evoked racist symbolism, either overtly or by innuendo.

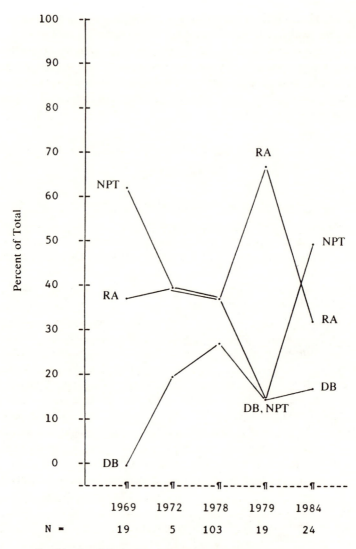

Note: RA = Remedial Action; DB = Delicate Balance; NPT = No Preferential Treatment.

Figure 2. Newsmagazine packages.

Cartoons

Remedial Action was the dominant package from the beginning. . . . The recurrent theme in the 1969 cartoons was the hypocrisy and covert racial discrimination of the opponents of affirmative action. . . . The cartoonists took for granted that blacks were excluded from the building trades and lampooned affirmative action opponents. . . .

Delicate balance enjoyed a brief peak at the time of Bakke, but the typical image here was really more one of *clumsy* balance. . . . The idea of balance or compromise was present in many, but that two *rights* were being balanced or traded-off was rarely very clear. The main point of many cartoons was simply the lack of clarity or confusion left by the decision, with no clear framing of affirmative action.

There were too few *no preferential treatment* cartoons to ask which version was most prominent. . . .

Opinion Columns[4]

Figure 3 shows the familiar peak for *delicate balance* at the time of Bakke and an especially sharp decline by the following year. *Remedial action* had only a slight edge over *no preferential treatment,* and this has completely disappeared by 1979.

In 1969, columnists displayed *no preferential treatment* by quoting union leaders or rank and file workers, but by 1972, *reverse discrimination* was displayed through interviews with articulate neo-conservatives. The few instances of *undeserving advantage* were by advocates of rival packages. . . .

By 1979, there was no contest left, and the *reverse discrimination* variation was part of *no preferential treatment* displays 93 percent of the time. In contrast, *undeserving advantage* appeared in only 27 percent of the columns that displayed the parent package.

Our findings in this study have utilized four different media samples with at least one time point missing for all except newsmagazines, but they form a coherent pattern. First, *remedial action* was once the dominant package but by 1984 had lost this initial advantage to *no preferential treatment.* Second, *delicate balance* had a brief flash of prominence at the time of the Bakke decision but faded and virtually disappeared after that. And finally, early opposition to affirmative action was frequently displayed as *undeserving advantage,* sometimes with overly racist symbolism. But more recent displays of *no preferential treatment* strongly favored *reverse discrimination* (65 percent) with a smattering of *blacks hurt* (4 percent)—two variations with anti-racist symbolism. The *divide and conquer* variation was very rare, occurring only 5 percent of the time that *no preferential treatment* was displayed and in only 2 percent of all displays.

TOWARD A THEORY OF PUBLIC DISCOURSE

The strong, though fading, media prominence of *remedial action* takes on added interest when we contrast this with public opinion polls from this period.

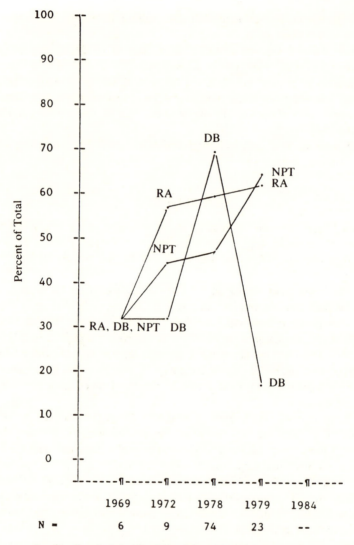

Note: RA = Remedial Action; DB = Delicate Balance; NPT = No Preferential Treatment.

Figure 3.   Columnist packages.

Lipset and Schneider (1978) review a substantial set of survey results, available at the time, to address the question of how the Bakke case would be decided at the bar of public opinion.

   The results are complex and cannot be summarized by any simple reference to a majority being for or against affirmative action. Responses swing widely, depending on how the question is framed. A 1977 Gallup poll posed a contrast between "preferential treatment" and selection on "ability, as determined by test scores" and found better than 80 percent chose the latter alternative (against 11 percent for "preferential treatment") (Lipset and Schneider, 1978). On the other hand, a *New York Times*/CBS News survey the same year found that more than two thirds of white respondents agreed (with 25 percent disagreeing) that: "The government should see to it that people who have been discriminated against in the past get a better break in the future" (Lipset and Schneider, 1978). Special training programs for victims of past discrimination gained substantial support as long as nothing in the question mentioned quotas, suggested anyone would be excluded thereby, or implied any costs for others.

Lipset and Schneider conclude (1978:41) that "Americans make a critical distinction in their minds between *compensating action* and *preferential treatment*." Since this distinction is anything but clear and demands an unrealistic level of political sophistication, it is certainly not literally true that most people carry it around in their heads. But it is a fair summary to say they respond as if such a distinction made sense. There is support for being race-conscious in providing opportunities, but not in allocating rewards.

The problem with this distinction is, as Lipset and Schneider acknowledge, that admission to college or professional school, or to special job training programs, is both an opportunity *and* a reward. Different packages focus attention on one or the other aspect. Public confusion and ambivalence are not surprising under the circumstances.

Delicate balance is probably the closest rendering of the complex array of poll results in the years before the Bakke decision. *Remedial action,* then, fared considerably better in media prominence than it did in public opinion. From its recent decline, it seems easier to argue that, for this issue at least, public discourse follows rather than leads popular thinking.

There is a second apparent discrepancy between public commentary on affirmative action and the way ordinary people think and talk about the issue. From preliminary evidence, we expect to be able to show that when the *no preferential treatment* package is displayed in conversations, it is generally the *undeserving advantage* or *divide and conquer* variations that are presented, and rarely *reverse discrimination*.

Why does *remedial action* do so well, then, in media commentary? And why, when *no preferential treatment* is displayed, is the *reverse discrimination* version of it so dominant? To answer these, we return to our more general model of public discourse.

It is useful to think of media prominence as the outcome of a value-added process. To illustrate this concept, consider the example of automobile production. Each stage—the mining of iron ore, smelting, tempering, shaping, assembling, painting, delivering, selling—adds its value to the final product. Furthermore, these stages may be thought of as determinants that, in combination, specify the final outcome. In this sense, they "explain" or account for whatever it is that is finally produced.

The production of issue cultures can be thought of as such a process. Our model postulates three broad classes of determinants that combine to produce particular package careers: sponsor activities, media practices, and cultural resonances.

Sponsor Activities

Much of the changing culture is the product of enterprise. Packages frequently have sponsors, interested in promoting their careers. Sponsorship is more than merely advocacy, involving such tangible activities as speech-making, advertising, article and pamphlet writing, and the filing of legal briefs to promote a preferred package.

These sponsors are usually organizations, employing professional specialists whose daily job involves interacting with journalists. Their job breeds sophistication about the news needs of the media and the norms and habits of working journalists. Indeed, many of these professionals began as journalists before moving to public relations jobs. . . .

The sponsor of a package is typically an agent of an organization, a person who is promoting some collective rather than personal agenda. Sponsors frequently draw on the resources of an organization to prepare materials in a form that lends itself to ready use. Condensing symbols are the journalist's stock and trade. Smart sources are well aware of the journalist's penchant for the apt one-liner and provide suitable quotes to suggest the frame they want.

Sponsor activities seem clearly to be adding important value to the careers of *remedial action* and *reverse discrimination*. From the outset, *remedial action* had official sponsorship. It was President Lyndon Johnson who used the signature metaphor of unshackling runners in a handicap race. Nixon Administration officials provided the rhetoric to justify the Philadelphia Plan, although they later changed their tune and provided no symbolic support from 1972 on.

Carter Administration officials again articulated this package and interpreted the ambiguous Bakke decision in its terms. Add to this official sponsorship, the sustained support of civil rights organizations that provided speeches, articles, interviews, and legal briefs on its behalf. The withdrawal of official sponsorship in the Reagan years and the diminution of private sponsorship activities on its behalf help to account for the decline observed in 1984.

In contrast, *delicate balance* has remained a package without sponsors. One might be tempted to say that the Supreme Court sponsored it in the Bakke decision, but only one Justice out of nine saw a meaningful distinction between the outlawed University of California, Davis admissions program and permissible ones such as Harvard's. More importantly, the Court does not normally engage in promotional activities to gain support for its decisions. Nor did any private organization take up this particular package. The result was that civil rights groups and Carter officials simply integrated the Bakke decision into *remedial action.* As the head of the EEOC put it, "We are not compelled to do anything differently from the way we've done things in the past, and we are not going to" (Eleanor Holmes Norton, *Time Magazine,* July 10, 1978:16).

Sponsor activities are also relevant to the rise of *no preferential treatment* and, especially, to the relative prominence of the *reverse discrimination* variation. This package and variation was actively promoted by a neoconservative network of interrelated journals (*The Public Interest, Commentary,* and *Public Opinion*), think-tanks (the American Enterprise Institute, the Hoover Institution) and organizations (the Coalition for a Democratic Majority). Advocates gave talks, wrote numerous articles and books, and presented it in legal briefs—in short, the full range of sponsor activities.

Other variations of *no preferential treatment* had either very modest or nonexistent sponsor activity. We were unable to identify any active sponsor for the *divide and conquer* variation. *Undeserving advantage* had some union sponsors in 1969 but, judging by the *amicus* briefs filed in the Bakke case, these sponsors had largely switched to *reverse discrimination* by 1978. This left active sponsorship in the hands of challengers such as the Ku Klux Klan and the John Birch Society.

Media Practices

That sponsors are active does not imply that journalists are passive. Journalists' working norms and practices add considerable value to the process. A number of students of news organizations have argued that journalists unconsciously give official packages the benefit of the doubt. In some cases, official assumptions are taken for granted; but even when they are challenged by sponsors of alternative packages, it is these competitors who carry the burden of proof. In a weaker form of this argument, journalists make official packages the starting point for discussing an issue. . . .

In addition to this tendency to fall into official definitions of an issue, journalists are especially likely to have routine relationships with official sponsors. Most reporting is the product of ongoing news routines. Sigal (1973) examined over a thousand stories from The *New York Times,* and The *Washington Post* and classified the channels by which the information reached the reporter. *Routine* channels included official proceedings, press releases, press conferences, and scheduled, official events. *Informal* channels included background briefings, leaks, nongovernmental proceedings, and reports from other news organizations. Finally, *enterprise* channels included interviews conducted at the reporter's initiative, spontaneous events which a reporter observed firsthand, independent research, and the reporter's own conclusions or analysis. He found that only about one quarter of the stories came from enterprise channels, while routine channels accounted for almost 60 percent.

Other media norms and practices favor certain rivals to the official package. First, there is a strong balance norm. . . . In news accounts, interpretation is generally provided through quotations, many of which contain the condensing symbols that concern us here. Balance is provided by quoting spokespersons with competing views. . . .

The balance norm is, of course, a vague one. The practices that it gives rise to tend to favor certain packages over others. There is a strong tendency, we hypothesize, to reduce controversy to two competing packages—an official one and (if there is one) the alternative sponsored by the most vested member of the polity. In many cases, this means that the chosen competitor to the official package will be one sponsored by the major opposition party, but when both major parties support the same package, established interest groups will do.

The balance norm, however, is rarely interpreted to include challenger packages, even when no other member alternative is available. Tuchman (1974:112) argues that balance in television news "means in practice that Republicans may rebut Democrats and vice-versa" but that "supposedly illegitimate challengers" are rarely offered the opportunity to criticize governmental statements.

The tendency to single out one alternative to juxtapose with the official package is built into media norms about proper story form. Epstein (1973:241) describes a memo that Reuven Frank sent to his staff at NBC News. "Every news story should, without any sacrifice of probity or responsibility, display the attributes of fiction, of drama". . . . One can meet the demands of form as well as the norm of balance by contrasting what officials say with one major protagonist. Hence, certain package sponsors become, for a given issue, the media-designated opposition.

Applying this model to affirmative action, we observe how media practices dovetail with sponsorship activities, amplifying *remedial action* and *reverse discrimination*. News routines point journalists to such official bodies as the EEOC, the Civil Rights Commission, and the Civil Rights Division of the Justice Department. Established civil rights groups are vested by the media with a legitimate interest, and their spokespersons were repeatedly sought for relevant comment. In most cases, they represented national organizations with Washington offices and were routinely available to journalists, many of whom knew them personally from earlier contact. Getting beyond sponsors of *remedial action* required a certain amount of journalistic enterprise.

Media practices, we argued above, call for one clear alternative to be contrasted with the official package. Journalists initially turned to union and ethnic group leaders, who tended to promote the *undeserving advantage* variation. But with the emergence of articulate neoconservatives, eager to be interviewed and willing to write op ed pieces themselves, there was no longer any journalistic need to turn to these earlier opponents to meet the balance norm.

Finally, media practices help us to account for the lack of staying power of the *delicate balance* package. It does not fit well with the dramatic form characteristic of American media. It provides no sharp contrast with the official position and blurs the element of conflict. This makes it an unappealing candidate for fulfilling the balance norm in spite of its popular appeal; furthermore, it requires special enterprise to locate spokespersons for it.

Cultural Resonances

Not all symbols are equally potent. Certain packages have a natural advantage because their ideas and language resonate with larger cultural themes. Resonances increase the appeal of a package; they make it appear natural and familiar. Those who respond to the larger cultural theme will find it easier to respond to a package with the same sonorities.

For affirmative action, two themes are of special interest—self-reliance and equality. The self-reliance theme concerns the relationship of the individual to collective life. The central issue for the theme is whether we are independent people who stand on our own feet or are dependent, sheep-like people who need and must rely on others. This theme has deep cultural roots and a host of symbols to invoke it—for example, the Horatio Alger hero.

Some affirmative action packages resonate with this theme while others do not. But it is possible for skillful sponsors to neutralize the effect of resonances by playing off the themes used by rival packages. There is no effective resonance, we hypothesize, when discordant packages play the same note.

Since cultural themes remain constant, it may be unclear how they can help us to explain changes in package careers. Resonances are the earliest stage in the value-added process. A package's resonances, we argue, facilitate the work of sponsors by tuning the ear of journalists to its symbolism. They add value to package careers by amplifying the impact of sponsor activities and media practices.

Media needs for conflict and dramatic form would be as well satisfied by singling out *undeserving advantage,* or *divide and conquer* as the official opposition to *remedial action.* Why does *reverse discrimination* do so much better? All are variations of no preferential treatment which resonate equally with larger themes of self-reliance and individualism. Furthermore, all tend to neutralize *remedial action's* resonance with equality and sympathy for the underdog. They directly compete over claims of victimization. . . .

The advantage for *reverse discrimination* is in its antiracist symbolism. As Lipset and Schneider (1978:41) observe, "Opponents who are well educated and of high status are shamefaced about trying to stop what appears to be a struggle for further equality, and much of the rest of the public basically feels the same way." *Undeserving advantage* has openly racist sponsors and little or no acknowledgment of past racial discrimination.

But *reverse discrimination* embraces "equality of opportunity" purporting to oppose only those programs in which "some are more equal than others." This appeal is strengthened even more by the addition of the blacks hurt variation. Far from being helped by affirmative action, it is claimed, the intended beneficiaries are stigmatized instead.

In sum, *reverse discrimination* had well-organized and articulate sponsors who actively promoted it. It met the news needs of working journalists for balance and dramatic form. Finally, it had strong positive resonances with larger cultural themes of self-reliance and individualism, and used antiracist and equality symbolism to neutralize the favorable resonances of its major competitor. No other alternative to remedial action had such a full array in its favor. . . .

ACKNOWLEDGMENT

The authors wish to acknowledge the support of the National Science Foundation, Grants SES-801642 and SES-8309343 in carrying out the research reported here.

NOTES

1.   Affirmative action for women involves similar issues but some important differences. We became convinced early in our research that the symbolism is sufficiently different that it requires separate analysis. Our attention here is confined to affirmative action for racial and ethnic minorities.

2.   Our sample was drawn from a list of the 200 largest circulation daily newspapers in the United States stratified into 5 regions: Northeast, Southeast, Southwest, Midwest, and West. We took equal numbers of papers from each region. The *New York Daily News, New York Times, Philadelphia Inquirer, Washington Post,* and *Boston Globe* were included among the ten from the East; the *Miami Herald, Atlanta Journal, Louisville Courier, Baltimore Sun,* and *New Orleans Times Picayune* were included from the Southeast; the *Chicago Tribune, Chicago Sun Times, Detroit News, Detroit Free Press, Kansas City Star, St. Louis Post Dispatch,* and *Milwaukee Journal* were included from the Midwest; the *Phoenix Republic, Houston Chronicle, Dallas Morning News,* and *Dallas Times Herald* were included from the Southwest; and the *Los Angeles Times, San Francisco Chronicle, Portland Oregonian, San Diego News Tribune, Denver Post* and *Seattle Times* were among those included from the West.

3.   The percentages for the variations add up to less than 100 because some displays of *no preferential treatment* present the generic package without invoking any particular subpackage.

4.   These are treated slightly differently in coding from the other samples. We treat each column as the unit rather than the individual utterances within it.

REFERENCES

Epstein, Edward Jay. 1973. News from Nowhere. New York: Random House.

Glazer, Nathan. 1975. Affirmative Discrimination. New York: Basic Books.

———. 1978. "Why Bakke won't end reverse discrimination: 2." Commentary 66:36–41.

Lipset, Seymour Martin and William Schneider. 1978. "The Bakke case: how would it be decided at the bar of public opinion?" Public Opinion March/April: 38–44.

Sigal, Leon V. 1973. Reporters and Officials. Lexington, MA: D.C. Heath.

Tuchman, Gaye. 1974. The TV Establishment: Programming for Power and Profit. Englewood Cliffs, NJ: Prentice-Hall.

26

Trends in Whites' Explanations of the Black–White Gap in Socioeconomic Status, 1977–1989

James R. Kluegel

Research on contemporary American race relations frequently notes a paradox. . . . On the one hand, white Americans increasingly endorse racial equality in principle. . . . On the other hand, whites show little or no support for policies and programs aimed at alleviating racial inequality. The paradox exists despite the fact that many whites acknowledge that such inequality results from a history of racial prejudice and discrimination.

To explain this paradox, some scholars argue for the persistence of widespread racial animosity on the part of whites. . . .

My previous work suggests that whites' beliefs about the causes of the economic gap between blacks and whites play an important role in sustaining this paradox (Kluegel 1985; Kluegel and Smith 1982, 1986). In the 1970s whites were strongly "individualistic" in their explanation of this gap. . . . A substantial majority believed that blacks' lower socioeconomic status was due all or in part to a lack of will or effort to achieve—what is often called "blaming the victim" (Ryan 1976). This contrasts with "structural" explanations that attribute the lack of achievement to historical or institutional causes.

Individualist and structuralist explanations of the black-white economic gap are not necessarily seen by whites as mutually exclusive. . . . Data for the 1970s (Apostle, Glock, Piazza, and Suelzle 1983; Kluegel 1985; Kluegel and Smith 1986) show some support for the coexistence within individuals of individualist and structuralist explanations for the black-white gap. . . .

I distinguish between two kinds of individualism—*traditional* and *motivational*. Traditional individualism involves a belief in the innate or genetic inferiority of blacks and is a component of common definitions of racial prejudice (Jones 1972; Pettigrew 1982). Motivational individualism involves attributing the

Excerpts reprinted with permission from the *American Sociological Review* 1990, vol. 55:512–589. Copyright © 1990 by the American Sociological Association.

black-white socioeconomic status gap to a lack of will or effort on the part of blacks without an accompanying belief in innate inferiority.

Motivational individualism may derive from a variety of sources. One may simply be an increasing sensitivity to race on the part of whites. Many white Americans now believe that since they are no longer racially prejudiced there are no barriers to opportunity for blacks. . . . This form of individualistic attribution may not reflect any particular animosity toward blacks, and in this sense is an "equal opportunity" interpretation (Sniderman and Hagen 1985), since whites apply the same interpretation to all "have-nots," regardless of race or other social characteristics. Opposition to policies to promote racial equality thus stems from the same source as opposition to all other policies for changing the economic status quo—a belief that structural factors are not the cause of economic inequality.

Motivational individualism may also stem from more recent sources of anti-black hostility, e.g., perceived economic or political threat (cf. Bobo 1983). Whites who feel threatened by programs to improve the economic status or political power of blacks may develop (or perhaps renew) antiblack sentiments that psychologically buttress opposition based in economic self-interest. The identification of blacks with contemporary social problems, e.g., "the welfare mess," has also been seen as a source of current hostility (Kinder and Sears 1981).

In this paper, I address three questions concerning contemporary whites' beliefs about the black-white gap in socioeconomic status. First, has the individualistic explanation of the sources of the black-white gap in socioeconomic status remained prevalent from the mid-1970s to recent times? . . . Second, what are the social and political characteristics of adherents to different beliefs about the causes of the black-white status gap? Third, how do whites' beliefs about the black-white economic gap influence support for policies to alleviate racial inequality? The influence of these beliefs relative to traditional prejudice is of particular interest. The paradox of contemporary race relations underscores that the *absence* of traditional prejudice is not sufficient to produce support for policies promoting racial economic equality. In addition to lacking prejudice, people must also attribute the black-white gap to structural causes before support for such policies follows (Apostle et al. 1983; Kluegel 1985; Sniderman and Hagen 1985).

DATA AND MEASURES

I employ data from five years of the General Social Survey (GSS): 1977, 1985, 1986, 1988, and 1989. . . . Analysis is limited to nonblack respondents, a total of 6,697 individuals (ages 18 and older) from all five years combined.[1] Because the questions used to form certain variables were not asked in all survey years, N's vary among analyses:[2]

The following question was asked in each of the five survey years: "On the average blacks have worse jobs, income, and housing than white people. Do you think these differences are . . .

A. Mainly due to *discrimination.*
B. Because most blacks have less *in-born ability* to learn.
C. Because most blacks don't have the *chance for education* that it takes to rise out of poverty.
D. Because most blacks just don't have the *motivation* or will power to pull themselves out of poverty."

Respondents were asked to respond "Yes" or "No" to each of the four subparts (A through D) of this question.

Two of the possible responses are individualist (B and D, inborn ability and motivation), and two are structuralist (A and C, discrimination and education). . . . The use of "mainly" and "most" in the wording of the four responses seems to imply that these answers should be mutually exclusive. However, many respondents answered as if the explanations were not competing alternatives.

A substantial fraction of the white public endorses *both* kinds of explanations. Nearly seven percent of whites choose both discrimination and inborn ability explanations; nearly one-fifth see the socioeconomic status gap as the product of discrimination and lack of motivation; 9.3 percent attribute the gap to lack of education and inborn ability differences; and roughly one-fifth see it as due to lack of education and lack of motivation. Clearly, structuralist and individualist explanations coexist among whites in the late 1980s as they did in the 1970s.

Prior research has employed categorical measures based on the joint configuration of endorsements of different causes, generally labeled "modes of explanation." The fact that a significant percentage of respondents view the black-white gap in both individualist and structuralist terms argues for constructing a similar measure from these data to characterize response patterns. Table 1 presents a seven-category measure of "modes of explanation" formed from the joint (four-way) distribution of the four explanations.

Four of these categories distinguish persons who employ purely individualist (Ability and Motivation) or purely structuralist explanations (Discrimination and Education). There are two mixed mode categories: the Mixed-Ability mode contains respondents who endorsed ability and one or both of the structuralist explanations. The Mixed-Motivation category includes those who endorsed motivation, deny the influence of inborn ability differences, and affirm the influence of one or both of the structuralist explanations. The final mode, "None," includes respondents who deny the influence of all four factors. . . .

Table 1. Response Patterns for "Modes of Explanation" for the Black-White
           Socioeconomic Gap

Modes of Explanation	Response Patterns			
	Individualist		Structuralist	
	Ability	Motivation	Discrimination	Education
Traditional Individualist				
Ability	Yes	Yes or No	No	No
Mixed-Ability	Yes	Yes or No	Yes (or)	Yes
Motivational Individualist				
Motivation	No	Yes	No	No
Mixed-Motivation	No	Yes	Yes (or)	Yes
Structuralist				
Discrimination	No	No	Yes	Yes or No
Education	No	No	No	Yes
None	No	No	No	No

TRENDS

[T]able 2 presents the distributions over all ages of whites' modes of explanation in 1977 and 1988–89. . . . The change in modes of explanation between
1979 and 1988–89 is limited to a decline in the percent of whites holding one of
the two inborn ability modes, and to an increase in the percent holding the
Education mode. The percentage distribution for the remaining four modes is
nearly the same in 1988–89 as it was in 1977. Individualistic modes prevail in
both periods—approximately 65 percent of white respondents in 1988–89 chose
an individualistic explanation (alone or in combination with a structural one),
compared to 68 percent in 1977. . . .

[E]ndorsement of individualistic modes predominate among the youngest cohorts. About 58 percent of whites under 40 years of age in 1988–89 endorse an
individualistic explanation of the black-white gap, alone or in combination with a
structural explanation. Only about 35 percent of these younger age whites adhere
to one of the two purely structural explanations.

[W]ith one exception, there has been little to no intra-individual change from
1977 to 1988–89 in adherence to modes of explanation among the four youngest
age cohorts. By 1988–89 these cohorts have essentially the same distributions for
five of the seven modes as they had when they were eleven years younger. The
one exception is found among cohorts ages 18–28 and 29–39 in 1977. Among
both of these cohorts, by 1988–89 the percent endorsing Education increased and
the percent endorsing Discrimination correspondingly decreased. Other things
equal, . . . whites' explanations of the black-white socioeconomic gap are likely
to remain predominantly individualistic in the near future. There will be a small

Table 2. Percentage Distribution by Mode of Explanation, 1977 and 1988–89

Mode of Explanation/ Prejudice Indicators	Year	All Ages
Mode of Explanation		
Traditional Individualist		
Ability	1977	12.6
	1988–89	10.1
Mixed-Ability	1977	14.4
	1988–89	10.7
Motivational Individualist		
Motivation	1977	20.7
	1988–89	20.4
Mixed-Motivation	1977	20.5
	1988–89	23.4
Structuralist		
Discrimination	1977	19.9
	1988–89	21.0
Education	1977	6.7
	1988–89	9.0
None	1977	5.2
	1988–89	5.5
Total	1977	100.0
	1988–89	100.0
N	1977	1209
	1988–89	1558

Note: The distributions by mode of explanation in 1977 and in 1988–89 differ significantly. $x = 19.00$. $p < .01$. The responses to indicators of traditional prejudice in 1977 and 1988–89 differ significantly. $p < .05$.

decline in the proportion of whites who make individualistic attributions, as the oldest cohorts are replaced, but the proportion should then level off at a high overall level.

SOCIODEMOGRAPHIC CHARACTERISTICS OF MODES OF EXPLANATION

[R]esearch based on data from the early to mid-70s . . . found that adherents of individualistic explanations of the black-white economic gap tend to be older, less well educated, more conservative politically, and more fundamentalist in their religious beliefs compared to supporters of more structural explanations. Our results support this pattern and show little change over time.

Persons endorsing the traditional individualist explanations are the most distinctive. They are about ten years older on average than all others, average less than twelve years of education, and have substantially lower incomes on average. They also tend to be more conservative than other groups—a higher percent rate themselves as politically conservative or believe the Bible is the word of God.

Persons who endorse the Education mode tend to fall at the other end of the socioeconomic spectrum from those who view ability as a cause of the socioeconomic gap. In both time periods, this group has the highest average income by a substantial margin, and the highest mean years of education. Supporters of the Discrimination explanation rank below Education adherents on mean years of education, but are clearly higher than the remaining groups. The mean family income for respondents in the Discrimination mode differs little from that for persons choosing either of the two motivation modes or the "None" category.

The Education group also is distinguished from the Discrimination group by its greater average political conservatism. They rate themselves more conservative and a higher percentage identify with the Republican party than those choosing Discrimination. They are less conservative than all other groups on the religion measure.

The general profile of the Education group suggests that this category may serve a particular function for privileged individuals who are also sensitive to racial inequality. . . . To see the economic gap as a result of the failings of educational institutions alone is consistent with the belief that economic institutions function fairly, permitting those who acquire the necessary educational credentials to occupy privileged positions if they work hard (see Jackman and Muha 1984).

Persons endorsing motivational individualism and "None" differ little from one another, and tend to occupy the middle ground in terms of age, socioeconomic status and conservatism. The Motivation group is an exception to this pattern only in its greater average self-rated political conservatism.

The data . . . show a remarkably stable profile of differences among adherents to different modes of explanation over roughly the past two decades.

SUPPORT FOR GOVERNMENTAL POLICIES

To complete the explanation of the paradox noted at the outset we need also to establish that whites' explanations of the black-white economic gap also shape their attitudes toward policies promoting racial equality. Questions concerning specific programs or policies to realize racial economic equality—affirmative action, job training, pre-school education, and so on—were not asked in the GSS. However, respondents to each of the five surveys were asked if the government was spending "too little," "about right," or "too much" on improving the conditions of blacks. In 1986, 1988, and 1989 only, respondents were also asked about

Table 3. Attitudes toward Government Spending and Government Assistance to Help Blacks by Mode of Explanation for the Black-White Socioeconomic Gap.

Mode of Explanation	Government Spending for Blacks			Government Aid to Black Standard of Living		
	Too Much	Too Little	N	Opposes (1 or 2)	Favors (4 or 5)	N
Traditional Individualist						
Ability	51.5	8.6	509	82.3	4.2	193
Mixed-Ability	26.6	21.1	593	58.8	13.3	218
Motivational Individualist						
Motivation	47.5	8.6	986	81.1	4.1	396
Mixed-Motivation	18.8	29.7	1,056	55.9	12.3	465
Structuralist						
Discrimination	7.0	47.5	992	30.2	33.2	370
Education	14.1	26.9	391	52.4	15.5	168
None	28.2	14.1	262	63.7	5.3	110

Note: Percentage differences for these two variables by Mode of Explanation are statistically significant at $p<.01$.

the obligation of the government to help improve the standard of living of blacks.[3] Thus, I can examine the association between whites' explanations for the black-white socioeconomic gap and support for government assistance *in general.*

Table 3 gives the distribution of whites' attitudes toward government spending to improve conditions for blacks and towards government assistance to improve the standard of living of blacks by modes of explanation for the black-white economic gap (based on pooled data from the five and three years available respectively for each measure of support for government assistance). The explanatory modes have the same ordering of support for both items. The Ability and Motivation modes have the highest levels of opposition to government assistance—nearly half of the whites in these modes believe that government spending to improve conditions for blacks is too high, and roughly 80 percent respond that they favor little or no government assistance to improve the standard of living of blacks. Whites in the two mixed explanatory modes and the Education mode have similar profiles of support for government assistance—they are substantially less hostile to government support than respondents in the Ability and Motivation modes, but they are not strong supporters. Whites in the "None" mode are somewhat more opposed to government assistance to blacks than those in either of the two mixed modes or Education, but they do not share the apparent hostility toward such policies as those in the Ability or Motivation modes. Finally, whites in the Discrimination mode have singularly high levels of support for government assistance. Nearly one-third are strong supporters (have scores of

4 or 5) and another third of respondents from this category favor at least some government assistance (have a score of 3) to help improve the standard of living for blacks. Nearly one-half believe that the government is spending too little to improve conditions for blacks.

Two characteristics of the distribution of support for government assistance by mode of explanation are especially noteworthy. First, though virtually all whites in the Ability mode also endorse lack of motivation as a cause of the black-white gap, and though no whites in the Motivation mode chose ability as a cause, these two groups are equally opposed to government assistance. Seeing the black-white economic gap in purely individualistic terms leads to categorical opposition to government assistance to blacks, regardless of whether it involves a belief in blacks' innate inferiority.

We can only speculate about why whites in the Education mode of explanation are no more supportive of government assistance than those in the mixed modes. Their lack of support for government assistance may stem from a view that *federal government* assistance is not needed . . . and that the solution to an education-based problem lies at the state or local level. Alternatively, their view that the black-white socioeconomic gap is the product of education but not discrimination may serve psychologically to exempt them from feeling that they are insensitive to race and from feeling any obligation to support structural solutions.

[V]ery little of the differences among modes in policy attitudes is a spurious result of correlations with traditional prejudice or sociodemographic variables. . . . How whites explain the black-white socioeconomic gap has important effects on their support for government spending and their support for government intervention to promote racial economic equality over and above the effects of prejudice and self-interest as represented in the sociodemographic variables.

DISCUSSION

Two major conclusions are supported: First, an individualistic perception of the causes of the black-white socioeconomic gap remains prevalent. Second, whites' explanations of the gap influence their attitudes toward government assistance to blacks aimed at realizing economic equality. These conclusions help explain the paradox of contemporary racial beliefs in which a belief in racial equality coexists with lack of support for policies to alleviate racial inequities.

The only substantial change between 1977 and the late 1980s in how whites view the black-white socioeconomic gap is a decline in the attribution of that gap to inborn ability differences. This decline parallels the trend of declining traditional prejudice, and correspondingly, one would expect that the proportion of whites who are traditional individualists will continue to lessen in coming years. The abatement of perhaps the most invidious explanation for the black-white status gap has not been accompanied by any noteworthy increase in attributions that favor efforts to provide equal opportunity for black Americans.

Of the two purely structuralist modes of explanation, only the tendency to attribute the gap to education has increased since 1977. Since adherents to this mode tend to have high socioeconomic status, and since the increase in adherence is principally due to intra-individual change among younger whites, the increased attribution to education may be a consequence of growing economic conservatism during recent times. In particular, this increase may result from the greater race sensitivity on the part of whites reared in the "post-traditional-prejudice era" (perhaps dating from the late 1950's onward) coupled with an increasing unwillingness to see the current black-white economic gap as the product of a flawed economic system. Attributing the racial status gap to lack of education alone allows privileged whites to avoid blame for the gap while endorsing an explanation commonly viewed as unprejudiced.

Though whites in the Education mode express the lowest level of traditional racial prejudice, they express no more support for policies promoting economic equality than whites in the mixed modes who express substantially higher prejudice. In short, whites in the Education mode fit one of the profiles of "victim-blamers" quite well (Ryan 1976).

Examining these trends by age suggests that if the forces currently shaping whites' explanations of the black-white economic gap continue, whites' beliefs will have much the same character in coming years as they have today. With the replacement of the oldest age cohorts in coming decades, the distribution of adherence to modes of explanation among whites will slowly approach a stable division of the population into roughly equal thirds in the purely individualistic, mixed, and purely structuralist categories.

This research shows that many people who otherwise lack traditional prejudice still hold individualistic explanations of the black-white economic gap. Thus, a decline in traditional prejudice need not bring an increase in structural attributions. Since explanations for the black-white gap strongly shape support for governmental assistance independent of traditional prejudice and socio-demographic factors, it follows that for many whites opposition to policies for improving the economic status of blacks stems solely from their interpretation of this gap.

Whites who attribute the black-white economic gap solely to discrimination stand out from all others in their support for policies promoting racial economic equality. Viewing the black-white gap as the result of any individualistic factor—ability or motivation—is sufficient to tip the scale toward opposition to such policies. . . .

ACKNOWLEDGMENTS

I would like to thank Lawrence Bobo and the anonymous reviewers of ASR for helpful comments, criticisms and suggestions concerning earlier versions of this paper. Responsibility for all conclusions, of course, rests solely with the author.

NOTES

1.   For convenience I refer to nonblacks as whites throughout, since groups other than whites make up only a small percentage of nonblacks and they are too few to support separate analysis.

2.   The GSS is the best source on nationally representative data for assessing trends in whites' explanations of the black-white economic gap. . . . The GSS is one of the few nationally representative surveys that simultaneously measures racial prejudice, explanations of the black-white economic gap, and attitudes toward government assistance for blacks.

3.   Respondents were asked: "Some people think that blacks have been discriminated against for so long that the government has a special obligation to help improve their living standards. Others believe that the government should not be giving special treatment to blacks. . . . Where would you place yourself on this scale or haven't you made up your mind on this?" (5-point scale, from (1) "I strongly agree that government is obligated to help blacks" to (3) "I agree with both answers" to (5) "I strongly agree that government shouldn't give special treatment.") For this analysis, responses were coded so that a high scored indicates greater support for government assistance.

REFERENCES

Apostle, Richard A., Charles Y. Glock, Thomas Piazza, and Marijean Suelzle. 1983. *The Anatomy of Racial Attitudes*. Berkeley, California: University of California Press.

Bobo, Lawrence. 1983. "White Opposition to Busing: Symbolic Racism or Realistic Group Conflict?" *Journal of Personality and Social Psychology* 45:1196–1210.

Jackman, Mary R. and Michael J. Muha. 1984. "Education and Intergroup Attitudes: Moral Enlightenment, Superficial Democratic Commitment, or Ideological Refinement." *American Sociological Review* 49:751–69.

Jones, James M. 1972. *Prejudice and Racism*. Reading, Massachusetts: Addison-Wesley.

Kinder, Donald R. and David O. Sears. 1981. "Prejudice and Politics: Symbolic Racism Versus Racial Threats to the Good Life." *Journal of Personality and Social Psychology* 40:414–31.

Kluegel, James R. 1985. "'If There Isn't a Problem, You Don't Need a Solution': The Bases of Contemporary Affirmative Action Attitudes." *American Behavioral Scientist* 28:761–84.

Kluegel, James R. and Eliot R. Smith. 1982. "Whites' Beliefs About Blacks' Opportunity." *American Sociological Review* 47:518–32.

Kluegel, James R. and Eliot R. Smith. 1986. *Beliefs About Inequality: Americans' Views of What Is and What Ought to Be.* Hawthorne, New York: Aldine de Gruyter.

Pettigrew, Thomas F. 1982. "Prejudice." Pp. 1–30 in *Dimensions of Ethnicity,* edited by Stephan Thernstrom, Ann Orlov, and Oscar Handlin. Cambridge, Massachusetts: Belknap Press.

Ryan, William. 1976. *Blaming the Victim.* New York: Vintage.

Sniderman, Paul M. and Michael Gray Hagen. 1985. *Race and Inequality: A Study in American Values.* Chatham, New Jersey: Chatham House.

27

Affirmative Action: Fair Shakers and Social Engineers

Morris B. Abram

I. INTRODUCTION

The civil rights movement has turned away from its original principled campaign
for equal justice under law to engage in an open contest for social and economic
benefits conferred on the basis of race or other classifications previously thought
to be invidious. This essay, written from my perspective as an early participant in
the civil rights cause, explains my view that this departure, however desirable to
some in the short run, violates the basic principles that hold together our heterogeneous society and secure our civil peace. The civil rights movement, by my
lights, should turn its attention back to first principles—the zealous regard for
equal opportunity and the promotion of color-blind law and social policy—and
away from color-conscious remedies that abandon principle and lead us further
from a society free of the bane of racial discrimination.

Between the mid-1940s and the mid-1960s, the civil rights movement grew
into a broad coalition united by moral principle and a shared vision of an American society without racial discrimination but with equal opportunity for all. The
overarching political goal of this movement was equality—an equality to be
reached by the elimination of discriminatory barriers that denied the individual
the opportunity to exercise his franchise effectively, to compete for housing and
employment, and to use public accommodations. Government, civil rights advocates agreed, was responsible for ensuring that each individual had access to all
spheres of public activity—social, economic, and political—regardless of race,
sex, or ethnic origin.[1] Because this original vision of the civil rights movement
was concerned with equality of *opportunity* and a fair shake for individuals, I will
label its advocates "fair shakers."[2]

The fair shakers were soon challenged, however, by a radically different vision

Excerpts reprinted with permission from the *Harvard Law Review* 99 (1986):1312–1326. Copyright
© 1986.

of civil rights. During the late 1960s, the civil rights community began to splinter and, certainly by the mid-1970s, much of its leadership had become preoccupied with equality of *results*. Those who focused on this type of equality attributed socioeconomic or political inequalities between minorities and whites, men and women, the disabled and the unimpaired, to discrimination—past and present. Absent discrimination, these result-oriented leaders claimed, all groups would be represented in the institutions and occupations of society roughly in proportion to their representation in the population. These leaders continue to believe that the only way to measure equality is in terms of such representation, and that it is the government's role to bring about proportional representation in short order. Because this new vision of the civil rights movement requires the attainment of predetermined ends, rather than the abolition of barriers to fair participation, I will call its adherents "social engineers."

My early experience in the civil rights movement now leads me to oppose the social engineers. . . . The role of government in securing racial justice, I came to believe, is best limited to vigilant concern with equal opportunity, procedural regularity, and fair treatment of the individual. I have not departed from my original fair shake view, but continue to believe that it is in keeping with our legal and political traditions; that the social engineers' advocacy of result-oriented and color-coded group rights is inconsistent with these traditions and violative of other democratic ideals and principles; and that adherence to the fair shake model is most likely to promote true racial equality and enlightened debate over our conceptions of social justice.

II. FAIR SHAKERS AND SOCIAL ENGINEERS

The fair shake principle is part of a long and respected American legal tradition. It was the force underlying the antislavery amendments to the Constitution, the series of laws passed in the wake of the Civil War that afforded protection of contract and property rights, and the guarantees of equality of opportunity in voting, employment, use of public accommodations, and housing in the mid-1960s.

Although the fair shake principle shaped our civil rights laws, it has, from an early date, been challenged by various forms of social engineering. In 1871, for instance, a black friend wrote to former slave Frederick Douglass, then the most prominent black leader in the country, arguing that blacks deserved government appointments based on their numbers. Douglass replied that "equality of numbers has nothing to do with equality of attainments" (Foner, 1955, p. 281). In a stunning rebuke to the concept of proportional representation on the basis of race, Douglass wrote:

The mulattoes, on a solid census basis, ought to have so many offices, the blacks so many, and the whites so many, the Germans so many, the Irish so many, and other classes and nationalities should have offices according to their respective numbers. . . . Upon your statistical principle, the colored people of the United States ought, therefore, not only to hold one-eighth of all the offices in the country, but they should own one-eighth of all the property, and pay one-eighth of all the taxes of the country. Equal in numbers, they should, of course, be equal in everything else. They should constitute one-eighth of the poets, statesmen, scholars, authors, and philosophers of the country (Foner, 1955, p. 280).

Because groups—black, white, Hispanic, male, and female—do not necessarily have the same distribution of, among other characteristics, skills, interest, motivation, and age, a fair shake system may not produce proportional representation across occupations and professions, and certainly not at any given time. This uneven distribution, however, is not necessarily the result of discrimination.[3] Thomas Sowell has shown through comparative studies of ethnic group performance that discrimination alone cannot explain these ethnic groups' varying levels of achievement. Groups such as the Japanese, Chinese, and West Indian blacks have fared very well in American society despite racial bias against these groups.

Moreover, although it is true that concern for qualifications has sometimes masked a purposeful intent to exclude individuals on the basis of race or other invidious criteria, the mere fact that some meritocratic devices have the result of excluding proportionally higher numbers of minorities does not in itself demonstrate that minorities are not getting a fair shake. And the fair shake principle, unlike the norm of proportional representation, is perfectly consistent with our meritocratic view of the relevant differences between individuals—a view through which our society rewards the individual for attainment and avoids patronage and spoils systems.

Yet many of those who opposed the use of social engineering to perpetuate segregation now depart from the fair shake model and actively advocate social engineering to achieve proportional representation. They now insist on a presumption that unequal results are due to intentional discrimination.[4]

[T]oday's social engineers, dissatisfied with the results of the fair shake model, invoke a new conception of justice. In their view, justice is less an individual's claim to equality before the law—an idea at the heart of our liberal tradition—than a particular distribution of social, economic, and political power among groups. This new conception of justice necessarily repudiates the ideal of the rule of law—a law that "would treat people equally, but . . . not seek to make them equal."[5] And to achieve this newly announced goal of group justice, the social engineers proclaim that it is necessary to abandon color-blindness (Fiss 1976, pp. 107, 129–156).

These social engineers call their plan for allocating social goods by race "affirmative action." But the term as they use it departs radically from the original intent of affirmative action—to give minorities a fair shake. Executive Order 11,246, for example, far from calling the merit system into question, attempted only to eliminate the institutional and informational barriers that stand in the way of the minority individual's ability to compete *equally* with others for jobs and promotions. Vice President Hubert H. Humphrey, who chaired the committee that drafted that order, was a committed fair shaker whose own Equal Employment Opportunity bill of 1964 described affirmative action and at the same time insisted on color-blind equal opportunity.

I believe that the social engineers' result-oriented conception of racial justice is both destructive of true racial equality and potentially harmful to society. Although the social engineers concede that their color-conscious and group-based approach may produce some injustice, they argue that extreme measures are at least temporarily necessary to eliminate discrimination. In my view, however, even the laudable goal of ending racial discrimination cannot justify the adoption of means incompatible with other ends of justice.

The social engineers' approach to affirmative action is without support in our Constitution and civil rights laws. . . . As Justice Douglas has observed:

> The Equal Protection Clause commands the elimination of racial barriers, not their creation in order to satisfy our theory as to how society ought to be organized . . . .
> So far as race is concerned, *any* state-sponsored preference to one race over another . . . is in my view "invidious" and violative of the Equal Protection Clause. (DeFunis v Odegaard, 416 U.S. 312, 342, 1972, Emphasis added)

Without doing violence to the principles of equality before the law and neutral decisionmaking, we simply cannot interpret our laws to support both color-blindness for some citizens and color-consciousness for others.

One possible, more practical, consequence of this social engineering is the decline of occupational and professional standards. For example, in 1981, the federal civil service exam for over 100 entry-level positions was suspended, because minorities were not passing it in sufficient proportions.[6] In order to make the minority passing rate on the written examination for Foreign Service Officers "relatively similar" to that for nonminorities, the Foreign Service Officers Examination Board simply adds 500 minority "near-passers" to the pool of candidates who actually passed and declares the whole group—"near-passers" and passers alike—qualified to go on to the next stage[7]. . . . The social engineers thus defy the existing distribution of skills and abilities—whether naturally present or socially developed—in order to achieve their objective.

Indeed, the social engineers' vision of affirmative action is, for all intents and purposes, a quota system. Though they usually repudiate the idea of "quotas" and insist on characterizing their preferred remedies as "goals and timetables," the effects of numerous enforcement actions and lawsuits brought by government agencies and civil rights groups belie the social engineers' characterization. . . .

Several civil rights policymakers have noted with dismay that, despite their good intentions, affirmative action has degenerated into a spoils system among competing racial and ethnic groups. . . .

The social engineers' approach also fails to confront the problem of *who decides* what groups are sufficiently disadvantaged to deserve special treatment. They offer no mechanism for neutral decisionmaking on this critical issue. America is a highly pluralistic and heterogeneous society that has had to expand continuously in order to accommodate different elements; many discrete groups have suffered discrimination here. Consequently, a major problem with addressing discrimination through race-conscious laws is the balancing of historical experiences. How and by whom shall the varying grievances of different groups be weighed and judged in order to decide what varying levels of compensation society should pay?

In the absence of any neutral decisionmaking mechanisms, the attempt to end discrimination through color-conscious remedies must inevitably degenerate into a crude political struggle between groups seeking favored status. Once we have abandoned the principles of fair procedure, equal opportunity, and individual rights in favor of the advancement of a particular group, we have opened wide the door to future abuses of all kinds. Bayard Rustin recently commented upon the charge of discriminatory results that blacks and Hispanics leveled at the New York City police sergeant's exam, an exam members of these groups had helped to devise:[8]

> This approach [of setting aside test scores simply because of disproportionate impact] says to blacks and Hispanics that you don't necessarily have to qualify to be included. Furthermore, if you have enough political pressure in New York City to get away with that, then what's going to happen 20 years from now in California when it is predominantly Hispanic? And then the Hispanics will say "we're very sorry but not enough Hispanics passed the test" so blacks and whites who passed have to go in another line now and wait to get called. Or what's going to happen when women, who far outnumber men in our society, begin to play this game.[9]

Further, the social engineers invite us to view people as statistics; they submerge personality, effort, and character under the blanket concerns of race, sex and ethnicity. In an already divided society, this approach results in a new set of classifications: those who got where they are by merit; those who were leveraged into position by race or gender preferences; those who do not owe their position to such engineering but are viewed as the recipients of preferences by others (and themselves) and are thus stigmatized; and finally those who originally earned their position without any favoritism but were displaced solely because of race, gender or ethnicity. In such a divided system, no one really wins.

Indeed, the social engineers' approach exacerbates divisions within society by implicitly assuming that white males—even the millions who have never finished high school—are the undeserving beneficiaries of special privileges at the expense of all others. This simplistic division of our complex society into white males and their victims was the hallmark of the United States Commission on Civil Rights when it was dominated by the social engineers. . . .

Perhaps the most ironic weakness of the social engineers' redistributive approach is that it fails to help those particular members of disadvantaged groups who are most in need of assistance. Blanket orders which blindly benefit groups defined by race, sex or ethnicity—especially when many members of such groups are prospering nicely—are an extremely crude and costly solution for social problems. While civil rights lobbyists frequently bolster their charge of continuing discrimination by pointing to the existence of the black underclass, many of their proposals can hardly have the effect of helping the millions of ghetto teenagers who lack the most basic entry level skills. . . .

III. TOWARD THE FUTURE

The civil rights movement has scored resounding victories and worked remarkable changes in American society through its commitment to principles of equal opportunity, fair treatment of the individual, and color-blindness. As Bayard Rustin remarked in a recent interview, the period between 1954 and 1968:

> was, perhaps, the most revolutionary period of any country in the world with regard to the achievement of justice for any minority group. In fact, in most of the world during that period, conditions worsened for many minorities. Racism was increasing in England. In the newly independent African countries, tribal hostilities were increasing. Ours was a most unique situation.[10]

The movement, to continue its record of success in uniting the American people behind the moral and legal principles at the heart of our democratic and liberal traditions, should redirect its energies toward eliminating racial discrimination and toward ensuring that *all* Americans, without regard to race, sex or ethnicity, are fairly equipped to compete for individual advancement in every arena.

We have the tools to achieve these goals. We have, for example, strict laws against intentional discrimination. The courts have broad remedial powers to eliminate such discrimination, including the authority to jail recalcitrant violators of the civil rights laws for contempt of court orders. The civil rights movement should press for the use of the courts' powers in a manner consistent with the fair shake principle.

Similarly, despite the mixed record of recent years, we as a society are capable of devising creative social and economic initiatives to aid the truly needy. We can target job training and remedial education programs to all individuals who need them, without regard to race, sex, or ethnicity. In this way we can address past inequities without abandoning the fair shake principle, and we can avoid perpetuating social divisions.

Although the mechanisms for change in our political system are far from perfect, this system has proven itself capable of correcting abuses and injustices with a minimum of violence and without curtailing freedom. The civil rights movement triumphed in this system because it united men and women in a just and principled cause and appealed to conservatives and liberals alike. It was, after all, a Republican President who appointed many of the judges who broke the back of white supremacy in the South.[11] This broad-based support finally created an atmosphere in which all Americans (some more willingly than others, of course) acknowledged the inevitable justice of equality of opportunity.

My participation in the civil rights struggle has shaped my deepest moral and political beliefs. Because the cause of civil rights has meant so much to me, I now feel compelled to register my strong dissent, unpopular though it may be, from what I see as the current direction of the movement. The mantle has now passed to those who believe in enforced equality of results, guaranteed social and economic rights for particular groups, and redistribution of income and jobs. Certainly we can debate ideas such as these in our free society. I ask only that the social engineers be open and candid about their vision for America, and desist from camouflaging their redistributive goals behind the label of "civil rights." Civil rights belong to all Americans; they are too important to be captured by a set of special interest groups.

ACKNOWLEDGMENTS

The authors of these Commentaries have not seen drafts of each other's pieces. The Commentary format is not meant to be a debate, but rather is meant to present different perspectives on current issues of public importance.

Mr. Abram gratefully acknowledges the assistance of Debra Livingston.

NOTES

1. Although in this essay I will speak primarily of racial classifications, my views on the use of invidious distinctions as a basis for social policy also extend to gender and ethnic classifications.

2. I am indebted to Professor James Blumstein of the Vanderbilt University School of Law for suggesting this term.

3. Social engineers ignore that it simply takes time for various groups to make their way fully into all sectors of society. For example, as recently as the mid-1960s, few Jews could be found in this country's executive suites. Discrimination is only part of the

explanation. Beginning with different kinds of abilities and skills, all the major ethnic groups staked out areas of advancement for themselves (the Italians in construction, for example, the Irish on the police force and in local politics, Jews in law and medicine). Members of such groups may require several generations to position themselves for more diverse and powerful roles.

4. For example, if test results show minority candidates passing at less than 80 percent of the nonminority passing rate, then the test is presumed discriminatory. *See* Uniform Guidelines on Employee Selection Procedures (1978), 29 C.F.R. § 1607.3 (1984) ("[p]rocedure having adverse impact constitutes discrimination unless justified"); id. § 1607.4 (1984) ("A selection ratio for any race . . . which is less than four-fifths of the rate for the group with the highest rate will generally be regarded . . . as evidence of adverse impact . . . ."). These provisions apply to persons subject to title VII of the Civil Rights Act of 1964, 42 U.S.C. § 2000e-2 (1982); Executive Order 11,246, 3 C.F.R. 339 (1964–65), *reprinted in* 42 U.S.C. § 2000e app. at 28–31 (1982) (order of President Johnson calling for "affirmative action"), or other equal employment opportunity requirements of federal law. See 29 C.F.R. § 1607.2(D) 1985).

5. D. Bell, *Liberalism in the Postindustrial Society,* in The Winding Passage: Essays and Sociological Journeys 1960–1980, at 228, 230–231 (1980) (discussing Hayek).

6. *See* Luevano v. Campbell, 93 F.R.D. 68, 80–81 (D.D.C. 1981).

7. Telephone interview with Frontis B. Wiggins, Executive Director, Board of Examiners for the Foreign Service, U.S. Dep't of State (Oct. 10, 1985).

8. New York City has chosen not to base its hiring solely on the test, but to accept quotas, promoting some 200 candidates who failed the examination. *See N.Y. Times,* Nov. 19, 1985, at B3, col. 1.

9. *An Interview with Bayard Rustin,* New Perspectives, Winter 1985, at 27, 31.

10. *An Interview with Bayard Rustin, supra* note at 27.

11. See generally J. Bass, *Unlikely Heroes* (1981) (discussing President Eisenhower's appointments to the Court of Appeals for the Fifth Circuit).

REFERENCES

Fiss, Owen. 1976. "Groups and the Equal Protection Clause." *Philosophy & Public Affairs* 5:107–77.

Foner, Philip S. 1955. *The Life and Writings of Frederick Douglass.* New York: International publishers.

28

Persuasion and Distrust: A Comment on the Affirmative Action Debate

Randall Kennedy

The controversy over affirmative action[1] constitutes the most salient current battlefront in the ongoing conflict over the status of the Negro in American life. No domestic struggle has been more protracted or more riddled with ironic complication. One frequently noted irony is that the affirmative action controversy has contributed significantly to splintering the coalition principally responsible for the Civil Rights Revolution. That coalition was comprised of a broad array of groups—liberal Democrats, moderate Republicans, the national organizations of the black and Jewish communities, organized labor and others—that succeeded in invalidating de jure segregation and passing far-reaching legislation in support of the rights of blacks, including the Civil Rights Act of 1964 and the Voting Rights Act of 1965.

For over a decade this coalition has been riven by bitter disagreement over the means by which American society should attempt to overcome its racist past. Opponents of affirmative action maintain that commitment to a nonracist social environment requires strict color-blindness in decisionmaking as both a strategy and a goal. In their view, "one gets beyond racism by getting beyond it now: by a complete, resolute, and credible commitment *never* to tolerate in one's own life—or in the life or practices of one's government—the differential treatment of other human beings by race" (Van Alstyne 1979, p. 809). Proponents of affirmative action insist that only *malign* racial distinctions should be prohibited; they favor *benign* distinctions that favor blacks. Their view is that "[i]n order to get beyond racism, we must first take race into account" and that "in order to treat some persons equally, we must treat them differently."[2]

Part I of this Commentary considers aspects of two principal objections to affirmative action: that it harms rather than helps Negroes in American society, and that it violates the Constitution. . . . I conclude that affirmative action should

Excerpts reprinted with permission from the *Harvard Law Review* 99 (1986):1327–1346. Copyright © 1986.

generally be retained as a tool of public policy because, on balance, it is useful in overcoming entrenched racial hierarchy.

Part II explores an issue widely ignored by academic commentators: whether covert motivations play a role in the political, judicial, and intellectual reaction against affirmative action. . . . I argue that division within the civil rights coalition is not the *only* conflict permeating the affirmative action controversy. Also involved is a much older conflict involving sectors of our society that have never authentically repudiated the "old style religion" of white supremacy. . . .

I.   THE EFFICACY AND LAWFULNESS OF AFFIRMATIVE ACTION

A.   The Case for Affirmative Action

Affirmative action has strikingly benefited blacks as a group and the nation as a whole. It has enabled blacks to attain occupational and educational advancement in numbers and at a pace that would otherwise have been impossible.[3] These breakthroughs engender self-perpetuating benefits: the accumulation of valuable experience, the expansion of a professional class able to pass its material advantages and elevated aspirations to subsequent generations, the eradication of debilitating stereotypes, and the inclusion of black participants in the making of consequential decisions affecting black interests. Without affirmative action, continued access for black applicants to college and professional education would be drastically narrowed. . . .

Furthermore, the benefits of affirmative action redound not only to blacks but to the nation as a whole. For example, the virtual absence of black police even in overwhelmingly black areas helped spark the ghetto rebellions of the 1960s. The integration of police forces through strong affirmative action measures has often led to better relations between minority communities and the police, a result that improves public safety for all. Positive externalities have accompanied affirmative action programs in other contexts as well, most importantly by teaching whites that blacks, too, are capable of handling responsibility, dispensing knowledge, and applying valued skills.

B.   The Claim that Affirmative Action Harms Blacks

In the face of arguments in favor of affirmative action, opponents of the policy frequently reply that it actually harms its ostensible beneficiaries. . . . The most weighty claim is that preferential treatment exacerbates racial resentments, entrenches racial divisiveness, and thereby undermines the consensus necessary for effective reform.[4] The problem with this view is that intense white resentment has accompanied every effort to undo racial subordination no matter how careful the attempt to anticipate and mollify the reaction. The Supreme Court, for example, tried mightily to preempt white resistance to school desegregation by directing that it be implemented with "all deliberate speed."[5] This attempt, however, to defuse white resistance may well have caused the opposite effect and, in any event, doomed from the outset the constitutional rights of a generation of black school children. . . . A second part of the argument that affirmative action hurts blacks is the claim that it stigmatizes them by implying that they simply cannot compete on an equal basis with whites. Moreover, the pall cast by preferential treatment is feared to be pervasive, hovering over blacks who have attained positions without the aid of affirmative action as well as over those who have been accorded preferential treatment. I do not doubt that affirmative action causes some stigmatizing effect. It is unrealistic to think, however, that affirmative action causes most white disparagement of the abilities of blacks. Such disparagement, buttressed for decades by the rigid exclusion of blacks from educational and employment opportunities, is precisely what engendered the explosive crisis to which affirmative action is a response. Although it is widely assumed that "qualified" blacks are now in great demand, with virtually unlimited possibilities for recognition, blacks continue to encounter prejudice that ignores or minimizes their talent. In the end, the uncertain extent to which affirmative action diminishes the accomplishments of blacks must be balanced against the stigmatization that occurs when blacks are virtually absent from important institutions in the society. The presence of blacks across the broad spectrum of institutional settings upsets conventional stereotypes about the place of the Negro and acculturates the public to the idea that blacks can and must participate in all areas of our national life. This positive result of affirmative action outweighs any stigma that the policy causes.

A third part of the argument against affirmative action is the claim that it saps the internal morale of blacks. It renders them vulnerable to a dispiriting anxiety that they have not truly earned whatever positions or honors they have attained.[6] Moreover, it causes some blacks to lower their own expectations of themselves. Having grown accustomed to the extra boost provided by preferential treatment, some blacks simply do not try as hard as they otherwise would. There is considerable power to this claim; unaided accomplishment does give rise to a special pride felt by both the individual achiever and her community. But the suggestion that affirmative action plays a major role in undermining the internal morale of the black community is erroneous.

Although I am unaware of any systematic evidence on the self-image of beneficiaries of affirmative action, my own strong impression is that black beneficiaries do not see their attainments as tainted or undeserved—and for good reason. First, they correctly view affirmative action as rather modest compensation for the long period of racial subordination suffered by blacks as a group. . . . Second, and more importantly, many black beneficiaries of affirmative action view claims of meritocracy with skepticism. They recognize that in many instances the objection that affirmative action represents a deviation from meritocratic standards is little more than disappointed nostalgia for a golden age that never really existed. Overt exclusion of blacks from public and private institutions of education and employment was one massive affront to meritocratic pretensions. Moreover, a long-standing and pervasive feature of our society is the importance of a wide range of nonobjective, nonmeritocratic factors influencing the distribution of opportunity. The significance of personal associations and informal networks is what gives durability and resonance to the adage, "It's not what you know, it's who you know" . . .

Finally, and most importantly, many beneficiaries of affirmative action recognize the thoroughly political—which is to say contestable—nature of "merit"; they realize that it is a malleable concept, determined not by immanent, preexisting standards but rather by the perceived needs of society. Inasmuch as the elevation of blacks addresses pressing social needs, they rightly insist that considering a black's race as part of the bundle of traits that constitute "merit" is entirely appropriate (See Fallon 1980).

A final and related objection to affirmative action is that it frequently aids those blacks who need it least and who can least plausibly claim to suffer the vestiges of past discrimination—the offspring of black middle-class parents seeking preferential treatment in admission to elite universities and black entrepreneurs seeking guaranteed set-asides for minority contractors on projects supported by the federal government. This objection too is unpersuasive. First, it ignores the large extent to which affirmative action has pried open opportunities for blue-collar black workers. Second, it assumes that affirmative action should be provided only to the most deprived strata of the black community or to those who can best document their victimization. In many circumstances, however, affirmative action has developed from the premise that special aid should be given to strategically important sectors of the black community—for example, those with the threshold ability to integrate the professions. Third, although affirmative action has primarily benefited the black middle class, that is no reason to condemn preferential treatment. All that fact indicates is the necessity for additional social intervention to address unmet needs in those sectors of the black community left untouched by affirmative action. . . . What is so remarkable—and ominous—about the affirmative action debate is that so modest a reform calls forth such powerful resistance.

C.   Does Affirmative Action Violate the Constitution?

The constitutional argument against affirmative action proceeds as follows: *All* governmental distinctions based on race are presumed to be illegal and can only escape that presumption by meeting the exacting requirements of "strict scrutiny."[7] Because the typical affirmative action program cannot meet these requirements,[8] most such programs are unconstitutional.

Among the attractions of this theory are its symmetry and simplicity. It commands that the government be color-blind in its treatment of persons, that it accord benefits and burdens to black and white individuals according to precisely the *same* criteria. According to its proponents, this theory dispenses with manipulable sociological investigations and provides a clear rule that compels consistent judicial application.

This view, however, is too abstract and ahistorical. In the forties, fifties and early sixties, against the backdrop of laws that used racial distinctions to exclude Negroes from opportunities available to white citizens, it seemed that racial subjugation could be overcome by mandating the application of race-blind law. In retrospect, however, it appears that the concept of race-blindness was simply a proxy for the fundamental demand that racial subjugation be eradicated. This demand, which matured over time in the face of myriad sorts of opposition, focused upon the *condition* of racial subjugation; its target was not only procedures that overtly excluded Negroes on the basis of race, but also the self-perpetuating dynamics of subordination that had survived the demise of American apartheid. The opponents of affirmative action have stripped the historical context from the demand for race-blind law. They have fashioned this demand into a new totem and insist on deference to it no matter what its effects upon the very group the fourteenth amendment was created to protect. *Brown* and its progeny do not stand for the abstract principle that governmental distinctions based on race are unconstitutional. Rather, those great cases, forged by the gritty particularities of the struggle against white racism, stand for the proposition that the Constitution prohibits any arrangements imposing racial subjugation—whether such arrangements are ostensibly race-neutral[9] or even ostensibly race-blind.[10]

This interpretation, which articulates a principle of antisubjugation rather than antidiscrimination, typically encounters two closely related objections. The first objection is the claim that the constitutional injury done to a white whose chances for obtaining some scarce opportunity are diminished because of race-based allocation schemes is legally indistinguishable from that suffered by a black victim of racial exclusion. Second, others argue that affirmative discrimination based on racial distinctions cannot be satisfactorily differentiated from racial subjugation absent controversial sociological judgments that are inappropriate to the judicial role.

As to the first objection, the injury suffered by white "victims" of affirmative action does not properly give rise to a constitutional claim, because the damage does not derive from a scheme animated by racial prejudice. Whites with certain credentials may be excluded from particular opportunities they would receive if they were black. But this diminished opportunity is simply an incidental consequence of addressing a compelling societal need: undoing the subjugation of the Negro. . . .

As to the second objection, I concede that distinctions between affirmative and malign discrimination cannot be made in the absence of controversial sociological judgments. I reject the proposition, however, that drawing these distinctions is inappropriate to the judicial role. Such a proposition rests upon the assumption that there exists a judicial method wholly independent of sociological judgment. That assumption is false; to some extent, whether explicitly or implicitly, every judicial decision rests upon certain premises regarding the irreducibly controversial nature of social reality. The question, therefore, is not whether a court will make sociological judgments, but the content of the sociological judgments it must inevitably make.

Prior to *Brown,* the Supreme Court's validation of segregation statutes rested upon the premise that they did not unequally burden the Negro. A perceived difficulty in invalidating segregation statutes was that, as written, such laws were race-neutral; they excluded white children from Negro schools just as they excluded Negro children from white schools. The Court finally recognized in *Brown* that racial subjugation constituted the social meaning of segregation laws. To determine that social meaning, the Court had to look past form into substance and judge the legitimacy of segregation laws given their intended and actual effects. Just as the "neutrality" of the segregation laws obfuscated racial subjugation, so too may the formal neutrality of race-blind policies also obfuscate the perpetuation of racial subjugation. That issue can only be explored by an inquiry into the context of the race-blind policy at issue, an inquiry that necessarily entails judicial sociology.

II.   THE QUESTION OF RACISM

Much has been written about the issues discussed in Part I of this Comment. However, there remains a disturbing lacuna in the scholarly debate. Whether racism is partly responsible for the growing opposition to affirmative action is a question that is virtually absent from many of the leading articles on the subject. These articles typically portray the conflict over affirmative action as occurring in the context of an overriding commitment to racial fairness and equality shared by all the important participants in the debate. . . . This portrait, however, of conflict-within-consensus is all too genial. . . . It obscures the emotions that color the affirmative action debate and underestimates the alienation that separates antagonists. It ignores those who believe that much of the campaign against affirmative action is merely the latest in a long series of white reactions against efforts to elevate the status of the Negro in American society. . . . They fear that the campaign against affirmative action is simply the opening wedge of a broader effort to recapture territory "lost" in the Civil Rights Revolution of the 1960s. And it is precisely this apprehension that explains the bitterness and desperation with which they wage the affirmative action struggle—emotions that are simply inexplicable in terms of the picture of race relations portrayed by conventional analyses.

The conventional portrait also implicitly excludes from consideration those whose opposition to affirmative action stems from racism. . . . [C]onventional scholarship leaves largely unexamined the possibility that the campaigns against affirmative action now being waged by political, judicial and intellectual elites reflect racially selective indifference, antipathy born of prejudice, or strategies that seek to capitalize on widespread racial resentments. . . .

A good way to begin setting the record straight is by assessing the motives of those in high public office. Suspicion characterizes the disposition with which I begin that assessment. My suspicion stems from the recognition that racism in America is an enormously powerful ideological institution, considerably older than the political institutions of our republic, and has often influenced the actions of the executive branch and indeed all levels of government. My preexisting distrust is heightened, however, by the particular background of the Reagan Administration and, more specifically, by the political biography of Ronald Reagan himself.

President Reagan now declares himself "heart and soul in favor of the things that have been done in the name of civil rights and desegregation . . . ." (Dugger 1983, p. 195). This commitment, he maintains, accounts for his opposition to affirmative discrimination. What justifies skepticism toward the President's account is his long history of suspect views on racial issues. His active opposition to racial distinctions *benefiting* Negroes is not matched by analogous opposition to racial distinctions *harming* Negroes. Indeed, a strikingly consistent feature of President Reagan's long political career is his resistance to practically every major political effort to eradicate racism or to contain its effects. During the height of the civil rights revolution, he opposed the Civil Rights Act of 1964, the Voting Rights Act of 1965 and the Open Housing Act of 1968, legislation that his own Assistant Attorney General has rightly described as "designed to make equal opportunity a reality" (Reynolds 1984, p. 999).

Of course, although opposition to this landmark legislation is itself tremendously revealing, limits exist to the inferences that one can properly draw from positions adopted over twenty years ago. But President Reagan has provided additional reasons for distrusting his explanation of his racial policies. Repeatedly his Administration has shown callous disregard for the particular interests of blacks and resisted measures designed to erode racial hierarchy. These actions include the Administration's opposition (1) to the amendments that strengthened and extended the Voting Rights Act, (2) to anything more than the most cramped reading of the Civil Rights Act of 1964, (3) to creating a national holiday honoring Dr. Martin Luther King, Jr., (4) to maintaining the integrity of agencies involved in federal enforcement of civil rights, and (5) to imposing sanctions on South Africa for its policy of apartheid. . . .

There are, of course, alternative explanations to the one advanced above. One could disaggregate the record of Ronald Reagan and his Administration and rationalize each position on a case-by-case basis, by reference to concerns having nothing to do with racist sentiments or strategies. . . .

The problem with this mode of defense is that it ignores the strong *systematic* tilt of the Administration's actions. It disregards as well the political milieu in which debate over affirmative action and other racial policies has been waged over the past decade—a period during which there has been a discernible attenuation of public commitment to racial justice and, even more troubling, a startling reemergence of overt racial animosity. The Reagan Administration's policies reflect, reinforce, and capitalize on widespread feelings that blacks have received an undeserved amount of the nation's attention. Unburdened by the inhibitions imposed by public office, ordinary white citizens have expressed quite openly the feelings that color their analysis of the affirmative action issue. The Reagan Administration has expertly tapped these feelings for political gain by dint of arguments for race-blindness that are, in fact, exquisitely attuned to the racial sensitivities of the dominant white majority. . . .

III. CONCLUSION

In the end, perhaps the most striking feature of the affirmative action debate is the extent to which it highlights the crisis of trust besetting American race relations. Proponents of affirmative action view their opponents with suspicion for good reason. They know that not all of their opponents are racist; they also know that many of them are. Such suspicions corrode reasoned discourse. . . . The only thing that will enable affirmative action—or any similarly controversial policy—to be debated in an atmosphere free of suspicion is for the surrounding social context to be decisively transformed. The essential element of this transformation is the creation of a sentiment of community strong enough to enable each group to entrust its fate to the good faith and decency of the other—the sort of feeling that in the 1960s impelled groups of black and white mothers to exchange their children during civil rights marches. Only the presence of such sentiment can enable the force of persuasion to supplant the force of distrust.

At this point, *even if* a demonstration of policy and fact decisively pointed toward eliminating affirmative action, many of its proponents might well refuse to recognize such a showing and continue to support preferential treatment. Their reaction would stem in large measure from their fears regarding the ulterior motives of their opponents. This is another reason why, as a practical matter, motive is so important. As long as suspect motivation justifiably remains a point of apprehension, inquiry into "the merits" of affirmative action will play a peripheral, instrumental role in the resolution of the controversy.

NOTES

1. Affirmative action refers to policies that provide preferences based explicitly on membership in a designated group. Affirmative action policies vary widely, ranging from "soft" forms that might include special recruitment efforts to "hard" forms that might include reserving a specific number of openings exclusively for members of the preferred group.

"Affirmative action," "preferential treatment," and "affirmative discrimination" are used as synonyms. At the level of semantics, "affirmative action" avoids the problem of preference that is inescapable if one uses the term "preferential treatment." It also avoids the problem of discrimination made salient by the term "affirmative discrimination." On all too many occasions, however, proponents of affirmative action have hurt their own cause by evading the difficulties posed and costs incurred by the policy they advance. These difficulties and costs will not disappear behind euphemistic terminology. To properly convince the public that these costs are worth shouldering, proponents of affirmative action will have to grapple straightforwardly with them—a process which involves, at the least, conceding their existence.

Finally, this Commentary is concerned solely with the debate over affirmative action for American blacks. I recognize that affirmative action programs often include other groups and exclude still others that arguably should be included. And I acknowledge that questions of fairness regarding the criteria by which preference is conferred constitute important issues in the controversy. While practical limitations prevent exploration of this issue, my basic position with respect to it is that the nation should use affirmative action policies to eradicate the oppression and isolation of any "specially disadvantaged group". . . .

2. See Regents of the Univ. of Cal. v. Bakke, 438 U.S. 265, 407 (1978) (Blackmun, J., plurality opinion).

3. To take one famous example, under the "regular" admissions program of the University of California at Davis Medical School, only one black applicant would have qualified for admission between 1970 and 1974; twenty-six were admitted due to affirmative action. *See Bakke,* 438 U.S. at 276 n.6. In the employment context, affirmative action has played a major role in upgrading the relative position of black workers. *See generally* Leonard (1983); Smith & Welch (1984).

4. This point has been advanced by commentators of varying political persuasions. *See, e.g.,* Glazer (1975); Kahn (1966).

5. The extent of white hostility, however, should not be exaggerated. Influential white voices in business, education and politics have strongly supported affirmative action. *See, e.g.,* Fisher 1985.

6. Some commentators have stated that beneficiaries of affirmative action feel guilty about their "tainted" achievements. . . . Blacks seem to be the primary targets of such ruminations. Justice Sandra Day O'Connor, the first woman to be appointed to the Supreme Court, was certainly not nominated because of her demonstrated mastery of federal law. Among the principal reasons for her elevation was her status as a competent *woman* jurist. . . . She appears, however, to have escaped the suggestion that she is silently suffering a crisis of conscience or confidence because her sex played an essential role in her appointment.

7. For a law to survive strict scrutiny, it must further a compelling state interest by the most narrowly tailored means available.

8. One reason why most public affirmative action programs would probably fail to pass muster under strict scrutiny is that they lack judicial, administrative or legislative findings of constitutional or statutory violations that are to be remedied by the program. See *Fullilove,* 448 U.S. at 497–98 (Powell, J., concurring).

9. *See* Loving v. Virginia, 388 U.S. 1 (1967) (invalidating an antimiscegenation statute even though it applied identical restraints to blacks and whites alike).

10. *See* Green v. County School Bd., 391 U.S. 430 (1968) (invalidating a "freedom of choice" pupil placement plan that failed to eliminate a racially identifiable pattern of public school attendance, even though the plan at issue was formally race-blind).

REFERENCES

Dugger, Ronnie. 1983. *On Reagan: The Man & His Presidency.* New York: McGraw-Hill.

Fallon, Richard H. Jr. 1980. "to Each According to His Ability, From None According to His Race: The Concept of Merit in the Law of Antidiscrimination." *Boston University Law Review* 60:815–77.

Fisher, Anne B. 1985. "Businessmen Like to Hire by the Numbers." *Fortune* Magazine, September 16.

Glazer, Nathan. 1975. Affirmative Discrimination. New York: Basic Books.

Kahn, Tom. 1966. "Problems of the Negro Movement." Pp. 144–69 in *The Radical Papers,* edited by Irving Howe. Garden City, NY: Doubleday & Co.

Leonard, Jonathan. 1983. "The Impact of Affirmative Action." Report submitted to the U.S. Department of Labor.

Reynolds, William Bradford. 1984. "Individualism vs. Group Rights." *Yale Law Journal* 93:995–1005.

Smith, James, and Finis Welch. 1984. "Affirmative Action and Labor Markets." *Journal of Labor Economics* 2:269–301.

Van Alstyne, William. 1979. "Rites of Passage: Race, the Supreme Court, and the Constitution." *University of Chicago Law Review* 46:775–810.

VIII
Conclusion

Social-scientific and legal analyses of labor market discrimination and public policy have taught us a great deal since Congress began considering EEO bills in the 1940s. We have learned that discrimination is not just a matter of individual employers acting on their prejudices when making decisions. Instead, discrimination is often the product of organized efforts to deprive groups of opportunities; its victims are frequently denied access to education and training as well as jobs, and are disadvantaged by employment criteria that make it difficult for them to compete on the basis of merit.

We have learned that although many scholars have predicted that discrimination would decline and eventually disappear in modern, democratic, free-market societies, their predictions have not been borne out, at least not so far. In fact, discrimination has at times gotten worse. Although competitive markets may exert powerful pressures against discrimination, other forces may exacerbate it. The desire of dominant groups to maintain their hold on good jobs, cultural beliefs about the "proper" place of particular groups, uncertainties in assessing productivity, and other factors, all institutionalized in organizational rules and maintained through organizational inertia, can prevent the advance of particular groups for decades or more.

We have also learned that labor market discrimination is difficult to eliminate. Although there is a considerable body of work suggesting that EEO laws reduce discrimination, no one argues that the laws have ended discrimination or that the reductions have been accomplished easily. Labor market discrimination will seemingly be with us for a long time to come and, consequently, so will the struggle against it.

The struggle for EEO has also stimulated significant theoretical, empirical, and political controversies. Social-scientific work on discrimination would have proceeded whether or not EEO had been a political issue, but there is no doubt that much scholarly work has been a response to policy concerns. The apparent failure of discrimination to disappear as Becker's theory predicted it would led to the development of new theories—most notably the theory of statistical discrimination—to supplement or replace it. In the last few years, sociologists as well as economists have developed theoretical approaches to labor market dis-

crimination. The result has been a period of intense activity among theorists and
the elaboration of some important controversies—perhaps the most intense are
those concerning how discrimination is maintained and under what circumstances it may be eliminated by competitive markets—but little sense that we are
at the point of agreeing that any single theory adequately explains discrimination.

Nor is there agreement on the consequences of EEO legislation. There is no
doubt that blacks, women, and other minorities have access to far more jobs than
they did thirty or forty years ago, and that the opportunities for them to rise to
positions of power and responsibility have increased significantly. What is less
clear is how much of the change to attribute to the EEO laws, and even whether it
makes sense to try to separate the impact of the EEO laws from the effects of
other civil rights laws, changes in public attitudes, the effects of the civil rights
and women's movements, and other social changes that have changed the circumstances of minorities and women.

Some of those social scientists—mostly economists—who have tried to gauge
precisely the impact of EEO laws have concluded that they have had a real but
modest positive economic impact on the groups they were intended to help.
Others see the laws as almost completely ineffective, however, and some have
even concluded that the laws have done more harm than good.

When the impact of EEO on the economy as a whole is considered, much of
the debate is carried on by journalists, politicians, and writers with strong ideological commitments. The resulting debate has been intense, but the amount of
credible evidence available is exceedingly small, and many of the claims made in
the debate far exceed anything that can be supported by solid evidence.

Probably the most intense controversies about EEO are those which raise
fundamental questions about the very definitions of terms at the heart of the fight
over EEO. What are *discrimination, affirmative action,* and *equal opportunity?*
On one side of the debate are those who believe that all three terms have plain,
intuitively obvious, and legally fixed meanings, given by law or history and not
subject to change. On the other side are those who believe that the definitions are
subject to change, and that they do change, as people improve their understanding of labor markets and policy implementation, and engage in political and legal
disputes about the definitions. The former tend to assume that labor markets
operate according to an inherent logic (or objective economic principles), with
discrimination an aberration the elimination of which requires no significant
change in the behavior of economic organizations. The latter often believe that
the formal and informal rules under which economic organizations operate are
socially constructed and that they are often biased (intentionally or not) to favor
the status quo and to disadvantage minorities or women; from this point of view,
discrimination is often built into the very structure of organizations, and eliminating it may require fundamental changes in their rules of operation.

All these controversies are bound to continue. The academic disputes are
important in their own right, but their intensity is at least in part the result of the

broader social and political struggles over EEO. Because jobs and the wages they bring are so important, the labor market has become one of the primary places in which Americans—and citizens of other countries as well—struggle over what place various groups will occupy in their society. Some want to maintain traditional patterns of discrimination; others want to bring about change, but find themselves involved in disagreements about what constitutes equality of opportunity and how to achieve it fairly and peacefully. The chapters of this book show that it is very difficult to achieve EEO, that demands for EEO are not likely to abate, and that EEO will therefore be a major political issue and a major challenge for modern societies for many years to come.

Selected References

American Council on Education. 1976. "The Cost of Implementing the Federally Mandated Social Programs at Colleges and Universities." Washington, DC: American Council on Education.

Arrow, Kenneth. 1973. "The Theory of Discrimination." Pp. 3–33 in *Discrimination in Labor Markets,* edited by Orley Ashenfelter and Albert Rees. Princeton: Princeton University Press.

Arthur Andersen & Co. 1979. "Cost of Government Regulation." Chicago: A. Andersen.

Ashenfelter, Orley, and Ronald Oaxaca. 1987. "The Economics of Discrimination: Economists Enter the Courtroom," *American Economic Review* 77:321–25.

Becker, Gary. 1971 [originally 1957]. *The Economics of Discrimination.* 2nd edition. Chicago: University of Chicago Press.

Belton, Robert. 1976. "Title VII of the Civil Rights Act of 1964: A Decade of Private Enforcement and Judicial Developments." *St. Louis University Law Journal* 20:225–307.

Belton, Robert. 1981. "Discrimination and Affirmative Action: An Analysis of Competing Theories of Equality and Weber." *North Carolina Law Review* 59:531–98.

Belton, Robert. 1990. "The Dismantling of the Griggs Disparate Impact Theory and the Future of Title VII." *Yale Law and Policy Review* 8:223–56.

Belz, Herman. 1991. *Equality Transformed: A Quarter-Century of Affirmative Action.* New Brunswick, New Jersey: Transaction Publishers.

Bielby, William T., and James N. Baron. 1986. "Men and Women at Work: Sex Segregation and Statistical Discrimination," *American Journal of Sociology* 91:759–99.

Brimelow, Peter, and Leslie Spencer. 1993. "When Quotas Replace Merit, Everybody Suffers." *Forbes* 151 (February 15):80–102.

Burstein, Paul. 1985. *Discrimination, Jobs, and Politics.* Chicago: University of Chicago Press.

Burstein, Paul. 1990. "Intergroup Conflict, Law, and the Concept of Labor Market Discrimination." *Sociological Forum* 5:459–76.

Burstein, Paul. 1991. "Legal Mobilization as a Social Movement Tactic: The Struggle for Equal Employment Opportunity." *American Journal of Sociology* 96:1201–25.

Burstein, Paul. 1992. "Affirmative Action, Jobs, and American Democracy." *Law and Society Review* 26:901–22.

Burstein, Paul. 1993. "Affirmative Action and the Rhetoric of Reaction." *The American Prospect,* number 14 (summer):138–47.

Burstein, Paul, and Susan Pitchford. 1990. "Social-Scientific and Legal Challenges to Education and Test Requirements in Employment." *Social Problems* 37:243–57.

Cohn, Samuel. 1985. *The Process of Occupational Sex-Typing*. Philadelphia: Temple University Press.

Cruz, Nestor. 1980. "Is Equal Employment Opportunity Cost Effective?" *Labor Law Journal* 1980:295–98.

Donohue, John J., III. 1987. "Further Thoughts on Employment Discrimination Legislation: A Reply to Judge Posner." *University of Pennsylvania Law Review* 136:523–51.

Dugger, Ronnie. 1983. *On Reagan: The Man & His Presidency*. New York: McGraw-Hill.

Ehrenberg, Ronald, and Robert Smith. 1991. *Modern Labor Economics*. 4th edition. New York: HarperCollins.

Epstein, Cynthia Fuchs. 1970. *Woman's Place*. Berkeley: University of California Press.

Epstein, Cynthia Fuchs. 1988. *Deceptive Distinctions: Sex, Gender, and the Social Order*. New Haven: Yale University Press.

Epstein, Richard A. 1992. *Forbidden Grounds: The Case Against Employment Discrimination Laws*. Cambridge: Harvard University Press.

Evans, M.D.R., and Jonathan Kelley. 1991. "Prejudice, Discrimination and the Labor Market: Attainments of Immigrants in Australia." *American Journal of Sociology* 97:721–59.

Fallon, Richard H., Jr. 1980. "To Each According to His Ability, From None According to His Race: the Concept of Merit in the Law of Antidiscrimination." *Boston University Law Review* 60:815–77.

Farley, Reynolds. 1990. "Blacks, Hispanics, and White Ethnic Groups: Are Blacks Uniquely Disadvantaged?" *American Economic Review* 80 (papers and proceedings):237–41.

Fiss, Owen. 1971. "A Theory of Fair Employment Laws." *University of Chicago Law Review* 38:235–314.

Fiss, Owen. 1976. "Groups and the Equal Protection Clause." *Philosophy & Public Affairs* 5:107–77.

Freeman, Jo. 1975. *The Politics of Women's Liberation*. New York: Longman.

Friedman, Milton. 1962. *Capitalism and Freedom*. Chicago: University of Chicago Press.

Gamson, William, and Andre Modigliani. 1989. "Media Discourse and Public Opinion on Nuclear Power." *American Journal of Sociology* 95:1–37.

Garrow, Davis. 1978. *Protest at Selma*. New Haven: Yale University Press.

Glazer, Nathan. 1978. *Affirmative Discrimination*. New York: Basic Books.

Glazer, Nathan. 1991. "Racial Quotas," pp. 3–28 in Nieli 1991.

Gold, Michael Evan. 1985. "Griggs' Folly: An Essay on the Theory, Problems, and Origins of the Adverse Impact Definition of Employment Discrimination, and a Recommendation for Reform." *Industrial Relations Labor Journal* 7:429–598.

Goldin, Claudia. 1988. "A Pollution Theory of Discrimination: Male and Female Differences in Earnings and Occupation." Manuscript, University of Pennsylvania.

Goldstein, Leslie Friedman. 1989. *The Constitutional Rights of Women*. Madison: University of Wisconsin Press.

Gordon, Milton. 1964. *Assimilation in American Life*. New York: Oxford University Press.

Gordon, Milton. 1981. "Models of Pluralism." *Annals of the American Academy of Political and Social Science* 454:178–88.

Greenhalgh, Roger. 1989. "The Law." Pp. 41–170 in *Discrimination in Employment*, by David Wainwright. London: Associated Business Press.

Harris, Barbara J. 1978. *Beyond Her Sphere: Women and the Professions in American History.* Westport, CT: Greenwood Press.

Harrison, Cynthia. 1988. *On Account of Sex: the Politics of Women's Issues 1945–1968.* Berkeley: University of California Press.

Heckman, James, and Brook S. Payner. 1989. "Determining the Impact of Federal Antidiscrimination Policy on the Economic Status of Blacks: A Study of South Carolina." *American Economic Review* 79:138–77.

Hirshleifer, Jack. 1976. *Price Theory and Applications.* Englewood Cliffs: Prentice-Hall.

Hunter, John E. 1986. "Cognitive Ability, Cognitive Aptitudes, Job Knowledge, and Job Performance." *Journal of Vocational Behavior* 29:340–62.

Hunter John E. and Frank L. Schmidt. 1982. "Ability Tests: Economic Benefits vs. the Issue of Fairness." *Industrial Relations* 21:293–308.

Jenkins, Richard, and John Solomos, editors. 1989. *Racism and Equal Opportunity Policies in the 1980s,* second edition. Cambridge: Cambridge University Press.

Jaynes, Gerald D., and Robin M. Williams, Jr., editors. 1989. *A Common Destiny: Blacks and American Society.* Washington, DC: National Academy Press.

Lawson, Steven F. 1976. *Black Ballots: Voting Rights in the South, 1944–69.* New York: Columbia University Press.

Laycock, Douglas. 1986. "'Nonpreferential' Aid to Religion: a False Claim About Original Intent." *William and Mary Law Review* 27:875–923.

Lehrer, Susan. 1987. *Origins of Protective Labor Legislation for Women, 1905–1925.* Albany: State University of New York Press.

Leonard, Jonathan. 1983. "The Impact of Affirmative Action." Report submitted to the U.S. Department of Labor.

Leonard, Jonathan. 1984. "Antidiscrimination or Reverse Discrimination: the Impact of Changing Demographics, Title VII, and Affirmative Action on Productivity." *Journal of Human Resources* 19:145–74.

Leonard, Jonathan S. 1986. "What Was Affirmative Action?" *American Economic Review* 76:359–63.

Leonard, Jonathan S. 1989. "Women and Affirmative Action." *Journal of Economic Perspectives* 3:61–75.

Leonard, Jonathan S. 1990. "The Impact of Affirmative Action Regulation and Equal Employment Law on Black Employment." *Journal of Economic Perspectives* 4:47–63.

Lieberson, Stanley. 1980. *A Piece of the Pie.* Berkeley: University of California Press.

Lundberg, Shelley J. 1991. "The Enforcement of Equal Opportunity Laws Under Imperfect Information: Affirmative Action and Alternatives." *Quarterly Journal of Economics* 106:309–26.

Lundberg, Shelly J., and Richard Startz. 1983. "Private Discrimination and Social Intervention in Competitive Labor Markets." *American Economic Review* 73:340–47.

Lynch, Frederick R. 1989. *Invisible Victims: White Males and the Crisis of Affirmative Action.* New York: Greenwood Press.

Maltz, Earl. 1980. "The Expansion of the Role of the Effects Test in Antidiscrimination Law." *Nebraska Law Review* 59:345.

Marshall, Ray. 1974. "The Economics of Racial Discrimination: A Survey." *Journal of Economic Literature* 12:849–71.

Marshall, T. H. 1964. *Class, Citizenship, and Social Development.* Garden City, NY: Doubleday.

Milkman, Ruth. 1987. *Gender at Work: The Dynamics of Job Segregation by Sex During World War II*. Urbana: University of Illinois Press.

Miyahara, Kojiro. 1988. "Inter-College Stratification: The Care of Male College Graduates in Japan." *Sociological Forum* 3:25–43.

Morello, Karen Berger. 1986. *The Invisible Bar: The Woman Lawyer in America, 1638 to the Present*. New York: Random House.

Munafo, Rachel Rossoni. 1979. "National Origin Discrimination Against Americans of Southern and Eastern European Ancestry." *Catholic Lawyer* 25:50–72.

Myrdal, Gynnar. 1962. *An American Dilemma*. New York: Harper and Row. Originally published 1944.

Nieli, Russell, ed. 1991. *Racial Preference and Racial Justice: The New Affirmative Action Controversy*. Washington, D.C.: Ethics and Public Policy Center.

1940 Office Firm Survey. 1940. National Archives, Record Group #86, Boxes 496–500.

Noda, Y. 1976. *Introduction to Japanese Law*. Translated and edited by Anthony H. Angelo. Tokyo: University of Tokyo Press.

Norwood, Janet L. 1985. "Perspectives on Comparable Worth." *Monthly Labor Review* 108 (December):3–5.

Phelps, Edmund S. 1972. "The Statistical Theory of Racism and Sexism." *American Economic Review* 62:659–71.

Pole, J. R. 1978. *The Pursuit of Equality in American History*. Berkeley: University of California Press.

Posner, Richard A. 1986. *Economic Analysis of Law*. third edition. Boston: Little, Brown.

"Race in the Workplace: Is Affirmative Action Working." 1991. *Business Week* (July 8):50–63.

"Rethinking *Weber:* The Business Response to Affirmative Action." 1989. *Harvard Law Review* 102:658–71.

Rosenfeld, Rachel A., and Arne L. Kalleberg. 1990. "A Cross-National Comparison of the Gender Gap in Income." *American Journal of Sociology* 96:69–106.

Rothman, Sheila M. 1978. *Women's Proper Place*. New York: Basic Books.

Rytina, Nancy F. 1981. "Occupational Segregation and Earnings Differences by Sex." *Monthly Labor Review* 104 (January):49–53.

Scales, Ann C. 1986. "The Emergence of Feminist Jurisprudence." *Yale Law Journal* 95:1373–1403.

Scalia, Antonin. 1991. "The Disease as a Cure," pp. 209–22 in Nieli 1991.

Schlei, Barbara Lindemann, and Paul Grossman. 1983. *Employment Discrimination Law*. Second edition. Washington, D.C.: Bureau of National Affairs.

Smith, James, and Finis Welch. 1984. "Affirmative Action and Labor Markets." *Journal of Labor Economics* 2:269–301.

Solomos, John. 1989. "The Politics of Anti-Discrimination Legislation." Pp. 30–53 in Jenkins and Solomos 1989.

Sowell, Thomas. 1984. *Civil Rights: Rhetoric or Reality*. New York: Morrow.

Stavisky, Leonard P. 1947. "The Origins of Negro Craftsmanship in Colonial America." *Journal of Negro History* 32:417–29.

Stavisky, Leonard P. 1949. "Negro Craftsmanship in Early America." *American Historical Review* 54:315–25.

Stevens, Charles. 1972. "Japanese Legal Systems and Traditions." Pp. 2–17 in *Current Legal Aspects of Doing Business in the Far East,* edited by Richard C. Allison. Chicago: American Bar Association.

Sunstein, Cass. 1991. "Why Markets Don't Stop Discrimination." *Social Philosophy and Policy* 8:22–37.

Takaki, Ronald. 1989. *Strangers from a Different Shore: A History of Asian Americans.* Boston: Little, Brown and Company.

Thomas, George M., John W. Meyer, Francisco O. Ramirez, and John Boli. 1987. *Institutional Structure: Constituting State, Society and the Individual.* Newbury Park, CA: Sage Publications.

Thomas, R. Roosevelt, Jr. 1990. "From Affirmative Action to Affirming Diversity." *Harvard Business Review* 90 (March–April):107–117.

Tolley, Michael Carlton. 1991. "Regulating Discrimination in Employment: The Judicial Enforcement of Civil Rights Statues in the United States and the United Kingdom." Paper presented at the annual meeting of the American Political Science Association, Washington, DC.

Treiman, Donald, and Heidi Hartmann, editors. 1981. *Women, Work, and Wages.* Washington, DC: National Academy of Sciences Press.

Turner, Margery Austin, Michael Fix, and Raymond J. Struyk. 1991. "Opportunities Denied, Opportunities Diminished: Discrimination in Hiring." Washington, D.C.: Urban Institute.

U.S. Department of Labor, Women's Bureau. 1920. *The New Position of Women in American Industry.* Bulletin of the Women's Bureau, No. 12. Washington, DC: U.S. Government Printing Office.

United States Department of Labor, Women's Bureau. 1934. *The Employment of Women in Offices,* by Ethel Erickson. Bulletin of the Women's Bureau, No. 120. Washington, DC: U.S. Government Printing Office.

United States Department of Labor, Women's Bureau. 1942. *Office Work in [Houston, Los Angeles, Kansas City, Richmond, and Philadelphia].* Bulletin of the Women's Bureau, Nos. 188–1, 2, 3, 4, 5. Washington, DC: U.S. Government Printing Office.

United States Equal Employment Opportunity Commission. 1968. "Hearings on Discrimination in White Collar Employment." Washington, DC: Government Printing Office.

United States Library of Congress, Congressional Research Service. 1976. "Costs of Affirmative Action in Employment." Washington, DC: Government Printing Office.

United States Office of Management and Budget. 1981. *Special Analysis: Budget of the United States Government, Fiscal Year 1981.* Washington, DC: Government Printing Office.

U.S. Office of Management and Budget. 1985. *Special Analyses: Budget of the United States Government, Fiscal Year 1986.* Washington, DC: Government Printing Office.

Wainwright, David. 1979. *Discrimination in Employment.* London: Associated Business Press.

Young, Michael K. 1984. "Judicial Review of Administrative Guidance: Governmentally Endorsed Consensual Dispute Resolution in Japan." *Columbia Law Review* 84:923–83.

Index